The Resources of the Third World

The Resources of the Third World

Guy Arnold

CASSELL

FITZROY
DEARBORN

PUBLISHERS

Cassell
Wellington House, 125 Strand, London WC2R 0BB

First published 1997

Published in the United States of America by
Fitzroy Dearborn Publishers
70 East Walton Street, Chicago, Illinois 60611

© Guy Arnold 1997

Guy Arnold is hereby identified as the author of this work as provided under Section 77 of the Copyright, Designs and Patents Act 1988.

British Library Cataloguing in Publication Data
A catalogue record for this book is available from the British Library.

ISBN 0 304 33249 6 (Hardback)

Library of Congress Cataloging-in-Publication Data
Arnold, Guy.
    The resources of the Third World/by Guy Arnold.
        p.   cm.
    Includes bibliographical references.
    ISBN 0-304-33249-6 (hc)
        1. Natural resources – Developing countries.   2. Developing
    countries – Population.   I. Title.
    HC59.7.A83358   1997
    3333.7'09172'2 – dc20   96–34108
                                                                            CIP

ISBN 1 57958 014 9 Fitzroy Dearborn

Typeset by York House Typographic Ltd, London
Printed and bound in Great Britain by Redwood Books, Trowbridge, Wiltshire

CONTENTS

MAPS

NOTE ON SOURCES

Country statistics have been derived from the following main sources:

BP Statistical Review of World Energy (1993, 1995). Group Media Publications

Britannia Book of the Year (1994, 1995, 1996). Encyclopaedia Britannica Inc., Chicago

The Gaia Atlas of Planet Management. Gen. Ed. Norman Myers, Pan Books, London, 1985

The Least Developed Countries 1996 Report. United Nations, New York and Geneva, 1996

Minerals in the World Economy. 1992 International Review, United States Department of the Interior, Washington DC.

The World Bank Annual Report (1994, 1995). The World Bank, Washington DC.

The World Development Report 1994. World Bank, Oxford University Press

The World Factbook 1993. Central Intelligence Agency, Office of Public and Agency Information, Washington DC.

INTRODUCTION: DEFINITIONS

The resources available to a country comprise a far more complex combination of factors than the term might suggest. They include agricultural capacity, minerals, the ability to add value to raw materials and the state of education and training of the population. A highly developed country may have only limited agricultural capacity and few minerals but will compensate for this lack with a well-trained and educated population which is capable of maximizing resources by adding value to them even if, in the first place, most of these have to be imported as raw materials – as is the case with Japan. A developing country may be blessed with rich resources, both agricultural and mineral, but lack the ability to add value and therefore to realize to the full its potential. Zaire illustrates this retarded state of development very well.

In the volume which follows the Third World or South (the terms are currently interchangeable) is broadly defined according to the classifications used by the World Bank in its annual *World Development Report*.[1] These classifications are: low-income economies ranging from a minimum of $80 per capita (1995) to $670 per capita; middle-income economies which are divided into lower-middle-income and upper-middle-income economies with per capita incomes ranging from $670 to an upper level of $7,510. Above these levels are the high-income economies (the rich or developed) which are broadly synonymous with the Organization for Economic Co-operation and Development (OECD) countries and for convenience these have generally been referred to in the text as the countries of the North although the term includes Australia and New Zealand. Prior to the break-up of the Soviet Union and communist bloc there was a further classification of centrally planned economies; since 1992, however, the successor states of the Soviet Union have been redistributed among the above classifications. In this volume Russia is treated as a member of the North along with its former European soviets – Belarus, Moldova, Ukraine and the three Baltic states (Estonia, Latvia and Lithuania) – but not Armenia or Georgia which, with the Asian soviets of Azerbaijan, Kazakstan, Kyrgyzstan, Tajikistan, Turkmenistan and Uzbekistan, have been included in the Third World.

There are anomalies: Kuwait with a per capita income above $23,000 is still rated as a Third World country, as are Israel and Singapore because of other particular circumstances; and Bermuda which is both a mini-state and a dependent territory but has an income that places it among the high-income economies is again included here because of its vulnerable status, the result of small size and a tiny population. On the other hand, a number of European countries with low per capita incomes – Bulgaria, Lithuania, Moldova, Rumania, for example – are nevertheless included among the countries of the North, partly for political–geographical convenience and partly because they have long been accepted as belonging to the North despite their relative poverty and backwardness.

During the twenty-first century we are likely to witness a search for resources and a battle for their control and exploitation that will be far more ruthless than anything that has happened hitherto. The pressures of expanding populations and the exhaustion of current assets as well as the effects of ecological and climatic changes will make all states, whether developed or developing, wary of surrendering to outsiders' control of the resources which they possess. These 'outsiders' will come mainly in the form of transnational corporations. Instead, most countries will want to exercise maximum control over what are seen, increasingly, to be steadily dwindling assets. Some of today's fears will, no doubt, turn out to be groundless as new mineral discoveries are made or technology enables us to tap the ocean beds but while agricultural capacity is renewable, mineral resources, ultimately, are finite: they run out. What does seem certain is that resources and their control will move to the top of the economic/political agenda during the course of the next century.

Agriculture has always been the basis of any nation's wealth and a country that can feed itself has an obvious advantage over one that is unable to do so. In the analyses that form the second part of this study agriculture is examined in relation to three questions: is a country able to feed itself; is it dependent upon food imports and if so by how much; and does it produce a surplus of either staples such as rice or wheat or tropical commodities such as cocoa or coffee for export.

Mineral resources from oil and coal for energy to copper and diamonds are the basis of industrialization and countries which are richly endowed with minerals are in a position, at least in theory, to create a strong manufacturing base. Here again, a number of questions have to be posed: to what extent are minerals being mined and exploited; who controls this process – the government of the country or a transnational corporation; is value added to the minerals in the country of origin or are they simply shipped abroad in their raw state for value to be added elsewhere; and how large are the total resources? Some countries may possess large deposits of minerals – copper in Afghanistan, bauxite in Malawi, for example – which are not being mined at all at the present time for reasons of either remoteness or civil war and political instability. Nonetheless, such resources may represent a long-term asset for the future when more readily accessible equivalents have been exhausted and the value has increased.

Resources alone do not guarantee either wealth or development. These come when value is added to raw materials and it is the capacity to add value that distinguishes the advanced from the developing economies. The advanced economies of the North all possess the capacity to add value while, in broad terms, the developing countries of the South do not. Those countries of the South such as Mexico which now have the capacity to add value on a substantial scale are the ones most likely to achieve the crossover from the status of a developing to the status of a developed country in the course of the next two decades. Adding value is as important for agricultural commodities such as coffee as it is for minerals such as copper and at the present time the greater part of all value-adding takes place after mineral or agricultural commodities have reached the advanced economies of the North in their raw or semi-processed state. Countries of the South that succeed in breaking this pattern by ensuring that their raw materials are fully processed at home before they are exported are most likely to break out of their current status as developing countries. Only a few seem on the point of doing this at the present time.

In Part II, the country surveys, the countries of the South or Third World have been divided under five headings as follows:

- Giant countries – Brazil, China, India – which are in a class of their own.

- The 'crossover' countries – the Asian 'Tigers' and the newly industrializing countries (NICs) – with the greatest chance of joining the ranks of the developed nations in the near or relatively near future.

- The oil states whose economies depend overwhelmingly upon the possession and export of the one commodity.

- The majority of Third World countries most of which have little prospect of changing their economic status very much if at all in the foreseeable future.

- The mini-states (many of them islands) which have few if any resources and must remain largely dependent upon aid or a single asset such as their attraction as tourist destinations. This category includes the world's remaining dependent territories or colonies.

The question of resources is inextricably bound up with the politics of North–South relations. In the aftermath of the Cold War, as strategic considerations have become less important, the rich countries of the North have demonstrated a marked tendency to withdraw even that interest which they formerly demonstrated in the welfare of the developing world and, for example, the volume of aid has fallen off sharply in real terms during the 1990s. Instead, the North is coming more and more to view the South only as a reservoir of resources or as a series of markets. The only Third World countries for which any real interest is now shown are the NICs or potential crossover countries and the oil states. There is little evidence that the North is eager to welcome newly developing economies into its ranks and a good deal to suggest that it would prefer to keep the countries of the South in a state of dependence – the way the debt problem is tackled (or, rather, not tackled) is sufficient evidence of this.

Some resources such as iron ore are in such abundant supply that for all practical purposes they will remain readily available for all users into the indefinite future. Other strategic minerals such as vanadium or the platinum group will become scarce much sooner. There is a misconception that the North cannot survive without the mineral resources of the South. Broadly, this is not the case. The South does possess certain minerals which are scarce and is the major or sole source of a small number that will become of increasing importance as the years pass. However, the expectation that the South will be able to use its minerals as an economic/political lever to obtain more equitable treatment from the advanced economies of the North – a spectre that was raised in 1973 at the time of the OPEC oil crisis – has turned out to be a chimera.

First, the North possesses large resources of most of the important minerals. Second, the oil scenario is now changing as oil under the sea and large new discoveries in former Soviet Asia – Azerbaijan and the Caspian Sea and Kazakstan – threaten to deprive the Gulf region of its near monopoly of surplus oil for trading. Third, what the North, and especially the USA which is by far the world's largest overall consumer, can do (and does) is stockpile: obtaining resources cheaply from the Third World while retaining its own 'in the ground' against a future when resources really do become scarce on a global scale.

As a general proposition the South needs to sell its resources to the North far more than the North depends upon obtaining such resources from the South.

In Part I: Overview which follows, a number of themes and their relevance to resources are briefly examined. These include population; agriculture; basic mineral resources; oil; the new dimensions offered by the exploitation of the oceans and the atmosphere; and the effect of changing communications – the globalization of the economy. The rapid changes taking place in a handful of Third World countries – described as the 'crossover' countries (the NICs and Asian Tigers) which are, hopefully, on the verge of making the crossover from the status of developing to developed economies – may well determine the direction of the world economy in the first years of the twenty-first century. There are not many countries in this group but their performance over the coming decades will be crucial to the concept of North and South or developed and developing. Depending upon their performance they will demonstrate whether or not the present members of the developing South can escape that condition.

An examination of ways in which the North manipulates international organizations such as the World Bank or IMF, or how it maintains the debt structures of Third World countries in order to exercise continuing 'control' over the South, concludes this section. Both the international drugs trade and the arms trade are important factors in this control. By emphasizing the responsibility of drug-producing countries for the trade and by offering to help them combat drug production, the North (principally the United States) shifts the blame away from itself (the North provides the drug markets) and on to the South; and by its readiness to sell arms to almost any regime in the South the North helps prolong wars or maintain chaos which, in turn, provides the *raison d'être* either for intervention or for withholding aid or investment.

Finally, if a global market does emerge, as pundits now confidently predict, will this in fact be a global market for everyone or are some countries, inevitably, going to be marginalized and excluded?

PART I

Overview

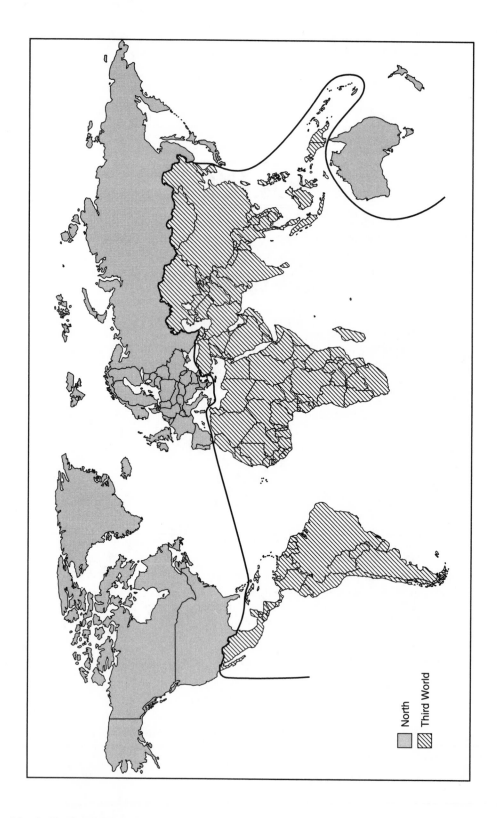

Map 1 North and Third World

OVERVIEW

THE RESOURCE OF POPULATION

The population factor determines everything else and in crude terms education is the equivalent of value-adding so that those countries with highly educated populations – North America, Europe, Russia, Japan, Australasia – maximize their population wealth while countries which have not yet achieved a high level of education are wasting, though not by choice, human assets that could greatly improve the general level of wealth.

In mid-1995 the world population had reached 5,702,000,000, an increase of 700 million over the figure for 1987 when the 5 billion mark was passed. Over this same period a slight decrease in the world birth rate was registered and this stood at 1.54 per cent in 1995. However, the growth of population in the less developed countries (LDCs) was by far the largest – 98 per cent of the total in 1995. That year, of approximately 88 million people added to the world total, 86.5 million were in the LDCs, the poorest nations least able to support them. This huge increase of population in the LDCs acts as a major impediment to constructive development since almost all economic gains are eaten up (more or less literally) by these increased numbers and cannot therefore contribute to a higher standard of living for the population as a whole.

The greatest concentration of the human race is to be found in Asia where approximately 60 per cent of the world's population occupies only 26 per cent of the world's area (including Oceania but excluding Australia and New Zealand). In 1995 Asia accounted for 3.5 billion of the total world population of 5.7 billion. Given Asia's resources and assuming that the level of education and productivity is proportionately increased in the coming years this region should become the world's richest and most influential in the relatively near future.

The time that a country requires to double its numbers is the best indicator of population trends. If the rate of increase is only 0.5 per cent, the doubling time will be 139 years; Table I.1 shows how the rate of population increase on a yearly basis is co-related to population doubling time.

Table I.1 Rate of annual population increase co-related to population doubling rate

Percentage increase a year	*Doubling time (years)*
0.5	139
1.0	70
2.0	35
3.0	23

However, the size of population base (the starting-point) is the controlling factor.

Asia will contain the preponderant share of the world's population from now on. In 1980 the population of Asia was greater than that of the whole world in 1950; by 2000 it will be equivalent to the whole world in 1970; and by 2025 to the whole world in 1980. However, other calculations have to be made and the most important are the relationship of numbers to land and other resources. Hong Kong and Singapore, for example, have very high densities of people to the square kilometre but are able to service such crowded populations because of their successful development of intense commerce and industry. In these two cases food self-sufficiency is not possible but this does not matter because each has achieved monetary self-sufficiency.

In predominantly rural countries with large rapidly increasing populations pressures upon available land are likely to become unbearable unless development of industry provides alternative wealth. Even so, industrialization and other modern developments take their toll of the land: new roads, airports and expanding cities each absorb agricultural land and often, moreover, the best land. Such land losses can be countered with improved techniques of food production, though there must be a limit to what can be achieved in this way.

The ratio of urban to rural population is another crucial determinant of development policies: for example, how much of the population is dependent upon food production in the rural areas. Most countries now recognize the importance of birth control although the application of successful birth control policies is another question entirely for it depends upon education, religious and other teachings and prejudices, the availability of good health services and contraceptives and an overall public acceptance of the need for birth control. One of the most important recent developments has been the growing awareness of the positive role that women could play in limiting population growth by asserting their right to control the size of the families they bear. Recent demands for the empowerment of women made at the 1994 Cairo Conference could have an enormous impact upon population growth patterns.[2] The UN International Conference on Population and Development held in Cairo during September 1994 was principally concerned with the role of women. Three problems were identified whose solution could be expected to have a major impact upon the rate of population increase:

- the need for improved access to contraceptives;
- the need to reduce child mortality;
- the need to promote women's rights to reproductive health.

Should these three areas be tackled effectively giant strides will have been made towards the empowerment of women.

Two opposed views highlight the core problem of population growth and its relation to resources. They were originally advanced at the first World Population Conference at Bucharest in 1974, unsurprisingly in the Cold War atmosphere of the time, by the USA on the one hand and communist China on the other. The first proposition is Western in origin and concept and was advanced by the USA: it claims, simply enough, that if countries with large populations and high birth rates exercised responsible birth control there would be less pressure worldwide upon resources and, as a result, more resources for all to share. The counter-argument, advanced on behalf of the developing countries by China, was equally simplistic: that if the advanced economies would curb their excessive consumption there would then be enough resources to enable everyone to enjoy a reasonable standard of living. In either case the onus is placed upon the other side to alter its approach to population growth on the one hand or resource consumption on the other. It is a sterile argument, although it is likely to become more acute in the future.

In 1995 the world population stood at 5.7 billion; it is expected to reach 6.2 billion by 2000 and of that total 4.3 billion will belong to the nations of the South while China and India between them will then account for well over half the South's total. Another nine countries with high populations accounted for just under a billion people in 1995: these were Bangladesh, Indonesia, Pakistan, the Philippines, Thailand and Vietnam in Asia; Brazil and Mexico in Latin America; and Nigeria in Africa. Between 1975 and 1980, while developed countries averaged 16 births per 1,000 of the population, developing countries averaged 33. The countries which can least afford to do so, therefore, have to cope with the fastest increases in population. There are enormous variations: in 1992 Japan had the highest life expectancy at 76 years for men and 82.1 years for women while infant mortality was at a low of only 4.6 per 1,000. At the same time Africa and parts of Asia faced a rate of infant mortality of 100 deaths per 1,000 of the population. By the year 2000 an estimated 84 per cent of the total world population will live in the countries of the South so that the countries least able to cope with the material needs of large numbers will be faced with the largest populations. Africa, the poorest continent, has the highest general rate of population increase with a number of countries growing by an increment of more than 3 per cent a year.

Over-population results in land degradation, soil erosion and sometimes unbearable pressures upon available resources; the rates of development and population increase are always precisely related to each other and where a population explosion is taking place a number of consequences follow. These include:

- the over-use of fertilizers to accelerate agricultural production which can do lasting damage to the soil;

- over-grazing of pastoral land;

- deforestation for fuel;

- an accelerated drift to urban areas in search of work leading (where no work exists) to an increase in urban problems of overcrowding, slums and crime; such drifts to urban areas have the added result of depriving the rural areas of their most productive manpower;

- the accelerated depletion of non-renewable resources.

Studies carried out between 1960 and 1990 have demonstrated a clear link between the growth of output per capita and the rate of population increase. In the period between 1985 and 1990 every 1 per cent reduction in population growth was associated with a 2 per cent increase in per capita incomes.[3] Further, a comparison of 41 countries with slow-growing populations and another 41 countries with faster-growing populations revealed the following results:

In the 1980s the 41 countries where population was growing more slowly managed an average income growth of 1.23 per cent a year. In the 41 countries with faster population growth, incomes *fell* by an average 1.25 per cent a year. The difference between these two groups was a massive 2.5 per cent per year.[4]

The importance of these studies is that they upset the theory that fast economic growth alone is the answer to population growth. Other means of population control are essential if development in LDCs is ever to outpace population growth.

The steady growth of the world's urban population, especially in the South, is not simply changing the balance between the urban and rural areas but is creating a series of new economic and social problems. In 1950 there were an estimated 287 million people worldwide living in urban areas; by 1980 the figure had increased to 1 billion and by the year 2000 it will reach an estimated 2 billion. In 1980 there were sixteen cities whose metropolitan areas were in excess of 5 million. By 1996 there were 280 cities worldwide with populations in excess of 1 million of which 31 were in China and seventeen in India while the USA, by comparison, had nine. The number of such cities is expected almost to double by 2015. Only nine of the world's 25 most populous urban (metropolitan) areas in 1994 were in the developed countries while sixteen were in developing countries and most of the latter were growing at a faster rate. The UN projects that a majority of the world population will be urban by 2005 and that by 2015 the cities of the developing world will be home to 3.2 billion of an estimated 4.1 billion city dwellers worldwide. The urban population is increasing much faster in developing countries than in the more developed regions.[5] The problems that arise, often in acute form, in the big cities include the growth of slums, health hazards, lack of social facilities, urban violence and crime, unemployment, poverty and confrontation with authorities. Precisely for these reasons governments tend to divert to them an unfair share of total resources to the neglect of the rural areas. Habitat, the United Nations agency, which is responsible for questions relating to cities, wants to link urban and regional development programmes rather than treating them as two separate areas of concern.

A highly skilled and motivated population can be a source of great strength; a large population that is poorly educated and lacks motivation is a source of national weakness. In either case, the size of population has to be related to available resources including land, the level of productivity which has been achieved and the capacity of the particular nation to add value to its resources while the rate of population growth is another crucial factor. The USA now has an estimated doubling time of 101 years and for most of the developed Western countries like Britain, France, Greece, Sweden or Switzerland the doubling time is for all practical purposes irrelevant since it is well in excess of 100 years. On the other hand, in 1995 the countries of the South accounted for 98 per cent of all population increases; it is in the South, therefore, that future population power lies (see Table I.2).

Any forward assessment of population in relation to resources must assume the political wish of the developing countries to catch up: that is, to achieve comparable standards of living to those enjoyed in the advanced economies and such determination is made all the stronger because almost everybody is able to see by means of the media and most notably television how people live in other parts of the world. The result will be constant, escalating pressures for better living standards accompanied by an accelerating determination of those who possess rare or scarce resources to hold on to them for their own development. A comparison of the USA and China yields startling figures to ponder. In 1995 the population of the USA stood at 263 million, its GNP at $6,738,000,000,000 and its per capita GNP at $25,850. By contrast China had a population of 1,206 million, a GNP of $581,109,000,000 and a per capita

Table I.2 Countries of the South with populations in excess of 50 million and estimated population doubling times[6]

Country	Population 1995	Doubling time (years)
Bangladesh	120,093,000	30
Brazil	155,822,000	58
China	1,206,600,000	63
Egypt	59,690,000	29
Ethiopia	55,053,000	—
India	935,744,000	37
Indonesia	195,283,000	47
Iran	61,271,000	21
Mexico	91,145,000	26
Nigeria	95,434,000	22
Pakistan	140,497,000	24
Philippines	70,011,000	30
Thailand	58,791,000	58
Turkey	62,526,000	35
Vietnam	74,545,000	—

GNP of $490. Thus the average American enjoyed an income 52 times greater than the average Chinese. If, in crude terms, we assume that GNP is the rough equivalent of resource consumption then China has to consume 52 times the resources it is now using in order to catch up or achieve a comparable standard of living for its people as that now enjoyed in the USA. If anything approaching that level of increase in resource use by China were to take place over the next 50 years the actual reduction of known resources would be immense. And if China showed that it could do it all the other countries of the South would attempt to do the same thing. This kind of equation ought to give pause to the world community as a whole: what needs to be planned is better use and better management of world resources now before fear of falling behind or being absolutely deprived sparks off a destructive scramble for control of the world's most valuable or scarce resources.

AGRICULTURE

Food shortfalls in 1996

Announcing a World Food Summit for November 1996, the FAO Director-General, Dr Jacques Diouf, said on February 1 1996: 'World food production will have to increase by more than 75 per cent over the next 30 years to keep pace with population growth. We must prepare now to feed about 9 billion people who will inhabit the world by 2030; that is up from 5.8 billion people today.'[7] 'Food for all' is to be the slogan for the summit. The Secretary-General also said:

> Unless the international community and national governments address the underlying causes of undernutrition, namely poverty, 15 years from now there still will be around 750 million hungry and undernourished people in the world. In Africa, the number of

chronically undernourished people is projected to swell by about 50 per cent to more than 300 million people by 2010. This the world can simply not allow or afford.[8]

World cereal production in 1995 at 1,891 million tons was 3 per cent or 58 million tons below the volume for 1994 and below the trend for the third year running.

Certain new trends became apparent in 1995–6 as the world's 30 million tonne store of reserve grains shrank to less than 5 million tonnes. Food stocks were lower in early 1996 than for years and, according to the FAO secretariat, were seen to be below the 'minimum necessary for world food security'. This anxiety about food stock levels has to be seen against an average annual population increase of 90 million, the great majority of whom are born in Third World countries which, often, cannot produce all their food requirements. There are three main reasons why after twenty years of over-supply the world faces grain shortages.

First, the USA and the European Union are in the process of reforming their support to farmers by forcing them to cut crop surpluses. This new policy is in order to reduce the huge tax subsidies to farmers that have been paid out under the Common Agricultural Policy (CAP) of the EU and its US counterpart of support for farmers. Second, changes in weather patterns, especially the heat waves and droughts of 1994 and 1995, have led to low harvests. (Such climatic changes are the least predictable factor.) The third pressure upon supplies comes from China which in 1996 was expected to import 20 million tonnes of grains or a tenth of total world supplies. This change is likely to be permanent as China industrializes and becomes more affluent, causing the eating patterns of its urban populations to change as a consequence of higher living standards. Good farmland in China is now being turned over to urban expansion: This trend is taking place in much of Asia (see above, under Population: urbanization).

Lester Brown, director of World-watch Institute, the Washington environmental think-tank, argues that huge tracts of once fertile land have now been lost to agriculture and that 'achieving a stable balance between food and people may now depend heavily upon policies that can dramatically slow population growth in the next few years'.[9] There are 88 poor countries which are net importers of cereals; 800 million people are chronically undernourished; 31 countries (16 in Africa) suffer from food emergencies (in 17 warfare is to blame).[10] Possibly of greatest significance is the fact that every year more grain is eaten by livestock, with the USA and EU turning two-thirds of their grain into meat. By the mid-1990s the world was in its worst period of grain scarcity since the early 1970s.[11]

As the World Bank points out in relation to food security: 'Access to, and availability of, food are major problems in many areas of the developing world. Given the limited possibilities for expansion of agricultural areas, increasing food security requires that the efficiency of food production within a sustainable biological and institutional framework be increased.'[12] At the same time that overall food security is becoming more precarious world trade in agricultural products is expected to grow by $84bn during the balance of the 1990s. This will result from higher consumption of such foods as beef in a more prosperous Asia and pressures by the World Trade Organization (WTO) to force the EU and the USA to cut subsidies. During 1996 the CAP is expected to cost the EU 41bn Ecus or $31bn which is equivalent to 47 per cent of the EU budget. Plans to enlarge Europe and take in the mainly agricultural economies of Eastern Europe as well as restrictions on subsidized exports will mean a cut-back in such subsidies. The US Farm Act also became law during 1996, restricting, though not abolishing, the level of agricultural subsidies.[13] The net result of these measures will be to lower the available cereal surpluses.

Assessment of problems

Overall, the world produces sufficient food to feed its entire population; malnutrition and famine are not the result of absolute food shortages but of local or regional conditions such as wars, climatic variations and poverty, since millions of people are simply too poor to purchase adequate food even when this is available. The politics of agriculture are complex. Many countries of the South possess sufficient potential cropland on which to produce all their food requirements; political, social or other considerations, however, may prevent its full utilization. For example, to maximize agricultural output a government may first have to embark upon the mass movement of people from an overcrowded region to virgin territories. Indonesia discovered just how difficult an operation such mass migrations can turn into when it attempted to transpose large numbers from overcrowded Java to Sumatra. Similarly, in the wake of the 1984–5 famine in Ethiopia, the government of Mengistu Haile Mariam attempted to transfer large populations away from the famine beset north and northeast to other parts of the country. The move turned into a disaster: people and cattle from highland regions fell victim to unfamiliar lowland diseases and ethnic groups which did not know each other were forced to compete for scarce land resources. Ethnic violence followed. The (relatively) easy option of food aid has made it possible for governments to avoid difficult decisions in relation to agricultural policies. The growth of food aid as an instrument of international policy – in its turn an easy option for the international community – has meant that countries which under different compulsions could grow their own food are able instead to appeal for food aid which is given, at least in part, for political rather than economic reasons.

Food emergencies now occur in an increasing number of countries. In 1994 Afghanistan, Liberia and Rwanda faced major food crises as the result of civil war while critical, sometimes famine conditions existed in Sudan, Tanzania and Uganda. Somalia, after a period of acute distress, was 'recovering' with the help of good harvests. The food situation in Angola was pronounced 'grave' by the UN while Kyrgyzstan, Swaziland and Yemen required emergency food aid and emergency conditions prevailed in Armenia, Azerbaijan, Georgia and Tajikistan.

Food Aid Committee (FAC) members pledged 7,320,000 tons of grain for emergencies in 1994–5 and of this amount the USA alone pledged 4,470,000 tons on an annual basis. The previous year (1993–4) a total of 13,340,000 tons of food aid in cereals had been provided. During the years 1986 to 1989 Africa had been the recipient on average of 47 per cent of disbursed food aid, Asia of 35 per cent and Latin America of 18 per cent. By 1993, however, the world pattern had changed and while the less developed countries (LDCs) received 64 per cent of the total assistance provided, former members of the Soviet bloc received 36 per cent. The principal sources of food aid (in kind or cash) are Australia, Canada, the EU, Japan, Norway, Sweden, Switzerland and the USA. They are followed by Argentina, China and India. The USA and EU normally hold major stockpiles of wheat and coarse grains.

Although food self-sufficiency is an obviously desirable goal, rapid growth of populations has often rendered it unobtainable. In much of Africa, parts of Latin America and Asia large segments of the population receive substantially less than the 100 per cent of their estimated calorific requirements.

Commodities

Food commodities for export such as cocoa, coffee or tea are always treated as development priorities. Staple foods, not normally exported, are too often neglected or given lower priority treatment and in many developing countries the require-ments of food production have been subordinated to the demands of the industrial sector while the agricultural sector is treated too easily as a source of revenues to be diverted to other uses. In the post-imperial age in which some 100 new countries became independent the need to earn hard currency to pay for development programme imports placed a premium upon commodity crops such as cocoa or coffee and in a number of instances such commodity exporting countries have faced growing problems in feeding themselves. Distortions of this nature may arise from deliberate political decisions, from incompetence or from a belief that the returns from cash crops will prove greater than losses incurred by reducing the land used to produce food staples. The principal commodity crops from the South which the North cannot produce are bananas, cocoa, coffee, tea, natural rubber, jute, hard fibres, coconuts and most spices.

Staple foods – cereals – are not a monopoly of the South. The major grain exporting countries, especially of wheat, are the USA, Canada, the EU, Australia and Argentina. Maize on the other hand is produced in both North and South, though Third World producers such as South Africa and Zimbabwe will face shortages in drought years. The principal rice exporters again include the USA; otherwise the main source of rice is Southeast Asia (Thailand and Burma) as well as China which produces over half the world's total rice crop – an average of 188 million tons a year during the 1990s.

The world pattern of food exports and surpluses could alter drastically as a result of any major reduction of farm subsidies in the USA and the EU. In the mid-1990s, however, US farmers were producing half of all traded agricultural products includ-ing 15 per cent of the world's wheat, 21 per cent of oats, 36 per cent of sorghum and 46 per cent of maize; the USA is also the lead producer for a range of other food crops and obtains this remarkable share of output on only 11 per cent of the world's cropland. American farmers achieve these huge harvests as a result of high techno-logy; there is a price to pay for such farming techniques, however, which may bring disaster in the future. At present five billion tons of topsoil are eroded every year from American croplands and such losses are accompanied by increasing pesticide pollution whose effects as yet are only partially understood. In addition, huge transport costs have to be met and these account for further levels of pollution.

The danger to land resources of monoculture farming dependent upon high technology and constantly increasing inputs of fertilizers and pesticides is now beginning to be appreciated. These include the erosion of genetic diversity as monocultures spread; the failure of pesticides to destroy their targets so that as much as 30 per cent of harvests are lost to pests; and the creation of new dustbowls as deforestation, overcropping and over-grazing take place. Irrigation consumes more than 70 per cent of global sweet water supplies while 40 per cent of grain is fed to 'meat' livestock. In addition, the growth of 'industrial' farming often has a calamitous impact upon the small farmer and the spread of large holdings in countries like Brazil leads to the contraction or crowding out of smallholdings which, on average, are more productive if less profitable than large plantations.

Finally, research tends to be geared to the needs of companies which operate plantations and in consequnce often bypasses the needs of small farmers who produce essential staples such as cassava, millet or sorghum. In the 'green revolution' days of the early 1960s huge efforts were made to increase harvests and the results were often spectacular; by the 1990s the main task facing agriculture had become that of safeguarding land resources from over-use.

THE MINERAL RESOURCE BASE

World mining in 1995

The mining industry did well through 1995 with the beginning of recovery in Russia and more general economic recovery worldwide while rapid development in China indicated that this potentially vast economy will soon become both a major importer and exporter of minerals. More importantly, from a resource viewpoint, a steady expansion of mineral exploration occurred throughout the year to reveal a substantial number of new finds, some of outstanding size and importance.

Brazil revised its 1988 legislation restricting foreign mining activity; Argentina, Chile and Peru each had large exploration programmes under way; in West Africa prospecting for gold was the main exploration activity in Burkina Faso, Ghana, Guinea and Mali; in Irian Jaya (Indonesia) what have been described as the largest and richest copper and gold deposits ever discovered were being opened up by the American company Freeport-McMoRan Copper & Gold Inc. Indonesia is also developing as a major coal producer and significant new reserves are being uncovered.

The strength of the sector and the mineral dependent position of most developing countries was illustrated by the fact that 75 nations have recently either revised old or introduced new legislation designed to attract foreign investment. During the year the British conglomerate RTZ and its Australian associate CRA announced plans to merge to create a $20 billion mining giant. They believed such a merger would strengthen their ability to expand more effectively into the mineral exploitation of Southeast Asia and the Pacific. The overall picture was one of huge new mineral resources coming on stream and a general easing of exploration and partnership conditions in the Third World so as to attract new investment into the sector.[14]

Many of the biggest new developments occurred in Australia and Canada: gold finds in Australia, nickel, copper and cobalt in Canada (Labrador) and diamonds in the Northwest Territories. Between them these confirmed the North's continuing pre-eminence in mineral resources as well as the fact that apart from oil, certain strategic minerals and the tropical food commodities, the great majority of minerals are abundantly available worldwide. The USA, Russia, Canada and Australia are leading world mineral producers and exporters while other countries such as France and Sweden are also heavily endowed.

The search for minerals in the Third World by the mining companies of the North is motivated more by arguments of comparative advantage and profit than because such minerals are not also available in the countries of the North. Most Third World countries are only too ready to welcome mining investment and exploitation from the North: they need the income and even if they would prefer to keep their minerals in the ground until able to exploit these fully themselves they are unable to resist the immediate gains that come with the surrender of at least partial control of their resources. Should political or economic conditions change (as they did for the OPEC countries in 1973) the North will be able to fall back upon its own resources (or alternatives) as the copper-producing countries of the South which formed CIPEC discovered when they attempted to emulate OPEC and increase the price of copper exports to the North. As a general rule, apart from the exceptions of oil and tropical food commodities, the countries of the South are far more dependent upon exporting their minerals to the North than are the countries of the North upon such imports.

The spread of mineral resources

Africa is richly endowed with minerals and possesses an estimated 30 per cent of the world's base metals (apart from the former communist bloc). It produces approximately 15 per cent of the world's copper and 70 per cent of its cobalt. South Africa is a storehouse of minerals and its output includes 30 per cent of the world's gold. Apart from Australia and Russia the main diamond-producing countries for both gemstones and industrial diamonds are located in Africa: these are, in order of output and value, Botswana, Zaire, South Africa, Namibia, Angola and Ghana, with smaller quantities being produced by such countries as the Central African Republic and Sierra Leone. Botswana, South Africa and Zimbabwe have vast coal reserves and South Africa is the world's leading producer of oil from coal by means of its SASOL plants, a capacity which may have great significance for the future. A number of African countries – Angola, Botswana, Congo, Gabon, Zaire, Zimbabwe – possess a range of minerals only some of which have yet been exploited, while long-term prospects in the remoter parts of the continent, including the huge countries of the Sahel belt such as Mali, Niger or Chad, are at best only partly surveyed. The continent possesses between 6 and 7 per cent of world oil reserves.

Latin America is also rich in minerals, especially silver, gold, copper, lead and zinc. Brazil, Peru and Venezuela are major producers of iron ore and Brazil accounts for 10 per cent of world output. Chile and Peru are leading copper producers and 25 per cent of the world's bauxite comes from three territories in the Caribbean – Guyana, Jamaica and Suriname. The region is responsible for 25 per cent of the world's antimony output, 27 per cent or more of its silver and 17 per cent of its tin. Latin America and the Caribbean possess just under 8 per cent of world oil reserves.

Asia, apart from the oil rich countries of the Middle East, presents a more complex picture. China, Indonesia and Kazakstan, for example, are storehouses of minerals while other countries such as Afghanistan have huge known resources, for example, of copper, although exploitation must await the resolution of political problems (civil war) while exploitation is also likely to be delayed until world demand changes since many of these resources are located in remote and largely inaccessible regions. Asia, however, accounts for the largest proportion of the world's population so that, far more than either Africa or Latin America, the greater part of all production is likely to be consumed at home as China, Indonesia and the Asian 'Tigers' industrialize and their living standards rise.

Over-dependence upon the mining and export of one or two minerals or the output of one or two agricultural commodities is a principal characteristic of the South's economic weakness. At the beginning of the 1990s (1991–2) 56 Third World countries were dependent upon one commodity for 50 per cent or more of their exports: of these twelve were dependent for 90 per cent or more, seven for 80 per cent or more, eleven for 70 per cent or more, ten for 60 per cent or more and sixteen for 50 per cent or more. Twenty-two of these depended upon petroleum and petroleum products and several, such as Bahamas and Seychelles, derived this dependence from the re-export of imported crude oil after it had been refined although not producing any petroleum of their own. Ten countries depended upon mineral exports (other than oil) and 24 upon agricultural (including forestry) exports.

Mineral round-up: conclusion

Approximately 80 minerals are used by industry and some such as iron ore and bauxite are in abundant supply while others are regarded as strategic – the supply is becoming critical. Platinum and cobalt are included in this category. The reserves of 75 per cent of these 80 minerals have lifespans stretching into the foreseeable future although about eighteen will present problems within two or three decades. These include lead, sulphur, tin, tungsten and zinc. Large areas of the world have yet to be surveyed adequately and many more resources will undoubtedly be uncovered as exploration during 1995 amply demonstrated. (A distinction has to be made between resources and reserves: the term resources covers all known mineral deposits; reserves those that are recoverable with existing technology.)

The USA is by far the largest consumer of minerals: it imports 100 per cent of its titanium, 97 per cent of its manganese and 90 per cent of its chromium, mainly from Third World countries. There now exists a growing range of recycling possibilities: for example, about 50 per cent of iron used in the manufacture of steel is recycled from scrap. Few developing countries, including those that are mineral rich, have the capacity to add value to more than a small proportion of their mineral output and this pattern seems unlikely to change very much in the foreseeable future except in a few cases and most notably among the Asian 'Tigers' or NICs.

OIL AND ITS IMPACT

Oil is the most valuable as well as the most widely used source of energy in the world whose possession gives to its owners greater economic returns than almost any other mineral. The largest share of the world's traded oil comes from countries of the South and for a brief period in the 1970s this group, consisting principally of the Arab oil states of the Middle East, came closer to bringing about a real change in international economic relations than has any other group or organization before or since that time.

During the 1990s the world market suffered from a glut of supplies; nor is there any likelihood that oil resources will dry up in the foreseeable future although in the longer term dwindling oil supplies will have to be replaced by coal (the most plentiful of the fossil fuels), natural gas and nuclear power. China, the USA and Russia between them possess 57 per cent of the world's coal reserves. The use of natural gas, a high proportion of which is currently flared off and wasted, will rise in proportion as oil reserves decline. Later still the world will become increasingly dependent upon the renewable sources of energy. These comprise hydropower, solar energy, power from the sea, geothermal power and wind power and though each is tapped and the technology to use them on a far larger scale exists, only hydropower makes a major contribution to present world consumption of energy. Already the use of hydro-power is on a vast scale yet the potential still to be tapped is enormous and in 1993, for example, 56 major dams worldwide were under construction of which eight were in China. A further eleven major dams were completed during 1992 or 1993. China and the USA each had 50 major dams under construction in 1994. Apart from hydropower, the other renewable resources are under-exploited and unlikely to be developed on any substantial scale for a number of years or until a really serious decline in oil reserves takes place.

Total proved oil reserves at the end of 1994 stood at 1,009,300,000,000 barrels of which 106,600,000,000 barrels or 10.6 per cent belonged to the OECD countries and 770,300,000,000 barrels or 76.3 per cent belonged to OPEC countries. A breakdown by regions, as at the end of 1994, is shown in the Table I.3.

Table I.3 Oil reserves by region, 1994[15]

Region	Barrels	%
North America (including Mexico)	88,300,000,000	8.7
Latin America	78,300,000,000	7.8
Western Europe	16,500,000,000	1.6
Eastern Europe (including Russia)	59,200,000,000	5.9
Middle East	660,300,000,000	65.4
Africa	62,200,000,000	6.2
Asia and Australasia	44,500,000,000	4.4

The oil-producing countries of the Middle East are the key: not only do they possess huge reserves in relation to those elsewhere but also in relation to their own needs, while the countries of North America, Europe and Japan are the principal consumers importing large quantities in addition to what they produce them-selves.

However, the present world oil balance may well change quite dramatically in the course of the next ten years depending upon the size of the new resources being uncovered in Central Asia, principally in Azerbaijan's section of the Caspian Sea and Kazakstan. So great are the expectations from this new source that the leading oil companies are manoeuvring for control and a political battle has developed over the way in which the oil from the Caspian Sea is to be delivered to its markets by pipeline – across Russia to the Black Sea, across Georgia to the Black Sea or through Turkey to the Mediterranean. Optimists have predicted that Azerbaijan could turn into a second Kuwait. Three fields are expected to yield 700,000 barrels a day and there are more to come. Both the USA and Russia have exerted extraordinary pressures upon Azerbaijan to ensure that they obtain at least a part of the coming bonanza, each supporting its own pipeline proposals.

More important than immediate economic considerations, however, are political questions concerning the balance of power in the region. Large Caspian resources will shift the oil balance away from the principal oil-producing Gulf states (Saudi Arabia, Kuwait and the UAE) and even more important could serve to isolate Iran. Already in the USA, Senator Bob Dole has suggested that it could diversify its sources of energy and reduce its dependence upon oil from the Middle East. At present the USA consumes 26 per cent of all global oil production: while producing 6.5 million barrels a day of its own oil it consumes a total of 18 million barrels a day and must continue to depend upon a growing ratio of imports to its total consumption as its own reserves run down.

The oil states of the Gulf now account for about 27 per cent of world oil production but the really important question concerns long-term performance. Just over 65 per cent of world reserves are in the Gulf: Saudi Arabia possesses 25.9 per cent, Iraq 9.9 per cent, Iran 8.8 per cent, Kuwait 9.6 per cent and Abu Dhabi (UAE) 9.1 per cent.[16] All members of OPEC combined account for 76.6 per cent of reserves (end 1994) while output for that year was as follows:

OPEC	26m b/d
Europe (OECD/non-OECD)	14m b/d
USA	9m b/d
Rest of world	16m b/d

Three Gulf oil states – Saudi Arabia, Kuwait and the United Arab Emirates – have such large reserves that, at present, by increasing output they can meet all increases in demand. At the same time the big consumers – the USA, Japan and the EU countries – remain extremely vulnerable to possible changes that might follow political upheavals in the Gulf region.

However, if the new finds being uncovered in the Caspian Sea and Kazakstan live up to their promise resources on an equal scale may tilt the balance away from the Gulf. Oil analysts believe, for example, that the Tengiz field in Kazakstan may hold up to 10,000,000,000 barrels.[17] In political terms what this could mean is the continuing isolation of both Iraq and Iran despite their huge share of oil reserves. At present no other resource is capable of creating such complex political calculations.

Other finds continue to be made and there are known to be substantial resources, for example, on the continental shelf round the Falkland Islands (Malvinas) awaiting development and exploitation. Moreover, despite the world rate of consumption total reserves are increasing. Thus, at the end of 1992 estimated world reserves stood at 1,006,800,000,000 barrels while two years later at the end of 1994 reserves had risen to 1,009,300,000,000. An annual rate of consumption averaging 3,128,400,000 tonnes over two years (1993–4) should have reduced overall reserves of 136,500,000,000 tonnes by 6,656,800,000 tonnes to 129,843,200,000 tonnes. Yet, at the end of 1994 total reserves had risen to 137,300,000,000 tonnes to give an increase over the two-year period of 7,456,800,000 tonnes in new reserves. Increasingly, exploration will move into deeper offshore waters (where perhaps 50 per cent of the world's oil resources are to be found) as advances in technology make deep sea operations more feasible. Deep sea drilling techniques have developed rapidly since 1976; in that year North Sea drilling was to depths of 150m. In 1993 using augur tension leg platforms American offshore drilling was down to 872m. In 1995, using a marine floating production system, offshore drilling in Brazil was down to 910m. It is now expected that in 1999 tension leg platforms will allow drilling at 1,200m and that in the year 2000 subsea remote rigs will operate at 1,650m depth while exploration drilling will be at a depth of 2,292m.[18]

The value of oil, once produced, has to be related to refining operations and at the end of 1992 world refining capacity where the main value is added to the product broke down as shown in Table I.4.

Table I.4 World oil refining capacity, 1992

Country/region	% share of refining
USA	21.7
Canada	2.3
Latin America	10.1
OECD Europe	20.8
Non-OECD Europe	13.7
Middle East	6.7
Africa	3.8
China	3.9
Japan	6.3
South Asia	2.1
Other Asia	7.3
Australia	1.2

Thus, the Middle East, which produces 28.4 per cent of the world's oil, only refines 6.7 per cent, while the USA, which produces 13.1 per cent, refines 21.7 per cent. In other parts of the world where oil is little used there is a fuel wood crisis and constant deforestation.

OPEC

Although OPEC was created at the beginning of the 1960s it was largely ineffective until in the early 1970s the new young leader of Libya, Muammar al-Gaddafi, decided to challenge the control over resources of the oil companies in his country. He did so by insisting upon a greater share of the oil wealth than his government was then receiving although tentative steps in this direction had been essayed before he came to power. Unlike the conservative pro-Western governments of most other Arab oil states at that time, Gaddafi was not afraid to take on the apparently formidable power of the Western oil companies: The result was to give OPEC teeth and his success in changing the terms upon which the oil companies operated led the other oil states in the region to follow suit and they too demanded new or revised partnership deals. OPEC power was born.

OPEC seized the opportunity offered by the Yom Kippur War of October 1973 between Israel and its Arab neighbours Egypt and Syria to quadruple the price of oil and operate a continuing cutback in supplies to Europe. This policy aimed to force the West to implement a more even-handed approach to Israel and its neighbours than had been customary up to that time.

The importance of this crisis was the use of oil as a lever with which to obtain both political and economic returns. Politically the Arab members of OPEC wanted a better deal from the West in relation to Israel; economically they hoped to redress the balance between themselves and the principal oil-importing countries of the West by linking rises in the price of oil to rises in the prices of a 'basket' of commodities, industrial goods and machinery, that the West exported to them in return for oil. It was a good try and for about two years the West went into a state of panic but the crisis passed once it became clear that the huge extra transfers of money to the oil states would have to return to the West to purchase the machinery and other goods which the OPEC states required for their own modernization (recycling became the jargon word).

OPEC's ability to influence events was based upon a simple enough equation: that its members controlled most of the world's surplus oil and that they would either put up the price or curtail supplies unless the main consumers, which meant the leading countries of the West, met some of their other political and economic demands. In real terms, OPEC as a cartel priced itself too high. It had to relate its reserves to two considerations: the first, OPEC's own needs which in the 1970s and subsequently were small scale; the second, the demand of the main consumers, and though this was very great two other factors came into play. The recession of the early 1980s had reduced demand from the high of the mid-1970s and alternative sources of supply had grown, with North Sea oil coming on to full stream by the end of the 1970s. Nonetheless, and despite divisions within OPEC and falling or stagnant world demand, OPEC was still meeting the main shortfalls in 1992: 7.3m b/d for the USA, 7.5m b/d for Europe and 5.5m b/d for Japan.

During the mid-1970s OPEC became the spearhead of demands by Third World countries for a New International Economic Order (NIEO) which, it was hoped, would redress the imbalances of the world economic power structures. Demands for an NIEO which became an important feature of international debates during the 1970s represented the only serious attempt by the South in the years since 1945 and its gradual appearance as a bloc to redress a balance that so far has always worked to the advantage of the rich advanced economies of the North. The assumptions behind calls for an NIEO were two: that the rich North was so heavily dependent upon the oil resources of the South that it would have to alter its policy to accommodate their demands; and, the corollary, that the members of OPEC would be prepared if necessary to withhold this resource long enough to force a change. It was also assumed by other countries of the South that OPEC would maintain solidarity with them and act as a spearhead in demanding global economic changes. Underlying the demands for an NIEO was the further assumption that those possessing preponderant power could somehow be persuaded willingly to surrender their advantage. This never happened and by the 1980s calls for an NIEO by the South had been dropped.

The rise of OPEC power in the mid-1970s and the confrontation between the rich advanced economies of the West and the oil states did cause a temporary blip in the more usual situation in which all the economic advantages lie with the 20 per cent of the world made up of the most advanced economies.

THE OCEANS AND CLIMATIC CHANGES

Seven-tenths of the world's surface is covered by seas and the ocean beds represent an enormous and as yet almost untouched and little understood realm of resources. We have just begun to tap the ocean beds for oil – that is, the more accessible shallower parts – and in places like the Gulf of Mexico have actually been doing so for a number of decades. But otherwise the floor of the oceans remains unexploited and what lies beneath must await the next century before receiving serious attention.

Predicting the results of climatic change is highly uncertain. Global warming is the result of industrialization and the consequent creation of carbon dioxide gases given off into the atrmosphere. What has happened, and is happening, is irreversible. One prediction, frightening in its envisaged scale, is that: 'By the middle of the next century, China's carbon-dioxide output will probably exceed that of the entire OECD.'[19] A return to the burning of coal as the main source of fuel seems inevitable as oil reserves are used up; coal reserves are equivalent to 70 per cent of the heat content of the world's fossil fuel reserves.[20] It is unrealistic to suppose that these huge stocks of coal will not be used when the need arises or that the effect of their use upon the world's climate will be avoided. It will not.

To prevent climatic changes in the future, action needs to be taken now and that means investment on a scale no nation seems prepared even to contemplate – the elimination of personal motor vehicles, for example. Otherwise, adaptation to climatic changes must take place as they occur. Meanwhile, water pollution kills more people than global warming does or is likely to do; soil erosion leaves more people hungry; the loss of species now taking place is irreversible; and deforestation is having a huge impact on climatic changes and living conditions for the affected populations.[21]

Apart from oil, the oceans have been seen largely as a source of fish and already there are increasing signs that this huge food resource is endangered from over-harvesting. In 1950 the world fish catch amounted to 21 million tons but from that year onwards the fish harvest taken from the oceans increased by between 6 and 7 per cent a year, a rate that was faster than the food improvements then being achieved on land by means of the 'Green Revolution'. By the early 1970s the fish catch had attained a level of 70 million tons a year. The world's richest fishing grounds such as the North Sea, the Grand Bank, the Mozambique Channel or the fisheries off the coasts of Namibia or South Africa have been ruthlessly over-fished. A number of poor countries of the South, Mozambique is a good example, entered into deals with fishing nations from the North (in Mozambique's case with the USSR) whereby they allowed factory ships to be stationed in their waters. Huge catches were taken which were quite beyond the capacity of local fishing fleets with the result that such waters became seriously under-stocked. The major fishing nations are by no means all from the North and in 1993 the top ten catching nations, in order, were China, Peru, Japan, Chile, the USA, the Russian Federation, India, Indonesia, Thailand and South Korea.[22] Frozen fish represent one of the world's most lucrative items of trade and countries with rich offshore fisheries see these as a resource for export along with other agricultural or mineral commodities.

The most up-to-date calculations suggest that the oceans can sustain an annual fish catch in the region of 100 million tonnes but since the catch recovered in 1992 came to 98,112,000mt this is perhaps no more than a calculation based upon existing reality rather than long-term sustainability. Nonetheless, it is given as the optimum catch which will allow fish to replenish stocks each year so as to maintain supplies for such a level of fishing. In 1993 the first UN Conference on Straddling Fish Stocks and Highly Migratory Fish Stocks took place in New York with the aim of identifying and assessing existing fishing problems and finding ways to improve co-operation between nations. During 1994 confrontations occurred between the three most important fishing nations of the EU – Britain, France and Spain – about the permissible length of fishing nets; Iceland sent gunboats against Norwegian trawlers; China and Taiwan disputed fishing rights off the island of Quemoy; Britain and Argentina were at odds over squid fishing rights off the Falkland Islands. Such disputes will intensify as competition for dwindling fish supplies becomes greater. The result of over-fishing has been to persuade more countries to extend their 200-mile offshore exclusive economic zones (EEZ) although poor countries, especially in Africa, do not have the means to protect these zones from predatory outsiders and a number of countries with highly efficient fleets consistently over-fish their waters.

The story of the whale illustrates just how hard it is to conserve anything in a world where pressure for resources constantly outweighs other considerations. Saving whales has become a highly emotive issue, but emotion and interest in this extraordinary mammal is not enough. In 1982 the International Whaling Commission (IWC) voted to ban all commercial whaling for a minimum period of five years from October 1985; the decision gave great hope to conservationists but they reckoned without the realities of the marketplace. Between the exercise of the ban and August 1987 (less than two years later) a minimum of 11,330 whales were slaughtered. A 1987 moratorium on whaling was then agreed but by 1994, although the IWC voted to create a sanctuary free from whaling in the waters south of Africa, South America and Australia, Japan voted against the measure and both Japan and Norway, the world's leading whalers, continued to defy the moratorium. Whales, like dolphins, may arouse human emotions in support that are not stirred by the cod but as a resource it is probable that they will become extinct unless a regime of conservation that is accepted by all fishing nations can be devised and enforced. The fortunes of the whale merely highlight the greater problems that control of the oceans is going to raise in the course of the next century.

Offshore oil and gas resources on shallow continental shelves have now been exploited for decades: in the Gulf of Mexico, in the North Sea, off Brunei and Indonesia, off the West African coast. As the technology improves, so the oil companies will move out into ever deeper waters. The technology for exploitation of the seabed at much deeper levels already exists although at present the costs are prohibitive. They will cease to be so during the twenty-first century when oil resources on land begin seriously to dwindle. Ocean technology is still in its early stages but will become a major growth industry in the twenty-first century. The world's continental shelves contain about half the world's oil and gas. Apart from oil, however, we have not yet obtained other minerals from the oceans.

So far most wealth from the seas has been obtained from the narrow coastal fringes of the oceans which are highly productive: first because their shallow waters enable ocean bed activities such as oil drilling to be carried out using relatively primitive technology; and second because these waters are subject to warm currents which provide the richest fishing grounds. The results have been over-fishing and pollution, the latter putting all sea life at risk. The world's coastal ecosystems are among the most valuable for marine life; they include salt marshes, wetlands in temperate zones and mangrove swamps in the tropics. Mangroves fringe over 50 per cent of all tropical shores which are rich in fish while the Nypa palm is a source of fruit, sugar, vinegar, alcohol and fibre. River estuaries are also highly productive regions, as are tropical coral reefs. These fringe areas where land and sea meet illustrate the potential wealth of all the world's waters.

Sea water contains about 70 elements of which the most important are salt, magnesium and bromine; of great future importance are the manganese nodules on the seabed. These contain between 25 and 30 per cent manganese, 1.3 per cent nickel, 1.1 per cent copper, 0.25 per cent cobalt plus molybdenum and vanadium. There are deposits of silver, copper and zinc in the mud of the Red Sea and an estimated 4 billion tonnes of uranium to be extracted from sea water (more than total known resources on land). The oceans are also a potential source of endless renewable energy in the form of tidal, wave and thermal energy each of whose possibilities have now been tested and in some cases are already providing energy.

A major political problem for the next century will be control of the oceans, the greater part of whose mineral wealth lies beyond the jurisdiction of individual nations. Dispute seems inevitable once mineral extraction becomes technologically feasible. The possibility of a scramble for ocean resources is real and is likely to mean that only the richest, most technologically advanced nations will stand to benefit unless international agreements have been forged to ensure that all nations are guaranteed a share in ocean wealth. How any such agreements could be enforced is another matter altogether.

Marine technology has so far been targeted at deep sea oil resources. Only a few nations have invested seriously in marine technology, including the USA, Japan, Germany, France and Britain. Many of the richest ocean nodule areas are outside national jurisdiction, for example, in the deep Pacific, and harvesting of the nodules will require costly retrieval techniques which only a handful of nations would be able to afford.

The Arctic and Antarctic regions are both rich in resources. The Arctic now provides 10 per cent of the global fish catch while the Antarctic and its surrounding seas is the greatest source of plankton upon which fish live. Arctic resources consist of fish, seals and minerals, including oil and natural gas; Antarctic resources consist of fish, whales, mineral ores and oil.

The need to manage the oceans with measures of conservation and control to prevent pollution becomes more urgent, as does the need for international resource control before a scramble for ocean bed resources takes place. There are few signs that workable international controls will triumph over the determined efforts of individual nations, led by the richest and most technologically advanced, to seize as much of the available resources for themselves as they are able to do with impunity.

COMMUNICATIONS: A WORLD SUPERHIGHWAY

What is described as the end or 'death of distance' may become the single most important economic fact in the first half of the twenty-first century. As tele-communications become an ever more integral part of our lives with technology constantly outstripping expectations, so the resulting information revolution will increasingly determine where people live and where they work while at the same time eroding older concepts of national borders and changing patterns of international trade. The effects of this rapidly developing revolution are already worldwide and pervasive. The new information 'superhighway' has been described as 'a network of computers and data-bases linked by high capacity telecommunications lines knitting the world's nations in a seamless electronic web'.[23]

The technology already exists to create a global information society that transcends geographical boundaries. Estimates in 1995 suggested that ITEC (information technology, electronics communications) would be worth 10 per cent of world GDP by the year 2000. Already in 1994 the ten largest telecommunications companies made greater profits than the world's 25 largest commercial banks and the industry was rapidly emerging as the world's pacemaker. Even more important for the future, the costs of telecommunications are being brought down. Although over the next two decades the industry will face huge upheavals as technological change continues to speed up, the lowering of costs will make it more readily available worldwide. Before long it will cost no more, for example, to telephone another continent than to telephone someone in the same town. The speed of these recent advances raises huge political questions: what will be the impact upon international relations and trade when the cost of communications has been reduced to next to nothing?

The death of distance means that any activity which relies upon screen or telephone for its commission can be carried on anywhere in the world. Moreover, an increasing number of diverse services or activities – the design of an engine, monitoring a security camera, selling insurance, running a secretarial paging service, for example – will become as exportable through this means as formerly manufactured parts were exported by more traditional means. The telecommunications revolution may also pose a major threat to white-collar workers in economically advanced societies whose jobs could be put at risk as educated workers in poor or developing countries find they have at their disposal for the first time the chance to obtain by such means a standard of living that formerly was open to them only by emigration. Countries seeking such advances must first bring down the costs of telecommunications although that will happen soon enough. When distance has been 'eliminated', bringing all communities closer together, they are likely to discover that the new ability to communicate has also undermined national sovereignty while there is less and less possibility of regulating the new information technologies.

How much nationalism will act as a bar to the spread of the superhighway and how much it will be able to prevent such a development remains to be seen. At present there is little political will and perhaps not a great deal of political understanding of just what is at stake. According to one authority the political will is at present lacking to allow suppliers such as AT&T of the USA or the UK's BT to connect up worldwide.[24] The World Trade Organization (WTO) has held talks with a view to bringing the telecommunications sector within the multilateral trading system and, if accomplished, this would represent a major step towards achieving a single global market in telecommunications. However, the WTO has found resistance on the part of the leading American and European systems to share markets – and information – with one another.

In February 1995 a ministerial conference of the Group of Seven (G-7) countries met in Brussels to discuss the implications of an information superhighway. The conference discussed ways of promoting fair competition, encouraging private investment, defining a regulatory framework and providing open access to networks. In combination these aims cover the range of obstacles and problems that have to be overcome if a smooth international system is to be put in place. The usual concern was expressed that a gap would develop between the 'have' and 'have not' nations. In response Charles Sirois (chief executive of the Canadian telecommunications company Teleglobe), suggested that one of the most effective ways to transfer knowledge and technology was through electronic networks and that a concessional rate for developing countries within a worldwide fee structure or through lines of credit arranged by the World Bank could meet that concern.[25] Some of these considerations may be premature for, according to one estimate, a true 'information society' in which global networks connect subscribers to a wealth of information and entertainment which is available on demand will not emerge before 2030.[26]

Telecommunications will greatly extend the reach of the computer – and be extended in their turn – as the two technologies converge. The integration of all forms of information is coming progressively closer as more and more material is processed, stored and manipulated by computers using graphic interface. An obvious immediate example is to be found in the way encyclopaedias are now becoming available on CD-Rom or through the World Wide Web as part of the Internet for multimedia use. A major side effect of this process – putting books or documents on the Internet – could be the end of copyright which will become almost impossible to control.

Parallel with these public concerns has been the rapid growth of private networks: for example, companies linking office telephones and personal computers. The European Commission reckons there are (1995) about 700,000 private networks in the USA but only some 14,000 in the EU. 'The proliferation of personal computers encourages companies to link them into networks which can cover anything from a single office to the whole world. Examples of global networks include those used by the banking and airline industries, or the Internet, the largest of them all.'[27]

India has built up a flourishing software industry round Bangalore; between 1990 and 1993 its exports doubled to US$270 million. India is now attracting major back-office work since it can supply efficient services at far cheaper costs than, for example, European countries. Airlines such as Swissair and British Airways now farm out various aspects of their operations such as accounts to Indian companies. This is becoming a normal pattern: more and more organizations whose headquarters and main operations are in one country (in Europe) site significant parts of their operations in other countries which offer the necessary services at a cheaper rate. Several leading Asian countries (NICs or Asian 'Tigers') are now investing heavily in the latest telecommunications networks and, given their stage of development, have relatively high densities of telephones. These countries, led by Malaysia and South Korea, will be the first from the developing or Third World to get 'on net' with the most advanced telecommunications centres.

As always, the advantages will lie with the countries which have the leading technologies. Although this poses well-rehearsed questions about the developed and less developed worlds, in fact the relationship is relative and may be illustrated by the dispute between the USA and France (towards the end of the long negotiations over the UNCTAD Uruguay Round) about American (Hollywood) films swamping the French market. Those who possess the best technology and can produce the most at the cheapest rates will always command the market unless artificial barriers are erected to prevent them from doing so. As telecommunications become more and more important and available the technology is likely to take over and dominate small markets, however much resistance is offered to a trend which threatens to bypass national controls.

The arrival of cyberspace – an artificial environment created by computers (virtual reality) – is part of this ongoing revolution and before long it is likely to become a region that could substantially alter the structure of our economies, the development of communities and the protection of rights as citizens. At present cyberspace is mainly concerned with networks of computers linked through telephone lines. The biggest, Internet, was first developed in the USA to assist military and academic research. By 1995 the Internet, which had operated almost unknown for years, had between 20 and 30 million private people using 30 terabytes a month – equivalent to the information contained in 30 million books of 700 pages each.[28]

Present predictions suggest that eventually the 'information superhighway' will absorb the functions of television, telephone and conventional publishing. If this turns out to be the case the information superhighway will have achieved an immense capacity for good or ill. The Internet has wide social implications and optimists see it re-creating a social cohesion that has largely been destroyed by the insulating qualities of television. Thus, since Internet depends on its users to supply and share information and act in co-operation with one another to make the system work, this process will assist social groups to come together. At least that is the theory. It will also have important implications for free speech and the passing of information on the Internet will become almost impossible for totalitarian governments to control. The converse of such arguments is the more pessimistic assumption that networks, rather than creating harmony or a global village, will instead emphasize differences – between rich and poor, of race, religion and politics – with the result that users will tend only to commune with compatible groups and not attempt to cross social or cultural barriers. There are other possibilities. The rapid increase in distance learning through the Internet could revolutionize educational systems while rural health systems in even the poorest countries could be immensely assisted by a network of telephone links. There will develop an increasing list of other similar possibilities.

At risk, inevitably, will be privacy and security of information as companies or individuals leave trails of data and information across the world. Further, Internet will lend itself, almost certainly, to increasing theft of ideas and copyright. Finally, it is unrealistic to suppose that so powerful a medium will not be used as a means of control by governments: it will be possible, initially, to make checks on spending and other apparently harmless habits. The (US) Electronic Frontier Foundation has called for vigorous protection of privacy rights on cyberspace. Just how this can be achieved is another matter entirely. The US government has already suggested a device to encrypt and decode messages on the Internet to protect privacy; but this could just as easily be used to allow governments to intercept and decode private messages.

THE CROSSOVER COUNTRIES: NICs AND TIGERS

Just why some countries manage to achieve highly developed status while others stand still or lag behind is far from easy to explain. Many strands go to making up the development process: these include possession of raw materials, capacity to feed the nation, levels of education and political stability; but, in the end, the most important is the ability to add value to raw materials and turn these into finished products either for use at home or for resale in a highly competitive world market. Per capita expenditure on education at all levels is one key to a country's performance and

Britain which spends considerably less per head than France or Germany of G-7 countries is beginning to fall behind them in performance, at least as this is reflected in per capita income. At the same time the British GNP which is now slightly more than US$1 trillion is equivalent to the combined GNPs of all the countries on the African continent plus China and India or, to put it another way, the workforce of Britain with a population slightly below 60 million is at present outproducing in terms of combined value of all products the output of a workforce of nearly 3 billion people in those territories. A comparison of American performance set against other regions of the world would present an even more one-sided picture.

The Group of Seven (G7)

The seven leading industrial or advanced economies – the USA, Japan, Germany, France, Italy, Britain and Canada – had a combined GNP in 1992 of $16,233,000,000,000 which came to just under two-thirds the total GNP for the world which then stood at $25,600,000,000,000. Their comparative standing is as shown in Table I.5

The Group of Seven will continue to set the world economic agenda for some time

Table I.5 Comparative standing of the G-7

USA
Population: 263,057,000 (1995)
GNP: (1994) $6,738,400,000,000, per capita $25,850

Japan
Population: 125,362,000 (1995)
GNP: (1994) $4,693,200,000,000, per capita $37,560

Germany
Population: 81,912,000 (1995)
GNP: (1993) $1,908,570,000,000, per capita $23,630

France
Population: 58,172,000 (1995)
GNP: (1994) $1,317,950,000, per capita $22,760

Italy
Population: 57,386,000 (1995)
GNP: (1993) $1,134,800,000,000, per capita $19,620

Britain
Population: 58,586,000 (1995)
GNP: (1993) $1,024,700,000,000, per capita $17,920

Canada
Population: 29,463,000 (1995)
GNP: (1993) $574,936,000,000, per capita $20,670

---

to come at conferences of the World Bank and IMF. Yet its ability as a group to control the world economy is fast being eroded as the statistics show a remorseless shift in industrialization and rates of growth away from North America and Europe to the newly industrializing countries (NICs) of Asia including the so-called Asian 'Tigers' of Hong Kong, Singapore, South Korea and Taiwan. These countries are now attracting heavy investment from Japan and the West and their rates of growth are far higher than those of the G-7. There are growing signs that the G-7 countries, huge as their lead may be, are nevertheless becoming ever more defensive as they see the system of world economic controls which they have dominated for so long gradually becoming irrelevant as the dynamic economies of Asia catch up.

The NICs and Asian Tigers

The centre of the global economy is shifting to Asia and the Western monopoly of modernity which has allowed it to maintain economic and political preponderance for centuries is now passing away. As Asian economies catch up they will not also or necessarily become more and more like those of the West. Rather, they will set new agendas of their own. The West, which in the heyday of its power never believed it could learn from Asia, is now admitting the possibility that it could after all be taught by the thrusting new economies of Southeast Asia, especially the so-called Asian 'Tigers'.

In 1993 when the USA hosted the Asia Pacific Economic Co-operation (APEC) conference in Seattle it gave the impression that it was the leading economy of the Pacific Rim. The Prime Minister of Malaysia, Dr Mahathir Mohamed, has other quite different ideas and is attracting a growing following for his theory that East Asia should act as a caucus against the USA, which he does not see as a natural part of the region. Powerful though it remains, the USA no longer plays the dominant role in Asia; that went with the end of the Cold War. Now the biggest motor for growth is intra-regional trade among Asian nations; this is expanding four times as fast as trade between the USA and Asia. The region no longer looks to the USA for investment; instead, it supplies an increasing proportion of its own capital requirements.

Asian economic growth since World War II has seen several stages: the first came in the 1950s with the rapid development of the original 'Tigers' – Hong Kong, Singapore, South Korea and Taiwan. These four were in the nature of special cases. Hong Kong's position off China during the long years of the Cold War when the communist giant was almost isolated from the rest of the world allowed it to become a booming entrepreneurial centre of enterprise and industry whose GNP in 1993 at $89,274,000,000 was equivalent to one-fifth that of China. Both South Korea and Taiwan were given massive US economic assistance in the 1950s which enabled them to industrialize effectively. A comparison of the two Koreas is instructive. In 1953 both were devastated as a result of the Korean War of the preceding three years; North Korea then embarked upon the communist path of the planned centralized economy while South Korea chose the free enterprise path, although with massive state direction and interventions from a government that was anything except democratic. Nonetheless, although they started from comparable bases in 1953, by 1993 the difference between them was enormous: North Korea, with a population of 23,067,000, had a GNP of $22,000,000,000; while South Korea, with double the population at 44,436,000, had a GNP fifteen times as great at $337,910,000,000. At the same time Singapore, with a population just under 3 million, had a GNP twice the size of North Korea's at $44,000,000,000.

Singapore's position at the hub of the booming ASEAN countries is one of the most advantageous in the world. In 1996 Singapore was admitted to membership of the Organization of Economic Co-operation and Development (OECD) after two decades of spectacular growth. It achieved this success with a mixture of policies that makes it impossible to assign its breakthrough to a single approach; rather, it combined authoritarian government, state controls and careful planning with free enterprise and compulsory savings which were used by government to create a modern infrastructure including a first-class telecommunications system and airline. Much of Singapore's success has depended upon its ability to attract ideas, capital and know-how from outside.

The second stage of economic advance in Asia saw the emergence of Malaysia and Thailand as thrusting NICs during the 1970s with high growth rates that have continued through to the 1990s. Third came the more recent breakthroughs of China and Indonesia. China's growth in the 1980s and 1990s has been phenomenal and by 2000, for example, it is expected to have issued 30 million credit cards (the equivalent to Britain) to its growing economic élite while an estimated 95 Chinese cities (far greater than official figures) now have populations in excess of 1 million. The European Commission calculated (January 1996) that 400 million Asians will have achieved disposable incomes as high as those in the West by the year 2000 while, according to World Bank estimates, China will have become the world's largest economy (ahead of both the USA and Japan) by the year 2020.[29]

Against this rapidly changing background European countries are now anxious to examine the performance of the Asian 'Tigers' and are especially interested in three areas: how they have achieved their dramatic economic growth; how they manage such comparatively low levels of public expenditure (25 per cent of GDP or less as opposed to 40 per cent in Europe); and how they fund welfare. As they move up in terms of technology the NICs of Asia will soon come close to Western levels of development.

The Asian NICs and Tigers are not the only countries on the threshhold of a crossover into the ranks of the advanced economies (see Country Surveys – parts one and two). One other example, Mexico, is worth examining here. The formation of the North American Free Trade Agreement (NAFTA) comprising the USA, Canada and Mexico, which was announced in August 1992, was hailed as a triumph for Mexico's President Carlos Salinas. Over a period of fifteen years the three countries will eliminate all trade and investment barriers. The agreement came into force in January 1994 yet already in early 1995 Mexico was rocked by a major financial crisis and it was far from clear whether NAFTA would provide a way for it to cross over from the South to join the ranks of the developed North or whether the agreement simply made the penetration and control of its economy by the USA easier to accomplish.

Economic predictions can go notoriously awry but in the mid-1990s all the most obvious indicators suggested a continuing shift to Asia: it has the resources, the people, the work capacity and seems set to reverse a world economic system which has been controlled by the West unchallenged for more than two centuries. At the same time the ability to cross over from developing to developed status does not mean parity in terms of per capita GDP. No matter how well its economy performs China will always include a huge population of great poverty into the foreseeable future. The most important aspect of the crossover from developing to developed status means the capacity to create wealth from internal savings without being dependent upon external assistance and this appears to be the main characteristic which the NICs or Asian 'Tigers' now have in common (see Table I.6).

Table I.6 Regional GNPs, 1993

Regional GNPs (1993)[30]	$
World	24,299,220,000,000
Africa	442,190,000,000
Americas	
USA/Canada	6,965,320,000,000
Latin America/Caribbean	2,320,496,000,000
Asia	
Eastern Asia (incl. China/Japan)	5,205,890,000,000
South Asia (incl. India)	361,170,000,000
Southeast Asia	458,010,000,000
Southwest Asia	709,480,000,000
Europe	
Eastern Europe	743,960,000,000
(of which Russia)	348,410,000,000
Western Europe	7,666,440,000,000
(of which the EU)	7,280,990,000,000
Oceania	367,360,000,000

MECHANISMS OF CONTROL: AID, THE IMF, DEBT

A range of political and economic mechanisms is used by the most advanced economies to manipulate and control the nations of the developing world or at least as large a proportion of them as is practicable. Aid and debt are two obvious means of control, as are multilateral institutions such as the World Bank and International Monetary Fund (IMF), which for all practical purposes are managed by the Group of Seven (G-7) or the European Union's Lomé Convention with the African, Caribbean and Pacific (ACP) countries. There are other, more subtle, less overtly obvious means of control as well; these include the arms trade, corruption, campaigns to fight the international drugs trade and the insistence upon certain (Western) standards of human rights as the prerequisite for aid or debt relief. The objective in almost every case is to ensure or prolong the capacity of the North to manipulate to its advantage the economies of the South.

Aid

Aid has rarely been about helping the developing countries of the South to achieve economic take-off; it has been provided to safeguard the investment, trade, strategic and other interests of the donors. The need for allies or at least for a sympathetically passive Third World was the primary consideration behind the flow of aid from North to South during the Cold War. In any case, flow is hardly the proper word to use since, in real terms, more resources in the form of aid repayments, interest and interest on investments flowed back from poor to rich than the other way round. Aid was a small annual price to pay to maintain a relatively quiescent relationship between 'have-not' and 'have' nations during a period of dangerous confrontation in the North, and without Cold War compulsions, as the events of the 1990s have already indicated, the outlook for the poorest nations has become even more stark. In terms of the interests of the North, they are expendable.

The cutback in aid began in the late 1980s and by 1995, for example, Britain was contemplating swingeing cuts in its programme of 12.5 per cent. Other donors were certain to follow. During the latter part of the 1980s, as a prelude to cutting aid, the North had begun to lecture the South about its political structures and its human rights record. No overt concern for these issues had been demonstrated during the Cold War years and this new insistence upon linking aid to such issues was to provide the donors with acceptable excuses for reducing their budgets. Aid was losing its political point.

By 1996 the USA was clearly set to cut back aid more or less across the board (except for Israel) and reduced its contribution to the International Development Agency (IDA), the 'soft arm' of the World Bank, by 40 per cent. Others would follow the American lead and most donors, in any case, were suffering from aid fatigue while questioning whether it was effective. It is easy to demonstrate that aid is wasted and undoubtedly much of it is, yet the big projects are the ones least likely to suffer because they represent major contracts in the donor countries where powerful business lobbies will ensure that they go through. The World Bank estimates that 20 per cent of loans to Africa have not achieved their objectives.[31]

Dialogue

For the short period following the Yom Kippur War and the rise of OPEC power there was a genuine dialogue between North and South when the South, led by the OPEC countries, was able briefly to talk on apparently equal terms with the North, but this did not last. By the beginning of the 1980s calls for a New International Economic Order (NIEO) became meaningless and though periodic meetings between North and South took place (for example, the Cancun Summit of 1981 in Mexico) these tended only to emphasize the power of the North and the weakness of the South, which once more was reduced to the role of suppliant for more aid. Back in the 1950s India's Nehru had been the founder figure of the Third World concept but he envisaged a Third Force that would represent an independent line from the two sides in the Cold War. The harsh realities of economics, however, made his approach impracticable and the terms Third World and then the South became synonymous with demands for economic assistance or aid from the developed economies of the North.

Raw material exports

Countries of the South which are dependent upon the export of raw materials were adversely affected in the ten-year period up to 1992 as prices paid for their export commodities steadily declined. Raw material prices fell by 20 per cent and the tendency increased at the beginning of the 1990s so that in 1991 the exporters of the South received, on average, only two-thirds of what they had obtained for raw materials in 1980. The effects upon their economies have been devastating. In the two-year period between 1990 and 1992 the wages paid to workers on palm oil plantations in Malaysia were halved and this in a country which is at the upper end of the lower-middle-income group of countries. Coffee exporting countries found the price halved between 1989 and 1992. In general, the more a country depends upon the export of raw materials, the poorer it is likely to be.

The end of the Cold War

The end of the Cold War saw attitudes towards the South change with abrupt speed. The 1992 *Human Development Report* of the UNDP[32] highlighted the change in both attitude and approach when it contrasted the West's unwillingness to write off Africa's debts with its readiness to reduce Poland's by 50 per cent, even though Poland's per capita income was five times the average for Africa. Here was very visible proof of how important the Cold War had been as a motive force behind aid. The switch of the West's economic interest (and readiness to provide either aid or investment) to Eastern Europe and subsequently to the southern tier of former Soviets such as Armenia, Azerbaijan or Kazakstan was immediate and striking: they were seen to have real potential for Western investment.

Debt

The heavy indebtedness of the South is a key to its continuing subservience to the economic policies of the North. An indebted country desperate for concessions is biddable. By the beginning of the 1990s the developing countries of the South were in debt to the North to the tune of $1,700bn with annual debt servicing amounting to $100bn and a net resource outflow from the developing countries of $80bn a year of which $70bn is from the most highly indebted countries. Between 1983 and 1989, for example, the rich creditor nations received $242bn in net transfers from the developing countries on their long-term lending.

In 1970 such debts stood at only $100bn; this figure had increased sixfold by 1980 to $650bn and then doubled during the 1980s to $1,350bn in 1990. Over half this debt is concentrated in only 20 countries, led by Brazil, Mexico, Argentina, India and Egypt. But at one level this concentration is irrelevant because the amount of debt has to be related to the size of the economy of the borrowing country as well as its ability to repay. Thus, the debts of Sub-Saharan Africa at $150bn, although just over a tenth of the total of the South's debts, are proportionately a far greater part of that region's GNP than are the far larger debts of Latin American countries to their region's GNP. The creditor nations change the rules depending upon the country with which they are dealing. Thus, according to World Bank criteria, a country with a per capita income below $700 should not be obliged to borrow at commercial rates. Yet India, with a per capita income of only $340, was obliged to borrow at commercial rates through the 1980s with the result that its debts rose from a mere $5bn in 1980 to $70bn in 1990 so that it joined the ranks of the most heavily indebted nations.

World Bank statistics for five heavily indebted countries – Philippines, India, Indonesia, Egypt and China – demonstrate how aid has created mammoth debt burdens.[33] (See Table I.7.)

Table I.7 Annual aid, cost and deficit: Philippines, India, Indonesia, Egypt, China

Country	Annual aid $m	Annual cost of debt $m	Annual deficit $m
Philippines	1,490	4,881	3,391
India	1,503	8,575	7,072
Indonesia	2,026	12,458	10,432
Egypt	2,304	4,749	2,445
China	3,273	9,296	6,023

The debt situation is made still worse by the way the North deals with loan requests from the South. Since it regards most developing countries as poor investment risks the North charges them exorbitantly for its loans. During the 1980s, for example, while the industrialized countries operated on interest rates of 4 per cent, developing countries were obliged to pay an average of 17 per cent on monies borrowed. A further tilt that leads to still greater imbalance results from the creation of a high protective wall of customs and excise duties and other barriers such as health regulations, industrial standards or agreements involving self-restraint which the North erects whenever it regards exports from the South as a potential danger to its own products. A UNDP estimate suggests that unequal access to world markets costs the South $500bn.

Throughout the 1980s institutional debts by the poorest countries, principally to the World Bank and IMF, rose steadily so that by the mid-1990s they were 400 per cent greater than in 1980 and, as a result, half of all interest payments made by the poorest nations go to multilateral creditors. Many developing countries in fact are standing still rather than developing because of their debt burdens which now represent the biggest obstacle to development with repayments taking 25 per cent of aid while unpaid interest (an increasingly frequent occurrrence) is constantly capitalized and added to the existing capital debt.

The IMF

The role of the International Monetary Fund (IMF) has become central to the North's control of the South. The IMF no longer performs the function for which it was created, to maintain monetary stability by sharing the burden of adjustment between surplus and deficit countries. The IMF has ceased to perform this function because it cannot control or exert authority over the rich industrial nations. Instead the rich nations – effectively the G-7 – have come to see it as their instrument (they can command a majority of the voting power). As a consequence the IMF, which ought to have been the guardian of the poor, has instead become the policeman of the rich.

A high proportion of all poor countries in the South, especially in Africa, operate IMF-inspired structural adjustment programmes (SAPs). In essence this means that the IMF instructs a government on how to manage its economy in return for debt relief, usually in the form of rescheduling. If the South could eliminate its debts it would thereby relieve itself of IMF interference, which is one reason why the North is content for the South to remain indebted. IMF conditionality is monetarist and deflationary, forcing governments to reduce imports by curtailing demand and so stifling growth.

Africa, the world's poorest region, is consistently bullied by the IMF which drained Sub-Saharan Africa of $700m a year between 1983 and 1989. The growing indifference of the rich North to the plight of the South was amply demonstrated in the aftermath of the Cold War when at the May 1992 conference of the IMF and World Bank in Washington the G-7 countries agreed to offer Moscow financial assistance to the tune of $24bn. The scale of the offer led to great bitterness among the poor countries of the South for if the rich Western donors could offer such a large sum so swiftly to Russia after 40 years of Cold War confrontation why could they not do a little better in relation to the indebted nations of the South? The extent of the offer simply underlined just how much aid for the South had always been subject to Cold War considerations.

Only in 1995–6 did the IMF finally acknowledge that massive indebtedness by the poorest nations to the multilateral institutions represented a major problem. The burden of constant pressures upon the weakest countries to repay debts by enforcing structural adjustment programmes always affects the most vulnerable members of such societies as food subsidies are cut, education and health budgets are slashed.[34] In Zambia, for example, an IMF programme led to redundancy among miners who were then faced with the doubling of staple food prices as subsidies were also cut. Uganda spends $3 a head on health and $17 a head servicing multilateral debts. Between 1990 and 1993 Zambia spent 35 times more repaying interest on debts than on its primary education. It had been obliged to introduce fees for both primary education and clinics with the result that over ten years child mortality rose by 20 per cent. Countries whose peoples face such problems or deprivations as a result of debt are unlikely to be able to develop effectively. Over fifteen years some 10,000 rescheduling negotiations have diverted the best skills of poor countries away from development.

The gap between North and South or rich and poor grew enormously in the 30 years from 1960 to 1992 (the end of the Cold War). In 1960 the incomes of the richest fifth of the world's population were 30 times greater than those of the poorest fifth; by 1991 the difference had doubled to 60 times greater.

Human rights

During the 1990s issues of human rights have been turned into a weapon by countries such as Britain whose Foreign Secretary, Douglas Hurd, wrote to the European Commission in August 1991 to urge it to cut aid to governments which violated human rights. The criteria that Mr Hurd pressed his European colleagues to adopt included respect for human rights and the rule of law, a movement towards democracy, accountable government and the rooting out of corruption, as well as the pursuit of sound social and economic policies. Behind this list of criteria was the unstated assumption that the donors would be the judges of whether or not such high standards had been met. The hypocrisy of such attitudes is borne out by the way a blind eye is at once turned to the human rights records of countries like Indonesia which also offer rich investment and trade opportunities to the advanced economies.

Corruption, which is endemic in most societies, is far more damaging to poor nations than to the rich in two respects: first, corruption in a developing nation may well siphon off the difference between effective development and standstill; second, its existence can be used as an excuse by rich nations to cut back on aid or otherwise interfere politically. The principal villains from the North are the major companies who fuel the culture of pay-off and backhander by paying commissions and bribes to safeguard their contracts; they justify such conduct by claiming that everyone does it and that they have no option. In this respect the arms business is probably the worst offender, not only because it is so large, but also because even the governments of the poorest countries are determined to buy arms and salesmen from the main Western countries have few scruples about what they sell or to which country. Annual arms sales to the South now come to approximately $30bn a year and as much as 15 per cent of this huge sum is estimated to cover bribes and various other forms of handout and pay-off.[35] The governments of the same companies from the North then accuse the developing countries of corruption and use behaviour which their own nationals have encouraged as an excuse to cut back on aid.

During 1995 the idea was mooted that debt relief should be linked to powers of monitoring for corruption. Countries would be relieved of debt in exchange for greater independent supervision of how they spent aid. The idea comes from Karl Ziegler, director of the Centre for Accountability and Debt Relief. There was no parallel suggestion of monitoring big business and its readiness to pay bribes to obtain contracts. Ziegler estimates that up to 5 per cent of public budgets in developing countries goes astray.[36] It is possible that the corrupt public sector in the developing world accounts for as much as $500 billion a year. The President of the World Bank, James Wolfensohn, wants to tie Bank aid to curbing corruption.

The Rio Earth Summit 1992

The question of resources and their control dominated the Rio Earth Summit of 1992. The squabbles between North and South which preceded the conference provided ample evidence of the way in which the world was dividing even more harshly into opposed camps of North and South. The rich developed nations, led by the USA, were determined not to have any restrictions placed upon their rates of consumption, while at the same time instructing the South as to how it should conserve resources. As Malaysia's Prime Minister, Mahathir Mohamed, argued cogently: if the wealthy nations wanted to assist the poor nations to cut back on logging or other activities which damaged the environment then they should be prepared to provide money and technological assistance to the poor nations. 'If the rich North expects the poor to foot the bill for a cleaner environment, Rio would become an exercise in futility,' he said. When the conference finally opened, the UN Secretary-General, Boutros Boutros-Ghali, succinctly expressed the differences between North and South when he said the planet was 'sick with over- and under-development'.

The summit agreed a treaty to combat global warming; a treaty to protect wildlife; moves towards a treaty to halt the spread of deserts; steps to tackle over-fishing and the pollution of the seas; Agenda 21 (an action programme for the next decade); and a Rio Declaration of Environmental Principles. There was no treaty on forests or their preservation. The summit was about the management and control of resources yet, despite the rhetoric and agreements, it was plain at the end that the North would continue to exploit as it wished and that the South would resist attempts to control the way it exploited what it had. In almost inverse proportion to the gravity of the assault upon resources worldwide so every nation reserved or attempted to reserve its position.

The Lomé Convention

In its *Human Development Report* of 1992 the UNDP posed the question: 'In a period of rapid economic globalisation, who will protect the interests of the poor?'[37] A new harsh attitude appears to be emerging in the North: that help for the poor will only be forthcoming if they are seen to be useful to the North. After fifteen months of wrangling by the members of the EU about the renewal of the Lomé Convention between Europe and the Africa, Caribbean and Pacific (ACP) group of countries, an agreement was finally reached at the beginning of November 1995 in Mauritius. The Lomé Convention was renewed for a further five years, but not before Britain had tried to slash its own contribution by 30 per cent. As the Prime Minister of Mauritius, Aneerood Jugnauth, said of the negotiations, the end of the Cold War meant that the strategic stake in Africa and other regions of the South had disappeared so that Europe was losing interest in the Lomé relationship: 'We are witnessing a growing movement towards the marginalisation of the South as the focus of the European Union's geopolitical interests seems to be increasingly directed towards other regions of the world.' That statement by the Mauritian Prime Minister is probably as accurate a summary of the North's (and not just the EU's) new attitude towards the South as we are likely to find. The full consequences of such an attitude have yet to be revealed but all the indications point in the same direction: that the North will regard the South as a source of commodities to be obtained as cheaply as possible. Moreover, the South's poverty will force it to sell its resources at prices set by the North. It is a grim outlook for the South and a divisive one for the world at large.

THE INTERNATIONAL DRUGS TRADE

At the beginning of the 1990s the international drugs trade was estimated to be the world's second largest in value after the arms trade and ahead of oil, although it may fall below oil depending upon price fluctuations. Between growers at one end of the trade through processing, middlemen, couriers and drug barons to street vendors and finally the users it generates an estimated annual turnover in the region of $500,000,000,000.

Illegal drugs come principally in three forms: cocaine, heroin and marijuana or cannabis, although there are other mild drugs such as qat which is found in Somalia and the Arabian Peninsula. The producers of the coca plant (the basis for cocaine) are in South America and the main sources are Bolivia, Ecuador and Peru, although most of the drug is processed in Colombia from whence it is shipped to its various international destinations.

Peru is the world's largest coca producer, followed by Bolivia and Colombia. Colombia is the leading world centre where coca is processed into the drug cocaine and its drug cartels wield great power. The principal markets for cocaine are the USA followed by Europe and then further afield including Russia.

Although, in recent years, the Latin American producers have begun to look at heroin (derived from opium) as an alternative to coca, the major producers of heroin are found in Asia. These are Afghanistan, Iran and Pakistan (the Golden Crescent) and Burma, Laos and Thailand (the Golden Triangle). Lebanon is also a producer, as is Mexico and Guatemala in Latin America.

China, Burma's neighbour to the north, produces its own opium for home consumption in about eighteen provinces and also acts as a transit country for opium from the Golden Triangle. Laos, another member of the Golden Triangle, is the world's third producer of opium as well as growing cannabis. Thailand is now only a relatively minor producer of the opium poppy due to eradication programmes but a major trafficker in opium, especially from Burma and Laos.

Afghanistan lies at the centre of the Golden Crescent and is the second opium producer after Burma as well as a major source of hashish. Iran produces opium for the international market and is also a transit country for heroin from Southwest Asia to Europe. Pakistan is the second largest heroin producer in Southwest Asia (after Afghanistan) and also produces hashish; the government eradication programme has had little impact. Turkey, which produces the poppy legally for medicinal drugs, is a major transit country for heroin and hashish to Europe and the USA with Istanbul acting as one of the world's centres for the international drugs trade. A number of other Asian countries are also heavily involved.

Africa is not a major source of drugs but in recent years a number of African countries have become important as transit countries and, for example, Nigeria has become notorious as a source of drug couriers. Côte d'Ivoire produces cannabis and is developing into an important transit point for drugs from Southeast Asia *en route* to Europe. Egypt is a major transit country for drugs from Southeast and Southwest Asia *en route* to Europe and the USA and is extensively used by Nigerian couriers while it provides a large domestic market for hashish and heroin from Lebanon and Syria.

Some 60 countries worldwide are listed by the CIA[38] for their involvement in the international drugs trade: either as producers or as transit countries and traffickers, or both. These 60 countries are apart from the main market or consumer countries for these drugs which are found in North America, Europe and the countries of the Commonwealth of Independent States (CIS), especially Russia, though a number of CIS countries are also producers.

In world resource terms drugs form an immensely valuable commodity which originates in the countries of the South while the principal markets are in the rich advanced economies of the North. The damage done to societies where substantial numbers of people are serious addicts is enormous, hence the efforts to curtail the trade and the severe penalties imposed upon traffickers.

In realistic terms there are three practical ways to tackle the international drugs trade: the first is to continue as at present. This entails a range of police methods in the consumer countries where drugs are illegal and penalties for trafficking can be very severe – Saudi Arabia, for example, imposes the death penalty for trafficking. The corollary of this approach is to launch eradication programmes in the principal producer countries and this has been done in a number of instances with substantial US financial assistance. Such programmes have largely failed for the simple 'market forces' reason that the trade is far too profitable to abandon.

The second approach would be to legalize drugs so that they become like any other agricultural commodity; the decriminalization of the trade would eradicate the present violence, lawbreaking and cartels which are now an essential part of the international drug business. Such a course of action, though sometimes discussed, is always dismissed in the main consumer countries where moral considerations and possibly other vested interests are opposed to legalization.

The third approach, which logically makes the most sense, would also be the most politically and economically costly: to attempt to eradicate in the principal consumer countries the social and economic reasons that turn so many people to drug abuse in the first place. There appears to be little sign that such a course will be followed.

Meanwhile, the international drugs trade continues as one of the three most widespread and profitable of the world's activities and allows the North, especially the USA, to fund drug eradication programmes in producer countries, thereby giving the impression that the South (the producers) rather than the North (the consumers) is to blame for the continuation of the trade.

THE GLOBAL MARKET

The end of the Cold War coincided, more or less, with an acceptance of the idea that we belong to a single world market. National boundaries are becoming increasingly irrelevant as both financial institutions and business companies cross boundaries to operate where it is most profitable to do so. There is a rapidly increasing fluidity about commercial operations with apparently fewer and fewer controls. The integration of world markets, however, could prove a disaster not only to the less developed countries but also to the poor in rich countries since the interaction of high technology communications and the deregulation of finances together create a fluid global economy that will be 'uncontrollable' in any narrow national sense. Globalization may excite businessmen and economists but the process will be fraught with political difficulties.

Money is now shifted rapidly from one country to another, always in search of the location where the highest, quickest returns can be found, and business follows the funds. The same products – brand names such as Coca-Cola or McDonald's – now appear worldwide, though produced locally under franchise, and the pervasive presence of the transnational corporations is more apparent than ever. The movement of money has become the key to the global market and an estimated $1 trillion is now moved round the world on a daily basis. Financial deregulation, which was the hallmark of the Reagan–Thatcher era, means that investors can now move their foreign direct investment (FDI) more or less anywhere in a world market that is both increasingly uncontrolled and harder to control so that money rather than trade has become the principal engine of growth. The creation of jobs will follow the movement of money.

Money is invested where labour is cheapest. The practice is not new: apartheid in

South Africa lasted as long as it did because the regulation of African labour ensured a cheap labour market that attracted investors who would have been forced to pay more elsewhere and their investment in the apartheid state assisted it to survive longer than would otherwise have been the case. What is new is the deregulation of money so that any amount may be shifted more or less overnight to finance operations in a new cheap market or environment. European companies may now employ more Asians (in Asia) as part of their workforces than they employ Europeans in the country where the company is domiciled and varying proportions – often the greater part of an item such as a car – may be made in Asia and then shipped to Europe for assembly as the finished European product.

Japan invested heavily in the rapidly developing economies of South Korea and Taiwan which a few years ago offered obvious advantages of cheap, highly motivated labour and proximity. Japan's companies are now redeploying to Malaysia and Thailand where wage costs are only a tenth, for South Korea and Taiwan have begun to move up the scale in terms of living standards, and wages, as a result, are rising. A British firm (Morgan Crucible) has moved operations from Germany and Japan to Eastern Europe and China. Labour costs in Eastern Europe may be as little as one-fifteenth of those in Germany while the enormous growth rates registered by China over the 1980s and into the 1990s were based upon some of the cheapest labour costs in the world. In 1995 rates of pay in industry in Japan were $31 an hour, in Germany $26 an hour, in Eastern Europe $1.50 an hour and in China (Shanghai) $1 a day.[39]

The commercial logic of following the cheapest labour markets is clear but there are other problems that have yet to be fully understood. On the face of it, for example, the arrival of a foreign company in China to provide employment where none existed before must represent a gain to that country. However, if the foreign company's operations lead to a rapid increase in living standards will this be followed by rising wage demands that persuade the foreign company to move on. If, on the other hand, standards do not rise wherein lies the advantage to China? The constant pursuit worldwide of locations where wages are low will create a climate in which wages are forced downwards and such situations produce their own political and social logic.

Reactions to the global economy are by no means all favourable and three deserve examination: the 'new protectionism' of the political right wing in advanced economies; cultural rejection of international capitalism in countries whose ruling castes feel threatened; and rejection by the less developed countries (LDCs) because they know the process will marginalize them.

The need to protect the old-established economies of Europe and North America from the threat of the new global capitalism is giving rise to demands for protectionism in Britain, France and the USA. If transnational corporations succeed in creating a single world economic system then the peoples of Western Europe or the USA will find themselves competing for employment with the lowest wage countries. A transnational may have its headquarters in New York or London but if the bulk of the employment it creates is in Mexico or China what advantage is that to the USA or Britain as opposed to the transnational corporation and its shareholders? Such a situation can be avoided by protection from the effects of going to the cheapest labour markets.[40] The new era of a globalized economy will be very different from that which has been dominated by the Group of Seven (G-7) and there will be no simple, easy hierarchy of the top economic nations: 'Instead, the world will be a far more complex place, there will be many players, intense competition and a constant process of borrowing, learning and leapfrogging.'[41] New protectionism of the kind advocated by Sir James Goldsmith in Britain who wants to detach Britain from Europe or Pat Buchanan and Ross Perot in the USA who see NAFTA allowing Mexico to take jobs away from Americans may become a powerful if reactionary creed opposed to the globalization of the economy.

The UN and its related institutions such as the World Trade Organization (WTO) have already accepted that the globalization of the economy is irreversible. The WTO is trying to establish global rules for business which would guarantee the rights of capital and property as these move offshore. There is a parallel move to take global action to secure social and environmental rights but these, as always, will take second place after capital and property rights have been secured.

A different form of protectionism altogether comes in the form of cultural rejection of what is seen as Western materialism. This is now becoming important in India and parts of the Muslim world. India represents the second largest long-term market in the world after China but Hindu nationalists do not wish to see their economy dominated by foreign transnationals. An Indian psychoanalyst, Sudhir Kakkar, says of this reaction: 'The ferment in Indian society isn't just economic. Many people feel the Western world is encroaching, that all traditional values are under siege – the family and relations between sexes.'[42]

The Islamic fundamentalism of Algeria and Iran is fuelled by antagonism to Western materialism and represents a conscious rejection of a global economy in which these countries would be minor players. Western consumerism, the vanguard of the global economy, can play havoc with the beliefs of a traditional society; as a result transnationals and their products are seen as dangerous invaders rather than welcome investors. Ironically, it was the oil wealth of the Gulf region that sparked off such reactions. As the Gulf oil states used their wealth to modernize they discovered they lacked two forms of labour: the first consisting of technical and technological expertise they could import from the West; the second consisting of unskilled labour they imported in large numbers from neighbouring but poor countries including Bangladesh, India, Pakistan and the Palestinians. These temporary workers made fortunes in their own terms and then returned to their home countries where they adopted lifestyles that had been impossible before their stint in the Gulf. In India this meant low-caste Hindus returning home with more wealth than higher-caste Indians who would not have soiled their hands with the kind of work on offer in the Gulf. The result is the beginning of a social revolution in India more powerful than all Mahatma Gandhi's pleas for an end to the caste system. The globalization of labour by such migrant movements is another aspect of the changing world economy.

The less developed countries (LDCs) are the third group which must fear the new global economy for in the most elementary sense these countries which, in any case, are at the bottom of the international 'pecking order' now stand to be marginalized, perhaps totally. Kevin Watkins, the senior policy adviser to Oxfam, argues that globalization is 'a euphemism for a race to maximise profit by lowering environmental standards and workers' pay and conditions'.[43] The contrary argument – that a growth of wealth, however achieved (the 'trickle-down theory'), is the best way to raise up the poor – would appear to be increasingly doubtful against the economic evidence of recent years. Despite huge creations of wealth the poor, on the whole, are worse rather than better off.

What is certain, however, is that the poorest nations are unable to escape the effects of economic globalization. There are inevitable imbalances. According to UNCTAD: 'International trade and production have not expanded at the same rate as international financial transactions, but production by transnational corporations has grown faster than trade.' Moreover, 'The principal driving force in the globalisation process today is the search of both private and publicly-owned firms – for profits worldwide.'[44] What puts the LDCs at a crucial disadvantage is the fact that they do not possess the necessary up-to-date capacity of international communications. As the same UNCTAD report says: 'With the ability to transmit virtually unlimited amounts of data at very low costs, firms can easily diversify geographically the various stages of production without losing managerial control.' That is not something within the capability of most LDCs.[45]

Globalization and liberalization feed on each other. Business organizations see the advantage in transnational production operations, but for these to be profitable they must exert ever greater pressures on governments to concede conditions that suit them. This means both the liberalization of international trade as well as the provision for incoming business of 'freedom of entry, right of establishment and national treatment, as well as freedom for international financial transactions, deregulation and privatisation'.[46] This is a great deal to ask of a small weak economy; it is also difficult for such economies which are desperate for investment to say no.

It seems unrealistic to suppose that the LDCs will be integrated into this new world economy and far more likely that they will be marginalized. Liberalization effectively makes the LDCs more vulnerable to economic penetration by the advanced economies and usually without any compensating advantage. As UNCTAD's *The Least Developed Countries 1996 Report* admits: 'In the absence of appropriate policy responses from the LDCs and the international community, globalization and liberalization may do little to alleviate the trend towards their marginalization from the world economy and may even accentuate it.'[47] In effect, the Report goes on to admit that apart from possible niche exports such as horticulture and tourism, the most likely role for LDCs is to attract a few enterprises that are labour intensive and in search of cheap labour.

The UNCTAD Report is honest if depressing about the prospects for most developing countries in the new globalized economy. It admits: 'There is currently much concern that globalization and liberalization are accentuating income disparities in the world economy, with most of the benefits accruing to the already industrialized economies and a relatively small number of newly industrialized economies (NIEs), while the weaker DCs become poorer and progressively marginalized.'[48] LDCs are in desperate need of capital to finance development yet: 'Their share of the total FDI flows to all DCs amounted to only 1.1 per cent in 1992-1994. FDI has been concentrated in the richer and more dynamic DCs, especially those in East Asia and Latin America.'[49] As the Report goes on to point out: 'The adjustment efforts of the LDCs require more support from the international community. A crucial role for the international community will be to provide adequate levels of concessional finance to fund the infrastructural and social development programmes of LDC governments and to provide the balance of payments and budgetary support to facilitate economic-reform programmes.' In fact such support was not forthcoming in the mid-1990s and the general cutback in aid suggests that it will not be available in the foreseeable future. Already unequal competition leads to an estimated loss of $500bn a year to developing countries at a time when aid which is running at $54bn a year faces either cutbacks or stagnation and, in any case, is quite inadequate to compensate for the trade disadvantages that developing countries face. In brutal terms, the advanced economies have no interest in bringing the LDCs into the global economy.

Many perceptions were changed with the end of the Cold War and during the 1990s the USA began to look at the Asian Rim in a new light while Europe became far more uncomfortably aware of the thrusting new economies of East Asia. For one reason, ideas now travel round the globe with incredible speed while intense competition forces countries and business to go in search of best practices wherever these are to be found for it is no longer possible to retain old business practices in face of the new pressures. When, in 1996, the leader of the British Labour Party, Tony Blair, visited Asia overtly to learn from the Asian Tigers his trip represented a startling admission (for Britain) that times had indeed changed and that in an environment of constant and rapid global changes there could be no room for complacency if Britain was to maintain its own in a highly competitive world. Europe will not find it easy to learn from Asia whose traditions are fundamentally different from its own but a new willingness to try to learn from other societies would now appear to be essential for any country that intends to keep abreast of the global business climate.

Much may be learnt from China which may well turn out to be the proving ground for the new global economy. The Chinese who are flocking to the fast-industrializing region between Hong Kong and Shanghai in search of work come from one of the poorest rural backgrounds in the world and to these people, at least for the time being, even a fifteen-hour day which earns them a pittance may seem better than the drudgery of subsistence agriculture. As business will argue (and is arguing already) the small wage which it offers represents an advance upon even worse conditions and it cannot afford to give more. Of course business could afford to give more but then it would be undercut by its competitors.

Western business will go to China because labour is so cheap and the Chinese government is unlikely to exert any pressures upon such incomers to increase wages when its primary aim is to produce cheap goods with which to break into new markets. China, moreover (or any other comparably placed country) would be still more reluctant to put pressure upon such companies if it knows their response will simply be to move elsewhere. The result, for the lowly paid, is a trap from which it will be exceptionally difficult to escape. The new global market, therefore, is going to be virtually impossible to control.

The veteran economist J. K. Galbraith responded to a question about the 'Asian Threat' by saying: 'This is part of the larger process of economic development and it is something to be welcomed. We must face the fact that certain industries will move to the newer countries, to the lower cost countries.'[50] As he has also pointed out, there is a new dialectic 'between the huge, economically and socially comfortable community that has come into being in the advanced economic society and those who live on the margins of the modern economy or outside'. Galbraith advanced this thesis in relation to the USA[51] but it has equal application to the West as a whole where two-culture societies are becoming more marked. Just as a growing divide is becoming evident in rich societies between those who are 'contented' and those who live on the margins, so the same divisions exist even more starkly in a world that is being made one by the global economy but in the process will marginalize many communities and countries (LDCs) which are unable either to catch up or stand the pace.[52]

NOTES

1   *World Development Report 1994*, World Bank, Oxford University Press.
2   International Conference on Population and Development (ICPD), Cairo, September 5–13 1994. (The conference, which was the outcome of a United Nations Economic and Social Council (ECOSOC) resolution, paid particular attention to the subject of the empowerment of women.)
3   Paul Harrison, Population facts that can spur women's well being, *People and the Planet*, 3(3), 1994, pp. 6–9.
4   Ibid.
5   *The State of World Population 1996*, United Nations Population Fund (UNFPA).
6   The figures are extracted from the country surveys in the *Encyclopaedia Britannica Book of the Year 1996*.
7   FAO News release PR96/3, February 1 1996, Rome.
8   Ibid.
9   *The Independent*, February 12 1996, The expanding appetite of a hungry world transforms food mountains into molehills, Nicholas Schoon.
10 Ibid.
11 *The Independent*, May 11 1996.
12 *The World Bank Annual Report 1995*, p. 25.
13 *The World in 1996*, The Economist Publications, The World in Figures.
14 *Encyclopaedia Britannica Book of the Year 1996*, Mining, p. 149.
15 *BP Statistical Review of World Energy*, June 1995, p. 2.
16 Ibid.
17 *The Independent*, May 18 1995, Russia's pipe dreams fuel oil rush on Caspian Sea, Andrew Higgins.
18 *The World in 1996*, The Economist Publications, Oil in 1996, p. 111.
19 *The Independent*, March 28 1996, Global warming won't cost the earth, Frances Cairncross.
20 Ibid.
21 Ibid.
22 *Encyclopaedia Britannica Book of the Year 1996*, Fisheries, Martin J. Gill, pp. 110–11.
23 *Financial Times*, February 27 1995, First steps towards a structure for global communications, Alan Cane.
24 *The World in 1996*, The Economist Publications, Sir Iain Vallance (Chairman of BT).
25 *Financial Times*, February 27 1995, First steps towards a structure for global communications, Alan Cane.
26 *Financial Times*, October 3 1995, International Telecommunications (survey) p. 21.
27 *The Economist*, September 30 1995, The end of monopoly (a survey of telecommunications), p. 10.
28 *Encyclopaedia Britannica Book of the Year 1996*, Special report, Cyberspace, Robert Everett-Green.
29 *The Observer*, January 7 1996, Asia's tiger economies earn their stripes, Barry Hugill.
30 *Encyclopaedia Britannica Book of the Year 1996*, National product and accounts, World Data.
31 *The World in 1996*, The Economist Publications. The death of foreign aid, p. 86.
32 *Human Development Report 1992*, United Nations Development Programme (UNDP), Oxford University Press.
33 *The World in 1996*, The Economist Publications, The death of foreign aid (extract of World Bank statistics), p. 86.
34 *The Independent*, February 22 1996, Third World death on the rise, Paul Vallely.
35 *The Observer*, October 22 1995, Muck and Brass, Michael Prest.
36 Ibid.
37 *Human Development Report 1992*, United Nations Development Programme (UNDP), Oxford University Press.
38 *The World Factbook 1993*, Central Intelligence Agency, Washington, DC.
39 *The Independent*, September 27 1995, How to halt the global money-go-round, Paul Vallely.
40 *The Independent*, June 12 1996, Inside the court of Sir James, John Rentoul.
41 *The Independent*, May 20 1996, Hunting down the Asian tigers, Martin Jacques.
42 *The Independent*, September 29 1995, India turns its back on Western ways, Tim McGirk.
43 *The Independent*, September 27 1995, How to halt the global money-go-round, Paul Vallely.

44 *Globalization and Liberalization*, Developments in the face of two powerful currents, UNCTAD 1996, New York, p. 6.
45 Ibid, p. 7.
46 Ibid, p. 7.
47 *The Least Developed Countries 1996 Report*, UNCTAD, p. II.
48 Ibid, p. IV.
49 Ibid, p. V.
50 *The Independent*, January 8 1996, Compassion comes before contentment (interview of J. K. Galbraith), Andrew Marr.
51 See *The World Economy since the Wars*, J. K. Galbraith, Sinclair-Stevenson, 1994.
52 See *The Culture of Contentment*, J. K. Galbraith, Houghton Mifflin, Boston, 1992.

PART II

Country Surveys

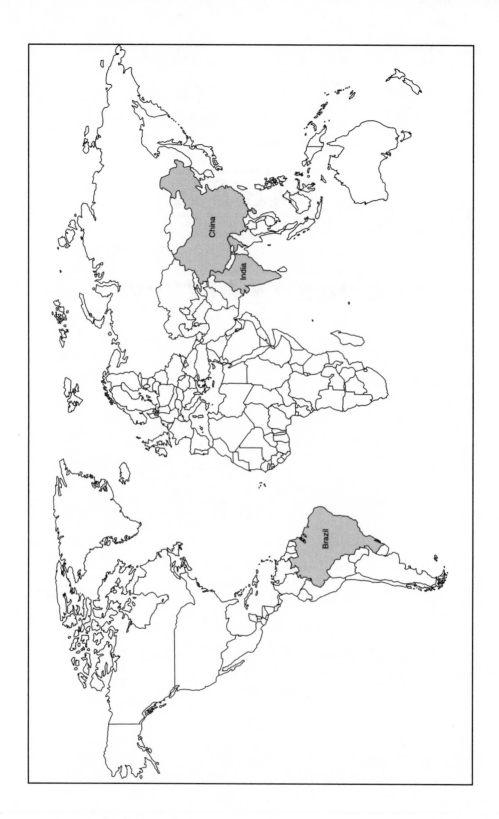

Map 2 The three giants

1 THE THREE GIANTS

INTRODUCTION

Although Brazil, China and India qualify for inclusion in the Third World or South in terms of their development, they are in a class of their own and stand apart from all the other countries considered in this survey by virtue of their size, population, resources and potential. Each is continental in size: Brazil, which covers 3,286,500 sq. miles, is roughly equivalent to the USA; China at 3,696,100 sq. miles is the world's third largest country (after Russia and Canada); and though India is much smaller at 1,222,243 sq. miles it is still vast. In terms of population China and India between them account for more than a third of the world's total population and numbers alone make them formidable. Brazil, at 155 million, has a more manageable population. Each of the three has huge resources although India is the least well endowed. The key to the future of these three giants is the rate of industrialization which they are able to achieve – the capacity to add value to their resources – and there is little doubt that they will achieve major economic breakthroughs over the coming decades. In effect, these three nations are big and powerful enough to go their own ways and each is likely in the foreseeable future to become a formidable economic force in its own right.

BRAZIL

Area. 3,286,500 sq. miles (8,511,996 sq. km).
Population. (1995) 155,822,000.
Capital. Brasília (1,598,415 – Federal District).
Other major cities. São Paulo (9,393,753 – metropolitan area – 15,416,416), Rio de Janeiro (5,473,909 – metropolitan area – 9,796,498), Salvador (2,070,296 – metropolitan area – 2,493,224), Belo Horizonte (1,529,560 – metropolitan area – 3,431,755), Recife (1,296,995 – metropolitan area – 2,871,261), Porto Alegre (1,237,223 – metropolitan area – 3,026,029), Manaus (1,005,634), Goiânia (912,136).
Language(s). Portuguese (official), Spanish, English, French.
Religion(s). Roman Catholic 90 per cent.
Date of independence. September 7 1822 (from Portugal).
GNP. (1993) $471,978,000,000, per capita $3,020.
Land and climate. The greater part of the country (the northern bulge) which includes the vast Amazon Basin consists of flat land or rolling lowlands; plains, hills and mountains are found in the south and there is a narrow coastal belt. The Amazon is the world's greatest river both in respect of its huge drainage area and the volume of its waters. The climate is mainly tropical though temperate in the south towards Argentina.

Introduction

Continental in size, Brazil is the fifth largest country in the world after Russia, Canada, China and the USA; it has a total of 14,691km of land boundaries with ten countries – Argentina, Bolivia, Colombia, French Guiana, Guyana, Paraguay, Peru, Suriname, Uruguay and Venezuela, as well as a coastline of 7,491km on the Atlantic. It possesses all the potential in terms of size of population, extent of mineral, agricultural and other natural resources including hydro-electric power (developed and undeveloped) and growing industrial capacity to become a major world economy and a possible economic superpower in the twenty-first century. Brazil's GNP ranks tenth in the world league and its industrial sector (even though it suffers many crises and reverses) is one of the fastest developing of any country in the South.

Historically, Brazil was Portugal's only colony in the Americas and its population is a mixture based upon the original Indian peoples, the Portuguese settlers and imported African slaves. It faces many problems arising out of its headlong rush to industrialize and modernize. These include inadequate controls over the activities of major companies and transnational corporations, massive pollution in the big cities, huge damage inflicted upon the ecology, accusations of genocidal practices against the indigenous Indian people, too rapid exploitation of natural resources and, in particular, the rate of depletion of Brazil's greatest natural asset, its vast rainforest. These economic, social and environmental problems arising out of too rapid development and possible over-exploitation of resources have to be considered alongside a rapid rate of population increase, a volatile political tradition which has included periodic interventions by the military and huge regional variations of wealth and development in the economy dominated by the 'industrial triangle' of São Paulo–Rio de Janeiro–Belo Horizonte.

Agriculture

The agricultural sector is large and varied with a particularly strong export division; agriculture accounts for 10.8 per cent of GDP and employs 22 per cent of the workforce. Forest accounts for 58 per cent of the land, meadows and pastures for 21.9 per cent, land under permanent cultivation up to 7.3 per cent, other 12.8 per cent. Most of the large agricultural holdings are private and government policy has been to channel finance into this sector. There are periodic conflicts, sometimes extremely violent, between large landholders and landless peasants.

The main crops (with production figures for 1994) are: sugarcane 279,822,000 metric tonnes (mt), maize 32,217,000mt, soybeans 24,855mt, cassava 24,058,000mt, oranges 17,978,000mt, rice 10,644,000mt, bananas 5,593,000mt, wheat 2,372,000mt. Other important crops are dry beans, potatoes, tomatoes, seed cotton, papayas, coffee (2,613,000mt), coconuts, pineapples, grapes, apples, tobacco leaves, cacao, cashews and palm oil. There is a national cattle herd of 153,000,000 and meat is a major export. There are also 33 million pigs, 19 million sheep and 6 million horses.

Brazil is the world's largest producer and exporter of coffee which has long been its staple foreign exchange earner and currently has about 24 per cent of the world market. It is also the largest world exporter of orange juice (concentrate). It is the second largest exporter of soybeans. Agricultural crop exports account for approximately 40 per cent of all exports.

Brazil possesses the world's largest resource of primary rainforest but its present policy of unrestricted logging or the cutting down of forests to provide new land for agriculture is depleting this huge resource at an alarming rate and deforestation is now causing major ecological problems as well as attracting the attention of world conservationists. Roundwood production (1993) stands at 272,078,000cu m.

There is a substantial (illicit) production of cannabis and coca (for cocaine) although these drugs are primarily for home consumption. There is a government programme of eradication; Brazil has become a transit country for Bolivian and Colombian cocaine to the USA and Europe.

Most of Brazil's food exports go to the USA, other South American countries, Europe and the Middle East.

Brazil is a leading member of the International Coffee Organization (ICO) and, as a major exporter of sugar, is also a member of the International Sugar Organization. Brazil has been a pioneer in producing ethanol from sugarcane juice and vehicles have been converted to run on ethanol so that by 1989 two-thirds of the country's cars used ethanol, although its development tends to depend upon the price of oil.

Brazil, apart from being a major commodity exporter, is self-sufficient in food except for wheat and it should have no difficulty in feeding its population into the foreseeable future despite its huge size and rapid rate of growth.

Minerals

Brazil has a huge range of mineral resources that includes iron ore, manganese, bauxite, nickel, uranium, phosphates, tin, gold, platinum, petroleum as well as vast hydro-power (actual and potential).

Of 25 major minerals, Brazil stands among the world's leading producers for no less than sixteen (see Table 1.1).

Table 1.1 Brazil, mineral production, 1992

Mineral	World placing	Output 1992
Bauxite	4	10,800,000mt
Aluminium	5	1,200,000mt
Chromite	7	340,000mt
Gold	9	76,000kg
Iron ore	2	146,000,000mt
Crude steel	9	24,000,000mt
Manganese ore	4	1,800,000mt
Silver	16	194mt
Tin	2	30,000mt
Zinc	16	140,000mt
Hydraulic cement	10	28,100,000mt
Diamonds	7	1,500,000 carats
Nitrogen ammonia	22	877,000mt
Phosphate rock	9	3,300,000mt
Salt	6	8,200,000mt
Elemental sulphur	22	282,000mt

Mineral production in 1992 included the following: iron ore (146,000,000mt), bauxite (10,800,000mt), manganese (1,800,000mt), kaolin (850,000mt), zinc (140,000mt), copper (37,000mt), tin (30,000mt), gold (2,450,000 troy ounces), diamonds (1,500,000 carats).

Brazil is not a major oil producer although in 1992 it produced 1 per cent of world output and consumed 1.9 per cent. Reserves, however, are small scale, perhaps one-quarter of a per cent of the total in Latin America. Crude oil production in 1992 was at the rate of 622,000 b/d with an additional output of 3,757,000,000cu m of natural gas.

Overall, Brazil's mineral resources are on a vast scale. There are an estimated 4,600 million tons of bauxite reserves while iron ore exports at the current level can continue into the indefinite future. Most important for Brazil, its wide range of minerals provides the flexibility upon which to base a rapidly expanding industrial economy while also making a significant contribution to export earnings. Even so, they only account for 1.7 per cent of GDP and employ less than 1 per cent of the labour force.

Manufacturing

The emergence of Brazil as a major industrial power has raised the economy to tenth place in world terms. The industrial sector is now widely diversified and currently contributes 25 per cent to GDP (1993) and employs over 9 million or 14.6 per cent of the workforce. Principal subdivisions of this sector include: chemicals, fabricated metals, food products, non-electrical metals, non-electrical machinery, electrical machinery, transport equipment, textiles, clothing and footwear, non-metallic mineral products, paper and paper products, plastics, rubber products, publishing and printing, pharmaceuticals, wood and wood products, furniture, beverages. Manufactures now contribute 30 per cent to exports with the USA, Europe and Japan as principal destinations.

Infrastructure

There are 28,828km of railways of which just over 24,000km are narrow gauge. Of 1,448,000km of roads 48,000km are paved. There are 50,000km of navigable inland waterways. Pipelines include 2,000km for crude oil, 3,804km for petroleum products and 1,095km for natural gas. The country is served by eleven major ports – Belém, Fortaleza, Ilheus, Manaus, Paranagua, Porto Alegre, Recife, Rio de Janeiro, Rio Grande, Salvador and Santos. There are 3,031 usable airports, 431 with permanent surface runways, two with runways over 3,659m and 22 with runways between 2,440 and 3,659m. There is a good overall system of telecommunications including 9.86 million telephones and a satellite system with three Atlantic Ocean INTELSTAT earth stations and 64 domestic satellite earth stations.

Political considerations

Brazil is now undergoing a major industrial revolution and moving towards the status of a potential economic super-power for the twenty-first century. Inevitably, there will be immense pressures by a range of interest groups – both internal and external – upon the political system. Alternating periods of democratic government and military interventions have characterized the half century since 1945. There is a wide range of political parties. Scandal in 1992 led to the impeachment of President Collor and his replacement by Itamar Franco.

Assessments

Brazil has now laid the basis of a dynamic industrial economy and has the infrastructure, the population and the expertise, the minerals and other resources as well as being self-sufficient in food so that it possesses all the obvious economic requirements to allow it to become a major world economy in the near future. Its huge, barely manageable international debts (standing at $87,000,000,000 in 1993) represent a temporary difficulty while high unemployment, at 15 per cent, is a more permanent problem, especially as the population is projected to reach 172 million in 2000 and 194 million in 2010.

CHINA

Area. 3,696,100 sq. miles (9,572,900 sq. km).
Population. (1995) 1,206,600,000.
Capital. Beijing (5,769,607 – 1990).
Other major cities. (1990) Shanghai (7,496,509), Tientsin (4,574,689), Shen-yang (3,603,712), Wu-han (3,284,229), Canton (2,914,281), Harbin (2,443,398), Chung-king (2,266,772), Nanking (2,090,204); there are another 13 cities with populations between 1 and 2 million.
Language(s). Mandarin Chinese (official), Cantonese, Shanghainese, Fuzhou, Hokkien-Taiwanese, Xiang, Gan, Hakka dialects and a number of ethnic minority languages such as Tibetan, Manchu, Mongol.
Religion(s). Non-religious 59.2 per cent, folk-religions 20.1 per cent, atheist 12 per cent, Buddhist 6 per cent, Muslim 2.4 per cent, Christian 0.2 per cent, other 0.1 per cent.
Date of independence. Creation of a unified China under the Ch'in Dynasty 221BC; the present People's Republic was established October 1 1949.
GNP. (1993) $581,109,000,000, per capita $490.
Land and climate. A predominantly mountainous country with high plateaux; deserts in the west; plains and deltas and hills in the east. China possesses two of the world's greatest rivers: the Yangtze (Chang Jiang) 3,430 miles (5,520km) and the Yellow River (Huang He) 2,903 miles (4,672km). The climate passes through huge variations from tropical in the south to subarctic in the far north. It is subject to a range of environmental problems including typhoons on the southern and eastern coasts, floods, earthquakes, deforestation and soil erosion as well as rapidly increasing industrial pollution.

Introduction

China, the birthplace of one of the world's three oldest civilizations, was also for centuries the world's wealthiest nation, a leader in both arts and technology. But it fell behind the rapidly developing nations of the West at the end of the Middle Ages and entered a long period of economic, social and political decline during the nineteenth century when it came close to being carved up by the Western imperial powers.

The present modern period begins with the triumph of the Chinese Communist Party in the revolution that brought Mao Zedong to absolute power over a unified China in 1949. During the Mao years (1949–76) social, political and economic experiments – 'Let 100 flowers bloom and diverse thoughts contend', the Great Leap Forward and the Cultural Revolution – as well as China's almost total isolation from the West meant that the country failed to keep abreast of modern industrial and technological developments or to realize its vast industrial–commercial potential in world (competitive) terms. But Mao's successor, Deng Xiaoping, embarked upon a policy of exposing China to more market-oriented policies with a relatively 'open door' policy in relation to the rest of the world. China now embarked upon a determined effort to increase production. Thus, between 1979 when Deng's new policy got under way and 1986 GNP was doubled. Foreign investment was encouraged by concessions to overseas investors in Special Economic Zones created in

1980 at Guangdong and Fujian. There followed a rapid expansion of foreign trade and in 1984, for example, fourteen coastal cities as well as Hainan Island were opened to technological imports, and joint ventures with foreign firms (so far mainly from Hong Kong) have been allowed since 1979. In 1986 a stock exchange was opened at Shanghai. Even so (and apart from political considerations and possible future changes of direction) China, with a per capita income of only $490 in 1993 (as compared with a US per capita income of $25,850 – a differential of 52) has an immense way to go before it even begins to catch up the world's leading economies.

Nevertheless, by 1995 it had become clear that huge and continuing changes were under way. There was greater personal liberty and mobility; the standard of living of the majority continued to rise; the number of rural poor had dropped from 200m to 80m. However, the gap between rich and poor continued to grow and there was a constant influx, by the millions, of rural Chinese into the coastal areas and towns in search of employment. The Ninth Five Year Plan (1996–2000) envisaged an 8–9 per cent rate of growth. China, by the mid-1990s, had become one of the world's leading trading nations with a $20bn trade surplus for 1994–5 and foreign reserves in excess of $64bn. Growing assertiveness in foreign affairs and a rapidly developing military potential already mark China as a major world power.

Located in eastern Asia, lying between India in the southwest and Mongolia in the north, China is the world's third largest country (after Russia and Canada). It has 22,000km of land boundaries and 14,500km of coastline and a total of sixteen neighbours: Afghanistan, Bhutan, Burma, Hong Kong (due to return to Chinese sovereignty from Britain in 1997), India, Kazakstan, North Korea, Kyrgyzstan, Laos, Macau, Mongolia, Nepal, Pakistan, Russia, Tajikistan and Vietnam.

Agriculture

Agriculture accounts for 22 per cent of GDP and employs 56.4 per cent of the labour force. China is a leading world producer of rice, potatoes, sorghum, peanuts, tea, millet, barley and pork. Production of the principal staples (grains) in 1993 was as follows: rice 187,211,000mt, wheat 105,005,000mt, maize 103,380,000mt. Other main staple crops include sorghum, millet, barley, oil seed, rapeseed, peanuts, sunflower seeds and a range of fruit and nuts. Other major crops include sweet potatoes (105,185,000mt), sugarcane (68,419,000mt), potatoes, sugar beet, cotton. Cotton and other fibres and oilseeds are the principal export crops and food and live animals accounted for 9.2 per cent of exports in 1993. The national herds include: pigs (393,000,000), sheep (97,000,000), goats (82,000,000), cattle (22,000,000), water buffalo (10,000,000). Roundwood production in 1992 came to 296,557,000cu m and the fish catch to 15,007,450mt.

Forested land comprises 13.6 per cent, meadows and pastures 42.9 per cent, agricultural land under permanent cultivation 10.4 per cent, and other 33.1 per cent. China is broadly self-sufficient in food production and with intense irrigation methods may produce three crops of rice in a year. In disaster years, floods, for example, China has been compelled to import grains.

Minerals

China is one of the world's greatest storehouses of minerals including coal, iron ore, petroleum, mercury, tin, tungsten, antimony, manganese, molybdenum, vanadium, magnetite, aluminium, lead, zinc and uranium. Of 26 major minerals China is a leading producer of 22 (see Table 1.2).

Table 1.2 China, mineral production, 1992

Mineral	World placing	Output 1992
Bauxite	8	3,000,000mt
Aluminium	6	950,000mt
Copper	6	375,000mt
Gold	6	140,000kg
Iron ore	1	194,000,000mt
Crude steel	3	80,000,000mt
Lead	3	385,000mt
Manganese ore	2	3,500,000mt
Nickel	6	37,000mt
Silver	18	170mt
Tin	1	43,000mt
Zinc	3	670,000mt
Hydraulic cement	1	304,000,000mt
Natural diamond	9	1,000,000 carats
Nitrogen ammonia	1	18,000,000mt
Phosphate rock	2	23,000,000mt
Salt	2	25,000,000mt
Elemental sulphur	4	5,970,000mt
Coal	1	1,110,000,000mt
Marketed natural gas	25	14,000,000,000cm
Crude oil	5	1,050,000,000 barrels
Refined oil	3	830,000,000 barrels

Reserves of major minerals are on a comparable scale: there are an estimated 770,000 million tonnes of coal, and 500,000 million tonnes of iron ore. China is the world's leading producer of wolfram (tungsten). In 1992 China produced 1,040,150,000 barrels of oil and after a consumption of 963,056,000 barrels had a surplus of 77,094,000 barrels for export. China possesses 2.4 per cent of estimated world resources, 24,000,000,000 barrels or 3,200,000,000 tonnes, equivalent to 22.2 years' output at the 1992 rate of production. China possesses 1 per cent of estimated world natural gas reserves equivalent to 1,400,000,000,000cu m or 92 years' output at current rates of production. China also possesses the world's largest hydro-electric potential.

Manufacturing

During the 1980s China's industrial/commercial sector experienced a phenomenal rate of growth which had reached 20.8 per cent by 1992. Manufacturing now accounts for 42 per cent of GDP and employs 17 per cent of the labour force. The principal manufacturing industries are cement, iron and steel including rolled steel, chemical fertilizer, paper and paper board, sulphuric acid, sugar, cotton yarn, cotton fabrics, cigarettes, consumer durables such as colour TV, washing machines and refrigerators, motor vehicles, construction, coal, industrial machines, armaments, petroleum and food processing. China became a nuclear power in 1964 with the explosion of her first bomb and went on to manufacture 600 nuclear warheads and with one of the world's largest military establishments has become a major producer of military equipment and weapons as well as a substantial exporter of weapons, including medium-range missiles, to other Third World countries.

In broad terms, by the mid-1990s, China had the capacity to produce a range of sophisticated industrial goods; with the opening up of the economy to Western investment it was also in measurable distance of catching up in a majority of mainstream industrial sectors. Manufactures in 1992 accounted for 40 per cent of all exports.

Infrastructure

Overall, the infrastructure is poor when related to the vast size of the country and the needs of its huge population, agriculture and rapidly developing industry. There are 64,000km of railroads of which 53,400km are 1.435m (standard) gauge and 6,500km are electrified while 10,000km are designated as industrial lines. There is just over 1 million km of highways (1,029,000km) of which 170,000km are paved, and there are 109,800km of navigable inland waterways. Pipelines include 9,700km for crude oil, 1,100km for petroleum products and 6,200km for natural gas. There are many ports on China's huge coastlime: the most important are Dalien, Guangzhou, Huangpu, Qingdao, Qinhuangdao, Shanghai, Xingong, Zhanjiang, Ningbo, Xiamen, Tanggpu, Shanton. There are 330 usable airports of which 260 have permanent surface runways and ten have runways above 3,500m and 90 have runways of 2,440m or more in length. The distribution of telecommunications facilities is uneven though these are becoming increasingly available in the developing industrial centres. There are an estimated 11 million telephones, 215 million radio receivers and 75 million TV sets.

Political considerations

China, the most populous nation on earth, possesses a formidable centralized system of government and is controlled by the single Chinese Communist Party (CCP). During 1994–5 the main political concern was the succession to the 90-year-old Deng Xiaoping with fears of a power struggle once he died. The military (imperial) tradition that has governed China for two thousand years (though periodically threatened by 'warlordism' as in the period of civil war and disintegration prior to the communist victory of 1949) seems set to continue and China has made plain since the June 1989 Tiananmen Square massacre of protesting students that its policy will not be swayed by external pressures. Whatever political policies are pursued internally (probably a continuation of a single party hierarchy – the CCP – holding overall authority) the Chinese leadership is also determined to modernize its economy and, where necessary, seek partnerships with Western industry in order to do so.

Assessments

One study has suggested that China could overtake the USA in industrial production during the first half of the twenty-first century. China possesses all the attributes required to turn it into an economic and political superpower: a huge, highly disciplined population which includes a well-trained élite at the top; vast mineral resources; the capacity to feed itself and produce surplus food for export; and a rapidly developing industrial sector that should soon turn it into one of the largest industrial powers in the world. It is one of the very few countries that in theory is capable of being genuinely autarkic.

On the other hand, it faces formidable development problems. First, the sheer size of the country and the vast population present the government with daunting problems of political control and organization while the faster the economy grows the greater will be the need for improved infrastructure. Second, almost all future plans could be jeopardized if population growth is not controlled. Current projections suggest the population will reach 1,323,000,000 by 2010 and that the population will double in 60 years. Popular resistance to central direction in recent years has weakened the population control programme. Third, there is the sheer extent of general poverty to overcome – a per capita income of only $490.

Despite these problems and an old Chinese tradition of self-sufficiency that turns its back on international contacts, China has all the makings of a new world superpower.

INDIA

Area. 1,222,243 sq. miles (3,165,596 sq. km).
Population. (1995) 935,744,000.
Capital. New Delhi (8,419,084).*
Other major cities.* Bombay (12,596,243), Calcutta (11,021,915), Madras (5,421,985), Bangalore (4,130,288), Hyderabad (4,253,759), Ahmadabad (3,312,216), Kanpur (2,029,889), Nagpur (1,664,006), Lucknow (1,669,204), Pune (2,493,987).
*Figures for city populations are for greater metropolitan areas.
Language(s). Hindi, English (official), Bengali, Telugu, Marathi, Tamil, Urdu, Gujarati, Malayalam, Kannada, Oriya, Punjabi, Assamese, Kashmiri, Sindhi, Sanskrit (the above languages are official in their appropriate states). There are 24 languages each spoken by more than 1 million or more people and many other languages and dialects.
Religion(s). (There is no official religion.) Hindu 80.3 per cent, Muslim 11 per cent, Christian 2.4 per cent, Sikh 2 per cent, Buddhist 0.7 per cent, Jain 0.5 per cent, other 3.1 per cent.
Date of independence. August 15 1947 (from Britain).
GNP. (1993) $262,810,000,000, per capita $290.

Land and climate. There is an upland plain in the south (the Deccan), a flat to rolling plain along the Ganges in the east, desert in the west and the Himalayas in the north. The Indus and the Ganges are among the world's greatest rivers. The climate varies from tropical monsoon in the south to temperate in the north.

Introduction

This vast, semi-continental country which now contains one-sixth of the earth's total population is the world's largest democracy and acts both politically and economically as a counterweight to Asia's other giant, China. Divided into 25 state and seven union territories, the average population of an Indian state is greater than the population of most other countries in the world. A land of great extremes, India has highly sophisticated heavy industries (including nuclear capacity) at one end of the scale and primitive subsistence village-based agriculture at the other. India's huge resources, industrial and economic potential are more than matched by the voracious demands of its expanding population which is projected to reach 1,189,396,000 by the year 2010.

India has six land neighbours: Bangladesh, whose territory, except for its sea coast, India completely surrounds; Nepal and Bhutan (two small landlocked countries that lie between India and China); Burma (Myanmar) in the east; Pakistan in the west; and China to the north. India has a 7,000km coastline on the Indian Ocean. In terms of GNP India ranks sixteenth in the world table; in terms of per capita income at $290 it remains among the poorest of low income-countries.

Agriculture

About 40 per cent of the population is too poor to afford an adequate diet and a high proportion of agricultural output is the result of traditional village farming. From the late 1950s to the 1970s India experimented with new strains of rice and then wheat (what was known at the time as the 'green revolution' to increase its harvest of staple grains and though no precise figures exist the output was greatly improved). India is basically self-sufficient in food although the country is subject to a range of natural and man-induced disasters including droughts, floods, deforestation, soil erosion, over-grazing, desertification and both air and water pollution. Agriculture accounts for 30 per cent of GDP and employs 61 per cent of the labour force (about 191 million). Principal agricultural exports are: tea (for which India has long been a major world supplier), cotton yarn, fabrics and thread (7.0 per cent of exports), leather and leather manufactures (6.0 per cent of exports), fish products (3.6 per cent of exports), oil cakes (3.3 per cent of exports). The national cattle herd at over 192 million is the largest in the world; other livestock include 118 million goats, 78 million water buffalo, 44 million sheep. Roundwood production in 1992 came to 282,359,000cu m. The fish catch at 4,324,231mt in 1993 ranks India among the top ten fishing nations. The principal staples are rice, wheat, sugarcane, groundnuts, kapoks, chickpeas, sorghum, maize, potatoes, beans (various kinds), lentils, sunflower seeds, vegetables and fruits, barley. Land use comprises forested 23 per cent, meadows and pastures 3.8 per cent, agricultural land under permanent cultivation 57.1 per cent, other 16.1 per cent.

Mining

Mining contributes 2.4 per cent to GDP but employs only 0.6 per cent of the workforce. The main minerals mined in 1993–4 were as follows: limestone 83,900,000mt, iron ore 56,400,000mt, bauxite 5,029,000mt, manganese 1,781,000mt, chromite 1,094,000mt, zinc 144,000mt, copper 45,000mt, lead 39,000mt, gold 62,300 troy ounces, gem diamonds 19,707 carats. Minerals do not contribute in any measure to exports. Of 26 principal minerals (raw and refined) India is among the world's top producers for twelve as shown in Table 1.3.

Table 1.3 India, mineral production, 1992

Mineral	World placing	Output 1992
Bauxite	5	4,475,000mt
Aluminum	10	500,000mt
Iron ore	7	54,000,000mt
Crude steel	10	18,000,000mt
Manganese	6	1,400,000mt
Zinc	14	148,000mt
Hydraulic cement	5	50,000,000mt
Nitrogen in ammonia	4	7,000,000mt
Salt	5	9,503,000mt
Elemental sulphur	22	243,000mt
Coal	6	225,000,000mt
Refined oil	16	345,000,000 barrels

India is a substantial oil producer (by world standards) although its output is all consumed at home. In 1993–4 oil production came to 225,700,000 barrels as opposed to consumption of 420,000,000 barrels.

Manufacturing

India is now one of the world's leading manufacturing nations and in 1993–4 manufacturing contributed 17.3 per cent to GDP and employed 9.1 per cent of the workforce. Principal manufactures were chemicals (including paints, soaps, drugs, medicines, industrial chemicals, fertilizers and pesticides); textiles, iron and steel, food products, electrical machinery, non-electrical machinery, transport equipment, refined petroleum, bricks, cement, tiles, metal products, rubber products, printing and publishing, tobacco products, paper and paper products, non-ferrous metals, plastics. Manufactures of all kinds account for more than 50 per cent of exports and are led by cut and polished diamonds and jewellery (18.6 per cent of exports). India is one of the world's leading manufacturing nations, is a substantial arms producer and has manufactured its own nuclear weapons. The Indian film industry in terms of quantity of films produced is far larger than that of Hollywood. In 1993 tourism netted $1,487,000,000; there is room for major expansion.

Infrastructure

Communications are continental in scale. There is a total of 61,850km of railroads of which 33,553km are broad 1.676m gauge; 24,051km are 1.000m gauge; and 4,246km are narrow gauge; 12,617km are double track and 6,500km are electrified. There are 1,970,000km of roads of which 960,000km are paved. Of 16,180km of inland waterways 3,631km are navigable by large vessels. There are 3,497km of pipelines for crude oil, 1,703km for petroleum products and 902km for natural gas. The country's principal ports are Bombay, Calcutta, Cochin, Kandli, Madras, New Mangalore (and Port Blair in the Andaman Islands). There are 285 usable airports of which 205 have permanent surface runways and two have runways over 3,659m in length while 58 are between 2,440 and 3,659m in length. Domestic telecommunications are poor; international telecommunications are adequate.

Political considerations

India's vast size and long-term potential ensure that it is treated as a major power and is not subjected to the kind of pressures exerted by the IMF and World Bank on smaller, more vulnerable Third World countries. There are two fundamental political problems which, inevitably, affect development. The first problem is communalism: the size of the states and their inevitable centrifugal pull away from New Delhi's control; the diverse and often dangerous religious tensions especially between Hindu, Muslim and Sikh communities; and the range and variety of ethnic groups with their distinctive cultures and demands for recognition – Tamils and Nagas to mention just two examples. The second problem is the sheer size of India. It may be possible for a small 'city state' such as Singapore to achieve a remarkable degree of efficiency but how does India control and provide efficient services for a continental-size country in which, for example, there are an estimated 750,000 rural villages many of which have remained for generations virtually untouched by any modernizing influence. India has to balance internal development problems with its role as an Asian regional superpower.

Assessments

India has the resources and the numbers as well as the technical–educational potential to become an economic–political superpower in the twenty-first century. If it can bring its rate of population increase under control it will the more easily be able to tackle its other problems. By way of comparison, on present projections, India will double its population in 36 years, China in 60 years.

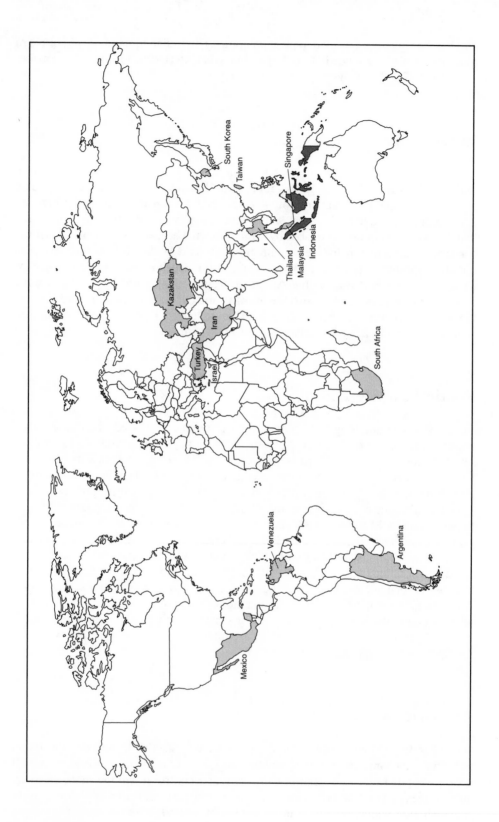

Map 3 The crossover states

2 THE CROSSOVER STATES

INTRODUCTION

This group of developing nations is either close to the point where the crossover could be achieved into the ranks of so-called developed nations or, at least, is in measurable distance of such a possibility. Fourteen countries are dealt with here and they comprise a most disparate group. The fourteen are:

- Argentina
- Indonesia
- Iran
- Israel
- Kazakstan
- South Korea
- Malaysia
- Mexico
- Singapore
- South Africa
- Taiwan
- Thailand
- Turkey
- Venezuela

Hong Kong would also qualify for inclusion here except that it is scheduled to revert to China in mid-1997. There are wide variations between these states in terms of economic strength, resources, stages of development in different sectors, size of population and regional influence yet each has in common with the rest the capacity to make the breakthrough to become a self-sustaining economy on its own. Whether or not they will succeed is another question entirely but the possibility is there.

It is worth looking briefly at their different stages of development since between them these fourteen countries provide apt illustrations of almost all the main problems faced by developing countries at the upper level of economic development in the Third World or South. They can be divided into seven categories as follows:

- Argentina, Mexico, Venezuela
- Indonesia
- Iran and Turkey
- Israel
- Kazakstan
- South Korea, Malaysia, Singapore, Taiwan, Thailand – the Asian Tigers
- South Africa

Each possesses relatively highly advanced and sophisticated industrial–commercial sectors; it is the nature of the other problems which may inhibit their ability to make the crossover to 'developed nation' status.

The Latin American group

At the beginning of the present century Argentina was regarded as a coming nation with a well-endowed, rapidly developing economy on a par with such British Dominions as Australia and Canada. Then for complex reasons, mainly political, Argentina fell behind. Today it possesses the resources, the basic industrial and commercial infrastructure and an educated population which together ought to ensure its rapid economic advance; political volatility rather than economic incapacity appears to be the main stumbling block.

Mexico is perhaps closer to making the crossover than any other major Third World country. It has a large resource base and a rapidly expanding sector that is now in the world class. Mexico's most acute problem concerns the size and rate of growth of its population which threatens to absorb all the gains from development that otherwise might be channelled into more constructive economic progress. Its decision to join the North American Free Trade Agreement (NAFTA) represents a crucial turning-point. If membership of NAFTA brings genuine prosperity and development all could be well; if, on the other hand, NAFTA turns out to be no more than a means of providing cheap Mexican labour for US industries then membership could turn into an economic and political disaster.

Venezuela with 6.2 per cent of the world's known oil reserves might have been included in the next section (Oil States). However, it has already created a substantial industrial–commercial sector independent of oil and unlike the Middle East oil states has a sound agricultural sector as well. The test for Venezuela now is whether over the next decades it uses its wealth to diversify fully away from over-dependence upon oil.

Indonesia

Indonesia with its vast size and huge population could be ranked with Brazil. It has the resources, including oil, which will ensure that it becomes an Asian and world industrial and commercial power and major sectors of the economy are well developed. As with Mexico, however, numbers are a constant restraint upon development and there is much poverty to eradicate while government faces enormous difficulties in administering a state that consists of 13,500 islands.

Iran and Turkey

Both Iran and Turkey were the centres of great historic empires and both have a sense of continuity which gives them important regional influence. Iran possesses 9 per cent of the world's oil reserves and oil made possible the economic advances which occurred under the last Shah. Despite its ongoing quarrel with the West which sees Iran as the source of fundamentalist terrorism it has the resources, the industrial base and the capacity to become a substantial self-sustaining economy in the relatively near future. Turkey enjoys far closer ties with both Europe and the USA and has formally applied for membership of the European Union. In many respects it is already an advanced economy.

Israel

Israel is a highly efficient mixed industrial economy and in other historic circumstances would have been deemed to have made the crossover to developed status. But its embattled situation of constant confrontation with its neighbours and consequent reliance upon massive annual injections of American aid (primarily for military purposes) as well as the ambivalent and dangerous position of both the Gaza Strip and the West Bank place it in a unique special category of its own.

Kazakstan

Kazakstan only emerged from the former USSR as a newly independent state at the end of 1991. It possesses vast resources and has the basis already in existence of a wide-ranging industrial sector as well as being self-sufficient in agriculture. Its problems are partly those of modernization and partly those of readjustment to a world market economy.

The Asian Tigers

Five Asian countries qualify as newly industrializing countries (NICs) or Asian Tigers. These are South Korea, Malaysia, Singapore, Taiwan and Thailand. Two of them – South Korea and Taiwan – received massive assistance from the USA in the early stages of the Cold War in Asia which made their rapid economic take-offs possible. Singapore has enjoyed the benefits of small size (it is a city rather than a country), unparalleled political stability (if over-authoritarian) and a unique strategic position which has enabled it to develop as the busiest port in the world. Malaysia and Thailand are each possessed of substantial, if varied, resources and have been led by determined governments which have pursued ambitious – and successful – paths of industrialization and modernization.

South Africa

South Africa represents a very special case on its own. As late as 1990 it could not have been considered as a potential crossover country with its huge undereducated and politically deprived black majority held precariously in place by the apartheid structures. It remains, as yet, two economies: the advanced industrial–commercial economy built up over the years by the white minority; and the Third World underdeveloped African economy created as a result of apartheid. The end of the apartheid divisions signalled by the elections of 1994 has transformed the country's economic possibilities. Provided that the two sides in this new equation work together, South Africa has the chance as well as the means in terms of its resource base and industrial infrastructure to move rapidly towards a position of self-sustaining growth that will be greatly helped by its ability to meet many of the development demands of the African continent to its north.

Despite their many problems these fourteen countries of the Third World seem those most likely to make the crossover into the ranks of the developed during the course of the next two decades.

ARGENTINA

Area. 1,079,518 sq. miles (2,780,400 sq. km).
Population. (1995) 34,587,000.
Capital. Buenos Aires (2,960,976 – 1991) (greater Buenos Aires has a population of 12,582,321).
Other major cities. Córdoba (1,179,067), Rosario (1,078,374), La Plata (542,567).
Language(s). Spanish (official), English, Italian, German, French.
Religions. Roman Catholic (91.6 per cent), other (8.4 per cent).
Date of independence. July 9, 1816 (from Spain).
GNP. (1993) $244,013,000,000, per capita $7,290.
Land and climate. Argentina falls neatly into three main zones: the rich plains of the pampas in the north; the flat, sometimes rolling plateaux of the south (Patagonia); the rugged Andes along the western border with Chile. It is a temperate climate.

Introduction

This vast country of more than 1 million sq. miles in South America, the eighth largest in the world, has never managed to achieve its full potential although it has often been referred to as one of Latin America's two giants (with Brazil). Argentina has five land neighbours – Chile, with which it shares one of the world's longest borders (5,150km), Bolivia, Paraguay, Brazil and Uruguay; and a seaboard on the South Atlantic of 4,898km that should be of great significance during the next century when access to the world's oceans is likely to be a feature of crucial importance as the search for minerals under the sea intensifies. Although the dispute with Britain over the Falkland Islands (Islas Malvinas) has a number of causes, the islands may well prove to be in the centre of a major oil-bearing region.

The country has a largely temperate climate which is arid in the southeast and sub-arctic in the southwest while the Andes region is subject to earthquakes and its vast plains are at risk from desertification. The country is rich in natural resources although, of the main minerals, Argentina is only among the top world producers for two of them – salt and natural gas. Argentina is a major food producer and exporter and has a highly literate population. Despite a comfortable trade surplus, Argentina has long been one of the world's most indebted countries. Agriculture is the mainstay of the economy and agricultural products account for 70 per cent of exports. There is a significant, diversified industrial–manufacturing sector.

Agriculture

Argentina is self-sufficient in food production and a major food commodity exporter as well, a position set to continue into the foreseeable future. Once the world's leading exporter of beef, this has declined in importance (not least because of EU subsidies to its own beef producers) and been replaced by grain exports which are crucial to the economy. Agriculture (including fisheries) now accounts for 40 per cent of foreign exchange earnings and between 16 and 17 per cent of GDP. The principal crops are wheat, soya, maize, sorghum, millet, oats, rye and barley; other major crops include rice, linseed, potatoes, tomatoes, cotton and tea. Grapes, produced in the Mendoza region, are the basis of the wine industry; Argentina is a major world wine exporter and became the fifth largest wine producer during the 1980s, although only a small proportion of total output is exported. Grains are the basis of the agricultural economy: in 1994 the main crops were sugarcane (17,500,000mt), soybeans (11,318,000mt), maize (10,246,000mt), and wheat (10,680,000mt). The national herd consists of 50 million cattle and 23 million sheep. Argentina is one of the world's top five exporters of both grains and beef and food products and live animals account for 40 per cent of exports. Approximately 1,200,000 or 12 per cent of the labour force work in the agricultural sector. The forestry sector is, as yet, underutilized and though Argentina has a huge Atlantic seaboard and rich fisheries potential this sector is also underdeveloped. Land use divides between forested 21.6 per cent, meadows and pastures 51.9 per cent, agricultural – under permanent cultivation 9.9 per cent and other 16.6 per cent.

Minerals

Although a range of minerals exists in Argentina, none is on a really major scale and the mining sector only accounts for about 2.3 per cent of GDP (1992) and employs less than 1 per cent of the labour force. Minerals include iron ore, zinc, uranium, copper, tin concentrates, silver, coal. Argentina has sufficient uranium stocks to sustain its own nuclear power programme. Silver and gold are the principal mineral exports.

Argentina is self-sufficient in oil and hydro-electric power. The oil field at Comodoro Rivadavia in the south (discovered 1907) supplies about 30 per cent of the country's needs; other fields are at Neuquen-Rio/Negro-La Pampa and Mendoza. Increasing attention is now being paid to offshore oil resources which exist under the continental shelf extending to the Falkland Islands. Crude petroleum output in 1993 came to 216,836,000 barrels. There are huge resources of natural gas, estimated reserves standing at 600,000m cu m. There is also huge hydro-electric potential (an estimated 30,000mw) derived from the Paraná and Uruguay river systems. Minerals make a useful contribution to the economy but, unless major new discoveries are made, will remain of secondary importance.

Manufacturing

Manufacturing now accounts for 21.9 per cent of GDP (1992) and the sector employs about 20 per cent of the labour force. The principal strengths of the sector lie in the motor industry, 'white' goods (such as refrigerators), pharmaceuticals, cosmetics, electronic equipment, fibres, cement, rubber, paper and wood products, in which Argentina is self-sufficient. Manufactures, including transport equipment, account for 25 per cent of exports.

Infrastructure

Argentina has the most sophisticated system of communications in Latin America with a total of 34,172km of railroads linking all the major cities; 208,350km of highways including over 47,000km which are paved. There are 11,000km of navigable inland waterways. The principal ports are Bahia Blanca, Buenos Aires, Comodoro Rivadavia, La Plata, Rosario and Santa Fé. There are 1,700 airports of which 137 have permanent surface runways, 31 with runways of 2,440–3,659m and one with a runway in excess of 3,659m. There is an extensive modern system of telecommunications.

Political considerations

Despite major economic potential and a highly educated population with a 95 per cent adult literacy rate, Argentina has yet to attain its true potential. It has had a troubled political life oscillating between popular dictatorships and periods of democratic rule with much emphasis on state control of large sectors of the economy. In addition, the economy has also been through decades of mismanagement and suffered from periodic bouts of high inflation. It is currently one of the world's most indebted nations ($61,534,000,000 in 1993). Since 1989, however, when President Carlos Menem and the Peronist party were elected, the country has adopted new economic policies of restructuring and placed Argentina on a path of (apparent) sustainable growth.

Assessments

The long-term economic future of Argentina is bright: it can feed itself; it is a major food exporter; it has a reasonable mineral base; it can meet all its energy requirements; it has an educated population. The biggest question mark concerns the volatile nature of Argentinian politics.

INDONESIA

Area. 741,052 sq. miles (1,919,317 sq. km).
Population. (1995) 195,283,000.
Capital. Jakarta (8,259,266).
Other major cities. Surabaya (2,421,016), Bandung (2,026,893), Medan (1,685,972), Semarang (1,005,316).
Language(s). Bahasa Indonesia (official), many dialects, English, Dutch (mainly in Java).
Religion(s). Muslim 87.2 per cent, Christian 9.6 per cent, Hindu 1.8 per cent, Buddhist 1 per cent, other 0.4 per cent.
Date of independence. Declared independence August 17 1945, legal independence December 27 1949 (from the Netherlands).

GNP. (1993) $136,620,000,000, per capita $730.

Land and climate. Most of the land consists of coastal lowlands while the larger islands have interior mountains. The climate is tropical, hot and humid, somewhat moderated in the highlands.

Introduction

This vast archipelago of 13,500 islands, the former Dutch East Indies, spans more than 3,000 miles from northern Sumatra in the west to New Guinea in the east, lies athwart the equator and controls the major sea routes between the Indian and Pacific Oceans. Only 6,000 islands are inhabited while many are tiny in size. Kalimantan (Indonesian Borneo) has borders with Malaysia (Sarawak and Sabah) while Irian Jaya (the Indonesian half of New Guinea) has borders with Papua New Guinea. There is a huge range in terms of population density with Java Island where the capital, Jakarta, and the greater part of the population are to be found, one of the most densely peopled territories anywhere in the world. The complexities of running a vast state comprising so many islands spread over such a wide area has tended to make Indonesian governments authoritarian by nature. Since 1975 when Indonesia annexed Timor it has been in dispute with Portugal while the United Nations has not recognized Jakarta's authority over the island. Indonesia is rich in mineral resources and agricultural potential and its forests represent 35 per cent of the world's tropical forest reserves of hardwoods.

Agriculture

Most staple food is produced by subsistence farming while export crops are grown by smallholder and plantation agriculture. The sector, including forestry and fisheries, accounts for just over 18 per cent of GDP and employs 46.2 per cent of the workforce (nearly 40 million people). Export crops include palm oil, rubber, copra, cocoa, coffee, pepper and spices. Roundwood production at 188,118,000cu m (1993) puts Indonesia among the world's top timber producers and plywood accounts for 11.6 per cent of exports. Rubber is an important crop and preparation rubber provides slightly under 3 per cent of exports. The annual fish catch is about 3.6m tonnes. The national cattle herd is 11,000,000 head. Staple foods are rice, sugarcane, cassava, maize. Formerly a major rice importer, Indonesia is now virtually self-sufficient in rice which is its most important grain; in 1994 rice production came to 46,245,000mt. Land use comprises forested 60.3 per cent, meadows and pastures 6.5 per cent, agricultural land under permanent cultivation 12.3 per cent, other 20.9 per cent.

Mining

Mining, including oil, accounts for 10.2 per cent of GDP but only employs 0.9 per cent of the workforce. Indonesia has a range of important minerals including petroleum, natural gas, tin, nickel, bauxite, copper, coal, gold, silver, iron sand. Of 26 major minerals Indonesia ranks among the world's top producers for seven as shown in Table 2.1.

Table 2.1 Indonesia, mineral production, 1992

Mineral	World placing	Output 1992
Gold	10	37,983 kg
Nickel	4	78,000mt
Tin	3	25,000mt
Hydraulic cement	18	17,280,000mt
Nitrogen in ammonia	7	2,700,000mt
Natural gas	8	45,000,000,000cu m
Oil	13	551,000,000 barrels

Crude and refined oil have long been the most important mineral exports and Indonesia has been an oil exporting country for a greater period than many Middle East producers. In 1992 oil production came to 1,540,000 barrels daily or 557,266,000 barrels for the year. Natural gas output in 1992 came to 51,809,000,000cu m. Crude petroleum accounted for 13.0 per cent of exports and natural gas for a further 11.0 per cent. Indonesia's proved oil reserves at the end of 1992 stood at 800,000,000 tonnes or 5,800,000,000 barrels representing 0.6 per cent of world reserves with an estimated life of 10.5 years at current rates of production. Natural gas reserves stood at 1,800,000,000,000cu m, equivalent to 1.3 per cent of world reserves with an estimated life at current rates of production of 34 years.

Other minerals produced in 1994 were nickel ore (2,300,000mt), bauxite (1,360,000mt), copper concentrate (1,065,468mt); also produced were iron sand, tin and silver. There are at least 100m tons of nickel reserves. Two ore bodies of copper have about 60m tons between them as well as associated gold and silver. There are major bauxite reserves and substantial tin reserves. Indonesia has estimated coal reserves of 22,500m tons (mainly low grade) but at present hardly any coal is mined.

Manufacturing

Manufacturing contributes 22.3 per cent to GDP and employs 13.2 per cent of the workforce. Principal manufactures are cement, fertilizers, newsprint, cigarettes, textiles, chemicals, plywood, foods and food processing, and rubber products. Garments account for 9.5 per cent of exports. The sector has grown very substantially since the late 1980s and in 1994 the overall rate of economic growth was 7 per cent.

Infrastructure

There is a total of 6,964km of railroads of which 6,389km are 1.067m gauge. Of 119,500km of highways, 11,812km are state and 34,180km provincial. There are

21,579km of inland waterways on the main islands of Sumatra, Java, Madera, Kalimantan, Sulawesi and Irian Jaya. There are 2,505km of crude oil pipelines, 456km for petroleum products and 1,703km for natural gas. The main ports are Cilacap, Cirebon, Jakarta, Kupang, Palembang, Ujungpandang, Semarang, Surabaya. Of 411 usable airports, 119 have permanent surface runways, one of which is over 3,659m and eleven between 2,440 and 3,659m in length.

Regarding telecommunications, there is an inter-island microwave system; domestic telecommunications are fair and international services are good.

Political considerations

Indonesia has been a unitary state since 1950: it is a republic with an executive president. The country has developed into a major Asian power and has played a leading part in the Non-Aligned Movement (NAM) since its foundation following the 1955 conference at Bandung which was presided over by former Indonesia President Ahmed Soekarno. It is a member of ASEAN, OPEC and APEC and its strategic position in Southeast Asia, huge size, large population and resources and the size of market which it offers give to it immense immediate and long-term influence and potential power.

Assessments

Economic controls are designed to encourage local processing of export materials which cover the range of Indonesia's products – logs, fertilizers, cement, reinforced iron, tyres, paper, asphalt, salt, wheat flour, and a variety of other foods and meat. Some goods cannot be exported; these include raw hide, unprocessed low-quality rubber, certain timber species, metal scrap, raw cotton and antiques of cultural value. Regulations ensure that foreign contractors have to counter-purchase a proportion of non-oil export goods against the value of their imported products. Foreign–local partnerships must become 51 per cent Indonesian owned within ten years.

Indonesia has the resources and numbers to allow it to become a major Asian and world industrial–commercial power. The principal restraints to development are the present level of poverty – the per capita income of $730 means it has only just entered the lower end of the middle-income economies. The large population of 191 million which is projected to increase to 236 million in 2010 represents the main problem inhibiting more rapid growth and development.

IRAN

Area. 632,457 sq. miles (1,638,057 sq. km).
Population. (1995) 61,271,000.
Capital. Tehran (6,475,527).

Other major cities. Mashhad (1,759,155), Esfahan (1,127,030), Tabriz (1,088,985), Shiraz (965,117), Ahvaz (724,653), Qom (681,253).
Language(s). Parsi (Persian) (official), Turkic, Kurdish, Luri, Baloch, Arabic, Turkish.
Religion(s). Muslim 99.1 per cent (Shi'a 93.4 per cent, Sunni 5.7 per cent), Baha'i 0.6 per cent, Christian 0.1 per cent, Zoroastrian 0.1 per cent, Jewish 0.1 per cent.
GNP. (1993) $111,008,000,000, per capita $1,940.
Land and climate. Iran is a rugged, mountainous country with a high central basin of desert and mountains, and small, interrupted plains along the coasts. The climate is hot, arid or semi-arid; it is subtropical along the Caspian Sea coast.

Introduction

This large Asian country, lying between the Caspian Sea and the Persian Gulf, has an uninterrupted history stretching back 2,500 years to Cyrus the Great. Its recent history has been extraordinarily turbulent: the revolution that led to the overthrow of the Shah at the beginning of 1979; the second revolution that turned Iran into an Islamic state under the Ayatollah Khomeini during the 1980s; the bitter war with Iraq (1980–88) that devastated many of its cities and did huge damage to the economy; its perceived role (in the West) as the source of Islamic fundamentalism and its semi-isolation by the West have each in their different ways ensured a unique international position for Iran.

The country has great mineral wealth, apart from its enormous oil resources, and the potential to become an important middle-level power. Iran has seven land neighbours: Afghanistan, Armenia, Azerbaijan, Iraq, Pakistan, Turkey and Turkmenistan; and a coastline of 2,440km stretching from the head of the Gulf to the Gulf of Oman, as well as a 740km coastline on the Caspian Sea. Its per capita income at $1,940 places it at the upper end of the middle-income band of countries.

Agriculture

Agriculture, including forestry and fisheries, accounts for just over 20 per cent of GDP and employs 22 per cent of the workforce. The principal crops are wheat (11,500,000mt in 1994), sugar beet (5,900,000mt), barley (3,100,000mt), rice (2,700,000mt); and grapes, sugarcane, apples, oranges, dates and pistachios. Only pistachios are important as an export crop and in 1994 accounted for 2.4 per cent of all exports. Iran is not self-sufficient in foods and is a substantial importer of grains. Roundwood production came to 7,467,000cu m in 1994 while the fish catch of 343,888mt was small for country with such a lengthy coastline, although caviar from the Caspian Sea is a luxury export. The national cattle herd is just under 7 million head but there are 45,000,000 sheep and wool is an important product. A great part of the sector consists of village agriculture (many of the great estates were broken up during the White Revolution under the Shah). Land use consists of forested 11 per cent, meadows and pastures 26.9 per cent, agricultural land, under permanent cultivation 9.2 per cent, other 52.9 per cent.

Mining

Iran's mineral resources include petroleum, natural gas, coal, chromium, copper, iron ore, lead, manganese, zinc and sulphur. Apart from petroleum and natural gas, mineral output in 1993 included 12,106,000mt of copper and 8,690,000mt of iron ore although only copper at 0.8 per cent of the total made a significant contribution to exports. Coal production at 1,500,000mt is consumed locally.

Iran's oil reserves are among the greatest in the world and petroleum exports first became important prior to World War I when Britain sought Iran's oil as fuel for her fleet. Petroleum output in 1993 came to 1,426,800,000 barrels or 3,909,000b/d; Iran consumed slightly above a quarter of this amount, the balance was exported. Natural gas production came to 34,400,000,000cu m but the greater part of this was consumed at home. Petroleum and natural gas production between them account for 17.6 per cent of GDP though only employing a fraction of the workforce. Petroleum and natural gas accounted for 79.3 per cent of exports for 1993–4. Iran's oil deposits are vast and at the end of 1992 oil reserves were estimated at 12,700,000,000 tonnes or 92,900,000,000 barrels equivalent to 9.2 per cent of the world's reserves with an expected life at current rates of production of 73.6 years. Natural gas resources are on a comparable (even larger) scale with reserves estimated at 19,800,000,000,000cu m, equivalent to 14.3 per cent of world reserves.

Although other minerals do not at present contribute a great deal to GDP, Iran has major deposits of lead-zinc ore in three locations with a combined potential of 600 tons of concentrates daily. Chromium from the Elburz mountains, red oxide, turquoise, sulphur and salt are all produced and exported. Iran is the leading sulphur exporter in the region. There are huge iron ore deposits in Kerman province, possibly 1,000m tons altogether and further reserves of 200m tons at Gol-e-Goha. Coal reserves are estimated at 6,000m tons, of which a third are readily exploitable. Major copper deposits have been discovered since 1967, amounting to 400m tons of reasonable grade copper with a further 400m tons of lower grade copper. In the mid-1970s important uranium finds were made in the northern and western regions and in 1984 additional deposits of 5,000 tons were found in central Iran. There are also mica and silica deposits. Ambitious plans to exploit these minerals, some dating back to the Shah's heyday in the early 1970s, have either been shelved or delayed as a result of the events of the 1980s – Iran's revolutions and the war with Iraq followed by Iran's long quarrel with the West and consequent semi-isolation.

Manufacturing

Manufacturing accounts for 14 per cent of GDP and employs slightly above 14 per cent of the workforce. Principal manufactures are textiles, food (especially sugar refining and vegetable oil production), bricks, tiles, cement, non-electrical machinery, iron and steel, non-industrial chemical products. Carpets and rugs, an ancient speciality of Iran, account for 7.7 per cent of exports. Much of the country's petrochemical capacity was destroyed or damaged during the war with Iraq in the 1980s but policy after the war has been to restore capacity as quickly as possible. Long-range plans to supply natural gas to Russia, Rumania, Bulgaria, India and Japan have been interrupted, in part by the war, in part through lack of investment capital. Iran's isolation (no diplomatic relations with the USA and only limited relations with Britain and the rest of the EU) have inevitably retarded industrial development plans.

Infrastructure

There are 4,852km of railways which is a small total for so vast a country: 4,760km are 1.432m gauge and 92km are 1.676m gauge while 480km of rail are under construction between Bafq and Bandar-e Abbas. There are 140,200km of highways of which 42,694km are paved. There is a total of 904km of inland waterways. The Shatt-al Arab which acts as the border between Iran and Iraq is navigable for maritime vessels for 130km and a channel has been developed to 3m depth. There are 5,900km of pipelines for crude oil, 3,900km for petroleum products and 4,550km for natural gas. The main ports are Abadan (largely destroyed in the war with Iraq), Banda Beheshti, Bandar-e Khomeyni, Bandar-e Torkeman (on the Caspian Sea), and Khorramshahr. There are 194 usable airports of which 83 have permanent surface runways, sixteen of over 3,659m and twenty between 2,440 and 3,659m in length. Internal telecommunications are reasonable and regional telecommunications are fair to good.

Political considerations

In the West, Iran has come to be seen as the source of Islamic fundamentalism, and the rejection of Western values that was a key aspect of Iranian policy under the Ayatollah Khomeini did much to isolate Iran. The succeeding government of President Hashemi Rafsanjani has gone some way to repair relations with the West and in early 1994 Rafsanjani conceded that the country faced serious economic problems. There remains a wide gulf between the modernists, many belonging to the prosperous middle class which rose to prominence under the Shah and the more conservative elements of society who were the principal supporters of the Islamic revolution. In July 1994 the US Secretary of State, Warren Christopher, declared Iran to be 'an outlaw nation' and the West especially feared what it saw as Iran's search for advanced weapons of mass destruction. Relations with Britain have been almost as bad as those with the USA, particularly over the Salman Rushdie affair, although Britain does maintain diplomatic relations with Tehran. The West appears very ready to blame Iran for international terrorism and the USA does not appear to have forgiven it for the hostage affair at the beginning of the 1980s.

Assessments

Iran has been a major regional power in southern Asia for more than 2,000 years and its influence upon its neighbours as well as upon the wider world of Islam is profound. Its quarrel with the West which has led to its partial international isolation cannot alter its long-term potential as a market. It is currently a middle-income country but further industrialization should raise it, before long, into the ranks of the upper-middle-income countries while its possession of vast mineral resources, especially oil and gas, ought to ensure long-term economic development.

ISRAEL

Area. 7,992 sq. miles (20,700 sq. km).
Population. (1995) 5,386,000.
Capital. Jerusalem (proclaimed capital in 1950 though Jordan claims part of the city); most embassies are located in Tel Aviv (566,500).
Other major cities. Tel Aviv-Yafo (357,400), Haifa (246,500), Holon (162,800), Peta Tiqwa (151,100), Bat Yam (143,200).
Language(s). Hebrew and Arabic (official), English.
Religion(s). Jewish 81.3 per cent, Muslim 14.2 per cent, Christian 2.8 per cent, Druze and other 1.7 per cent.
Date of independence. May 14 1948 (from Britain which held the League of Nations mandate).
GNP. (1993) $72,667,000,000, per capita $13,760.
Land and climate. The land divides neatly into the southern Negev desert, the coastal plain, the central mountains and the Jordan Rift Valley which contains the Dead Sea. It is a temperate, eastern Mediterranean climate, hot and dry in the southern and eastern desert regions.

Introduction

This tiny country at the eastern end of the Mediterranean was proclaimed the State of Israel in May 1948 under a United Nations plan for the division of the British mandated territory of Palestine. The formation of Israel, however, was vehemently opposed by the surrounding Arab peoples as well as by the Palestinian Arabs with the result that Israel was born in a state of war with its neighbours (1948–9). In subsequent years Israel was to remain in a state of permanent, often terrorist-dominated, tension with its neighbours, and was to fight further wars in 1956 (Suez), 1967 (the Six-day War), 1973 (the Yom Kippur War) and 1982 (the invasion of southern Lebanon). In the war of 1948–9 Jordan annexed the West Bank; this was taken back by Israel in 1967 when it also occupied the Gaza Strip. These Arab territories of the West Bank and the Gaza Strip were (1995) under negotiation in the Arab–Israeli peace process that got under way on May 17 1994 when Israel ended its occupation of the Gaza Strip and Jericho in the West Bank, allowing Palestinian police to move in to take control. Subsequent violence on both sides by Israeli and Palestinian extremists put the peace process at risk and meant that the process would be likely to continue for years before a final resolution of Arab and Israeli differences (which in real terms means the emergence of a fully independent Palestinian state) can be expected to take place.

Israel, as a state, came into being under especially dramatic and traumatic conditions; at one level it does not qualify as a developing country at all for it has a highly sophisticated mixed economy. But its peculiar historical position and the constant influx of Jews from other parts of the world as well as its 'war footing' economy place it in a class of its own so that it makes sense to deal with it as part of the developing world, more especially as it includes the two Palestinian 'attachments' of the Gaza Strip and the West Bank whose future has yet to be resolved. Israel has land boundaries with Egypt, the Gaza Strip, Jordan, Lebanon, Syria and the West Bank and a Mediterranean coastline of 273km.

Agriculture

Agriculture only contributes 2.3 per cent to GDP and employs a mere 3.1 per cent of the workforce, yet it plays a more significant role in the national economy than such figures would suggest. Citrus and other fruits and processed foods are important exports and accounted for 5.0 per cent of the total in 1994. The main products are citrus and other fruits, vegetables, cotton, beef, dairy and poultry products. Israel is largely self-sufficient in food except for grains which have to be imported. Land use consists of forested 5.5 per cent, meadows and pastures 7.2 per cent, agricultural land, under permanent cultivation 21.5 per cent, other 65.8 per cent.

Mining and manufacturing

The mining sector is insignificant and consists largely of the extraction of phosphate rock, potash, lime, bromine and bromine compounds. The manufacturing sector is highly diversified and covers food processing, diamond cutting and polishing, textiles, clothing, chemicals, metal products, military equipment (including nuclear weapons), transport equipment, electrical equipment, miscellaneous machinery, high-technology electronics. Tourism is a major industry, earning $2,110,000,000 in 1993 but this figure is more than matched by the expenditure of Israelis abroad ($2,313,000,000). Manufacturing and mining contribute 20.9 per cent to GDP and employ 19.6 per cent of the labour force.

Infrastructure

Israel has 600km of 1.435m gauge single track railway; 4,750km of paved highways; 708km of oil pipelines, 290km of petroleum products pipelines and 89km of natural gas pipelines. Ashdod and Haifa are the country's ports. There are 46 usable airports, 28 with permanent surface runways of which seven have runways between 2,440 and 3,659m in length. Telecommunications are the most highly developed in the Middle East.

Political considerations

Given Israel's history of confrontation with its Arab neighbours, defence and aid have become major aspects of both planning and the economy. About 9.4 per cent of GNP goes on defence (three times the world average) and Israel is heavily dependent upon aid (principally from the USA, private and government) for both development and defence purposes. Debts in 1992 stood at $54,742,000,000.

Assessments

Israel has demonstrated its capacity to become a highly efficient mixed industrial economy. The long-term future security, however, must depend upon the achievement of a just settlement with the Palestinian Arabs.

The Gaza Strip

Israel took control of the Gaza Strip in the 1967 war. The population in 1993 was 705,834. The economy depends, overwhelmingly, upon employment over the border in Israel and when the peace process faltered in 1995 Israel closed the border with the Strip to prevent Palestinian workers crossing into Israel. In April 1995 Western countries agreed to provide $130m to fund Yasser Arafat's Palestinian Authority to the end of the year. In addition, Israel was preventing goods from entering or leaving the territory.

The West Bank

In the West Bank, according to the May 1994 peace process agreement, control of Jericho was also handed over to Arafat's Palestinian Authority. But the Israeli military authorities continue to control the West Bank (and refuse to stop Israeli settlements). Until Israel relinquishes control of the region and also makes peace with Syria, which must include a restoration to that country of the Golan Heights, there can be no long-term solution to the Palestine question (which means an independent Palestine State) and no long-term security for Israel.

Prosperity in the State of Israel is not enough if it is permanently at war or on the brink of war with its neighbours.

KAZAKSTAN

Area. 1,049,200 sq. miles (2,717,300 sq. km).
Population. (1995) 16,669,000.
Capital. Almatey (Alma-Ata) (1,156,200).
Other major cities. Karaganda (608,600), Chimkent (438,800), Semipalatinsk (344,700), Pavlodar (342,500).
Language(s). Kazak (official), Russian.
Religion(s). No official religion, believers mainly Sunni Muslim, some Christian (Russian Orthodox and Baptist).
Date of independence. December 16 1991 (from the USSR).
GNP. (1993) $26,440,000,000, per capita $1,540.
Land and climate. Kazakstan consists mainly of a vast plateau/plain stretching from the Volga to the Altai Mountains and from western Siberia to the oasis and desert of Central Asia. It has borders on the Caspian and Aral seas; the latter sea is drying up as a result of pollution. The climate is one of continental extremes, arid or semi-arid.

Introduction

This huge landlocked country of Central Asia emerged from the break-up of the USSR as the ninth largest territory in the world. It is a storehouse of minerals and has the potential to develop into an economic power of the second rank in the relatively near future. The possibility of huge oil and gas concessions ensured that it obtained immediate Western investment interest after 1992. The main political problem is one of achieving ethnic balance with the Muslim Kazaks making up 41 per cent of the population and the Russians 37 per cent; tensions between these two groups were brought to a head during the elections of March 1994. Western aid in 1994 came to $1bn. Kazakstan also faces a range of economic problems: these include the contraction of the economy during 1993 by over 12 per cent and a 2,000 per cent rate of inflation. In April 1994 Kazakstan embarked upon a privatization plan involving 3,500 enterprises (about 70 per cent of the country's state-owned firms) which were to be auctioned off over the succeeding fifteen months. In January 1995 Kazakstan and Uzbekistan announced plans for an economic merger. Russia has demanded a share in the development of Kazakstan's oil and gas resources. The country has over 12,000km of land boundaries with China, Kyrgyzstan, Russia, Turkmenistan and Uzbekistan.

Agriculture

Agriculture accounts for 28.6 per cent of GDP and employs 24 per cent of the workforce. Grains are principal crops and in 1994 output included 9,052,000mt of wheat and 7,060,000mt of maize. It is also a major cotton producer with an annual crop of 207,000mt of seed cotton. Other important crops are potatoes, sugar beets, oats, rye, rice, fruit, sunflower seeds, grapes. The national cattle herd stands at over 8 million head while there are more than 33 million sheep and goats. Grain, wool and meat are important exports. The country is broadly food self-sufficient. Land use divides between forested 6.3 per cent, meadows and pastures 68.7 per cent, agricultural land, under permanent cultivation 13.1 per cent, other 11.9 per cent.

Mining

Kazakstan has a huge range of minerals including oil, natural gas, coal, iron ore, manganese, chromite, lead, nickel, cobalt, zinc, copper, titanium, bauxite, gold, silver, phosphates, sulphur, uranium, molybdenum. In 1993 output of iron ore came to 17,000,000mt, chrome 2,900,000mt, copper 250,000mt, manganese 200,000mt. Oil production that year came to 141,400,000 barrels (home consumption was 117,300,000 barrels). At the end of 1992 Kazakstan possessed an estimated 5,200,000,000 barrels of recoverable oil, equivalent to 0.5 per cent of world reserves, and at current rates of extraction this will last for 26.5 years.

Of 26 major world minerals Kazakstan is a leading source and producer for eleven as shown in Table 2.2.

The mineral potential of Kazakstan is enormous and further discoveries seem likely.

Table 2.2 Kazakstan, mineral production, 1992

Mineral	World placing	Output 1992
Chromite	1	3,600,000mt
Copper	9	350,000mt
Gold	14	24,000mt (cu c)
Iron ore	11	20,000,000mt
Lead	5	240,000mt
Silver	7	900mt
Uranium	3	3,000mt
Zinc	8	200,000mt
Phosphate rock	5	7,000,000mt
Coal	10	127,000,000mt
Natural gas (marketed)	27	9,000,000,000cu m

Manufacturing

Manufacturing, with mining, contributes 28.9 per cent to GDP and together they employ 24 per cent of the workforce. However, the sector suffers from backward technology, high pollution and little or no experience of international marketing. Kazakstan lacks investment capital and managerial skills and seeks assistance from the West to modernize its industrial production. At present Kazakstan's huge oil prospects act as an attraction to Western investors. Major manufactures include steel, rolled ferrous metals, mineral fertilizers, textiles, carpets, shoes, bulldozers, metal cutting machines, forge press machines, excavators. Formerly, when Kazakstan was part of the USSR, its role was to produce natural resources and heavy machinery in return for finished consumer and industrial goods. The country remains heavily dependent upon trade with Russia and, for example, oil exports have to pass through pipelines across Russia.

Infrastructure

There are 14,460km of railroads of 1.520m gauge as well as some industrial lines; 189,000km of highways of which 108,100km are hard-surfaced or paved; 2,850km of pipelines for crude oil, 1,500km for refined products and 3,480km for natural gas. There are 152 usable airports, 49 with permanent surface runways, eight of which are 3,659m in length and 38 between 2,440 and 3,659m in length. The internal telephone service is poor, regional and international telecommunications are moderate to fair.

Political considerations

Kazakstan faces all the immediate problems of decommissioning a command economy and entering into international economic relations. It must modernize its technology and the economic system. While performing these tasks it must also deal with an explosion of ethnic rivalries with the largely Muslim Kazaks, now the dominant group, and the Russians who are almost as many in numbers but are now regarded with enmity as the former imperialists. Kazakstan has still to work out a new, post-independent relationship with its Russian neighbour for, whatever differences or suspicions may exist, it will remain heavily dependent upon Russia as its principal trading partner into the foreseeable future.

Assessments

If Kazakstan can find working solutions to its most pressing political and economic problems, its long-term economic prospects are bright. It has vast resources, the basis of a wide-ranging manufacturing sector and broad self-sufficiency in agriculture with major food commodity export potential. Nor does it face a population problem; the estimated doubling time for its 17 million people is 58 years.

SOUTH KOREA

Area. 38,330 sq. miles (99,274 sq. km).
Population. (1995) 44,834,000.
Capital. Seoul (10,612,577).
Other major cities. Pusan (3,798,113), Taegu (2,229,040), Inch'on (1,817,919), Kwangji (1,139,003).
Language(s). Korean (official), English.
Religion(s). Religious 54 per cent (divided between Buddhist, Protestant, Roman Catholic, Confucian, Wonbulgyo, Ch'ondogyo) and non-religious 46 per cent.
Date of independence. August 15 1948 (from US occupation following Japanese surrender).
GNP. (1993) $337,910,000,000, per capita $7,670.
Land and climate. Mainly hills and mountains with wide coastal plains in the west and south. The climate is temperate with heavier rain in summer than winter.

Introduction

As with North Korea, its southern neighbour was also part of the Japanese colony from 1911 to 1945 and, following partition along the 38th parallel after World War II, was to come into the US sphere of influence in the rapidly developing Cold War. It emerged devastated from the Korean War of 1950–53 but then became, for a crucial period of reconstruction, the recipient of massive injections of US aid. South Korea established a pattern that was to be followed by a number of Asian countries: it combined authoritarian, near dictatorial rule under three presidents – Rhee (1948–60), Park (1961–79) and Chun (1980–87) – with remarkably free rein, successful market force economic policies. The result has been a massive transformation, from a per capita GNP of only $90 in 1961 to one of $7,670 in 1993 while the total GNP in the latter year at $337,910,000,000 placed the country among the world's top fifteen economies. Korea has only one land neighbour, North Korea, while three-quarters of the country is surrounded by seas – the Yellow Sea and the Sea of Japan.

Agriculture

Agriculture accounts for 7.5 per cent of GDP and employs 14.4 per cent of the labour force. South Korea is self-sufficient in food production except for wheat. The principal crops (1994) are rice (7,056,000mt), cabbages, onions, apples, tangerines, garlic, barley, soybeans. The national cattle herd is just over 3,200,000 head and meat, pork, poultry, eggs and dairy products make an important contribution to total food supplies. The fish catch in 1993 was 2,648,977mt and places South Korea at the top end of the scale of fishing countries with the world's seventh largest annual catch. Roundwood production is slightly above 6,000,000cu m a year. Land use is divided between forested 65.5 per cent, meadows and pastures 0.9 per cent, agricultural land, under permanent cultivation 21 per cent, other 12.6 per cent.

Mining

South Korea does not possess mineral resources on the scale of North Korea and mining only contributes 0.4 per cent to GDP and only employs 0.3 per cent of the labour force. Principal minerals mined in 1994 were copper (224,000mt), iron ore (191,313mt), zinc (14,243mt), lead (4,345mt). Gold is also mined and in 1992 output came to 21,000kg.

Manufacturing

South Korea's greatest economic strength lies in what is now a highly developed manufacturing sector. Between 1962 and 1987 the country increased its exports from $55,000,000 worth, mostly primary products, to $44,000,000,000, mainly manufactures. Between 1987 and 1993 the value of exports was almost doubled to $82,235,900,000. Starting with only a base of cheap labour South Korea at first exported textiles and simple manufactures. Today, however, its principal manufactures are small cars, a range of domestic appliances, silicon chips, computer-related products and electronics. The top three markets are the USA, Japan and the EU. Manufacturing now accounts for 29 per cent of GDP and employs 23 per cent of the labour force. Cement output in 1993 came to 47,313,000mt and pig iron to 21,870,000mt. In 1992 only twelve countries registered a higher GNP than did South Korea. In the range and sophistication of manufactures it has become a highly competitive modern economy.

Infrastructure

There are 3,091km of railroads of which 3,044km are 1.435m standard gauge. The country's 63,201km of roads are classified as follows: 1,551km expressways,

12,190km national highways, and 49,460km as provincial and local roads. Inland waterways are restricted to small craft. There are 455km of pipeline for petroleum products. The main ports are Pusan, Inchon, Kunsan, Mokpo and Ulsan. There are 93 usable airports, 59 with permanent surface runways of which 22 are between 2,440m and 3,659m in length. Both domestic and international telecommunications are excellent and there are over 13 million telephone subscribers.

Political considerations

South Korea, in many respects, has made the crossover to the status of an advanced economy. A major long-term problem concerns its relations with North Korea, from which it was split in 1945 and with which it is still technically at war. The bitter row between the two countries in 1994 when both the International Atomic Energy Agency (IAEA) and the USA accused North Korea of diverting nuclear materials from peaceful to war purposes and North Korea's threat (in the subsequent arguments) to treat the application of sanctions to it by South Korea as an act of war did nothing to lessen long-standing tensions. Nor did South Korea's refusal to send any official condolences to North Korea on the death of Kim Il Sung make relations any easier. The tensions continued into 1996.

Assessments

Self-sufficient in food production (except for wheat) and one of the world's most efficient manufacturing countries, South Korea's future should be assured as that of an economy in the second rank. It must, however, pay constant attention to the growing competition it faces from two of its giant Asian neighbours, China and Indonesia, which are industrializing fast, to the enormous capacity of Japan to capture its markets (though South Korea is a major supplier to Japan for a range of manufactures) as well as increasing competition from Asia's other newly industrializing countries (NICs) such as Taiwan, Singapore and Malaysia.

MALAYSIA

Area. 127,584 sq. miles (330,442 sq. km).
Population. (1995) 19,948,000.
Capital. Kuala Lumpur (1,145,075).
Other major cities. Ipoh (382,633), Johor Baharu (328,646), Melaka (295,999), Retaling Jaya (254,849).
Language(s). Malay (official), English, Chinese, Tamil, tribal languages.
Religion(s). Islam (official) 52.9 per cent, Buddhist 17.3 per cent, Chinese folk religions 11.6 per cent, Hindu 7 per cent, Christian 6.4 per cent, other 4.8 per cent.
Date of independence. August 31 1957 (from Britain).

GNP. (1993) $60,141,000,000, per capita $3,160.

Land and climate. Both the Peninsula and East Malaysia have coastal plains which rise into interior hills and mountains and over half the land is forested. The climate is tropical and is subject to the annual southwest monsoon (April to October) and the northeast monsoon (October to February).

Introduction

A mixed economy whose public sector is efficiently managed, Malaysia achieved one of the world's best rates of growth during the latter years of the 1980s and into the 1990s of between 8 and 9 per cent a year. With a per capita income above $3,000, Malaysia is an upper-middle-income economy and bids to move out of Third World status in the relatively near future. The country is blessed with both mineral and agricultural wealth and potential and can be classified among the Southeast Asian newly industrializing countries or NICs. Malaysia consists of a federation of the eleven states of the Peninsula (Malaya) and the two states of Sarawak and Sabah on the Island of Borneo (Kalimantan). All these territories formerly belonged to the British Empire: Malaya came to independence in 1957 following a ten-year war against communist (Chinese) insurgents. The Federation of Malaysia was formed in 1963 with Singapore and the two Borneo territories, Sabah and Sarawak, although Singapore was to break away as an independent state two years later (1965). Malaysia is a constitutional monarchy but under a unique system whereby, every five years, the head of state is elected from among the nine hereditary rulers of the Peninsula. It is a multiparty democracy.

Situated in possibly the most strategic position in South east Asia, Malaysia's dual territories (the Peninsula and the Borneo states) have a combined coastline on the South China Sea of 4,675km. Malaysia has three land neighbours: Thailand to the north of the Peninsula; the double enclave of Brunei in Sarawak; and the border between East Malaysia and Indonesia (Kalimantan).

Agriculture

Agriculture, including forestry and fisheries, is dominated in both the Peninsula and East Malaysia by rubber which has long been a key product and export. Production in 1994 came to 1,074,000mt. A second export commodity is palm oil with an annual production of more than 7,000,000mt. Sarawak is an important producer of pepper. Other export crops include cocoa, pineapples, coconuts. All regions produce rice, the main grain crop, but not in sufficient quantities to meet the country's needs and a proportion has to be imported. Pigs and chickens are important as a source of meat. Malaysia is a major producer of tropical hardwoods (over 54,000,000cu m a year) and controversy attaches to the rate of deforestation now taking place, especially in Sarawak. Much production, particularly in Sabah, is by subsistence farming. The fish catch is slightly above 600,000mt a year. Palm oil, wood and wood products and rubber are the main agricultural exports. Agriculture contributes 15 per cent to GDP and employs 21 per cent of the labour force. Land use is divided between forested 57.8 per cent, meadows and pastures 0.1 per cent, agricultural land, under permanent cultivation 14.9 per cent, other 27.2 per cent.

Mining

Mining contributes 7.4 per cent to GDP although only employing 0.4 per cent of the labour force. The main minerals are tin, petroleum, copper, iron ore, natural gas and bauxite. Tin is declining in importance although Malaysia is still one of the world's leading producers; output in 1994 came to 6,458mt. Iron ore output in 1994 came to 202,682mt, bauxite 161,919mt, copper 106,468mt. Although Malaysia is only a small oil producer in world terms, petroleum exports in the 1970s (after the OPEC-induced price rises) played a significant role in boosting the country's economic performance and growth. In 1993 oil production came to 233,685,000 barrels while home consumption at 82,477,000 barrels was just under a third of this figure, leaving the balance for export. There are large commercial deposits of natural gas to be found offshore from both the Peninsula and Sarawak and output in 1993 came to 21,399,000,000cu m (three times home consumption requirements).

Manufacturing

The manufacturing sector in Malaysia has seen consistent growth since 1960 with vigorous encouragement from the government and by the end of the 1980s machinery and transport equipment accounted for a third of all export earnings. Light industry now includes electronics and cars and in 1993 machinery and transport equipment earned just under 48.5 per cent of foreign exchange. Other manufactures include cement, refined sugar, wheat flour, other processed foods, fertilizers, plywood, radio receivers, automobile tyres. Industrial production has been growing at up to 13 per cent a year and in 1994 the sector accounted for 31.4 per cent of GDP and employed 23 per cent of the workforce. Singapore, the USA and Japan are the three most important export destinations. A range of incentives such as reduced duties apply to imported raw materials for the production of goods for export. For conservation reasons the export of 27 wood species is banned, as are exports of sawn logs over 40cm in diameter. There are only minimal controls on invisibles activities. Foreign investment is encouraged (up to 100 per cent) in export-oriented activities.

Infrastructure

There are 1,665km of 1.04m gauge railway in the Peninsula and 136km of 1.000m gauge railway in Sabah; none in Sarawak. The Peninsula has 23,600km of roads of which 19,352km are paved; Sabah has 3,782km of roads, Sarawak 1,644km. There are 7,296km of inland waterways and these are of particular importance in Sarawak. There are 1,307km of crude oil pipelines and 379km of pipelines for natural gas. The main ports are Tanjong Kidurong, Kota Kinabalu, Kuching, Pasir Gudang, Penang,

Port Kelang, Sandakan, Tawau. Malaysia has 102 usable airports, 32 with permanent surface runways of which one is over 3,659m in length and seven between 2,440 and 3,659m. Telecommunications on the Peninsula are good, in East Malaysia fair between cities and the general international service is good.

Political considerations

A constitutional monarchy and multiparty democracy, Malaysia's politics have been controlled since independence by the National Front, a federation of political parties dominated by the United Malays National Organization Baru (UMNO Baru). Following the end of the communist insurgency and independence in 1957, Malaysia has proved to be one of the most politically stable countries in Southeast Asia and a pillar of the Association of Southeast Asian Nations (ASEAN). Rising prosperity should help maintain this record.

Assessments

Malaysia's drive to industrialize and maximize the value of its considerable natural resources (both mineral and agricultural), has produced a steady increase in living standards with a per capita income that places it in the upper-middle-income group of countries. With an expanding economy (as a successful NIC) there is no reason why Malaysia should not make the crossover into the ranks of so-called developed countries in the relatively near future. However, there are wide differentials between the various regions and Sarawak and Sabah are far less advanced than the Peninsula.

MEXICO

Area. 756,066 sq. miles (1,958,201 sq. km).
Population. (1995) 91,145,000.
Capital. Mexico City (9,815,795).
Other major cities. Guadalajara (1,650,042), Ciudad Netzahualcoyotl (1,255,456), Monterrey (1,068,996), Puebla (1,007,170), Juárez (789,522), León (758,279), Tijuana (698,752), Mérida (523,422), Chihuahua (516,153).
Language(s). Spanish (official), Mayan dialects.
Religion(s). Roman Catholic 89.7 per cent, Protestant 4.9 per cent, other 2.2 per cent, none 3.2 per cent.
Date of independence. September 16 1810 (from Spain).
GNP. (1993) $324,951,000,000, per capita $3,750.
Land and climate. The country is a mixture of high rugged mountains, low coastal plains, high plateaux and desert with a climate that ranges from tropical in the south through desert and temperate modified by altitude.

Introduction

This major country of Latin America lies uneasily between the two worlds of the developed North represented by its huge US neighbour and the Third World or South to which all the countries of Central and Southern America still belong, although at widely varying stages of development. Mexico, which became independent of Spain in 1810, experienced a violent revolutionary history for much of the succeeding century until this phase came to an end in the late 1920s. For the last 60 or more years Mexico has been a relatively stable democracy although always dominated by the Institutional Revolutionary Party (Partido Revolucionario Institucional, PRI) which, yet again, won the elections of 1994.

In terms of GNP Mexico ranks fifteenth in the world league and is a major industrial producer. It is also one of the world's leading storehouses of minerals, including oil. On the other hand it can no longer feed its huge population of 90 million which is expected to double over the next 26 years and it faces many problems of poverty, unemployment or underemployment, overpopulation and lack of skills commonly associated with membership of the Third World. Its adherence to the North American Free Trade Agreement (NAFTA) with the USA and Canada in 1994 (NAFTA became operational on January 1 1995) could be seen as a quantum leap that would take Mexico from the status of a developing country to that of a developed country although the immediate effect was to trigger off a massive economic crisis in January 1995. On the other hand, it is far from clear whether NAFTA really represents a vehicle that will assist Mexico's advance into the ranks of the North. Instead, it may turn out to be a trap whose main result is to make cheap Mexican labour the more readily available to US companies without also providing commensurate advantages.

Mexico has a border of 3,326km with the USA to the north across which a constant flow of emigrants, both legal and (mainly) illegal, represents one aspect of its economic problems. It has far shorter borders with its two southern neighbours, Belize and Guatemala, and over 9,000km of coastline, most of it on the Pacific shore (including the long inlet created by the Mexican Panhandle) and a much shorter coastline on the Gulf of Mexico where the offshore oil is to be found.

Agriculture

Agriculture accounts for only 7.4 per cent of GDP and employs 26 per cent of the workforce. During the 1980s the rapid growth of population at more than 1 million increase a year outstripped food production. Even so, Mexico remains a major food producer with both big estates and smallholder farmers. Cash crops include cotton, coffee and a range of fruits and tomatoes although processed foods and beverages only account for 3 per cent of exports. The main crops and output (1994) are sugarcane (41,106,000mt), maize (19,193,000mt), sorghum (3,869,000mt), wheat (3,589,000mt), followed by oranges, bananas, mangoes, avocados, dry beans, lemons, canteloupes, apples, barley, grapes, soybeans, rice, pineapples and strawberries. The national cattle herd is over 30,000,000 head followed (in numbers) by pigs, goats, horses, turkeys, sheep, mules and asses. Roundwood production is in excess of 23,000,000cu m a year while the fish catch at 1,200,686mt (1993) places Mexico among the top twenty fishing countries with shrimps and sardines as important exports. Mexico also cultivates (illicitly) opium poppy and cannabis despite an active programme of eradication and the USA is the principal market. Mexico is also a trans-shipment country for cocaine from South America to the USA. Land use is divided between forested 21.5 per cent, meadows and pastures 39 per cent, agricultural land, under permanent cultivation 13 per cent, other 26.5 per cent.

Mining

Mexico is a major source of minerals apart from oil; these include silver, copper, gold, lead, zinc, natural gas. Mexico derived half its income from its mines for the three centuries from 1600 to 1900, especially from silver, and in 1983 following the opening of the Real de Angeles silver mine the country once more regained its position as the world's leading silver producer. Only modest quantities of iron ore and coal are mined.

Of 26 major minerals Mexico is a leading producer for 16 of them as shown in Table 2.3.

Table 2.3 Mexico, mineral production, 1992

Mineral	World placing	Output 1992
Copper	11	320,000mt
Gold	19	10,000 kg
Iron ore	16	7,380,000mt
Crude steel	21	8,435,000mt
Lead	7	174,000mt
Manganese	9	407,000mt
Silver	1	2,316mt
Zinc	6	279,000mt
Hydraulic cement	11	26,900,000mt
Nitrogen in ammonia	9	2,222,000mt
Salt	8	7,600,000mt
Elemental sulphur	8	1,600,000mt
Marketed natural gas	11	33,000,000,000cu m
Natural gas plant liquids	5	165,000,000 barrels
Crude oil	6	978,000,000 barrels
Refined oil	9	575,000,000 barrels

Despite this high level of mineral production only oil is a significant export earner and oil has not proved an unmixed blessing. Petroleum was found at the turn of the century and given a major boost by the demands of World War I. For a short period in the 1920s Mexico was second only to the USA as a world producer. But slump was to follow and then in 1938 Mexico nationalized the petroleum industry, in the process isolating itself from the mainstream petroleum-using countries, most notably the USA and Britain, which actually considered military intervention against Mexico for her action. In the 1950s and 1960s, before major new discoveries were made, Mexico had to import oil to meet all its requirements but from 1972, after new wells had revealed huge fields, Mexico was again able (1975) to produce oil surplus to its requirements.

In 1976 President José Lopez Portillo made a decision to reverse the earlier policy of conserving oil for Mexico's future and, instead, expanded production for export to increase development income; unfortunately this also led to the rapid accumulation of oil-based debts (borrowing on the basis of oil to come) and Mexico has yet to escape from this debt problem. About 40 per cent of the oil is refined in Mexico. As at the end of 1992 proved reserves of oil were 51,300,000,000 barrels, equivalent to 5.1 per cent of world reserves while natural gas reserves stood at 2,000,000,000,000cu m. Petroleum output in 1992 at 975,000,000 barrels was only slightly in excess of home consumption of 968,000,000 barrels; nonetheless, crude oil exports accounted for 16.1 per cent of all export earnings.

Manufacturing

Border assembly plants and tourism geared to the US market are the two main sources of foreign exchange earnings after oil. The USA is Mexico's principal trade partner accounting for nearly 75 per cent of both imports and exports. Manufacturing accounts for 22.5 per cent of GDP and employs over 5 million workers or 15 per cent of the workforce. Mexico is now a substantial industrial economy and the main manufacturing sectors cover metal products, chemicals, food, beverages and tobacco, textiles and apparel, iron and steel, non-metallic mineral products, paper and printing, wood and wood products, non-electrical machinery and transport equipment, electrical machinery. The total value of Mexico's exports in 1994 came to $60 billion and well over half this amount (58.0 per cent) was derived from metallic products, machinery and equipment including automobiles, with the USA taking 83 per cent of all exports. Tourism, which is aimed overwhelmingly at the US market, earned $6,167,000,000 in 1993.

Infrastructure

There are 24,500km of railroads, 212,000km of roads of which 65,000km are paved and 2,900km of inland waterways. Mexico has a vast network of pipelines: 28,200km for crude oil, 10,150km for petroleum products, 13,254km for natural gas and 1,400km for petrochemicals. The main ports are Acapulco, Altamira, Coatzacoalcos, Ensenada, Guaymas, Manzanillo, Mazatlan, Progreso, Puerto Vallarta, Salina Cruz, Tampico, Tuxpan, Veracruz. There are 1,478 usable airports, 200 with permanent surface runways of which three are over 3,659m and 35 between 2,440 and 3,659m in length. There is a highly developed system of telecommunications which was privatized in 1990.

Political considerations

Although Mexico would like to be seen as a truly modernized state, this is not yet the case and in many ways the period January 1994 to January 1995 revealed the extent of its problems. Even so, Mexico is closer than most Third World countries to the point at which it can make the crossover from developing South to industrialized North. In January 1994 Mexico was faced with the Zapatista rebellion of Indians in the remote southern province of Chiapas; they were deeply unhappy with the way they believed themselves to be exploited by the centre. A year later, in January 1995, following her adherence to the North American Free Trade Agreement (NAFTA), Mexico was faced with a devastating economic crisis. There were a number of reasons for this but underlying them was uncertainty as to whether NAFTA really represented the best route for Mexico to follow. In the event of the crisis the USA was obliged to mount an $18bn rescue package as well as making additional loan guarantees in the region of $40bn. Mexico faced the unpalatable fact that the country is still seen in the developed world, and most especially in the USA, as only really being valuable for its cheap labour and raw materials, particularly its oil, rather than for its internal market, although multinational corporations and private financial institutions are quick enough to move in and out of Mexico as conditions dictate to make quick, and often huge, profits. When the crisis occurred in January 1995 $10bn of US investment fled the country. Doubts about the real value of NAFTA are the cause of current Mexican uncertainties: will it be the means of drawing Mexico into the advanced economies of the North; or is it a device to allow its powerful US neighbour the more easily to penetrate the Mexican market and utilize its cheap labour?

Assessments

Mexico possesses huge resources and, for example, at current rates of production can make its known oil reserves last another 50 years. There are vast mineral resources apart from oil. It is at least possible that with greater concentration upon the agricultural sector Mexico could again achieve food self-sufficiency. Most important for the future, Mexico has established a wide industrial base. But the country also faces several daunting problems: the first concerns the rapid rate of population increase and, with a doubling time of only 26 years, Mexico will have 180 million people by 2020. Second, and more short term, is the size of its international debt obligations: $86 billion outstanding at the end of 1993 before the huge rescue operation mounted by the USA in January 1995. Debts on this scale are bound to inhibit important development projects. Third, Mexico is likely to find that the expectations of the people (raised by the current belief that the country is close to the point of moving away from its Third World development status) may outrun anything the government is able to deliver and it could face dangerous political instability as a result. Nonetheless, of all major Third World countries Mexico is probably one of the closest to the point of genuine economic take-off into the ranks of the advanced economies of the North.

SINGAPORE

Area. 247.5 sq. miles (641 sq. km).
Population. (1995) 2,989,000.
Capital. Singapore (there are no other city/town divisions on the island).

Language(s). Chinese, Malay, Tamil, English (all official).
Religion(s). Buddhist, Taoist, other traditional beliefs 53.9 per cent, Muslim 15.4 per cent, Christian 12.6 per cent, Hindu 3.6 per cent, non-religious 14.5 per cent.
Date of independence. August 9 1965 (from Malaysia).
GNP. (1993) $55,372,000,000, per capita $19,310.
Land and climate. Singapore is a low-lying island with an undulating central plateau which includes a water catchment area. The climate is tropical, hot, humid and rainy.

Introduction

Founded by the British imperialist Sir Stamford Raffles in 1819 as an entrepôt port, Singapore's principal asset is its geographical position and deep sea port on what has become the busiest sea lane in the world, making it the world's premier port in terms of the number of vessels which pass throught it annually. Perhaps it would be more accurate to describe Singapore as a city state rather than as a country. When Britain withdrew from the last of its Asian possessions it created a federation to comprise Malaya, Singapore and the Borneo territories of North Borneo and Sarawak but in 1965, after only two years, Singapore broke away from the Federation of Malaysia, believing it would be more viable on its own. Under its long-term prime minister Lee Kuan Yew, Singapore developed as a highly efficient entrepôt and industrial powerhouse so that by 1993 the people enjoyed an average per capita income of $19,310 and Singapore was close to the point of making the crossover from the status of a developing to a developed nation. The island is situated at the southern tip of the Malay Peninsula to which it is connected by a causeway.

Agriculture

Agriculture is of minor importance to Singapore, contributing only 0.2 per cent to GDP and employing only 0.2 per cent of the workforce. The major crops produced are rubber, copra, fruit and vegetables and it is self-sufficient in eggs and poultry. Most foodstuffs have to be imported.

Minerals

Similarly, minerals are of minimal importance to the Singapore economy, the only mineral of any importance to be quarried being granite.

Manufacturing

During more than a century of British rule Singapore was seen as a great entrepôt for her imperial role in the Far East and its fall to Japan in 1942 was symbolic of the collapse of the British and other Western empires in the Far East. Singapore was of such importance to imperial Britain because of its geographic location and port facilities and these advantages have been utilized to full effect by the successor independent government that came to power in 1965.

Manufacturing accounts for 28.3 per cent of GDP and employs 25.6 per cent of the workforce. The principal manufactures are electronic products, transport equipment, refined petroleum products, metal and chemical products, non-electrical machinery, printing and publishing. Computer-related components are a key manufacture and export. The importance of Singapore's location is reflected in the Asian destinations of a high proportion of its exports which go to Malaysia, Hong Kong, Japan, Thailand and Taiwan. The USA, however, is the biggest single export destination and Germany and Britain in Europe are also important.

Financial services are another vital aspect of Singapore's success and prosperity and account for 27 per cent of GDP.

Infrastructure

There is a single 38km 1.000m gauge railway line and 2,644km of roads. Singapore, the only port, is one of the most up to date and busiest in the world. Many ships registered under the Singapore flag are foreign owned. There are ten usable airports, all with permanent surface runways of which two are over 3,659m and another two between 2,440 and 3,659m in length. Telecommunications, both domestic and international, are good.

Political considerations

A unitary multiparty republic, in fact Singapore has been ruled along authoritarian lines for most of the period since 1965 and has achieved a high degree of internal discipline as well as a strong work ethic as a result. These attributes have contributed markedly to its economic success. Growing prosperity and the crossover to developed economy status that ought to take place in the near future will bring new problems and government will probably find it harder to maintain its rigid disciplinary control over the population. Singapore has become a transit point for heroin from the Golden Triangle on its way to the USA, Western Europe and other destinations in the Third World. Singapore is a founder member of the Association of Southeast Asian Nations (ASEAN) and operates an open economic system with few bars to investment or the movement of funds.

Assessments

Its unique location, first-class port facilities and major economic achievements, including its position as one of the world's growing financial centres, should ensure a bright future for Singapore which represents one of Asia's major success stories.

SOUTH AFRICA

Area. 472,281 sq. miles (1,223,201 sq. km).
Population. (1995) 41,465,000.
Capitals. Pretoria (executive) (1,080,187), Bloemfontein (judicial) (256,000), Cape Town (legislative) (2,350,157).
Other major cities. Johannesburg (1,916,063), Durban (1,137,378), Port Elizabeth (853,204).
Language(s). Afrikaans, English, Ndebele, Pedi, Sotho, Swazi, Tsonga, Tswana, Venda, Xhosa, Zulu (all official).
Religion(s). Christian 78 per cent (a variety of denominations), traditional religions 10.5 per cent, Hindu 1.7 per cent, Muslim 1.1 per cent, Jewish 0.4 per cent, other 8.3 per cent.
Date of independence. May 31 1910 (from Britain).
GNP. (1994) $118,961,000,000, per capita $2,930.
Land and climate. The interior of South Africa consists of a vast uplifted plateau which is surrounded by rugged hills. There is a narrow costal plain. The climate is semi-arid although subtropical along the coast. Temperatures are moderate with sunny hot days and cool to cold nights.

Introduction

Not far short of half a million square miles in size, South Africa occupies the whole southern extremity of the African continent from the Atlantic to the Indian Ocean although within its borders is enclosed the small enclave territory of Lesotho. Apart from Lesotho, South Africa has boundaries with five countries to its north – Botswana, Mozambique, Namibia, Swaziland and Zimbabwe, and a coastline of 2,881km (one of the longest in Africa). The history of South Africa has been one of clashing cultures: between Boer and Briton, European settler and African, Zulu and Xhosa. The formation, after the Anglo-Boer War of 1899–1902, of the Union of South Africa comprising the four territories of Cape Province, Natal (British colonies of settlement), the Orange Free State and Transvaal (Boer republics) in 1910 provided the framework for modern South Africa.

The election victory of the National Party in 1948 ushered in the apartheid era and from that date until 1990 with the policy of apartheid being attacked every year in the UN, South Africa became increasingly a pariah state, isolated and defiant, as its white minority enforced the apartheid system and the black majority sought international support to overthrow it. By the mid-1980s the structures of apartheid were collapsing and following his election victory of September 1989, the new President and leader of the National Party, F. W. de Klerk, came to terms with political realities when on February 2 1990 he gave a speech unbanning the African National Congress (ANC) and 33 other banned organizations. Just over a week later he released the ANC leader Nelson Mandela from prison and following four complex and sometimes violent years of negotiations, universal franchise elections were held for the first time in South Africa's history in April 1994; they were followed by the formation of a transitional government of national unity which was dominated by the ANC while Nelson Mandela became the first black president of South Africa.

Agriculture

Agriculture only contributes 4.6 per cent to GDP while employing 13.3 per cent of the labour force yet South Africa is both self-sufficient in food and a substantial food exporter as well, although in drought years it faces a shortfall of maize, the main staple. Production includes poultry, eggs, meat (beef–South Africa is a meat exporter–sheep and goat) from the livestock sector, maize (a surplus for export in good years), wheat, sugarcane, citrus fruits, grapes, tobacco. Fine quality wines are produced at the Cape and with the lifting of apartheid these were becoming a major export item in 1995. There is a substantial output of roundwood, just short of 20,000,000cu m in 1993, while South Africa has rich offshore fisheries with an annual catch in excess of 500,000mt with fish making an important contribution to exports. Altogether, agricultural products account for 7 per cent of all exports. Water conservation measures are essential as there are few major rivers. Land use is divided between forested 3.7 per cent, meadows and pastures 66.6 per cent, agricultural land, under permanent cultivation 10.8 per cent, other 18.9 per cent.

Minerals and mining

South Africa is one of the world's great storehouses of minerals and these have long played a crucial role in the country's economy. Mining contributes just under 9 per cent to GDP but only employs 3 per cent of the workforce. Gold, diamonds, coal and the platinum group of metals dominate the sector. Gold has long been the most important mineral with South Africa accounting for up to 50 per cent (and sometimes more) of total world output. Gold also represents 50 per cent of all minerals mined in the country (in value) although gold production is now declining. Diamonds are also in decline and South Africa has fallen from first to fifth place as a world producer. Since 1945, however, South Africa has expanded production of a wide range of minerals including uranium, platinum, nickel, copper, coal, antimony, vanadium, asbestos, iron ore, fluorspar, chromium, manganese and limestone as well as other minerals on a lesser scale.

Of 26 principal minerals, South Africa is a leading world producer of 14 of them as shown in Table 2.4.

Mineral exports, in order of value, are gold, diamonds, coal, the platinum group, iron ore, copper, manganese, lime and limestone, and chrome. In 1993 gold accounted for 28 per cent of exports, gem diamonds 12.8 per cent, base metals 12.5 per cent, coal 6 per cent. South Africa's exceptionally large mineral base will continue to act as a principal arm of the economy into the foreseeable future.

Manufacturing

Manufacturing now accounts for 23.5 per cent of GDP and employs 16.7 per cent of the workforce. Principal manufactures are food and beverages, soaps, paints, pharmaceuticals, refined petroleum, iron and steel, transport equipment, metal products, non-electrical machinery, paper and paper products. South Africa is now a substantial arms producer and exporter. There is a major construction industry.

Table 2.4 South Africa, mineral production, 1992

Mineral	World placing	Output 1992
Chromite	2	3,361,000mt
Copper	15	167,000mt
Gold	1	613,000 kg
Iron ore	9	28,226,000mt
Crude steel	20	9,061,000mt
Lead	9	75,000mt
Manganese	3	2,404,000mt
Nickel	8	28,000mt
Silver	17	172mt
Uranium	6	2,222mt
Diamonds	5	10,156,000 carats
Phosphate rock	10	3,051,000mt
Elemental sulphur	14	604,000mt
Coal	8	176,000,000mt

Although South Africa has no oil or natural gas it is the leading world producer of oil from coal (through its SASOL plants) and these provide approximately half the country's petroleum requirements. The industrial sector is the most advanced and sophisticated on the African continent. The financial sector, including the Johannesburg Stock Exchange, is an important contributor to the country's wealth. South Africa has huge tourist potential (it earned $1,190,000,000 in 1993) but the sector needs to make major improvements to realize its full potential. South African citizens spend more abroad than the country receives from visitors.

Infrastructure

There are 20,638km of rail track, almost all 1.067m gauge; 183,309km of roads of which 54,013km are paved; 931km of pipeline for crude oil, 1,748km for petroleum products and 322km for natural gas. The main ports are Durban, Cape Town, Port Elizabeth, Richard's Bay, Saldanha and Mosselbai. There are 713 usable airports of which 136 have permanent surface runways and of these five are over 3,659m and ten are between 2,440m and 3,659m in length. Telecommunications are highly developed. South Africa possesses the best overall system in Africa and the main cities – especially Johannesburg, Cape Town and Durban – are geared for international business.

Political considerations

The ending of the apartheid system and the holding of universal franchise elections in April 1994 launched South Africa upon a new and hopeful era. The country faces enormous problems of which the two most difficult are the question of provincial powers (the extent to which the country will move towards a federal system) especially with regard to the Zulus under their volatile leader Chief Mangosuthu Buthelezi; and the question of meeting the expectations of the mass of the population for improved living standards and employment opportunities now that apartheid has come to an end. At present about 45 per cent of the black population is unemployed. If the government can deal successfully with these problems its long-term future should be bright.

Assessments

South Africa has huge mineral resources; it is food self-sufficient and a food exporter as well; it possesses the most highly developed industrial sector on the continent; and it has the best general infrastructure in Africa. After the long isolation of the apartheid years there is urgent need for the economy to catch up with developments outside Africa and readjust to an international economic system that has moved dramatically over the last decades and left South Africa behind. South Africa urgently seeks to attract international investment but will need to adjust its tax laws and eventually end foreign exchange control in order to obtain the range of investments it would like to see enter the country. The high unemployment and low educational levels of the majority of the African labour force represent another long term problem. There exists the danger that the economic divisions created by the apartheid system could continue in the form of a two-tier society – the developed economy that is part of the wider international global economy on the one hand, and the underdeveloped (mainly African) economy that is still very much part of the Third World on the other. The advanced sector possesses the capacity to forge a single dynamic economy which could become a motor force for the African continent as a whole. The possibility is there.

TAIWAN

Area. 13,969 sq. miles (36,179 sq. km).
Population. (1995) 21,268,000.
Capital. Taipei (2,652,000).
Other major cities. Kao-hsiung (1,416,160), T'ai-chung (836,560), T'ai-nan (702,704), Chi'ung (365,312).
Language(s). Mandarin Chinese (official), Taiwanese, Hakka dialects.
Religion(s). Chinese folk religions 48.5 per cent, Buddhist 43 per cent, Christian 7.4 per cent, Muslim 0.5 per cent, other 0.6 per cent.
Date of independence. (Taiwan is regarded in Beijing as part of China.)
GNP. (1994) $244,650,000,000, per capita $11,629.
Land and climate. The west of the island consists of gently rolling plains, the eastern two-thirds of rugged mountains. The climate is tropical marine, affected by the southwest monsoon from June to August; there is persistent cloud year round.

Introduction

The defeated army of the Chinese Nationalist government (the Kuomintang) fled to Taiwan in 1949 as the Chinese Communist Party and its army under Mao Zedong took complete control of mainland China. As the Cold War escalated during the 1950s the USA gave both military and economic assistance to the Nationalist Chinese on Taiwan and this enabled the government to set out on its path of massive economic growth so that it developed first into a newly industrializing country (NIC) and subsequently came to be regarded as one of the so-called Asian 'Tigers'. With a small economic base (agricultural and mineral) Taiwan concentrated upon building up an export-oriented industrial sector (beginning with textiles) and was greatly assisted in this because of three principal factors: massive US support including economic aid; a highly authoritarian regime (democracy has only been gradually introduced in Taiwan since the mid-1980s); and a strong general work ethic which, however, now appears to be on the wane. As a result, over the years 1950 to 1990, Taiwan created a dynamic capitalist-oriented economy, although with important government guidance over questions of investment and foreign trade, as well as substantial government ownership of a number of banks and industrial companies.

By the 1990s Taiwan had come to be ranked as the thirteenth trading country in the world; meanwhile, more and more labour-intensive industries have been replaced by capital and technology-intensive industries. In 1992 Taiwan's exports passed $82bn while imports at $72bn produced a healthy trade balance in her favour. Taiwan imports most of its raw material requirements and stands as a classic illustration of how wealth can be created by the process of adding value to raw materials or semi-manufactured goods. The island of Taiwan lies off the south-eastern coast of China between Japan and the Philippines and has a total coastline of 1,448km.

Agriculture

Agriculture only contributes 3.6 per cent to GDP although employing 10.7 per cent of the workforce. The sector has been heavily subsidized by the state. Principal crops are sugarcane, rice, citrus fruits, maize, pineapples, bananas, sweet potatoes. The principal livestock are pigs. The fish catch of 1,286,750mt (1994) places Taiwan among the world's major fishing nations. The country is not self-sufficient in wheat, maize or soybeans. Land use is divided between forested 55 per cent, agricultural land, under permanent cultivation 25.7 per cent, other 19.3 per cent.

Minerals

Mining only contributes 0.3 per cent to GDP and employs 0.2 per cent of the workforce. There are small deposits of oil and natural gas, coal, limestone, marble and asbestos and a limited output of silver.

Manufacturing

Manufacturing contributes 29 per cent to GDP and employs 27.4 per cent of the workforce, and manufactures of all kinds account for the great majority of Taiwan's exports with machines and electronics as the main export earners. Taiwan has 65 per cent of the world's shipbreaking market. The principal manufactures are cement, steel ingots, paperboard, fertilizers, synthetic fibre, polyvinyl chloride plastics, electronic calculators, sound recorders, sewing machines, desktop computer systems. Taiwan's phenomenal industrial success has seen its products penetrate all the main industrial markets of the world; it has also become a major source of investment for China, Thailand, Indonesia, the Philippines and Malaysia. Tourism now earns nearly $3bn a year.

Infrastructure

There are 4,600km of railways of which 1,025km have 1.067m gauge track while the balance consists of industrial lines owned and operated by government enterprises. There are 20,041km of roads of which 17,095km are paved; 615km of pipelines for petroleum products and 97km for natural gas. The country is served by five main ports: Kao-hsiung, Chi-lung, Hua-lien, Su-ao and T'ai-tung. There are 38 usable airports, 36 with permanent surface runways of which three are over 3,659m and sixteen between 2,440 and 3,659m in length. Taiwan has the best-developed communications system in Asia apart from Japan with slightly above one telephone for every three people and excellent international connections. Taiwan (1995) is in the middle of a $300,000,000,000 programme to improve the island's overall infrastructure.

Political considerations

Beijing regards Taiwan as part of mainland China and intends to reclaim the territory at some future date; what happens in Hong Kong after its reversion to China in 1997, therefore, will have vital implications for the future of Taiwan and events there will be closely monitored from Taipei. Meanwhile, Taiwan faces a number of problems that, ironically, arise out of its industrial–commercial success. These include a slackening of the work ethic which has sustained the country during its rise; and an influx of immigrants (both legal and illegal) to take advantage of its prosperity. Future development must be closely related to the rapid economic growth now taking place in mainland China and the relations that the 'two Chinas' establish over the next ten or so years.

Assessments

The huge success of Taiwan (which at the beginning of the 1950s relied upon agriculture for 90 per cent of its exports) in transforming itself into the thirteenth-ranked industrial trading nation in the world must, in part, be attributed to the special circumstances of the Cold War over the period 1950 to 1970 when it could rely upon immense US backing. Nonetheless, it is a prime illustration of how an economy with a minimal resource base can turn itself into a major industrial power by adding value to resources most of which are imported either in the form of raw materials or as semi-manufactured goods. Taiwan's per capita income of $11,629 places it just below the high-income group of OECD countries.

THAILAND

Area. 198,115 sq. miles (513,115 sq. km).
Population. (1995) 58,791,000.
Capital. Bangkok (5,620,591).
Other major cities. Nonthaburi (264,201), Nakhon Ratchasima (202,503), Chiang Mai (161,541), Khon Kaen (131,478).
Language(s). Thai (official), English, various local and regional dialects.
Religion(s). Buddhist 94.8 per cent, Muslim 4 per cent, Christian 0.5 per cent, other 0.7 per cent.
Date of independence. 1238 (traditional date of the foundation of the Kingdom).
GNP. (1993) $120,235,000,000, per capita $2,040.
Land and climate. There is a central plain, an eastern plateau and surrounding mountains. The climate is tropical: the rainy warm southwest monsoon runs from May to September and the dry cool northeast monsoon from November to March. The southern isthmus is always hot and humid.

Introduction

One of the few Asian countries never to be colonized, Thailand pursued a delicately balanced middle course through the years of the Cold War though its sympathies were always inclined towards an open market system. Well endowed with natural resources, both mineral and agricultural, it has achieved major economic success during the 1980s and 1990s and is well on the way to becoming an industrialized nation. In 1994 it led the world with a 9 per cent increase in GNP and a 16 per cent increase in exports. A constitutional monarchy with two legislative houses, Thailand has faced a range of political challenges and unrest in recent years although in 1995 it appeared relatively stable under a democratically elected government. Thailand is located in the centre of the so-called 'golden triangle' of drug-producing countries and is a major trafficker in heroin from Burma and Laos as well as being a major drug money laundering centre. Thailand has four neighbours: Burma, Cambodia, Laos and Malaysia and coastlines on either side of its long southern peninsula on the Indian Ocean (Andaman Sea) to the west and the Gulf of Thailand to the east.

Agriculture

Agriculture contributes just under 12 per cent to GDP and employs 55.5 per cent of the workforce. Rubber, rice, cassava (tapioca), and vegetables as well as fish and fish products are the sector's principal exports. Thailand, long known as the rice bowl of Asia, is a major exporter of rice and produces over 18,000,000mt a year as it also does of cassava (tapioca) which is another big export. Other staple crops are sugarcane, maize, bananas, coconuts, soybeans, dry beans, cabbages and sorghum. Livestock includes 7,593,000 cattle and 4,257,000 buffalo. Roundwood production exceeds 38,000,000cu m a year and includes some of the major hardwoods. The fish catch in excess of 3,000,000mt is one of the largest in the world and fish and fish products account for between 9 and 10 per cent of exports. Apart from wheat, Thailand is self-sufficient in food. Land use is divided between forested 27.4 per cent, meadows and pastures 1.6 per cent, agricultural land, under permanent cultivation 45.3 per cent, other 25.7 per cent.

Minerals

Mining contributes 1.5 per cent to GDP and employs 0.2 per cent of the workforce. The main minerals mined are limestone, gypsum, zinc, marble, fluorite, lead and tin. Other resources include natural gas, tungsten, tantalum, lignite. Precious stones make an uneven contribution to the sector but in 1993 accounted for 4.4 per cent of exports. A small output of oil and natural gas is consumed locally.

Manufacturing

It is in the manufacturing sector that Thailand has made the greatest strides in recent years and turned the economy into one of the fastest growing in the world. Manufacturing now accounts for 28.3 per cent of GDP and employs 12 per cent of the workforce. Principal manufactures include cement, refined sugar, chemical fertilizer, synthetic fibre, jute products, motorcycles. Leading exports (1993) were electrical machinery 14.4 per cent, textiles and apparel 11.7 per cent. It is the process of adding value that is transforming the Thai economy. Tourism is a major earner of foreign exchange, receipts in 1993 coming to $5,014,000,000.

Infrastructure

There are 3,940km of 1.000m gauge railway; 77,697km of roads of which 35,855km are paved; 3,999km of important inland waterways (and many additional minor ones); 350km of pipelines for natural gas and 67km for petroleum products. The country's main ports are Bangkok, Pattani, Phuket, Sattahip, Si Racha. There are 95 usable airports, 51 with permanent surface runways of which one is over 3,659m and fourteen are between 2,440 and 3,659m in length. The domestic system of tele-communications is inadequate; the international system is reasonable.

Political considerations

In the centre of a highly volatile political region, Thailand has long learnt the art of political compromise which has allowed the country to maintain its political independence and not be drawn into conflicts in neighbouring states. Two developing problems may cause setbacks in the near future. First, there is a growing need to increase the output of college graduates with technical training as well as skilled workers if Thailand is to maintain the pace of its economic expansion. Second, an alarming report of 1995 revealed that there are now an estimated 800,000 Thais infected with Aids and the effects of the disease could be devastating in the quite near future.

Assessments

Thailand has made very rapid strides over the two decades of the 1970s and 1980s and into the 1990s with the emphasis upon developing the industrial sector; the result has been to bring the country more into line with the smaller, so-called Asian 'Tigers'. With a per capita GNP of $2,040 Thailand is now at the upper end of the lower-middle-income group of countries and if the right priority is given to improving skill levels it should soon progress into the upper-middle-income group.

TURKEY

Area. 300,948 sq. miles (79,452 sq. km).
Population. (1995) 62,526,000.
Capital. Ankara (2,719,981).
Other major cities. Istanbul (7,331,927), Izmir (1,920,807), Adana (1,010,363), Bursa (949,810), Gaziantep (683,557), Konya (558,308).
Language(s). Turkish (official), Kurdish, Arabic.
Religion(s). Sunni Muslim 80 per cent, Alevi 19.8 per cent, Christian 0.2 per cent.
Date of independence. October 29 1923 (when modern Turkey became the successor state to the Ottoman Empire).
GNP. (1993) $126,336,000,000, per capita $2,120.
Land and climate. A rugged mountain country with narrow coastal plains and a high central plateau (Anatolia). The climate is temperate with hot dry summers and mild wet winters with harsh (continental) conditions in the interior.

Introduction

Modern Turkey is the successor state to the Ottoman Empire which finally collapsed following its defeat in World War I. The country's history stretches back into antiquity. Turkey owes its secular rather than Islamic bias to the modern reforming leader Kemal Ataturk who ruled the country through the 1920s and 1930s. During the Cold War Turkey was a staunch member of NATO. It became an associate of the

EEC in 1964, when it was envisaged that Turkey would eventually become a full member of what is now the EU, and in April 1987 formal application was made to join. The end of the Cold War and the subsequent break-up of the Soviet Union made this question more urgent and more complex as the EU considered its new relationship with the countries of Eastern Europe, many of which also wished to join the EU. Since that time the EU has stalled on the issue of full Turkish membership: partly on purely pragmatic grounds – how to integrate so large an economy and population into the communities; and partly on grounds of Turkey's alleged poor human rights record as well as objections by Greece, which has always opposed Turkey's accession to the EU. But more important, and underlying the other objections, is the fact that the Turkish population is predominantly Muslim. Given growing European suspicions, misunderstandings and antagonisms towards Islam which have emerged especially during the 1990s, Turkey's religious orientation may prove an insuperable obstacle to its membership of the EU in the foreseeable future. Turkey has the basic requirements – agricultural and mineral resources, population and industrial base – to develop into a substantial economic power in the near future and so make the 'crossover' from developing to developed economic status. Turkey has eight neighbours: Armenia, Azerbaijan, Bulgaria, Georgia, Greece, Iran, Iraq and Syria and a total of 7,200km of coastline on the Black Sea, Aegean and Mediterranean. It claims an exclusive economic zone over part of the Black Sea. Turkey's geographic position straddling Europe and Asia gives it an influential role in two major regions.

Agriculture

Agriculture accounts for 16.3 per cent of GDP and employs 40 per cent of the workforce. Turkey is a major wheat producer (17,500,000mt in 1994). Other principal crops are sugar beet, barley, potatoes, grapes, maize, apples, oranges, cotton seed, sunflower seeds, lentils, cotton (lint), olives, tobacco, hazelnuts, sultanas, raisins, attar of roses. Fruits account for 6 per cent of exports. Attar of roses is used as a base for perfumes and Turkish tobacco is famous. Livestock herds include 37,541,000 sheep and 11,916,000 cattle. Roundwood production averages 15,000,000cu m a year and the fish catch (1993) is 556,000mt. Turkey is normally self-sufficient in food. Land use is divided between forested 26.3 per cent, meadows and pastures 11 per cent, agricultural land, under permanent cultivation 36 per cent, other 26.7 per cent.

Mining

Although mining only contributes 1.3 per cent to GDP and employs less than 1 per cent of the workforce, Turkey is richly endowed with minerals which include large resources of bauxite, borax, coal, chromium, copper, sulphur, iron ore and manganese, as well as antimony and mercury. Coal and about 60 per cent of other mineral extraction is controlled by state enterprises. Turkey is a leading world producer of chromite (556,000mt in 1993), iron ore (5,300,000mt), crude steel

(10,343,000mt), hydraulic cement (28,607,000mt), salt (1,500,000mt) and coal (55,000,000mt). Total coal reserves are estimated at 5,000m tons. Turkey has limited resources of heavy grade oil in the southeast of the country (discovered in 1950) accompanied by natural gas; output in 1994 came to 26,355,000 barrels of oil providing a surplus for export over home requirements and 199,500,000cu m of natural gas. Most of Turkey's mineral resources have a long lifespan ahead.

Manufactures

Manufacturing contributed 20.1 per cent to GDP in 1994 and employs 13.8 per cent of the workforce. The sector is relatively widely diversified. Principal manufactures include refined petroleum products (there are four refineries), textiles, food products, motor vehicles, industrial chemicals, non-electrical machinery. Textiles and clothing accounted for 34.7 per cent of exports in 1994, iron and steel for 13.1 per cent, electrical machinery for 3.8 per cent. Tourism is a major contributor to the economy, earning $4,321,000,000 in 1994. Of Turkey's six major export destinations (Germany, former USSR, USA, Britain, France and Italy) four are in the EU.

Infrastructure

There are 8,429km of 1.435m standard gauge railways; 320,611km of roads of which 31,200km are limited access expressways or main highways; 1,200km of inland waterways; 1,738km of crude oil pipelines, 2,321km of petroleum product pipelines and 708km of natural gas pipelines. The main ports are Iskenderun, Istanbul, Mersin, Izmir. There are 102 usable airports, 65 with permanent surface runways, three over 3,659m and 32 with runways between 2,440 and 3,659m in length. The telecommunications system, both international and domestic, is reasonable.

Political considerations

Domestic politics have seen swings between democracy and military takeovers although the military has always handed power back to the civil authorities. A major problem concerns the Kurdish minority of slightly over 6 per cent of the total population (about 3,660,000) in eastern and southeastern Turkey. The Kurdish Workers' Party (PKK) has been carrying out terrorist attacks and conducting a civil war against the government for years. In 1994 this led to the launch of an all-out military offensive against the Kurds, including attacks on PKK bases in northern Iraq. The results were inconclusive. Turkey also has to resolve tensions between progressives and traditionalists (Islamic) who oppose some of the changes inevitable under a rapid process of industrialization and modernization. These problems naturally affect Turkey's efforts to become a full member of the EU. Following the collapse of the USSR Turkey has attempted to forge a common policy with the

Turkic republics of the former Soviet Union such as Turkmenistan and this has caused friction with Russia.

Assessments

Turkey has the infrastructure and the agricultural and mineral base to become a substantial economic power. Her industrial development is considerable and, for example, her multi-billion dollar programme to build dams along the Tigris and Euphrates river valleys to generate power and extend irrigation for agriculture demonstrates the confidence of a rapidly growing economic power. Per capita income above $2,000 places Turkey at the upper end of the lower-middle-income group of countries. Debts at $52bn are well below 50 per cent of GNP. Turkey occupies a pivotal position between Europe, the members of the former USSR and the Arab nations to her south and east which gives her an especially influential role and her fast-developing economy should mean that she becomes an important regional power in the first years of the twenty-first century.

VENEZUELA

Area. 352,144 sq. miles (912,050 sq. km).
Population. (1995) 21,844,000.
Capital. Caracas (1,822,465).
Other major cities. Maracaibo (1,249,670), Valencia (903,621), Barquisimeto (625,450), Maracay (538,616)
Language(s). Spanish (official), Amerindian dialects.
Religion(s). Roman Catholic 92.1 per cent, other 7.9 per cent.
Date of independence. July 5 1811 (from Spain).
GNP. (1993) $58,916,000,000, per capita $2,840.
Land and climate. The Andes Mountains meet the Maracaibo lowlands in the northwest; the centre of the country consists of plains (llanos); in the southeast are the Guyana highlands. The climate is tropical, hot and humid though moderated by altitude.

Introduction

Venezuela has had a long history of alternating authoritarian and democratic rule but from 1935 has evolved along modern democratic lines although with a period of military rule from 1948 to 1958. For many years coffee was Venezuela's principal export but the discovery and exploitation of oil had, by the mid-1930s, changed the economic orientation of the country and oil has remained the principal product and export ever since. Oil wealth has produced spectacular changes in social, political and economic life and its effects have been widely spread across the population; it has also allowed Venezuela to exercise significant influence in both Latin America and the Caribbean region. The country has three neighbours – Brazil, Colombia and Guyana – and a 2,800km coastline on the Caribbean Sea.

Agriculture

Agriculture accounts for just under 5 per cent of GDP and employs 10 per cent of the workforce. Export crops include coffee, cocoa, bananas. Staples are sugarcane, maize, rice, sorghum, plantains, cassava. The national cattle herd is 15,000,000 strong and Venezuela exports meat and meat products. The fish catch is 390,333mt (1993). Apart from meat, Venezuela is not self-sufficient in food and despite extensive forests only has a relatively small roundwood output (2,245,000cu m in 1993). Land use is divided between forested 33.9 per cent, meadows and pastures 20.1 per cent, agricultural land, under permanent cultivation 4.4 per cent, other 41.6 per cent.

Minerals

Apart from oil, Venezuela possesses a wide range of minerals, some in abundance. There are large resources of iron ore, bauxite, coal; there are substantial deposits of gold, diamonds and silver. In addition, there are deposits of zinc, lead, copper, phosphates, nickel and uranium. Venezuela has huge iron ore reserves but at present only a moderate output in the region of 18,000,000mt a year. Production of bauxite in 1994 came to 4,667,000mt and aluminium ore to 635,000mt while gold output reached 9,944kg. Iron ore accounts for 1.8 per cent of exports.

Petroleum, natural gas and mining account for 22.4 per cent of GDP although only employing 0.9 per cent of the workforce. Crude oil and petroleum products account for 77.5 per cent of exports (1993). In 1993 crude oil output came to 851,641,000 barrels which allowed a surplus of 500,000,000 barrels for export. At present natural gas output is consumed by the domestic market. Venezuela, which is a member of OPEC, is its highest petroleum refiner with a total of twelve refineries. Her most important customer is the USA. At the end of 1992 proved oil reserves stood at 62,600,000,000 barrels, equivalent to 6.2 per cent of world reserves with an estimated lifespan of 70 years while natural gas reserves at 3,600,000,000,000cu m were equivalent to 2.6 per cent of world reserves.

Manufacturing

Manufacturing contributes 16.3 per cent to GDP and employs 14 per cent of the workforce. Venezuela has a relatively sophisticated and wide-ranging manufacturing sector which includes petroleum refining and downstream products, construction materials, food processing, textiles, steel, aluminium, motor vehicle assembly, chemicals, metal products, electrical machinery, paper and paper products. To take one example, the value added to base metals by manufacturing is equivalent to $354,000,000. There is a relatively small tourist industry although Venezuelans spend three and a half times as much abroad as the country receives in tourist income. The USA is, by far, Venezuela's most important trading partner taking 56 per cent of all exports and supplying 46 per cent of imports.

Infrastructure

There are 542km of railroad of which 363km are 1.435m standard gauge; 77,785km of roads of which 22,780km are paved; 7,100km of inland waterways; 6,370km of pipelines for crude oil, 480km for petroleum products and 4,010km for natural gas. The principal ports are Amuay Bay, Bajo Grande, El Tablazo, La Guaira, Puerto Cabello and Puerto Ordaz. There are 331 usable airports, 133 with permanent surface runways of which fifteen are between 2,440 and 3,659m in length. There is a modern system of telecommunications which is being expanded.

Political considerations

Oil has allowed governments to keep taxes low and spread benefits widely; it has also led to immense government patronage. Venezuela plays an important regional role in the Caribbean and, for example, in 1990 was granted observer status on the Caribbean Common Market (CARICOM); and it has formed a number of bilateral trading agreements with other Latin American states. Venezuela has become a major transit country for cocaine from Colombia as well as a centre for money laundering.

Assessments

Great oil wealth and the size of its reserves should allow Venezuela over the coming decades to industrialize and diversify sufficiently to create a reasonably rounded economy against the time when the oil comes to an end. There is, however, the danger that oil wealth will persuade governments to adopt easy options (both political and economic) and not diversify enough or in time during the good (oil) years. International debts (1993) at $26,856,000,000 are equivalent to just under 50 per cent of GNP. Venezuela is in the upper-middle-income bracket of countries.

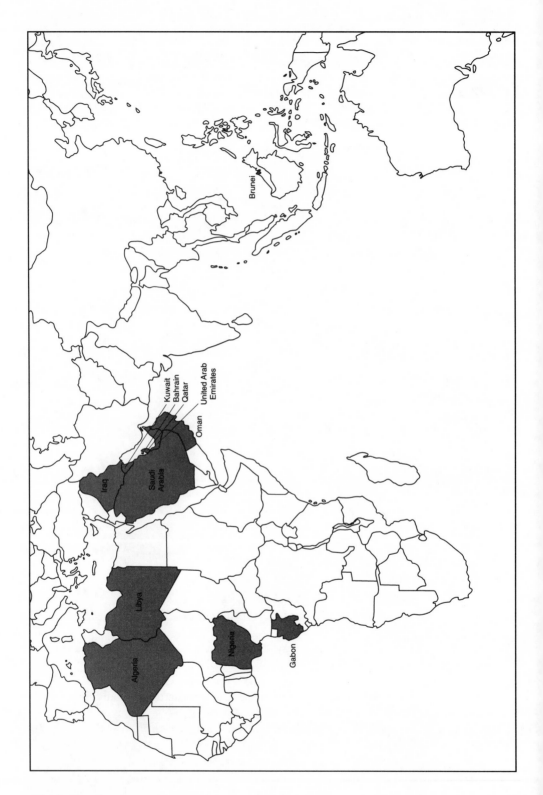

Map 4 The oil states

3   THE OIL STATES

INTRODUCTION

The significance of this group of countries lies in their overwhelming dependence upon the production and sale of the one commodity of oil (and associated gas) for their income. Twelve states are included here:

- Algeria

- Bahrain

- Brunei

- Gabon

- Iraq

- Kuwait

- Libya

- Nigeria

- Oman

- Qatar

- Saudi Arabia

- United Arab Emirates (UAE)

Two other states which are members of OPEC and are generally regarded as oil states are Iran and Venezuela; they, however, have been placed in Part II The Crossover States. Other developing countries such as Mexico are significant oil producers but do not rely upon the one resource to the same extent. Ten of these twelve countries belong to OPEC though Brunei and Oman do not. Algeria, in particular, is more dependent upon its huge gas deposits than oil and has a ready market for these in Europe. Nigeria was agriculturally self-sufficient with significant food exports as well before it discovered oil and unlike most of the other countries in this group does not have to rely upon food imports. Saudi Arabia possesses a quarter of the world's known oil reserves and when these are combined with those of Iraq, Kuwait and the UAE the four countries together control 54 per cent of the world's total oil reserves.

ALGERIA

Area. 919,595 sq. miles (2,381,741 sq. km).
Population. (1995) 27,939,000. (There are an additional 2.5 million Algerians resident in France.)
Capital. Algiers (1,507,241).
Other major cities. Oran (609,823), Constantine (440,842), Annaba (222,518), Batna (181,601).
Language(s). Arabic (official), French, Berber.
Religions. Muslim (Sunni) 99.9 per cent, Christian 0.1 per cent.
Date of independence. July 5 1962 (from France).
GNP. (1993) $44,347,000,000, per capita $1,650.
Land and climate. Mainly mountains and desert, Algeria accounts for approximately 25 per cent of the Sahara Desert. The climate (except for the coastal region) is arid or semi-arid with hot summers and cold winters. The coast enjoys a Mediterranean climate of wet winters and hot dry summers.

Introduction

A huge country (Africa's second largest) with a 600-mile Mediterranean coastline, Algeria has six land neighbours: Tunisia, Libya, Niger, Mali, Mauritania and Morocco (including Western Sahara). There is a narrow coastal plain which is separated by the barrier of the Atlas mountains from the vast plateaux which form part of the Sahara Desert. The country is subject to increasing desertification and earthquakes in the mountains. Algeria became independent from France in 1962 after a brutal eight-year war of liberation in which an estimated 1 million people were killed. Following the aborting of the elections by the military at the end of 1991 and subsequent proscription of the fundamentalist Islamic Salvation Front (FIS), whose supporters were winning the elections, the country has been plunged into a civil war between fundamentalists and government supporters (including the armed forces).

Oil and natural gas are the principal sources of mineral wealth; they contribute above 95 per cent of foreign exchange earnings, account for about 30 per cent of government revenues and contribute 25 per cent of GDP. Algeria is a member of OPEC. Other minerals include iron ore, phosphates, lead, zinc, antimony, uranium. Only 3 per cent of the land is arable and agricultural production is mainly confined to the coastal (Mediterranean) region. Although great emphasis has been placed upon developing the agricultural sector Algeria is not food self-sufficient and has to import a substantial proportion of its total food requirements.

Petroleum and natural gas account for 96 per cent of all exports with pig iron and wine as the only other substantial earners. The main imports are machinery (electrical and other) 30 per cent, food and beverages 20 per cent, transportation equipment 13–14 per cent.

Agriculture

In 1993 agriculture contributed 10.9 per cent to GDP while the agricultural labour force at 907,490 was equivalent to 15.9 per cent of the total labour force. Despite its rich resources of oil and gas Algeria remains a basically agricultural economy; the agricultural sector was given priority in the 1985–9 Plan. However, there are only 7.5 million hectares of cultivable land. Land use divides as follows: arable 3 per cent, permanent crops 0 per cent, meadows and pastures 13 per cent, forest and woodland 2 per cent, other 82 per cent.

The main crops are wheat, barley, oats, grapes, olives and citrus fruits. In 1994 wheat production came to 1,350,000 tonnes, barley 800,000 tonnes, potatoes 1.2 million tonnes, tomatoes 515,000 tonnes, grapes 250,000 tonnes. Grapes are crucial to the profitable wine sector and account for about two-thirds of agricultural exports. Other export crops are citrus fruit (oranges), olives, figs, dates, tobacco. Staple foodstuffs consist of wheat, barley, oats, maize, sorghum, millet, rye and rice. Livestock herds include sheep 17,850,000, goats 3,800,000, cattle 1,370,000. Production of roundwood stands at 2,250,000cu m per year (forests cover 4.4m hectares) and the fish catch at just over 90,000 tonnes is very small.

Algeria is a net importer of food and the principal imports are grains, vegetable oils and sugar. By 1980 Algeria was only producing 30 per cent of her food requirements; the ratio had declined, partly as a result of the rush to industrialize following independence, and also because of the rapid increase in population. However, government then gave greater priority to agricultural development and set the target of achieving 80 per cent food self-sufficiency by the year 2000.

Apart from political considerations, agricultural development has to take account of the rapid increase in population which is expected to pass 40 million in 2010. There is a conflict of interests between the demands of the highly profitable vine (wine producing) sector and the needs of the cereal producers for more land. Control of the land is a mixture: small farmers, state-controlled estates and private estates; farmers who bring desert land under cultivation automatically obtain title to the land. It is unlikely that Algeria will ever achieve full food self-sufficiency.

Minerals

Although Algeria possesses a range of minerals, oil and gas have provided the basis for the development of its modern economy and government strategy since independence has been to build up a heavy industrial sector dependent upon oil and gas that remains in government hands. The first petroleum was produced in 1958 (prior to independence) and by the 1970s production was running at 1m b/d. However, production had fallen off by 17 per cent by the late 1980s. At the end of 1992 Algeria's proven oil resources at 1,200mt (9,200m barrels) were equivalent to 0.9 per cent of world resources.

At the end of 1992 natural gas resources were estimated at 3,600,000 million cu metres (128,000,000 million cu ft.) equivalent to 2.6 per cent of the world's resources, the fourth largest in the world. In 1992 Algeria produced 56 billion cu m of natural gas and was the world's sixth largest producer. Algeria is a member of OPEC and is usually regarded as a price 'hawk' and the country has borrowed heavily on the strength of its oil and gas resources. Exports of petroleum and natural gas account for more than 96 per cent of foreign exchange earnings; the main customers are Italy, USA, France, Germany and Spain. When oil runs out, possibly in about 22 years, natural gas will replace it as the principal earner of foreign exchange. It has an expected life of 70 years at current rates of exploitation. There is a petrochemical plant at Skikda.

Other minerals include iron ore, phosphates, lead, zinc, antimony. Iron ore is found at a number of sites: Beni-Saf, Zaccar, Timezrit, Ouenza and Bou Khadru. About 75 per cent of production comes from Ouenza. There are also huge iron ore reserves (2 billion tons) at Gara Djebelit in the west of the country but these are in territory claimed by Morocco. Most of the ore is graded at between 50 and 60 per cent. Production of iron ore reached a high of 2 million tons in 1974 but fell thereafter. Italy and the UK are the main customers for iron ore.

Zinc deposits are found on the Algeria–Morocco border at El-Abed-Oued Zounder and lead is also mined there. Huge phosphates deposits are sited at Djebel-Ouk, some 340km from Annaba where exploitation began in 1960 and production has exceeded 1 million tonnes pa. The phosphates provide the base for the Arzew fertilizer plant; the balance is exported to Europe (mainly France and Spain). Other minerals to be fully exploited include tungsten, manganese, mercury, copper and salt. Exploration for minerals is proceeding in the southern Hoggar range of mountains where tungsten, gold and uranium are present. Production of minerals in 1993 included: iron ore 2,311,000 tonnes, phosphate rock 718,000 tonnes, mercury 545,000 kg. Mining, including oil and gas, accounts for 21 per cent of GDP (1993) and oil and gas employ 55,000 workers or 1 per cent of the total workforce. The mining industries are controlled by the state.

Manufacturing

The manufacturing sector accounts for 10.8 per cent of GDP and light industries generally are in private hands. Major reforms were initiated in 1988 (after years in which the centralized economy had been mismanaged and spurred on by falling oil and gas prices) but though some privatization of public sector companies followed, the process was put on hold as the political crisis became worse in the early 1990s. There are hopes that the oil and gas sector will allow private companies to operate in it.

Infrastructure

Algeria has a total of 4,060km of railways and 90,000km of highways of which 58,868km are concrete or bitumenous. There are the following oil and gas pipelines: crude oil 6,162km; petroleum products 298km; natural gas 2,948km. The country is served by eleven ports on the Mediterranean; these include Algiers, Annaba, Arzew, Mers el Kebir, Oran and Skikda. There is a merchant marine of some 75 vessels. The country is served by 141 airports of which 124 are usable while 53 have have permanently usable runways. Telecommunications are among the best in Africa: there are 822,000 telephones, 26 broadcast stations and 18 television stations.

Algeria is connected to Italy, France, Spain, Morocco and Tunisia by microwave radio. There are a number of earth satellite stations.

Political considerations

A move back to multipartyism was begun in 1988, following nationwide riots, and the process was to lead to the effective political demise of the Front de Libération Nationale (FLN) which had ruled Algeria as a one-party state since independence in 1962. When the fundamentalist Islamic Salvation Front (FIS) won the first round of open elections at the end of 1991 the army stepped in to abort the result; it then removed President Chadli Benjedid who was replaced by a High State Council. Thereafter, violence escalated for the supporters of the FIS would not accept the military intervention as final and between 1992 and 1994 an estimated 10,000 people were killed on either side of the new political divide while the government's failure or inability to stop the violence increased its unpopularity. Given the growing strength of fundamentalist movements throughout the Islamic world, as well as the deliberate targeting of foreigners in Algeria, there would appear to be little likelihood of an early end to what by late 1994 had developed into a civil war situation. Further, there are signs of a widening conflict: in March 1993, for example, the government broke diplomatic relations with both Iran and Sudan on the grounds that their governments were supporting fundamentalist dissidents in Algeria. There are a good many indications that the fundamentalist-inspired violence is set to continue for some time and as long as this is the case, with foreign workers targets for death squads, Algeria is unlikely to attract new investment.

Assessments

Algeria is unlikely ever to be able to feed itself completely. It has major natural gas resources that will provide an income into the foreseeable future and is blessed with a number of other mineral resources while large parts of the Sahara as well as the Hoggar Mountain range in the south have yet to be fully explored.

BAHRAIN

Area. 268.4 sq. miles (695.3 sq. km).
Population. (1995) 579,000.
Capital. Manama (140,401).
Other major cities. ar-Rifa (45,956), al-Muharraq (45,337).
Language(s). Arabic (official), English, Farsi, Urdu.
Religion(s). Islam (Shi'a 70 per cent, Sunni 30 per cent).
Date of independence. August 15 1971 (from Britain).
GNP. (1993) $4,283,000,000, per capita $7,870 .
Land and climate. The island consists mainly of a low desert plain with a central escarpment; it is arid although it enjoys mild winters but very hot humid summers.

Introduction

This small island in the Arabian Gulf has risen to prosperity as a result of oil. Formerly the centre of the Gulf pearl fisheries (a traditional occupation that has now virtually disappeared), Bahrain's economy depends upon oil, both the production from its own modest wells and major refining activities. It also acts as an entrepreneurial centre for trade with other Gulf states. Formerly a Trucial State under British protection, Bahrain belongs to the moderate group of Gulf states with close economic ties to the West. Resources consist of oil, natural gas and fish.

Agriculture

Only 2 per cent of the land is arable and producing permanent crops while another 6 per cent consists of meadows and pastures. The rest is desert. Agriculture, including fisheries, accounts for under 1 per cent of GDP. The principal products are fruit and dates, vegetables, poultry, dairy products and fish. About 10,000sq km have been irrigated. The fish catch (1993) came to 8,958mt. Livestock includes 17,000 goats and 16,000 cattle from which there is a substantial production of fresh cow's milk. Bahrain is not food self-sufficient.

Minerals

Minerals consist of oil and natural gas (both associated and non-associated with the oil). Oil reserves are now small and much of Bahrain's oil wealth is derived from its refining activities; it imports Saudi crude to refine and re-export and has a refining capacity of 245,000 b/d. There are substantial reserves of natural gas equivalent to 0.1 per cent of the world's reserves (1992) which at current rates of production (and without the benefit of any new discoveries) will last for 22 years. Oil, refined oil and natural gas exports between them account for 76.2 per cent of foreign exchange earnings as well as 60 per cent of government revenues and 31 per cent of GDP.

Manufacturing

Bahrain imports alumina from Australia for its aluminium refinery and re-exports are worth about 7 per cent of foreign exchange earnings. Otherwise, Bahrain has long acted as an entrepôt for trade with Saudi Arabia. A substantial part of its economic activity consists of re-exports.

Infrastructure

There are 200km of bitumen highways including a 25km bridge-causeway to Saudi Arabia. There are 56km of pipelines for crude oil, 16km of pipeline for refined petroleum products and 32km of pipeline for gas. There are three ports – Mina' Salman, Manama and Sitra (where the refinery is situated). There are three airports two of which have runways over 3,659m in length. The telecommunications system is modern and includes 98,000 telephones (one for every five people) and excellent international communications including microwave radio relays and satellite earth stations. Import regulations are light and Bahrain, generally, is geared to international trade and has an open economy.

Political considerations

A moderate Arab state, Bahrain is susceptible to political pressures from more powerful neighbours and though, for example, Iran's claim to Bahrain was settled in Bahrain's favour by the UN in 1970, it could be revived. During 1993 Bahrain made some tentative steps towards establishing a more democratic system of rule but by 1996 faced growing unrest as demands for a full democratic constitution escalated. Like other moderate Arab states in the region, it is nervous about the possible rise of Islamic fundamentalism. The island has great strategic importance since its position in the Gulf means that a large proportion of Western purchased petroleum passes through it.

Assessments

In ideal conditions Bahrain should continue as a reasonably well-off small economy indefinitely, given its position in the centre of the oil world of the Gulf although it will never be able to feed itself. Problems may arise due to the extreme political volatility of the region.

BRUNEI

Area. 2,226 sq. miles (5,765 sq. km).
Population. (1995) 291,000.
Capital. Bandar Seri Begawan (45,867).
Other major cities. Kuala Belait (21,163), Seria (21,082).
Language(s). Malay (official), English, Chinese.
Religion(s). Muslim 66.5 per cent, Buddhist 11.8 per cent, Christian 8.9 per cent, other/non-religious 12.8 per cent.
Date of independence. January 1 1984 (from Britain).
GNP. (1993) $2,001,000,000, per capita $14,530.
Land and climate. A flat coastal plain which rises to mountains in the east and hilly lowlands in the west. Four-fifths of the land is still covered by forest or woodland and the climate is tropical: hot, humid and rainy.

Introduction

This tiny enclave of territory on the northwest coast of the island of Borneo is entirely surrounded by Malaysia (a salient of whose territory divides Brunei in two) except for a 161km coastline on the South China Sea. Its wealth is derived from its large oil and natural gas deposits which give the tiny population one of the highest per capita incomes in the world. However, over-dependence upon oil wealth is likely to create problems for the future when oil output declines.

Agriculture

Agriculture only accounts for 3 per cent of GDP and employs 1.9 per cent of the total workforce. Land use is divided between forested 40.8 per cent, meadows and pastures 1.1 per cent, agricultural – under cultivation 1.3 per cent, other 56.8 per cent. The principal crops are rice and cassava while the main livestock consist of buffalo and pigs. About 80 per cent of food requirements now have to be imported.

Minerals

The economy is almost entirely dependent upon exports of crude oil and natural gas which, with some refined products, account for 99.1 per cent of all exports and contribute 50 per cent of GDP. In 1994 Brunei produced 57,758,000 barrels of oil, equivalent to 0.3 per cent of total world output. Proved reserves stand at 1,300,000,000 barrels and represent 0.1 per cent of world reserves; at current rates of production they should last for 20 years. At the same time Brunei produced 8,548,000,000cu m of natural gas and her reserves of 400,000,000,000cu m represent 0.3 per cent of world reserves and should last 40 years at current rates of extraction. Brunei ranks 28 for marketed natural gas. There are no other known mineral resources.

Manufacturing

Apart from oil-related activities there is only a tiny manufacturing sector. Since 1986 attempts have been made to create new private sector industries so as to diversify away from over-dependence upon oil and gas. Brunei has a considerable income from overseas investments.

Infrastructure

There are 13km of narrow gauge private rail line, 1,090km of highways of which 370km are paved, 209km of inland waterways and 135km of pipeline for crude oil, 418km for petroleum products and 920km for natural gas. There are two ports, Kuala Belait and Muara, and two airports, one of which has a runway of 3,659m and a permanent surface. There are adequate telecommunications and good contacts with neighbouring Malaysia.

Political considerations

There has existed a state of emergency since 1962 (under the British) which was continued by the Sultan after independence and though the country is described as a constitutional sultanate it tends to be heavily autocratic. Like many direct-rule states there exist inherent dangers that autocracy will invite rebellion though it has been stable since independence.

Assessments

Since the economy is so dependent upon oil and natural gas, the long-term concern must be the extent to which new industries can be created from the oil wealth while this source lasts.

GABON

Area. 103,387 sq. miles (267,667 sq. km).
Population. (1995) 1,156,000.
Capital. Libreville (419,596).
Other major cities. Port-Gentil (78,225), Franceville (75,000).
Language(s). French (official), Fang, Myene, Bateke, Bapounou, Banjabi.
Religion(s). Christian 96.2 per cent, traditional 2.9 per cent, other 0.9 per cent.
Date of independence. August 17 1960 (from France).
GNP. (1993) $5,002,000,000, per capita $4,050.
Land and climate. There is a narrow coastal plain and savanna country to the east and south while most of the interior is hilly and forested. The climate is tropical, hot and humid at all times. Deforestation is taking place.

Introduction

This small country on the equator is sandwiched between Equatorial Guinea, Cameroon and Congo with a coastline of 880km on the Atlantic. Gabon is rich in minerals and with the exploitation of its oil resources has achieved the second highest per capita income, after Libya, on the African continent. Like too many oil countries it has become over-dependent upon oil revenues; unlike most of them, however, it has a range of other resources that can be developed more fully once the oil runs out. The greater part of the land is still covered by virgin forest.

Agriculture

The agricultural sector has been stagnant for some years and despite lucrative forestry business is in decline so that Gabon is one of the very few countries in Africa where the contribution of minerals to GDP is more important than agriculture as a whole. Agriculture, forestry and fisheries only contribute 8.8 per cent to GDP although employing 41.6 per cent of the workforce. Only timber is important as an export and in 1993 roundwood production came to 4,436,000cu m with wood accounting for 9 per cent of exports. Okoumé, the tropical softwood, is the most important timber. Other cash crops, although on a very small scale, are cocoa, coffee and palm oil. Livestock numbers are minimal (only 30,000 head of cattle) and the annual fish catch is in the region of 30,000mt. Staple food crops are cassava, yams, sugarcane, plantains, maize, peanuts, bananas. Gabon is not self-sufficient in food and food and agricultural products account for more than 14 per cent of imports. Land use is divided between forested 74.2 per cent, meadows and pastures 17.6 per cent, agricultural land under permanent cultivation 1.7 per cent, other 6.5 per cent.

Mining

Mining accounts for just over 30 per cent of GDP but until the 1970s, with the development of oil, Gabon depended upon manganese as its main export. Although exploration for oil began in 1957 it was only ten years later when the Gamba-Ivinga deposits and the offshore Anguille field were exploited that oil came to dominate the economy. Fluctuations in oil demand and price affected the economy through the 1980s but in 1989 the relatively massive onshore field at Rabi-Kounga came into production and soon reached an output of 50,000b/d. In 1993 crude petroleum output was 110,072,000 barrels and oil accounted for 80 per cent of exports. Gabon and Nigeria are the only two sub-Saharan African countries which belong to OPEC. At the end of 1992 proved reserves stood at 700,000,000 barrels and were equivalent to 0.1 per cent of total world oil resources.

Apart from oil, Gabon mines manganese and uranium. There are huge manganese deposits (about 200mt), an estimated 25 per cent of known reserves outside the former USSR, and exploitation began in 1962. During the 1980s manganese exports were at the rate of 2.3mt a year. In 1993 production came to 1,460,000 tons and manganese ore and concentrates accounted for 7 per cent of exports. The extraction of uranium at Mouanana began in 1961 and the business is largely controlled by French interests through Compagnie des mines d'uranium de Franceville (COMUF) in which the Gabon government has a 25 per cent stake. Uranium output varies substantially according to demand; it reached a high of just over 1,000 tons in 1983. Output in 1993 came to 509 tonnes. Known reserves at 35,000 tons are equivalent to about 40 years' production.

Gabon also possesses vast iron ore deposits (among the largest in the world) at Bélinga in the northeast of the country but their exploitation awaits the completion of the Trans-Gabon railway. In any case, there is a current surfeit of iron ore worldwide. Other minerals known to exist are lead, zinc and phosphates and prospecting for both gold and diamonds is under way. Mabounie has deposits of niobium, phosphates, rare earths and titanium and the European Investment Bank

(EIB) is examining the possibility of financing the development of this region. Other minerals include barytes and talc. In 1988 the government passed legislation to stimulate the search for gold and diamonds.

Manufacturing

Manufacturing remains small scale, its growth inhibited by the tiny size of the home market. In 1991 manufacturing accounted for only 7.4 per cent of GDP and with mining and construction only employed 11.5 per cent of the labour force. The main manufactures are cement, flour, refined sugar, beer, soft drinks, cigarettes and textiles. Manufactures of all kinds are a major part of imports.

Infrastructure

The saga of building the Trans-Gabon railway has dominated the Bongo presidency: finance for the first 340km stretch of the line was hard to find. Work on the railway began in May 1974 and the first stretch from Owendo to Booué was completed in 1983. The second 330km stretch from Booué to Franceville was inaugurated in 1986 by which time the railway had cost $3,000m. The third (projected) stretch from Booué to Belinga (where the iron ore deposits are located) awaits finance. The 648km Libreville–Franceville link is now fully operational. There are 7,500km of highways of which 560km are paved and there are extensive plans to pave further stretches of the road system. There are 1,600km of inland waterways, 270km of pipeline for crude oil and 14km for petroleum products. The country is served by three ports – Owendo, Port-Gentil and Libreville. There are 56 usable airports, two with runways between 2,440 and 3,659m in length. The telecommunications system is adequate.

Political considerations

Since independence in 1960 Gabon has maintained close relations with France and sought external investment. Like a number of African leaders, however, President Bongo attempted to maintain an over-authoritarian system and in 1994 the government came close to collapse when all the opposition groups refused to accept the election results of December 1993. Relations with France deteriorated in the wake of Bongo's harsh repressive measures but, following a peace conference in Paris held during September 1994 between the government and opposition parties, a coalition government was formed in November 1994 with a mandate to govern until the holding of new elections.

Assessments

Gabon is rich in resources but needs to develop agriculture while the oil wealth lasts. Although debts are equivalent to 60 per cent of GDP, servicing them does not present a problem. The country's mineral wealth, with indications of possible new finds to come, and the tiny population should together mean long-term prosperity.

IRAQ

Area. 167,975 sq. miles (435,052 sq. km).

Population. (1995) 20,413,000.

Capital. Baghdad (4,044,000, metropolitan area, 1990).

Other major cities. Basra (616,700), Mosul (570,926), Irbil (339,903), al-Sulaymaniyah (279,424).

Language(s). Arabic (official), Kurdish (official in the Kurdish autonomous region), Assyrian, Armenian.

Religion(s). Shi'a Muslim 61.5 per cent, Sunni Muslim 34 per cent (Islam is the official religion), Christian 3.7 per cent, Yazidi syncretist 0.8 per cent.

Date of independence. October 3 1932 (from Britain which held the League of Nations mandate).

GNP. (1991) $12,640,000,000, per capita $710.

Land and climate. Iraq consists mainly of wide plains with reedy marshes in the southeast and rugged mountains in the northern Kurdish region adjoining Turkey and Iran. It is a desert climate with mild cool winters and hot dry summers. The mountains of the north suffer from bitter winters and periodic heavy snows.

Introduction

Created as a mandate by the League of Nations from the dismemberment of the Ottoman Empire at the end of World War I, Iraq was placed under British control and only became independent in 1932. Occupying the region between the two rivers, the Tigris and Euphrates which was formerly known as Mesopotamia, modern Iraq, nonetheless, regards itself as the heir of ancient Babylon. Under the ambitious Saddam Hussein who became president in 1979, Iraq entered upon a devastating and costly war with its neighbour, Iran, in 1980; this was supposedly about their joint frontier along the Shatt-al-Arab river but in fact was about dominance in the Gulf region. The war was fought to a stalemate and cost Iraq all its financial reserves as well as putting it heavily in debt. The combination of this loss of wealth and the huge reconstruction requirements that followed the end of the war were a major reason (though not the only one) for Hussein's August 1990 invasion of Kuwait. He hoped to add that small state's huge oil resources to those of Iraq, a combination (had it survived) that would have given him control of just under 20 per cent of the world's total oil reserves.

The UN-sponsored, US-led coalition which assembled huge military forces in the Gulf in the latter half of 1990 and then drove the Iraqi forces out of Kuwait in the first months of 1991 still left Saddam Hussein in control of Iraq at the end of hostilities. Subsequently, UN sanctions were applied to Iraq; these limited the sale of its oil to amounts that were just sufficient to pay for food and other humanitarian imports. The situation remained volatile, however, with Saddam Hussein pushing UN (allied) patience to the limit in the period between 1991 and 1995 as he continued to defy the world body by his treatment of the Kurds in the north of Iraq, the Shia Muslims (Marsh Arabs) in the south and his evasion of demands for compliance with UN disarmament conditions. Iraq has six neighbours – Iran, Jordan, Kuwait, Saudi Arabia, Syria and Turkey, and a 58km coastline at the head of the Gulf.

Agriculture

Agriculture accounts for 28 per cent of GDP and employs 11.6 per cent of the workforce. The principal crops are wheat, barley, rice, vegetables and fruit (watermelons, grapes, cucumbers, tomatoes, oranges) and maize. Dates are an important export crop and account for 1.8 per cent of a total of 2.2 per cent of agricultural exports (1992). Although a high proportion of economic activity is state controlled agriculture is left largely to private enterprise and peasant farming. The country is not self-sufficient in food production. The national cattle herd is just over 1 million head although there are 6 million sheep. Neither roundwood production (155,000cu m) nor the fish catch of 23,500mt make a significant contribution to the sector's output. Agricultural products account for 60 per cent of imports and nearly half that consists of cereals. Land use is divided between forested 4.3 per cent, meadows and pastures 9.1 per cent, agricultural land, under permanent cultivation 12.5 per cent, other 74.1 per cent.

Mining

Although there are phosphates, sulphur and gypsum deposits which are mined, oil and natural gas are the mainstay of the economy and Iraq is one of the world's leading oil producers. However, production figures since 1990 when Iraq invaded Kuwait in an effort to double its oil reserves, have not reflected the extent of the country's reserves or its productive capacity. UN sanctions have effectively limited Iraq to producing only sufficient oil for export to pay for necessary food and humanitarian imports (such as medicines). During 1993 Iraq only produced 175,000,000 barrels of crude oil. Its reserves, however, are vast (on a par with those of Iran). Proved reserves of oil (at the end of 1992) were 13,400,000,000 tonnes or 100,000,000,000 barrels, equivalent to 9.9 per cent of world reserves. Iraq's natural gas reserves are equivalent to 3,100,000,000,000cu m, or 2.2 per cent of world reserves. When Iraq's political differences with the world community have been resolved and the country returns to full production, it could be at a rate of more than 4,000,000b/d. Exports in 1992 accounted for 97.8 per cent of the total.

Manufacturing

Manufacturing contributes only 4.2 per cent to GDP and employs 8.2 per cent of the workforce. Principal manufactures are petroleum and chemical products, non-metal mineral products, food, textiles, paper products, printing and publishing, beverages, footwear, electrical machinery, non-electrical machinery and tobacco. The country faces large reconstruction tasks in the wake of two highly destructive wars.

Infrastructure

There are 2,457km of railroads of 1.435m standard gauge; 34,700km of roads of which 17,500km are paved; and 1,015km of inland waterways of which the Shatt-al Arab is navigable for 130km by maritime traffic. Both the Tigris and Euphrates have stretches navigable by shallow draft craft. There are 4,350km of pipelines for crude oil; 725km for petroleum products; and 1,360km for natural gas. There are three ports – Um Qasr, Khawr al Zabayr and Basra (closed since 1980). There are 99 usable airports, 74 with permanent surface runways of which nine have runways of 3,659m and 52 have runways between 2,440m and 3,659m in length. Most tele-communications damaged during the 1991 war (Desert Storm) have been rebuilt and the overall system is fair to reasonable.

Political considerations

There has been no indication since 1991 that the government of Saddam Hussein intends to be any more accommodating, either with its regional neighbours or with the Western world, than it is obliged to be as a result of UN sanctions, so that a state of tension between Iraq and her neighbours and Iraq and the West seems set to continue until there is a change of regime and policy in Baghdad.

Assessments

Iraq's population of 20 million is heavily dependent upon food and other imports which it can only pay for with oil exports; the economy is overwhelmingly dependent upon oil and likely to remain so for decades to come. Nonetheless, the sheer size of Iraq's oil resources should mean that long before these run out the wealth they have created ought to have been translated into various forms of industrialization.

KUWAIT

Area. 6,880 sq. miles (17,818 sq. km).
Population. (1995) 1,691,000.
Capital. Kuwait City (31,241).
Other major cities. al-Jahra (139,476), al-Salimiyah (116,104), Hawalli (84,478), al-Farwaniyah (47,106).
Language(s). Arabic (official), English.
Religion(s). Islam 90 per cent (Sunni 63 per cent, Shi'ah 27 per cent) (official), Christian 8 per cent, Hindu 2 per cent.
Date of independence. June 19 1961 (from Britain).
GNP. (1993) $34,120,000,000, per capita $23,350.

Land and climate. Kuwait consists of flat or slightly undulating desert plain; it is a dry desert climate with extremely hot summers and short cool winters.

Introduction

Ruled by a hereditary monarchy, the al-Sabah family, since the mid-eighteenth century, Kuwait sits uneasily at the head of the Gulf between Saudi Arabia and Iraq, two of the most powerful and predatory powers in the region. From 1899 to 1961 Kuwait was a British protectorate; subsequently, fully independent, it has been ruled by the Sheik with an elected National Assembly though the latter has had little power and was dissolved in 1986. In August 1990 Iraqi forces invaded and occupied Kuwait. Iraq could advance certain historical claims to Kuwait but the primary reason behind the invasion was to secure Kuwait's vast oil resources which would have had the effect of doubling Iraq's total reserves and given it much needed extra income for the immediate reconstruction it faced as a result of the devastating war it had fought with Iran (1980–88). But Western opposition to any absorption of Kuwait by Iraq crystallized in the formation of the UN-sponsored, US-led coalition which, in the 'Desert Storm' operation, rapidly drove the Iraqi forces out of Kuwait in March 1991 after a month of intense aerial bombardment. The royal family was restored to power as was the National Assembly and Kuwait then faced the task of massive reconstruction of its oil sector following the damage done to it as a result of the fighting, and especially by the retreating Iraqis. By the end of 1992 oil production was up to a level of 2 million barrels a day.

In October 1994 Iraq carried out threatening troop movements on Kuwait's border; these brought a rapid response from the USA and Britain and the deployment of ground and air forces including 40,000 US troops. Iraq then withdrew and in a decree of November 10 recognized the sovereignty of Kuwait. The economy of Kuwait, in real terms, means oil.

Agriculture

There is virtually no agriculture and up to 75 per cent of potable water has to be distilled or imported. The sector (tomatoes, cucumbers, gherkins, onions, eggplants and 150,000 sheep) contributes only 0.4 per cent to GDP and employs 1.6 per cent of the labour force. Over 90 per cent of the land is desert.

Mining

Oil and gas represent the wealth (and political *raison d'être*) for modern Kuwait. During 1992 Kuwait produced 388,700,000 barrels of oil, gradually increasing production through the year to a level of 2,000,000b/d. At the end of 1992 Kuwait's total proved oil reserves stood at 94,000,000,000 barrels equivalent to 9.3 per cent of the world's reserves (only Saudi Arabia and Iraq have greater reserves). Her natural gas resources stand at 1,500,000,000,000cu m, equivalent to 1.1 per cent of world reserves. The vast oil wealth gives the people of this little country one of the highest average per capita incomes in the world and should last for 70 years or more at likely rates of production once Kuwait has fully recovered from the effects of the Gulf War. Sulphur and lime are also mined.

Manufacturing

The manufacturing sector which accounts for 14.6 per cent of GDP and employs 7.1 per cent of the workforce is considerably more important than agriculture. Principal manufactures are cement, cement slabs, ammonia, flour, bread, bran, concrete pipes, liquefied caustic soda, chlorine gas, biscuits, detergents, hydrochloric acid, sodium hydrochloride (a mix of cement products, chemical by-products of oil and food processing).

Infrastructure

There are 3,900km of roads of which 3,000km are paved; 877km of pipelines for crude oil, 40km for petroleum products and 165km for natural gas. There are three ports: Ash Shu'aybah, Ash Shuwaykh and Mina'al'Ahmadi. The country has four usable airports with permanent surface runways between 2,440m and 3,659m in length. The telecommunications network was badly damaged in the war of 1990–91 and reconstruction is still under way, while mobile satellite ground stations provide international communications.

Political considerations

Kuwait faces three major political problems. The first concerns its neighbours and primarily Iraq which could easily renew its pressures upon Kuwait, especially once the allied forces (which means the Americans) leave the Gulf. Kuwait is also vulnerable to pressures from Iran and Saudi Arabia, the other two major regional powers. The second problem concerns the nature of the political system which is nominally a constitutional monarchy but in fact dominated by the al-Sabah family which at best makes gestures towards democracy. Revolutionary pressures from below could upset the system. The third problem concerns the make-up of the population of whom more than half (56.4 per cent) consist of non-Kuwaitis. These incomers include other Arabs, South Asians (Pakistanis, Indians and Bangladeshis) and Palestinians; they come for the work and high wages but could upset the political balance. It is at least open to question whether the state of Kuwait as now constituted will outlast its oil wealth.

Assessments

The sheer size of Kuwait's oil reserves related to its tiny population and conservative state structures as well as its strategic position at the head of the Gulf make it an attractive proposition for aggression by its neighbours. In theory its wealth could be used over the next half century to turn Kuwait into an important mini-industrial state.

LIBYA

Area. 678,400 sq. miles (1,757,000 sq. km).
Population. (1995) 5,407,000.
Capital. Tripoli (591,000).
Other major cities. Benghazi (446,250), Misurata (121,700), az-Zawiyah (89,338).
Language(s). Arabic (official), Italian, English.
Religion(s). Sunni Muslim 97 per cent, other 3 per cent.
Date of independence. December 24 1951 (from Italy).
GNP. (1994) $32,900,000,000, per capita $6,510.
Land and climate. Mainly flat to undulating plains and plateaux with depressions; Libya enjoys a Mediterranean climate along the coast but the interior is dry, extreme desert.

Introduction

This huge sparsely populated country which is 90 per cent desert was among the poorest in the world, unable to meet its annual budget or development costs during the 1950s, prior to the discovery of oil which transformed its economic prospects. Nominally part of the Ottoman Empire at the beginning of the century, it was invaded and colonized by Italy just prior to World War I and achieved independence in 1951.

The coup of 1969 which overthrew the conservative King Idris and brought the charismatic Gaddafi to power changed Libya's political direction to make it one of the most radical countries of North Africa and the Arab Middle East. The combination of huge oil resources and small population have enabled Gaddafi both to carry out major social and economic reforms at home and exercise international influence out of all proportion to the country's capacities were it not for its oil wealth. Libya has six neighbours – Algeria, Chad, Egypt, Niger, Sudan and Tunisia – and a 1,770km coastline on the Mediterranean.

Agriculture

Agriculture contributes 7.5 per cent to GDP and employs just over 19 per cent of the workforce. Principal crops are wheat, barley, olives, dates, citrus fruits, peanuts. Even with its tiny population Libya is only able to produce a small proportion of the food it requires and imports 75 per cent of its needs, amounting to 20 per cent of all imports. Land use is divided between forested 0.4 per cent, meadows and pastures

7.6 per cent, agricultural land, under permanent cultivation 1.0 per cent, other (mainly desert) 91 per cent.

Mining

Although small quantities of lime, gypsum and salt are mined and there exist extensive gypsum deposits, the sector really only consists of oil. Important oil strikes were first made in 1957 and by 1967 Libya had become the fourth largest exporter of oil in the world. Libya built up a system of ocean terminals connected to its various oilfields by pipelines. At the beginning of the 1970s Libya took a lead among OPEC countries in demanding full (national) participation in petroleum activities with foreign companies and entered into disputes with both British Petroleum and Bunker Hunt. Through the 1970s Libya went much further than other OPEC countries in applying Libyanization of the oil industry and was also a price 'hawk' in OPEC.

In 1992 crude petroleum output reached 519,400,000 barrels and crude petroleum accounted for 99.8 per cent of all exports (1991) with Italy, Spain, Germany and France as the main destinations. Libya's proven oil reserves at the end of 1992 came to 22,800,000,000 barrels equivalent to 2.3 per cent of world resources with a lifespan (at current rates of production) of 42 years. Reserves of natural gas at the end of 1992 amounted to 1,300,000,000,000cu m equivalent to 0.9 per cent of world reserves. All other aspects of the economy and economic development depend upon the oil industry, the world oil price and the rate of production that provides Libya with surpluses for investment in the other sectors of its economy. Although mining contributes 26 per cent to GDP the sector only employs 2.4 per cent of the workforce.

Manufacturing

Apart from oil-related manufactures – distillate fuel, jet fuel, gasoline – the principal manufactures consist of cement, crude steel and meat products. Manufacturing contributes just under 8 per cent to GDP and employs just over 9 per cent of the workforce. The Great Manmade River which is designed to bring fresh water from the huge aquifers under the Sahara to Libya's coastal cities is the largest water development project in the world.

Infrastructure

Earlier existing railroads had been dismantled by 1965 and at present Libya has no railway system. There are plans for a railway to be constructed from the Tunisian border to Tripoli and then on to Misurata and inland to Sabha in the centre of the country which is situated in a mineral-rich area. Of 19,300km of roads 10,800km are metal surfaced. There are 4,383km of pipelines for crude oil, 1,947km for natural gas and 443km for petroleum products including liquefied petroleum gas. The principal ports are Tobruk, Tripoli, Benghazi, Misurata, Marsa al Burayqah, Ra's Lanuf, Ra's al Unif. There are 124 usable airports, 56 with permanent surface runways of which nine are over 3,659m and 27 between 2,440 and 3,659m in length. Libya has a modern system of telecommunications which is constantly being expanded.

Political considerations

Huge oil revenues in relation to a small population have allowed Libya's leader, Colonel Gaddafi, great latitude to support a variety of causes worldwide; his interventions have not made him popular with most of his Arab and African neighbours or with the leading Western powers. The US bombing of Tripoli in 1986 in retaliation for an alleged Libyan terrorist bombing incident, and the US and British insistence upon blaming Libya for the Lockerbie bomb outrage of December 1988 in which a total of 270 people were killed (despite mounting evidence through the 1990s that responsibility lay elsewhere) have led to Libya's semi-isolation and the application of UN sanctions. Despite such enmity, Libya's oil resources ensure her continued economic development.

Assessments

Libya enjoys the highest per capita income in Africa and will continue to reap the benefits of huge oil revenues for decades to come. Development is constrained by lack of adequate numbers of trained technicians so that it remains over-dependent upon foreign workers and, despite UN sanctions, continues to import foreign skills from the West. Despite the recession of the 1980s Libya managed to avoid becoming a heavily indebted nation, is not dependent upon aid and normally operates a trade surplus. The development of all other sectors of the economy, however, depends to a large extent upon the oil revenues. A change in Libya's political relations with the West and an end to UN sanctions (imposed in the wake of the Lockerbie bomb disaster to force Libya to hand over two suspects for trial in the West) could lead to a boom in the country's development.

NIGERIA

Area. 356,669 sq. miles (923,768 sq. km).
Population. (1995) 95,434,000.
Capital. Abuja (Federal Capital Territory).
Other major cities. Lagos (1,347,000), Ibadan (1,295,000), Kano (699,900), Ogbomosho (660,600), Oshogbo (441,600), Ilorin (430,600).
Language(s). English (official), Hausa, Yoruba, Ibo, Fulani.
Religion(s). Christian 49 per cent, Muslim 45 per cent, other 6 per cent.
Date of independence. October 1 1960 (from Britain).
GNP. (1993) $32,517,000,000, per capita $310.
Land and climate. The south consists of lowlands which merge into the central hills and plateaux; the north consists of extensive plains. There are mountains in the southeast. The confluence of the Niger and its main tributary, the Benue, in south-

central Nigeria effectively divides the country into three while the Niger delta is one of the great river deltas of the world. The climate ranges from equatorial in the south through tropical in the centre to arid in the north. The country is subject to desertification in the north, and soil degradation and rapid deforestation.

Introduction

This large country of West Africa, the size of France, Britain and the Netherlands combined, is by far the most populous on the continent with 50% greater population than Egypt. At independence in 1960 it was an agriculture-based society both feeding itself and exporting a range of cash crops led by cocoa and groundnuts. The discovery and exploitation of oil transformed the economy but also created many new problems: oil wealth has not been translated into new industries as was hoped in the 1970s while over-dependence upon the one commodity has led to the neglect of agriculture which was and still must be the backbone of the economy.

Nigeria has experienced a troubled political history since independence in 1960: multiparty democracy, a civil war and rule by the military, a return to civilian rule, then the return of the military again; by the 1990s the country was ruled by an increasingly corrupt military, bankrupt of ideas and clinging on to power. Endemic corruption has added to the country's problems. Yet the potential exists to make Nigeria a prosperous society: apart from oil there are other minerals; the agricultural base is both sufficient to feed the huge population and produce commodities for export; and there are plenty of educated and trained Nigerians with a long and successful entrepreneurial tradition. Despite these advantages, however, Nigeria remains one of the world's poorest countries on a per capita basis. It has four land neighbours – Benin, Cameroon, Chad and Niger; and a coastline on the Bight of Benin and the Gulf of Guinea. The Niger which traverses the country is one of Africa's greatest rivers.

Agriculture

Agriculture accounts for 33.5 per cent of GDP and employs 43 per cent of the workforce although a great part of production comes from inefficient small-scale farming. Once (at independence) a major food exporter, Nigeria is now a food importer. There are a number of explanations for this: the huge growth of population, neglect of agriculture despite periodic political 'back-to-the-land' campaigns and changing patterns of consumption, especially among the élite, which have led to demands for the import of foods such as wheat that cannot be grown in Nigeria. The country could feed itself – good agricultural land is available – and should continue to be a major exporter of a variety of cash crops. These include cocoa, groundnuts, palm oil and rubber. The main food crops are yams (22,000,000mt), cassava (21,000,000mt), sorghum, millet, rice, plantains and bananas, maize and sugarcane. Livestock herds include 25,497,000 goats, 16,717,000 cattle and 14,455,000 sheep. Roundwood production at 118,052,000cu m (1993) places Nigeria among the world's top wood-producing countries. Fisheries contribute an annual catch in excess of 250,000mt. Land use is divided between forested 12.4 per cent, meadows and pastures 43.9 per cent, agricultural land, under permanent cultivation 35.6 per cent, other 8.1 per cent.

Mining

Nigeria possesses a range of minerals including petroleum, tin, columbite, iron ore, coal, limestone, lead, zinc and natural gas but petroleum is the key to the economy. Petroleum has dominated Nigeria's economic activities since the early 1970s when, in the wake of the civil war, the country benefited from the OPEC-induced oil price rises of 1973. The subsequent windfall enabled Nigeria to launch Africa's largest-ever development plan which was then scheduled to cost 42 billion naira. Currently, Nigeria produces approximately 669,900,000 barrels of oil a year and if this rate is maintained it will be able to continue doing so for another quarter century. At the end of 1992 Nigeria's proved reserves stood at 2,400,000,000 tonnes or 17,900,000,000 barrels equivalent to 1.8 per cent of world reserves. With Gabon, Algeria and Libya, Nigeria is one of Africa's four members of OPEC.

Nigeria also possesses vast resources of natural gas: 120,000,000,000,000cu ft. or 3,400,000,000,000cu m, equivalent to 2.5 per cent of world reserves. In 1992 Nigeria produced 4,900,000,000cu m of natural gas but this was all consumed at home. Crude petroleum accounts for 97.9 per cent of exports (1992) while mining as a whole (which really means petroleum) accounts for 37.6 per cent of GDP (a higher percentage than agriculture) although only directly employing 6,800 workers or 0.1 per cent of the workforce. Other minerals mined include limestone, marble and tin and about 95,000mt of coal (though far greater amounts of coal have been mined in the past).

Manufacturing

During the heyday of oil (1973–80) when national income was constantly increasing Nigeria launched a number of ambitious industrial projects based on the new oil wealth. Unfortunately, many of these had to be modified or abandoned during the 1980s when the world price of oil slumped and depression followed so that, despite the hopes of industrialization raised at that time, manufacturing still only accounted for less than 6 per cent of GDP at the beginning of the 1990s and then only employed 4 per cent of the workforce. Apart from oil and mining activities, the principal manufactures concern primary processing – palm oil, groundnuts, cotton, rubber, wood, hides and skins; and textiles, cement, building materials, food products, footwear, chemicals, printing, ceramics and steel. Given the size of the Nigerian market which is the largest in Africa there is room for huge manufacturing/industrial expansion.

Infrastructure

There are 3,505km of 1.067m gauge railway (north–south), and 107,990km of roads of which 30,019km are paved. With the Niger and its huge delta as well as the Benue and many tributaries Nigeria has 8,575km of inland waterways. Pipelines include 2,042km for crude petroleum, 500km for natural gas and 3,000km for petroleum products. The main ports are Lagos, Port Harcourt, Calabar, Warri, Onne and Sapele. Of 63 usable airports, 34 have permanent surface runways, one of more than 3,659m and fifteen between 2,440m and 3,659m in length. The telecommunications system is good but suffers from poor maintenance.

Political considerations

During the 35 years since independence (up to 1995) Nigeria has experienced nine years of civilian rule and 26 years of rule by the military and by the mid-1990s the latter had clearly acquired the taste for power so that, despite periodic gestures and promises, showed no intention of relinquishing control to the civilians. The year of 1994 was deeply troubled and violent with Moshood 'MKO' Abiola, the man seen to have won the aborted 1993 elections, imprisoned by the military. Corruption appears to have become endemic to Nigeria. Economic reforms that could provide a real impetus to growth seem unlikely to be implemented until the country returns to civilian rule.

Assessments

Oil should provide the wealth to be used over the next quarter century to transform the manufacturing base of the economy although this will depend in part upon world conditions and in part upon the political situation in Nigeria; judging by performance between 1970 and 1995 the outlook cannot be any too certain. More important in the long run, Nigeria possesses abundant agricultural land and ought both to feed itself (despite its large population) and produce a healthy surplus of staple foods and commodity products for export.

Bars to efficient development appear to be political rather than economic and include the habit which has developed since the oil boom of the mid-1970s of over-dependence upon oil to solve all the nation's problems. The urgent need to translate oil wealth into other forms of economic growth must be reinforced by the fact that Nigeria's 1994 population of 95 million is expected to double in only 22 years. In 1994 Nigeria's total external debts stood at $29,496,000,000 which was slightly less than GNP. Although Nigeria is open to foreign investment, difficulties in repatriating money act as a disincentive to would-be investors.

OMAN

Area. 118,150 sq. miles (306,000 sq. km).
Population. (1995) 2,163,000.
Capital. Muscat (100,000).
Other major cities. Nizwa (62,880), Sama'il (44,771), Salalah (10,000).
Language(s). Arabic (official), English, Balochi, Urdu.
Religion(s). Islam (official) 86 per cent, Hindu 13 per cent, other 1 per cent.

Date of independence. 1650 (following the expulsion of the Portuguese).
GNP. (1993) $9,631,000,000, per capita $5,600.
Land and climate. There is a large central desert plain enclosed by mountains in the north and south. The climate is a hot dry desert one except on the coast where it is hot and humid while the far south is affected by the summer southwest monsoon (May to September). Natural freshwater resources are scarce and the interior is subject to sand and dust storms.

Introduction

Long regarded as one of the most conservative and reactionary closed societies in the world, Oman moved to become a modern state following the overthrow in 1970 of Sultan Said bin Taimur by his son, Sultan Qaboos bin Said. Oil was discovered in the 1960s and was first exported in 1967 since when oil has transformd the country's economic prospects. Politically, Oman remains an absolute monarchy although there is a consultative assembly with limited influence. Britain is the most important external power in the Sultanate which historically came within the British sphere of influence. Oman occupies the southeast corner of the Arabian Peninsula and has three neighbours – Yemen, Saudi Arabia and the United Arab Emirates – and a coastline of more than 2,000km on the Indian Ocean.

Agriculture

Agriculture only contributes 3.3 per cent to GDP although employing 27.7 per cent of the workforce. Less than 2 per cent of the land is cultivated and most production is the result of subsistence farming. The principal crops are vegetables, melons, watermelons, dates, bananas, mangos, onions, papayas, tobacco leaf. Fishing is important, yielding an annual catch in excess of 100,000mt. Livestock herds are small scale: goats 739,000, sheep 148,000, cattle 144,000, camels 96,000. Land use is divided between meadows and pastures 4.7 per cent, agricultural land, under permanent cultivation 0.3 per cent, other (mainly desert) 95 per cent.

Mining

Petroleum was first discovered in 1964 and commercial production began in 1967 when the operator was Petroleum Development Oman Ltd (a subsidiary of Royal Dutch/Shell). Initially, exports ran at 200,000b/d, a figure that increased to 300,000 b/d through the 1970s. There are two main oil-bearing areas: southwest of Muscat; and in Dhofar. Oman has estimated reserves (1992) of 4,500,000,000 barrels equivalent to 0.4 per cent of world reserves and at the current rate of production (269,869,000 barrels in 1992) a lifespan of 17 years if no new discoveries are made. Recoverable reserves of natural gas are estimated at 6,300,000,000,000cu ft. although at present all production is consumed locally. Crude oil accounts for 76.3 per cent of annual exports (1994). Oman is associated with the group of non-OPEC oil producers (NOPEC) which includes Angola, China, Colombia, Egypt, Malaysia,

Mexico, Norway and Yemen. Generally, these countries support the production restraints favoured by OPEC in order to maintain high foreign exchange earnings.

Other mineral resources include copper, asbestos, marble, limestone, chromium and gypsum although desert conditions have retarded exploitation. Copper and gypsum are both mined and in 1993 copper output came to 12,000mt. Small quantities of silver and gold are also mined. Mining (which in real terms means oil) accounts for just under 40 per cent of GDP although employing only 0.5 per cent of the workforce.

Manufacturing

Manufacturing accounts for just over 5 per cent of GDP and employs 6 per cent of the workforce. Apart from mining-related activities, manufactures include textiles and apparel, metal products, machinery, chemicals, food and beverages, wood and paper products. Fish, processed copper and textiles are export items.

Infrastructure

There are 26,000km of highways of which 6,000km are paved; 1,300km of oil pipelines and 1,030km of natural gas pipelines. The country is served by three ports: Mina' Qabus, Mina' Raysut and Mina' al Fahl. There are 130 usable airports, six with permanent surface runways of which only one is over 3,659m in length and nine are between 2,440 and 3,659m in length. Oman has a modern system of telecommunications.

Political considerations

Although Sultan Qaboos bin Said is seen as a modernizer he is still, in essence, an absolute monarch and during 1994 serious dissidence by civil servants and businessmen upset the apparently even control of the system. The disturbances led to about 500 arrests and prompted a government statement condemning 'treacherous people intent on overthrowing the government while using Islam as a cover'. The statement could be taken as a summary of Oman's potential political problems: demands for greater democracy; and militant Islam.

Assessments

Foreign capital is welcomed and investment encouraged, for example, by five-year tax holidays, especially in relation to heavy industry and manufacturing. Foreign exchange repatriation and invisible earnings are not restricted. As with many oil-rich countries, the problem for Oman must be to maximize manufacturing and increase agricultural production by modern methods while the oil wealth lasts.

QATAR

Area. 4,412 sq. miles (11,427 sq. km).
Population. (1995) 579,000.
Capital. Doha (236,131).
Other major cities. ar-Rayzan (99,939), al-Wakrah (25,747).
Language(s). Arabic (official), English.
Religion(s). Muslim (Sunni) 92.4 per cent, Christian 5.9 per cent, Hindu 1.1 per cent, other 0.6 per cent.
Date of independence. September 3 1971 (from Britain).
GNP. (1993) $7,871,000,000, per capita $15,140.
Land and climate. The peninsula consists mainly of flat barren desert; the climate is hot dry desert with humid summers.

Introduction

An independent sheikdom which has been ruled by a single dynasty, the Al-Thani family, since the eighteenth century, Qatar was also a British protectorate from 1916 to 1971. Sheikh Khalifa al-Thani carried out a bloodless coup in 1972 and then instituted a programme of economic and social reforms. He was ousted in a similar coup by his son in 1995. Qatar forms a thumb-like peninsula jutting out from mainland Saudi Arabia into the centre of the Red Sea towards Iran. Its principal source of wealth is oil.

Agriculture

Agriculture contributes less than 1 per cent to GDP and employs only 1.6 per cent of the workforce. The agricultural area is small and government owned. Crops consist mainly of vegetables, fodder and fruit; sheep, goats and some cattle provide dairy products and meat while fishing is of growing importance. Most food has to be imported.

Minerals

Oil is the basis of the Qatar economy, accounting for 85 per cent of exports and 38.4 per cent of GDP, although only employing 0.5 per cent of the workforce. At the end of 1992 Qatar's oil reserves stood at 3,700,000,000 barrels, equivalent to 0.4 per cent of world reserves with an expected lifespan of 21.6 years. Natural gas reserves stood at 6,400,000,000,000cu m, equivalent to 4.6 per cent of world reserves. Apart from oil and natural gas Qatar produces limestone and moderate quantities of sulphur and gypsum as well as sand and gravel.

Manufacturing

Manufacturing accounts for 11.2 per cent of GDP and employs 3.6 per cent of the workforce. Qatar has used its oil wealth to create a range of industries including steel and aluminium manufactures for export as well as a number of lighter industries. The collapse of oil prices and the consequent drop in the production of natural gas affected these industries at the end of the 1980s, however, and held back development of major natural gas finds. The principal manufactures (1992) are chemicals, petroleum products, fabricated metal products, machinery, food, beverages, tobacco, paper and paper products, furniture, wood products, clothing and textiles. There are almost no restrictions on trade and no foreign exchange regulations or limits on invisible trade. Most imports and exports are freely allowed and foreign investment is encouraged when 51 per cent of the capital is controlled by Qatar nationals.

Infrastructure

There are 1,500km of roads of which 1,000km are paved; 235km of pipelines for crude oil and 400km for natural gas. The country is served by three ports – Doha, Umm Sa'id, Halul Island. There are four usable airports, one with a permanent surface runway which is over 3,659m in length. The telecommunications system which is centred upon Doha is modern with good international links.

Political considerations/assessments

An authoritarian monarchy rules Qatar and there are no political parties or parliament although an advisory council can debate legislation and make recommendations to the government. As a tiny oil-rich state in a politically troubled region, Qatar is uneasily poised between the big powers of the Gulf – Saudi Arabia, Iraq and Iran – and must constantly take account of their policies. At home it is a conservative regime tempered by the problems created by the influx of workers from other parts of the Gulf or elsewhere. Its main long-term economic policy is to create an alternative manufacturing-based structure while the oil wealth lasts.

SAUDI ARABIA

Area. 865,000 sq. miles (2,240,000 sq. km).
Population. (1995) 17,880,000.
Capital. Riyadh (1,800,000).
Other major cities. Jiddah (1,800,000 – 1983), Mecca (550,000), at-Ta'if (300,000).
Language(s). Arabic (official).
Religion(s). Islam 100 per cent.
Date of independence. September 23 1932 (unification, formerly part of the Ottoman Empire).

GNP. (1994) $173,100,000,000, per capita $9,510.

Land and climate. Saudi Arabia consists of a vast expanse of undulating sandy desert, mainly uninhabited, with a harsh dry climate of great temperature extremes. There are no permanent sources of water or perennial rivers and a major programme of coastal seawater desalination is crucial to the provision of the country's sweet water requirements.

Introduction

Occupying the main portion of the huge Arabian peninsula, Saudi Arabia's international importance rests upon its possession of 25 per cent of the world's known oil resources, a fact that gives to it extraordinary influence out of proportion to its general stage of development. An Islamic society, Saudi Arabia also holds a unique position as guardian of the two most holy cities of Islam – Mecca and Medina – and therefore plays host to an annual influx of many thousands of Muslim pilgrims from all over the Islamic world. Large numbers of foreign workers and technicians upon whom the economy depends – especially in the oil and banking sectors – represent a possible political problem for the future. Saudi Arabia's vulnerability was demonstrated in 1990–91 at the time of Iraq's invasion of Kuwait when it felt quite unable to defend itself and relied upon the massive UN-sponsored, US-led coalition for its defence.

Modernization of a traditional Islamic society which is still ruled by an absolute monarchy has produced increasing strains so that, for example, through 1994 growing demands for greater civil rights, more liberties and political and economic reform were the dominant activities of the year. In the north Saudi Arabia has three neighbours: Jordan, Iraq and Kuwait; to the east (in the Gulf) its neighbours are Qatar and the United Arab Emirates (UAE); to the southeast Oman and to the south Yemen. It has a total of 2,640km of coastline on the Red Sea and the Gulf.

Agriculture

Agriculture contributes just over 6 per cent to GDP and employs just under 10 per cent of the workforce. The principal crops are wheat, barley, dates, tomatoes, watermelons, grapes, cucumbers, potatoes, eggplants, pumpkins and citrus fruits. The national livestock herd consists of 7,257,000 sheep, 4,150,000 goats and smaller numbers of camels and cattle, as well as chickens. Agricultural activity is subsidized by the government and the use of irrigation and plastic covers has enabled Saudi Arabia to approach self-sufficiency in a range of foodstuffs. Land use is divided between forested 0.9 per cent, meadows and pastures 55.8 per cent, agricultural land, under permanent cultivation 1.7 per cent, other 41.6 per cent.

Minerals

Mining and the oil sector contribute 36.7 per cent to GDP although employing less then 1 per cent of the workforce. Saudi Arabia produces small quantities of gypsum and gold but effectively mining means oil. The Arabian American Oil Company (Aramco) was given a concession to search for oil in 1933 and discovered oil in commercial quantities in 1938; by 1945 four oil fields had been discovered and a number of other American companies had bought into Aramco.

There was a spectacular growth of Saudi oil production during the 1970s and when OPEC became a formidable cartel in the period 1973–6 Saudi Arabia's vast productive capacity meant that it automatically assumed the position of the organization's 'swing' country: that is, Saudi Arabia was able by increasing or decreasing production to regulate and control total OPEC output. At the end of 1992 Saudi Arabia's oil reserves stood at 35,100,000,000 tonnes or 257,800,000,000 barrels of oil, equivalent to 25.6 per cent of total world reserves with an estimated life (at current rates of production) of 82 years. In 1993 Saudi Arabia produced a total of 2,915,000,000 barrels of oil or 7,986,000 b/d. On the other hand Saudi Arabia possesses only modest stocks of associated natural gas, an estimated reserve of 5,200,000,000,000cu m or 3.7 per cent of world reserves. It is upon its great oil wealth that Saudi Arabia has based its development plans which include major industrialization for the future.

Manufacturing

At present manufacturing contributes 8.4 per cent to GDP and employs 6.5 per cent of the workforce. Saudi Arabia, which is determined to remain a traditional Islamic society, is nonetheless encouraging private enterprise to help turn the country into a modern industrial state. The main industrial products are cement, steel, fuel oils, gasoline, naptha, diesel oil, jet fuel, asphalt and related products, fertilizer and plastics. Apart from these oil-related products and steel the great bulk of manufactured goods are imported, principally from the USA, Britain, Germany, Switzerland, Italy, France, South Korea and Taiwan.

Infrastructure

There are 1,399km of 1.435m standard gauge railway, 74,000km of roads of which 35,000km are paved. The oil pipeline system includes 6,400km for crude oil, 150km for petroleum products, 2,200km for natural gas. The country is served by seven ports on the Red Sea and Gulf: Jiddah, Ad Dammam, Ras Tanura, Jizan, Al Jubayl, Yanbu al Bahr, Yanbu al Sinaiyah. There are 193 usable airports, 71 with permanent surface runways of which fourteen are over 3,659m and 36 between 2,440 and 3,659m in length. The telecommunications system is modern and extensive.

Political considerations

There are no political parties. The country is ruled by the Saudi royal family whose extensive membership effectively controls all aspects of government and commerce and the country is ruled according to Islamic Sharia law. Growing demands for civil liberties including democratization of the system pose a developing threat to the existing royal monopoly of power. The spread of education, invitably, will lead to increasing challenges to the status quo which is seen to be more and more anachronistic in the modern world. In addition, of a population just short of 18 million (1995), some four and a half million are non-citizens and, as in neighbouring Kuwait, their presence may well prove a political embarrassment in a future political crisis. Saudi Arabia is seen to be strategically vital to the USA because of its huge oil resources but this very fact renders it vulnerable both to Western interference and to jealousy on the part of its often highly volatile Middle East neighbours. The future must be an uneasy one.

Assessments

Oil wealth will continue to give Saudi Arabia major economic and political importance into the foreseeable future. If it is able to use its wealth to diversify the economy and industrialize before the oil resources begin to decline and is also able gradually to modernize its political system at the same time, its long-term future could be reasonably assured.

UNITED ARAB EMIRATES (UAE)

Area. 32,280 sq. miles (83,600 sq. km).
Population. (1995) 2,195,000.
Capital. Abu Dhabi (363,432).
Other major cities. Dubayy (585,189), al-Ayn (176,411), ash-Shariqah (125,000), Ras al-Khaymah (42,000).
Language(s). Arabic (official), Persian, English, Hindi, Urdu.
Religion(s). Muslim 94.9 per cent (official – Sunni 80 per cent, Shi'ite 20 per cent), Christian 3.8 per cent, other 1.3 per cent.
Date of independence. December 2 1971 (from Britain).
GNP. (1993) $38,420,000,000, per capita $22,470.
Land and climate. The UAE consists of a flat barren coastal plain that merges into the rolling sand dunes of the interior desert; there are mountains to the east bordering Oman. The climate is desert, cooler in the east.

Introduction

The UAE consists of seven small states that formerly had been brought under British protection in 1853 and were known as the Trucial States; from 1892 to 1971 Britain controlled their defence and foreign policy. Prior to independence in 1971 the seven states negotiated a federal structure to form the UAE. In part the decision of the seven rulers to come together reflected their fears of much more powerful neighbouring states in the Gulf. The seven states which make up the UAE are: Abu

Dhabi, Dubai, Sharjah, Ras al-Khaimah, Fujairah, Ajman and Umm al Qaiwain. There is a Federal Council while the president is elected from among the seven hereditary rulers. The UAE has borders with Oman to the east and Saudi Arabia to the south and a coastline of 1,318km on the Gulf. Oil is the basis of the economy.

Agriculture

Agriculture contributes only 2.5 per cent to GDP although employing about 6 per cent of the workforce. It is nonetheless important to the economy as a whole. Principal crops are dates, tomatoes, eggplants, cabbages, lemons and limes, pumpkins and squash, cauliflowers, cucumbers, peppers and mangoes. Dates, fruit and vegetables are exported. Livestock includes 861,000 goats, 333,000 sheep, 148,000 camels and 65,000 cattle. The fish catch averages 92,000mt a year. Food and live animals account for about 13.5 per cent of imports. Land use is divided between meadows and pastures 2.4 per cent, agricultural land, under permanent cultivation 0.5 per cent, other 97.1 per cent.

Minerals

Mining accounts for 33.4 per cent of GDP though the sector only employs 1.5 per cent of the workforce. Although mining really means oil, a few other minerals are also exploited. These include small quantities of gypsum, sulphur, lime and marble shale. Oil, however, is the basis of UAE wealth. At the end of 1992 the UAE had an estimated 98,100,000,000 barrels of oil with a projected lifespan of 100 years. The oil divides between Abu Dhabi with 92,200,000,000 barrels and Dubai and the northern emirates with 5,900,000,000 barrels. Combined, this represents 9.8 per cent of world reserves. Production in 1993 was at the rate of 2,030,000 barrels a day or 741,300,000 barrels in the year. Crude petroleum provides 65 per cent of all exports while refined products contribute about another 15 per cent. The UAE has an estimated 5,500,000,000,000cu m of natural gas, equivalent to 4 per cent of world reserves although at present a high proportion of production is consumed locally. Given its projected lifespan, the oil should enable this small Gulf state to industrialize fully against the time when the resource runs dry.

Manufacturing

Manufacturing now accounts for 8.3 per cent of GDP and employs 9.2 per cent of the workforce. Diversification away from oil has not been very fast: there is an aluminium smelter in Dubai and steel and chemical plants and a developing petro-chemical complex, also in Dubai. A free trade zone was established in 1985 at the man-made port of Jebel Ali. The main manufactures in 1993 were cement, aluminium and processed foods, apart from petroleum-related products.

Infrastructure

There are 2,000km of roads of which 1,800km are paved; 830km of pipelines for crude oil and 870km for natural gas and gas liquids. There are seven ports: Al'Fujayrah, Khawr Fakkan, Mina' Jabal 'Ali, Mina' Khalid, Mina' Rashid, Mina' Saqr, Mina' Zayid. There are 34 usable airports, twenty with permanent surface runways of which seven are over 3,659m and five between 2,440 and 3,659m in length. The UAE has a modern system of telecommunications.

Political considerations

There are two kinds of political problem: that of external pressures; and those of domestic change. The Gulf is a highly volatile political region and the UAE is surrounded by far more powerful neighbours – Saudi Arabia, Iraq, Iran; at any time in the future one of these (as did Iraq against Kuwait in 1990) might see the UAE as a small, defenceless yet rich prize worth seizing for its oil wealth. In domestic terms the UAE is an anachronism – seven emirates ruled by hereditary sheikhs who have made only limited concessions to modern political aspirations. The general wealth – one of the highest per capita incomes in the world – may be seen as a substitute for real participation in politics but that state of affairs cannot last indefinitely.

Assessments

The wealth of the UAE places its population (on a per capita basis) on a par with the rich OECD countries. The projected lifespan of the oil resources should enable the UAE to industrialize fully before the oil runs dry.

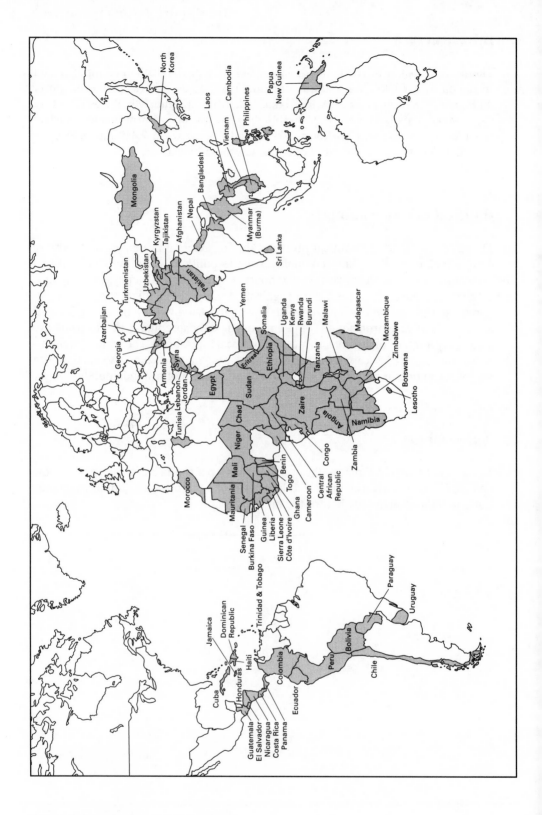

Map 5 Low- and middle-income economies

4 LOW- AND MIDDLE-INCOME ECONOMIES

INTRODUCTION

This section covers 80 countries: they include a handful with substantial potential such as Angola and Sudan whose economic development has been held back disastrously as a result of long-lasting civil wars and others such as Bangladesh whose economic advances are always swallowed up by a huge and rapidly increasing population. A few more such as Egypt or Zimbabwe face great problems of poverty but, on the other hand, possess relatively well-developed infrastructures and their futures depend upon the extent to which they can build up and increase their manufacturing capacities. The greater number of these 80, however, are unlikely (short of the discovery of major new resources such as oil) to achieve any real change in their present economic standing, not at least in the foreseeable future. They include 34 out of the 48 countries which the United Nations designates as less developed countries (LDCs) – the remaining fourteen LDCs are to be found in Part V Mini-states – and a majority of all these states at the very least face the prospect of being marginalized by the new international economic forces of so-called liberalization and globalization (see Introduction).

AFGHANISTAN

Area. 251,825 sq. m (652,225 sq. km).
Population. (1995) 18,129,000. There are, in addition, 1.5m Afghan refugees in Pakistan and 1.8m in Iran.
Capital. Kabul (700,400).
Other major towns. Kandahar (225,500), Herat (177,300).
Language(s). Pashtu (35 per cent), Dari (Persian) (50 per cent), Turkic languages.
Religions. Sunni Muslim (74 per cent), Shi'ite Muslim (25 per cent), other (1 per cent).
Date of independence. August 19 1919 (from Britain).
GNP. (1988) $3,100,000,000, $220 per capita.
Land and climate. A highland mass mainly above 1,200m though with many mountain ranges exceeding 6,000m, broad valleys some of which are extremely fertile, undulating plateaux and wide river basins. Most of the country is arid or semi-arid and averages 100mm–150mm rain a year. It suffers extremes of temperature.

Introduction

Landlocked between six Asian neighbours – Iran, Pakistan, China, Tajikistan, Turkmenistan and Uzbekistan – Afghanistan is one of the world's poorest nations. A rugged land of high mountains and plains and subject to earthquakes in the northern Hindu Kush region, it also faces environmental problems including desertification, over-grazing, deforestation and flooding. Fully independent (from British interference) since 1919, its recent history has been politically deeply troubled. The country became a republic on the overthrow of the monarchy in 1973; in 1979, following a coup by Babrak Kermal, Soviet forces invaded the country to provide him with support and for the next decade Afghanistan was subject to a brutal civil war with the Soviet-backed Marxist government fighting various Islamic and traditionalist groups. Soviet troops finally withdrew in 1989 but the civil war continued. In 1992 the communist President, Mohammed Najibullah, was finally overthrown by a rebel coalition and in 1993 the country became an Islamic state with Burhannudin Rabbani as President and Gulbuddin Hekmatyr as Prime Minister. The civil war between rival Islamic groups continued.

Although it possesses a range of mineral resources, exploitation is inhibited by continuing political instability, poor infrastructure and inaccessibility. Agriculture is the mainstay of the economy and accounts for half the national income and the majority of exports. Principal exports include dried fruit and nuts (49.6 per cent), carpets and rugs (23.6 per cent), wool and hides (6.7 per cent) and cotton (1.3 per cent). Principal imports include machinery (37.7 per cent), general manufactures (18.3 per cent), minerals and fuels (10.9 per cent). The country is likely to be aid dependent into the foreseeable future. As a result of the long years of civil war there are no reliable statistics.

Agriculture

Agriculture accounts for slightly more than half GDP and 80 per cent exports and employs a labour force of 2,777,000 equivalent to 61 per cent of the total labour force. Land use is divided as between forested (2.9 per cent), meadows and pastures (46 per cent), agricultural and under permanent cultivation (12.4 per cent) and other (38.7 per cent); of 65m hectares of land 8m are suitable for arable farming while only 2.6m ha of irrigated land provide 85 per cent of all crops. Principal agricultural exports are dried fruit and nuts, carpets and rugs, wool and hides, cotton, karakul fur skins. The principal cash crops, in addition to the above, are wheat and mutton. Otherwise, agriculture is largely subsistence farming or nomadic animal husbandry.

Estimated agricultural production in 1994: wheat 1,750,000mt, maize 360,000mt, rice 350,000mt, grapes 330,000mt, potatoes 228,000mt, barley 180,000mt. Livestock include sheep 14,200,000, goats 2,150,000, cattle 1,500,000 as well as asses, horses, camels and chickens. There are small wood and fisheries sectors.

However, potential capacity is much greater. Prior to the 1970s which were first affected by drought and then civil war, wheat production was up to 3,000,000mt a year, maize 800,000mt, barley 400,000mt; similarly, figures for livestock were much higher: karakul sheep 6.5m, ordinary sheep 15m, cattle 3.7m.

At present Afghanistan is obliged to import wheat while the years of civil war have disrupted normal agricultural production which has been greatly reduced. According to UN estimates Afghanistan is the world's leading opium grower (2,000 tons in 1992) and a major source of hashish and cannabis.

Cotton is a state monopoly and other products such as skins, wool, roots, raisins and liquorice require the surrender to the state of part of the foreign exchange earnings.

Minerals

Natural gas is the only mineral that is currently being exploited on any scale and in 1993 output came to 188,000,000cu m. Natural gas is a state monopoly and exports to the former Soviet Union have accounted for as much as 55 per cent of all exports. It is, at present, the one mineral that is relatively easy to exploit and in the mid-1980s (1983–4) exports to the USSR were running at 2,400m cu m a year, although exact figures are hard to calculate since the pipeline meters were on the Soviet side of the border and the pipelines were repeatedly blown up by guerrillas. Unless new finds are made the gas fields may be exhausted by the end of the century.

Other minerals include petroleum, coal, copper, talc, chromium, silver, gold, fluorite, mica, barites, sulphur, lead, zinc, iron ore, salt, precious and semi-precious stones including lapis lazuli. There are an estimated 1,700m tons of iron ore (62 per cent high grade) at Hajigak in Bamian province although it is located at a height of 3,500m. Copper resources near Kabul are estimated to be equivalent to 2 per cent of world copper supplies at 4.7m tons. There is some uranium (exploited on a small scale during the 1980s for export to the USSR) and two small oil fields though with only 12m tons of resources.

Infrastructure

Afghanistan is landlocked and has no seaport and no railways; its infrastructure generally is primitive. There are 21,000km of roads of which 2,800km are hard

surfaced. There are 41 airports (36 in use). Telecommunications (telephone, telegraph and radio broadcasts) are limited.

Political considerations

The civil war of the 1980s and continuing strife into the 1990s disrupted every aspect
of development and drastically reduced output; as of 1994 there are few reliable
statistics. As of 1993 there were still 3.8m refugees (the largest number in the world),
principally in Pakistan and Iran, although the UN hoped that the 1.5m in Pakistan
would have been returned home by the end of 1995. Afghanistan is in the centre of
the Islamic belt of Asian countries and is affected by the politics of Islamic
fundamentalism.

Under a law of 1974 – Foreign and Domestic Private Investment Law – up to 49
per cent of foreign ownership of a company may be encouraged. Foreigners in
Afghanistan are obliged to convert a proportion of their salaries into afghanis at the
official rate of exchange. Afghanistan will qualify for and require substantial foreign
aid for development into the foreseeable future.

Assessments

A period of sustained peace and stable government should enable Afghanistan to
increase agricultural production to cover its own food needs while this sector will
continue to provide the bulk of exports. Although it has extensive mineral resources,
especially iron ore and copper, exploitation is inhibited by access and poor infrastructure and they are unlikely to be developed on any major scale while other more
readily available resources exist elsewhere.

ANGOLA

Area. 481,354 sq. miles (1,246,700 sq. km).
Population. (1995) 11,558,000.
Capital. Luanda (1,134,000).
Other major cities. Huambo (203,000, 1983), Benguela (155,000, 1983), Lobito
(150,000, 1983).
Langauge(s). Portuguese (official), various Bantu languages.
Religion(s). Christian 90 per cent, traditional 9.5 per cent, other 0.5 per cent.
Date of independence. November 11 1975 (from Portugal).
GNP.(1989) $6,010,000,000, per capita $620.
Land and climate. A tropical to subtropical climate tempered by altitude (the
greater part of the country lies above 1,000m); the south tends to be arid and the
Namib Desert extends up the southern coast above Namibe. Apart from the Cuango
(up to 193km) Angola's rivers do not provide access to the interior. The coast is arid
and semi-arid. The average density of population of this huge country is only 8.8
persons per sq. km (22.7 per sq. mile). The river systems (falling off the central
plateau) provide huge hydro-electric potential for development.

Introduction

A huge country of just under half a million square miles in southern Africa, Angola has an Atlantic seaboard of 1,000 miles and four land neighbours: Congo, which virtually surrounds the Cabinda enclave lying to the north of the Zaire River mouth, Zaire, Zambia and Namibia. Apart from the narrow coastal plain the country consists chiefly of a huge interior plateau. After fifteen years of bitter warfare against the colonial power, Portugal, Angola became independent in 1975 only to be plunged into civil war thereafter. A ceasefire of May 31 1991 was followed by internationally monitored elections in 1992 which gave the victory to the ruling Popular Movement for the Liberation of Angola (MPLA) whereupon the opposition National Union for the Total Independence of Angola (UNITA) went back to the bush and resumed the civil war. However, a peace agreement of November 20 1994 between the government and UNITA held through to mid-1996.

The country has large mineral resources and most notably oil, followed by diamonds and iron ore as well as a number of other minerals yet to be exploited. There is good arable land that in normal times should enable Angola both to feed itself and to produce a range of export crops as well (Angola was Africa's second coffee exporter under the Portuguese). But development (or redevelopment) of these resources requires peace so that international investment can be attracted into the country. Principal exports in 1991 consisted of petroleum (89.8 per cent) and diamonds (5.5 per cent) while imports consisted of general manufactures and capital goods.

Agriculture

Twenty years of civil war have so disrupted both the people and the land they farm that it is impossible to do more than speak in generalities about agricultural potential. Angola should be self-sufficient in food as well as a major exporter of a range of cash crops (that had been developed under the Portuguese) for the land and climate are suitable for major agricultural production. But famine, malnutrition and the need simply to survive in a war situation have affected up to 50 per cent of the population since the mid-1980s and by 1991 (when the first ceasefire was agreed) 1.8m people were threatened by shortages and food aid had become essential for the economic survival of a substantial proportion of the population. In 1990, for example, the UN Special Relief Programme for Angola estimated a cereal deficit of 565,000 tons.

Although slightly more than 70 per cent of the labour force, totalling 2,892,000 (in 1991), works on the land, mainly as subsistence farmers, agriculture only accounts for 10.3 per cent of GDP. The principal staple crop is cassava with an output of 986,000mt in 1994; this is followed by maize at 201,000mt (only two-sevenths the figure of 700,000mt in the early 1970s when maize was an export crop); sugarcane (220,000mt), bananas (25,000mt). Other crops include sweet potatoes, millet, palm oil, beans and peanuts.

Prior to independence Angola was Africa's second producer of coffee with an annual crop of 200,000mt of robusta (in 1992 production was a mere 5,000 tons) which was a major export item. Other exports included: sisal at 66,719mt in 1974

141

(Angola was Africa's second producer again) but this had dropped to a mere 1,000mt in 1987–90; cotton production reached 104,000mt in 1974 but by 1983 Angola was obliged to import cotton for the first time. Sugar was another important export crop and this was maintained, in part, during the civil war with Cuban aid but the withrdawal of the Cubans led to a collapse of sugar production (plantation agriculture under the Portuguese was reorganized as workers' co-operatives).

Cattle is mainly confined to the drier south of the country (the north is subject to tsetse fly) and in 1994 livestock consisted of 3,280,000 cattle, 1,570,000 goats, 830,000 pigs.

Cash crops in time of peace include coffee, sisal, maize, cotton, sugarcane, manioc and tobacco. Food crops are cassava, maize, vegetables, plantains, bananas. Livestock accounts for 20 per cent, fishing 4 per cent and forestry 2 per cent of total agricultural output.

Angola should be both food self-sufficient and a major exporter of cash crops including coffee but a return to such a condition must await an end to the civil war. Meanwhile, food has to be imported. Land use is divided between forested 41.7 per cent, meadows and pastures 23.3 per cent, agricultural (under cultivation) 2.7 per cent, other 32.3 per cent.

Minerals

Throughout the civil war the Angolan government has largely sustained itself with its oil production (and to some extent diamond output). Principal minerals are oil, diamonds, iron ore while other minerals include gold, phosphates, feldspar, bauxite and uranium.

At the end of 1992 proved reserves of oil were 200 million tons or 1,500 million barrels, equivalent to 0.1 per cent of world reserves. A new oil field of an estimated 6,000 b/d capacity was discovered offshore in 1990 and continuing offshore exploration is expected to reveal further resources. In 1991 oil accounted for 89.8 per cent of all exports and crude petroleum output came to 18,205,000 barrels. Most of the oil comes from the Cabinda enclave but present indications suggest that offshore oil will soon predominate. Angola is Sub-Saharan Africa's second oil producer after Nigeria.

Diamond production in 1994 came to 1,350,000 carats and accounted for 5.5 per cent of exports in value. Diamond reserves are estimated to be among the world's highest and, following a permanent cessation of the civil war, production is expected to increase nine or tenfold. Diamond sales, worth $230m at the end of the 1980s, fell back to $178m in 1991.

The third mineral is iron ore. Mining began in 1956 with annual production averaging 700,000 to 800,000 tons during the 1960s. The Cassinga mines in Huila province have proven reserves of 1,000m tons to high-grade ore and a railway spur was constructed to link the mines to a new harbour north of Namibe. An annual rate of production of 6m tons had been achieved when the civil war put the Cassinga mines out of action in 1976. Although the mines had been rehabilitated by 1986 a standstill to further mining followed, in part due to the depressed state of world markets, in part because of the continuing civil war.

Angola is believed to be one of the richest sources of minerals in southern Africa and much prospecting and exploration remains to be done; its mineral future is seen to be bright. Other minerals which have been identified (and in some cases part exploited) include copper, which has been found in four provinces; feldspar in the south; manganese, which was mined in 1973; phosphate rock in the Zaire and Cabinda provinces; uranium on the border with Namibia; and some gold. In 1991 mining contributed 58.2 per cent to GDP although only employing a fraction of the total labour force.

Apart from mining there is, at present, only a minuscule manufacturing sector.

Infrastructure

The country's overall infrastructure has suffered major neglect as a result of more than 30 years of continuous warfare; for much of that time, for example, its main railway line across the centre of the country, the Benguela Railway, has been out of action. There are 3,189km of rail track of which 2,879km are 1.067m gauge and 310km 0.600m gauge. Of 73,000km of highways and roads only 8,517km have bitumenized surfaces. There is a single oil pipeline of 179km and the country is served by four ports – Luanda, Lobito, Namibe and Cabinda. Of 302 airports just over half are at present usable and two have international-length runways. High-frequency radio has been extensively developed for military purposes; other telecommunications facilities are limited.

Political considerations

Through twenty years of civil war the government has always managed to keep the oil industry fully operational and that has provided the great bulk of its revenues. Most other sectors of the economy, coffee, for example, have collapsed and are unlikely to be effectively rehabilitated until a lasting peace is achieved. Then Angola will require substantial inputs of economic and technical assistance if it is to achieve a rapid and full economic recovery. Yet, despite the civil war, the attractions of the economy to outsiders were demonstrated in 1993 when Italy announced it was prepared to finance an oil terminal at Cabinda and Chevron and Elf announced plans to expand their operations there while the government said it was prepared to award new exploration contracts to Exxon and Royal Dutch Shell.

Assessments

In terms of both mineral resources and agricultural potential Angola should realize a bright long-term economic future. It has the capacity to feed itself (and to do so, moreover, for a much larger population than at present) as well as produce a range of commodity crops such as coffee for export. It should be able to create a substantial manufacturing sector based upon its mineral resources. Full exploration is likely to reveal extensive new mineral resources.

ARMENIA

Area. 11,506 sq. miles (29,800 sq. km).
Population. (1995) 3,548,000.
Capital. Yerevan (1,283,000).
Other major cities. Gyumri (163,000, prior to the 1988 earthquake), Kirovakan (76,000).
Language(s). Armenian (official), Russian.
Religion(s). Armenian Orthodox (94 per cent).
Date of independence. September 23 1991 (from the USSR).
GNP. (1993) $2,462,000,000, per capita $660.
Land and climate. With a continental climate subject to drought, Armenia consists of high plateau with mountains. There is good arable soil in the Aras river valley.

Introduction

Armenia is a small, landlocked country in eastern Europe that emerged as a newly independent state in 1991, as a result of the break-up of the Soviet Union of which it had been a part. It has four land neighbours: Azerbaijan, Georgia, Iran and Turkey. Armenia has limited natural resources and, while part of the USSR, had been developed as an industrial centre to supply other Soviets with textiles and a range of machinery and other goods. In its turn it was heavily dependent upon other Soviets for its raw materials and energy. Since independence it has been engaged in a bitter war with its neighbour, Azerbaijan, over the mainly Armenian-populated enclave of Nagorno-Karabakh inside Azerbaijan.

Agriculture

Agriculture accounts for between 56 and 57 per cent of GDP. About 29 per cent of the land is arable though none is under permanent crops; meadows and pastures account for a further 15 per cent of the land while the remainder (mainly mountain terrain) has little agricultural use. About 3,000 sq. km of land has been irrigated (1990). Approximately 30 per cent of the labour force is employed in agriculture. The principal crops are vegetables, potatoes, milk, wheat, grapes. The national herd consists of 500,000 cattle and 736,000 sheep and goats. Armenia is more or less self-sufficient in foodstuffs. Brandy and other liqueurs are produced in the Yerevan vineyards.

Minerals

There are no outstanding major mineral resources though there are deposits (unexploited) of bauxite, copper, zinc and molybdenum.

Manufacturing

This sector was the mainstay of the economy when Armenia was a part of the USSR; industries included metal-cutting machine tools, forging-pressing machines, electric goods, tyres, textiles, washing machines, chemicals, trucks, watches and a range of light industries. However, the economic and political upheavals which have followed the disintegration of the USSR have put at risk Armenia's former stable markets. Manufacturing and mining contributed 30.5 per cent to GDP in 1993 and employed 23 per cent of the labour force.

Infrastructure

In the short period since independence in September 1991, the infrastructure of Armenia has been adversely affected by the war with its eastern neighbour, Azerbaijan, and the civil war in its western neighbour, Georgia. There are 840km of railways, 11,300km of roads of which 10,500km are hard surfaced. Of the twelve airports only two are serviceable. The telecommunications system is reasonable and includes 260,000 telephones and 100 per cent access to Armenian and Russian television.

Political considerations

The political outlook in 1995 improved as relations with Azerbaijan stabilized and those with Russia made significant progress when on March 25 the two countries signed a 25-year agreement which allows Russia to maintain two military bases in Armenia. But no long-term settlement has yet been reached with Azerbaijan over Nagorno-Karabakh and Armenia is very conscious of the fact that its most important land communications to Russia, its principal market, pass through its two neighbours – Azerbaijan and Georgia – with neither of whom does it enjoy good relations.

Assessments

Armenia is a small country of limited resources whose main markets have either been lost or put at risk since independence while its economy has also been badly affected by the earthquake of 1988 which destroyed 10 per cent of industrial capacity and housing. These deficiencies have not been repaired because of the war with Azerbaijan. As a landlocked country three of whose neighbours – Azerbaijan, Iran and Turkey – are Muslim and potentially antagonistic, Armenia faces an immediate and longer-term future that looks at best fraught with problems.

AZERBAIJAN

Area. 33,400 sq. miles (86,600 sq. km).
Population.(1995) 7,525,000.
Capital. Baku (1,080,500).
Other major cities. Gyandzha (282,200), Sumgait (236,200), Mingechaur (90,900).
Language(s). Azeri 82 per cent, Russian 7 per cent, Armenian 5 per cent, other 6 per cent.
Religion(s). Muslim 87 per cent, Russian Orthodox 5.6 per cent, Armenian Orthodox 1.8 per cent.
Date of independence. August 30 1991 (from the USSR).
GNP. (1993) $5,428,000,000, per capita $730.
Land and climate. There is a large lowland area (much below sea level) but with the Caucasus Mountains in the north and the Karabakh Uplands in the west. It has a dry, temperate semi-arid steppe climate and is subject to drought.

Introduction

A newly independent successor state to the USSR, Azerbaijan is landlocked (although possessing an 800km coast on the Caspian Sea) and has five land neighbours: Armenia, Georgia, Iran, Russia and Turkey. Recent oil discoveries in the Caspian Sea may transform its economic situation but, oil aside, it is a relatively underdeveloped country (less developed than either of its neighbours, Armenia or Georgia) with a low per capita income, low standard of living and high unemployment. It is heavily dependent upon agriculture. During the Soviet period it was a centre for a number of heavy industries. It now faces major problems in effecting the change from a command economy to a market economy. International aid, especially for the development of the oil sector, may prove of crucial importance in the immediate future. Meanwhile, Azerbaijan faces a major and dangerous crisis and armed conflict with its neighbour, Armenia, over the Armenian-claimed enclave of Nagorno-Karabakh. The majority of the population are Muslim and a section of Azeris look to Iran with its Azeri population for possible closer ties.

Agriculture

Agriculture contributes 29.4 per cent of GDP and employs just over 1 million of the total labour force (33.4 per cent). The principal crops are cotton, grains, rice, grapes, other fruit, vegetables, tea and tobacco. Livestock includes 4,539,000 sheep and goats and 1,621,000 cattle. Food commodity exports are substantial, accounting for about 33 per cent of total exports in value. Azerbaijan also produces quantities of cannabis and opium for the drugs trade, mainly to Russia, and is in receipt of aid in the form of wheat from Turkey. Cotton is the most important agricultural product and export commodity.

Minerals

Apart from petroleum and natural gas, Azerbaijan has substantial iron ore deposits and produced 300,000mt in 1993. The oil and gas fields of the Caspian Sea have long been the principal source of mineral wealth and in 1992 crude petroleum output came to 77,698,000 barrels while natural gas output came to 7,800,000,000cu m. The Caspian field had been in decline for some years; now, however, new developments are underway. On 20 September 1994 the Azerbaijan government signed an $8bn oil investment deal with an oil consortium led by Britain's BP (with a 17 per cent stake in it). It is a 30-year production agreement. Russia is opposed to it although Lukoil, the Russian oil conglomerate, holds a 10 per cent stake in the deal. There are also five US companies participating in the consortium.

The oil reserves in the Caspian Sea are now believed to be equivalent to those of one of the Gulf oil states. These resources were not fully developed earlier because the USSR lacked experience in offshore oil drilling which is the reason for the BP-led consortium. The importance of the agreement is twofold: it will open up a large oil resource and provide Azerbaijan with Western oil technology; and it is the most attractive and clear-cut investment opportunity in this former Soviet republic for Western capital. Apart from BP, other members of the consortium include Pennzoil and Amoco from the USA and Azerbaijan's Socar Company which retains 20 per cent, although the National Oil Company of Iran, which was an original member of the consortium, was later excluded through US pressure.

Russia's claim to a major stake in the consortium is based upon the assertion that the Caspian Sea is a lake jointly owned by all the states on its shores and on October 5 1994 it informed the UN that unilateral action by a single state on the Caspian Sea was unlawful and would be resisted. The consortium deal, nonetheless, was ratified in November 1994 by the Azerbaijan parliament. It will allow the exploitation of an estimated 500 million tonnes of oil in the Caspian Sea. If development is now able to proceed it could make a substantial long-term difference to the generally troubled state of the Azerbaijan economy.

Manufacturing

As a member of the USSR, Azerbaijan (apart from its oil industry) produced oilfield equipment, steel, cement, chemicals, petrochemicals and textiles and accounted for between 1.5 and 2 per cent of the capital stake and output of the USSR. Figures for 1993 show that mining, manufacturing and public utilities combined accounted for 45.6 per cent of GDP. Since its independence in 1991, however, Azerbaijan has suffered from high inflation while industrial production has declined by more than a quarter. Most of its manufacturing exports depend upon the Russian market or those of other former Soviets and, given the state of their economies, such export markets are in doubt at the present time.

Infrastructure

There are just over 2,000km of railways (excluding industrial lines) and 36,700km of roads of which 31,800km are hard surfaced. There are 1,130km of oil pipelines, another 630km of petroleum product pipelines and 1,240km of pipelines for natural gas. The country's only port is Baku on the Caspian Sea. Only 33 of 65 airports are usable and eight of these have runways between 2,440 and 3,659m. Telecommunications are inadequate: there are approximately 644,000 domestic telephone lines while domestic and Russian television is locally available; Turkish and Iranian television is also available through an Intelstat receiver-only station.

Political considerations

Like the other successor states of the former USSR, Azerbaijan faces a difficult phase of adjustment: as it searches for new markets outside the old Soviet sphere; as it switches from a command to a market economy; and as it works out a new political direction – democracy (in some form) in place of one-party Communist control. The most pressing problem, however, concerns the conflict with Armenia over Nagorno-Karabakh; in 1994 this absorbed 25 per cent of the country's resources and has created many thousands of refugees. Until the dispute is settled on a long-term basis Azerbaijan is unlikely to be able to attract the foreign investment it needs to push forward its development. Both Turkey and Iran of its southern neighbours are showing substantial interest in becoming politically involved in the affairs of Azerbaijan: partly in response to the fact that Azerbaijan is, overwhelmingly, a Muslim country; partly for ethnic reasons, since the Azeris of Azerbaijan have close links with the Azeris of Iran; and finally, because these two powers (Turkey and Iran) are vying for influence in the region.

Assessments

Azerbaijan will never be a rich economy but it could be a reasonably self-sustaining one if, first, it can overcome the conflict relating to Nagorno-Karabakh and then rebuild its shattered economy and infrastructure; and, second, if the exploitation of its oil and gas resources in the Caspian Sea (with international investment from the oil consortium) is allowed to proceed unhindered to provide the economic means for wider industrial development.

BANGLADESH

Area. 57,295 sq. miles (148,393 sq. km).
Population. (1995) 120,093,000.
Capital. Dhaka (6,105,160, 1991).
Other major cities. Chittagong (2,040,663), Khulna (877,388), Rajshahi (517,136).
Language(s). Bengali, English.
Religion(s). Muslim 86.8 per cent, Hindu 11.9 per cent, other 1.3 per cent.
Date of independence. December 16 1971 (from Pakistan).
GNP. (1993) $25,882,000,000, per capita $220.
Land and climate. Bangladesh has a tropical monsoon climate of cool dry winters and hot humid summers. Most of the land is a flat alluvial plain, much of it forming

the delta of the Ganges–Brahmaputra rivers. In the east are the Chittagong hills, mainly jungle covered.

Introduction

Carved out of British India in 1947 to form the eastern half of Muslim Pakistan, Bangladesh was born out of the war of 1971 when, with massive Indian assistance, it broke away from West Pakistan (the dominant half of the state) to become the independent state of Bangladesh. Situated at the head of the Bay of Bengal with a 580km coastline, it is otherwise almost entirely surrounded by India except for a small border with Myanmar (Burma). Possessing only a small land area in relation to its huge population, Bangladesh is one of the most densely populated countries in the world with more than 775 persons to the square kilometre. The country has few resources apart from its people and is subject to annual flooding during the monsoon season (sometimes on a devastating scale) and otherwise suffers from droughts and deforestation.

Agriculture

Agriculture accounts for about 30 per cent of GDP and employs 65 per cent of the labour force. The economy as a whole is overwhelmingly dependent upon the agricultural sector and Bangladesh is the world's foremost producer of jute which in 1993–4 accounted for 10 per cent of all exports. Rice is the principal crop and a total of 27,537,000 tonnes was produced in 1994. Other main crops are wheat, tea, sugarcane, followed by potatoes, beef, milk and poultry. The fish catch is substantial and came to 1,047,170 tonnes in 1993. Livestock includes a national cattle herd of 24,130,000 and 28,000,000 goats. Special emphasis is now placed upon increasing the production of wheat which is both cheaper to produce and more nutritious as a staple than rice. Wheat output in 1993 came to 1,131,000 tonnes. Sugarcane is a major export and production is in excess of 7,000,000 tonnes a year. In addition to jute and jute products, Bangladesh also exports fish and prawns, hides, skins and leather and tea. It is obliged to import approximately 10 per cent of its food grains.

Although the soil is rich and Bangladesh came close to achieving food self-sufficiency in the 1980s and production of food grains is steadily rising, the aim of self-sufficiency is constantly deferred because of the huge annual increase in population. Jute, the principal crop for export, has faced a series of crises – poor quality crops, constant climatic variations, milling problems and fluctuations in world demand. Some 33 million or more members of the workforce are engaged in agriculture.

Minerals

Apart from modest quantities of natural gas which, so far, have not been properly exploited, Bangladesh has almost no minerals. Its sources of power are also insufficient so that it has to import coal from India. Marine salt and industrial limestone are the only exploited minerals. In 1993 it produced 5,960,000,000cu m of natural gas. There are hopes of offshore oil finds.

Manufacturing

The manufacturing sector, including mining, accounts for 9.7 per cent of GDP (1993) and employs 11.6 per cent of the labour force. Most industries are related to jute or cotton textiles (ready-made garments account for 60.2 per cent of exports) and food processing. There are also steel and fertilizer industries.

Infrastructure

There are 2,892km of railways which divide between 1.000m gauge (1,914km) and 1.676m gauge (978km); there are 7,240km of highways of which half (3,840km) are paved. Bangladesh has over 5,000km of inland waterways, half of which are main cargo routes. There are 1,220km of gas pipelines. Of sixteen airports, twelve are currently usable and four have runways of between 2,440 and 3,659m. Telecommunications both internal and international are adequate.

Political considerations

A politically volatile society (its first two presidents were assassinated), subject to considerable political violence, Bangladesh, nonetheless, is a democracy whose principal problem is the level of its poverty which is exacerbated by the rate of population increase. Beset by hunger, disease and overpopulation it is also subject to constant natural disasters in the form of cyclones and floods. A Muslim country, Bangladesh pursues a non-aligned stance in international politics and remains one of the poorest states in the world. The government establishes an annual import policy and more than 350 items are prohibited imports either for religious reasons or to safeguard home industries.

Assessments

Although in 1993, for example, Bangladesh almost produced enough grain to meet its total requirements and thus food self-sufficiency, the constant battle is always to meet the needs of a rapidly expanding population. The 1993 population of 115 million is expected to reach 132 million in the year 2000 and 161 million in 2010 so that food self-sufficiency at a level which would provide a reasonable standard of living appears unlikely. It is and will remain into the indefinite future one of the poorest countries in the world. Bangladesh is heavily dependent upon inputs of international aid.

BENIN

Area. 43,500 sq. miles (112,680 sq. km).
Population. (1995) 5,409,000.
Capital. Porto-Novo (177,660).
Other major cities. Cotonou (533,212), Djougou (132,192), Abomey-Calavi (125,565), Parakou (106,708).
Language(s). French (official), Fon, Yoruba and other tribal languages.
Religion(s). Traditional beliefs 62 per cent, Roman Catholic 21 per cent, Protestant 2.3 per cent, Muslim 12 per cent, other 2.7 per cent.
Date of independence. August 1 1960.
GNP. (1993) $2,182,000,000, per capita $420.
Land and climate. A flat, undulating country with some hills and low mountains. The climate is tropical, hot and humid in the south, semi-arid in the north which is affected by the dusty harmattan wind. Both deforestation and desertification are taking place.

Introduction

A small wedge-shaped country on the west coast of Africa with a short coastline on the Bight of Benin and sharing boundaries with Togo, Burkina Faso, Niger and Nigeria, Benin is one of Africa's poorest countries and is mainly dependent upon agriculture. It has experienced a volatile political life since independence but returned to multiparty politics in the 1980s. Apart from the official economy, much economic life in fact depends upon the unofficial subsistence sector which includes large-scale cross-border trade with Nigeria. There is only a small mineral sector.

Agriculture

Agriculture contributes about 33 per cent of GDP and employs 60 per cent of the labour force. The principal export crop is cotton which accounts for about 25 per cent of all exports. Other commodity crops include cocoa, coffee, palm kernel oil, palm oil and fruits. The principal staple foods are yams, cassava, maize, millet and sorghum. About 12 per cent of the land is arable and 4 per cent under permanent crops. There is a national cattle herd of 1 million head and similar numbers of sheep and goats. Benin is not food self-sufficient and approximately 20 per cent of imports are foodstuffs, and 10 per cent of this consists of grains.

Minerals

Although a number of minerals are present in small quantities – phosphates, chromium, iron ore, rutile, limestone, marble, gold and petroleum – only the offshore petroleum (and associated natural gas), limestone, marble and small quantities of gold have been exploited. The phosphates, chromium, iron ore and rutile are all located in the north of the country. Offshore oil (near Cotonou) was first produced from two wells in 1982. By 1985 production had reached 10,000b/d. Several international oil companies – from Norway, Switzerland, the USA (with financial backing from the IDA amd EIB) – have been involved in the development of this oil but by the early 1990s a number of plans had been abandoned and the outlook (against poor world demand) for anything other than small-scale development remains gloomy. Output of crude oil in 1993 was negligible and there was no natural gas production. At best, on present showing, Benin's future mineral output will do no more than contribute to a marginally more prosperous economy. The manufacturing sector is minuscule.

Infrastructure

There are 578km of 1.000m gauge single track railway, and 5,050km of roads of which 920km are paved. Cotonou is the country's port. There are five usable airports, one of which has a permanent runway of between 2,439 and 3,659m. There is a fair system of telecommunications.

Political considerations

Benin, formerly Dahomey, had a troubled political history in the years following independence in 1960: this included a number of coups and the establishment of a one-party state as well as a sharp move to the political left. However, at the end of the 1980s the country reverted to multipartyism and held elections in April 1990 when the Benin People's Revolutionary Party was replaced by the Union of Forces of Progress. In the following year (1991) President Mathieu Kerekou was defeated in free elections and replaced by Nicephore Soglo.

Assessments

Benin is heavily dependent upon aid to balance its recurring trade deficit. Its principal long-term problem is poverty which is exacerbated by a rapid population increase (the estimated doubling time is only 21 years). Unless major mineral discoveries are made, the economy will only just suffice to maintain equilibrium with development needs that will also require aid to be effective.

BOLIVIA

Area. 424,164 sq. miles (1,098,581 sq. km).
Population. (1995) 7,414,000.
Capitals. La Paz (administrative) (711,036, 1992), Sucre (judicial) (130,952).
Other major cities. Santa Cruz (694,616), El Alto (404,367), Cochabamba (404,102), Oruro (183,194), Potosí (112,291).

Language(s). Spanish, Aymara, Quechua.
Religion(s). Roman Catholic (95 per cent).
Date of independence. August 6 1825 (from Spain).
GNP. (1993) $5,472,000,000, per capita $770.
Land and climate. Set in the high Andes, much of Bolivia rises to 10,000ft or more above sea level. The western high Cordillera range that marks the boundary with Chile has many peaks of 5,500m or more while the central plain or altiplano (enclosed by high mountains) also lies between 3,660m and 3,800m in height and contains Lake Titicaca (shared with Peru). To the west lowland plains merge into the Amazon region. The climate varies between humid and tropical to cold and semi-arid depending upon altitude.

Introduction

One of South America's only two landlocked countries, Bolivia has nearly 7,000km of borders with five neighbours – Brazil, Paraguay, Argentina, Chile and Peru. A large country of rugged mountains and harsh terrain, it is one of the poorest in Latin America. The economy is largely based upon mineral extraction and its two principal exports are zinc and natural gas, followed by tin. With the dubious record, up to 1980, of sustaining 190 coups over 155 years of history since independence in 1825, Bolivia has had an uneasy political record of alternating military and civilian rule although it has enjoyed civilian rule since the early 1980s. It is much less developed economically than its neighbours. Argentina is Bolivia's principal trading partner. Bolivia is a leading (illegal) producer of coca and with Peru and Colombia is the main source of cocaine in South America (and the world).

Agriculture

Agriculture accounts for 17 per cent of GDP and employs 39 per cent of the workforce. Sugarcane, potatoes, bananas and plantains are the main crops, followed by maize, cassava, soybeans. Rice, oranges, tangerines and wheat are also important. The national cattle herd is 6,000,000 strong; there are 7,789,000 sheep and 1,517,000 goats. Just over 51 per cent of the land is forested and roundwood is an important product; meadows and pastures account for 24.5 per cent of the land while agricultural land under cultivation accounts for 2.1 per cent. Bolivia is food self-sufficient (during the 1960s and 1970s food production increased faster than population growth). Export commodities include coffee, cotton, sugar and timber.

Bolivia is also the world's second largest producer of coca (from which cocaine is derived) after Peru with approximately 47,900ha under coca cultivation. Despite voluntary and forced programmes of eradication, output between 1989 and 1992 rose from 74,700mt to 82,000mt. Cocaine is exported through Colombia and Brazil to the USA and other markets. Coca is the main crop for half the country's farmers and the drug industry accounts for an estimated 15 per cent of revenues.

Minerals

Following the defeat of the Inca Empire by Pizarro and the discovery of silver in 1545, Bolivia's wealth was built upon this precious metal and silver production did not peak until the late nineteenth century. Bolivia then became the world's second largest producer of tin (after Malaya) although in recent years it has dropped to fourth place behind Indonesia and Thailand.

Mining now accounts for 7.7 per cent of GDP and employs 2 per cent of the workforce. Most mining is found in the high Andes region although oil and natural gas are found in the area round Santa Cruz and further south. Principal mineral output in 1993 consisted of zinc (122,640mt), lead (21,240mt), tin (18,624mt); other minerals include antimony, silver and gold. Bolivia now ranks twelfth in world terms as a producer of silver with an output of 46,344 kg in 1993.

Crude oil production is currently running at 8m barrels a year (1992) (enough to meet domestic requirements) while natural gas production is in the region of 3 billion cu m pa, although this is only equivalent to 0.1 per cent of world output. There are substantial reserves of natural gas. The principal mineral exports (1993) are zinc 15.8 per cent, natural gas 12 per cent, tin 11.1 per cent, gold 10.1 per cent. Other minerals include tungsten and copper. Bolivia is a member of the International Tin Council and the Association of Tin Producing Countries.

Manufacturing

Constraints upon the manufacturing sector include the small population and size of the home market, poverty and limited export markets since Bolivia's neighbours are more economically advanced and enjoy larger markets and higher living standards. The manufacturing sector accounts for 16 per cent of GDP and employs 8 to 9 per cent of the workforce. Apart from mining-related activities, smelting and refining, the principal manufacturing enterprises are concerned with food and beverages, tobacco, handicrafts and clothing.

Infrastructure

There are 3,684km of narrow gauge railways (government owned) and 38,836km of roads of which only 1,300km are paved. There are 10,000km of commercially navigable waterways and 1,800km of pipelines for crude oil, 580km for petroleum products and 1,495km for natural gas. Maritime outlets are in Chile (Arica and Antofagasta) and Peru (Matarani and Ilo). There are 1,225 airports of which just over 1,000 are usable and nine have runways over 3,659m in length. Telecommunications are fair and the microwave radio relay system is being expanded.

Political considerations

Bolivia has a long political history of coups and alternating military and civilian rule as well as left–right revolutionary movements. It returned to multiparty rule in the

1980s. Bolivia's landlocked position and poverty are principal constraints upon development; the population is expected to reach 12,700,000 in 2010 and the doubling time is only 24 years. The important role that coca (cocaine) plays in the economy could well prove a destabilizing factor in the future, depending especially upon US anti-drug policies but also according to relations with outlet countries (Brazil and Colombia). Bolivia has considered joining the Mercosur group of countries, Argentina, Brazil, Paraguay and Uruguay (especially as Argentina is its leading trading partner), although the group is wary of Bolivian membership. All imports require import control forms although import licences are only needed for a few goods.

Assessments

Short of major new discoveries, Bolivia possesses sufficient minerals to provide it with the means for modest if slow development alongside its agricultural self-sufficiency. Apart from tin and natural gas, it is a small-scale mineral producer in world terms. Its substantial (hidden) dependence upon coca and cocaine exports could backfire in the future if there are changes in US and world approaches to the international drugs trade.

BOTSWANA

Area. 224,607 sq. miles (581,730 sq. km).
Population. (1995) 1,549,000.
Capital. Gaborone (133,791).
Other major cities. Francistown (65,026), Selebi-Pikwe (39,769), Molepolole (36,928), Kanye (31,341).
Language(s). English (official), Setswana.
Religion(s). Indigenous beliefs 50 per cent, Christian 50 per cent.
Date of independence. September 30 1966 (from Britain).
GNP. (1993) $3,631,000,000, per capita $2,590.
Land and climate. A flat or gently rolling tableland which is characterized by underground rivers and salt flats; much of it in the southwest consists of the Kalahari Desert. The climate is semi-arid with warm winters and hot summers.

Introduction

Landlocked in central–southern Africa, Botswana has four neighbours – Zambia, Zimbabwe, South Africa and Namibia. One of Africa's poorest countries at independence in 1966 when the economy effectively depended upon the national cattle herd, the situation was transformed by the discovery of diamonds and copper which by the 1980s were providing Botswana with one of the highest per capita incomes on the continent and a currency (the pula) stronger than the rand of neighbouring South Africa. Much of the land is arid, desert (the Kalahari) or semi-desert and, apart from cattle, Botswana is never likely to be food self-sufficient. A large country in relation to its small population, Botswana has remained politically one of the most stable countries on the continent ever since independence.

Agriculture

Agriculture accounts for just over 5 per cent of GDP although with cattle herding it provides a livelihood for 22 per cent of the population. Most Batswana are subsistence farmers and a majority owns a small number of cattle only while a tiny minority of wealthy farmers controls huge herds. Botswana produces about 20 per cent of its total food requirements while the rest has to be imported and food and beverages account for about 8 per cent of all imports. Beef accounts for about 3.5 per cent of all exports and with Zimbabwe Botswana is one of the only two African countries that has a regular quota agreement to sell beef to the European Community; the majority of its beef goes to Europe, the balance to South Africa. About 19 per cent of the land is forested, meadows and pastures (often sparse) account for another 58.2 per cent of the land while only 2.5 per cent is under permanent cultivation. There are serious risks of desertification as more land is brought into pasture for the growing cattle herd which stands at 2.8 million head. Botswana is never likely to be food self-sufficient.

Minerals

Botswana was only found to be a storehouse of minerals after independence. The east of the country has been well mapped geologically but in the west the overlying Kalahari sands hinder geological exploration although the area is believed to be rich in minerals. There are abundant reserves of diamonds, coal, copper-nickel, soda ash, potash, sodium sulphate, salt, plutonium, some gold and silver, and a number of other industrial minerals.

Diamonds now account for 78.8 per cent of exports (1992). The Orapa mine went into production in 1971 to be followed in 1977 by the Letlhakane pipe and then the Jwaneng mine in 1982. Diamond mining is controlled by the De Beers Botswana Co (Debswana), a venture jointly owned by the government of Botswana and De Beers Consolidated Mines of South Africa. Botswana is now the world's third producer of diamonds (in volume) and the first in value. In 1990 output reached 16 million carats. There are large reserves in the existing pipes and more may be discovered.

Copper-nickel matte accounts for 7.2 per cent of exports. Other minerals currently being exploited include coal with 17,000m tons of reserves though, so far, production at Moropule has been limited to about 500,000 tons a year for power generation purposes. The exploitation of Botswana's large deposits of soda ash got under-way in the second half of the 1980s when Africa Explosives and Chemicals Industries (AECI) of South Africa began talks with the Botswana government and BP (which then had the option to develop) and modest production began in 1991 at a rate of 62,000 tons a year. Small-scale gold mining has been carried out in Botswana for many years.

The strength of the Botswana economy rests on its range of minerals, led by diamonds; there is every indication that extensive new finds will be made once it becomes a viable proposition to explore the Kalahari region. At present diamonds, copper-nickel, coal, salt, soda ash, potash are being actively exploited. There are a number of uranium traces.

Manufacturing

Botswana depends for 90 per cent of its manufactures upon imports from South Africa; the manufacturing sector is very small, contributing only 8.5 per cent of GDP and employing only 6 per cent of the labour force. The country does, however, possess substantial tourist potential at the upper end of the market with the attractions of its game parks and, in particular, the huge but remote Okavango delta area.

Infrastructure

The principal transport route consists of the 712km stretch of 1.067m gauge railroad along the eastern border of the country that connects Botswana with Zimbabwe in the northeast and South Africa, through to the Cape, in the south. There are 11,514km of roads of which only 1,600km are paved. There are 87 usable airports (out of 100), eight with permanent surface runways and one with a runway of between 2,440 and 3,659m length. Telecommunications are fair and there are 26,000 telephones.

Political considerations

Since independence in 1966 Botswana has remained one of the most stable countries in Africa, retaining its multiparty system without change. Between 1966 and 1990 its delicately poised relationship with apartheid South Africa was always the first priority and it was more than once subjected to South African destabilizing tactics including cross-border raids. Following the end of apartheid and the all-race elections of April 1994 in South Africa, the problem has changed its nature. Now Botswana's chief concern is not to allow its small but strong economy to be submerged in that of its giant neighbour. At home the chief problems are two: unemployment which is added to every year by more school-leavers coming on to the market than there are jobs to match; and the need to prevent the development of a two-tier society of wage earners in the towns and mining sector whose standard of living gets further away from the subsistence farmers of the rural areas. Botswana is an open economy which welcomes investment. It is a member of the Southern African Customs Union (SACU) with South Africa, Lesotho, Namibia and Swaziland; it is also a member of the Southern African Development Community (SADC), the former SADCC. Its principal trading partners are SACU and the EC.

Assessments

The long-term mineral wealth of Botswana has yet to be fully established but its known mineral resources, especially diamonds and coal, are very great and it possesses a wide range of other minerals as well. Its economic potential, based upon minerals, is clearly substantial. However, now that apartheid is ended, Botswana is likely to become part of a greater South Africa-dominated regional market or economic system. The possibility of constructing a railway east to west across the country from Francistown to Gobabis in Namibia so as to link the two systems has long been considered: this would enable both countries to open up on their respective western and eastern borders what is believed to be a major region of untapped mineral wealth.

BURKINA FASO

Area. 105,946 sq. miles (274,400 sq. km).
Population. (1995) 10,324,000.
Capital. Ouagadougou (441,514, 1985).
Other major cities. Bobo-Dioulasso (228,668), Kondougou (51,926).
Language(s). French (official), Sudanic tribal languages.
Religion(s). Traditional beliefs 44.8 per cent, Muslim 43 per cent, Christian 12.2 per cent.
Date of independence. August 5 1960 (from France).
GNP. (1993) $2,928,000,000, per capita $300.
Land and climate. It is mainly a land of flat, undulating plains with some hills in the west and southeast; the climate is tropical with warm dry winters and hot wet summers. It is subject to drought, desertification and deforestation.

Introduction

One of the poorest countries of both Africa and the world, Burkina Faso is landlocked between six West African neighbours – Benin, Ghana, Côte d'Ivoire, Mali, Niger and Togo. Lacking resources and over-populated in relation to its land, it is basically a subsistence economy.

Agriculture

Agriculture accounts for 34 per cent of GDP and employs 84 per cent of the labour force. It is basically a subsistence economy whose principal staples are sorghum, millet and maize while cotton, groundnuts, shea nuts and sesame are the major export crops, of which cotton is the most important. In 1994 there was a harvest of 171,000 tonnes of seed cotton while raw cotton accounted for 23.8 per cent of exports. The national cattle herd is just over 4 million strong with hides and skins accounting for 5.4 per cent of exports and live animals for a further 4.1 per cent.

Forestry provides the third source of exports in the form of roundwood. Land use is divided between forested 23.9 per cent, meadows and pastures 36.5 per cent, agriculture and permanent cultivation 13 per cent, other 26.6 per cent. It is not self-sufficient in grains.

Minerals

There is a number of minerals present including zinc, silver, manganese, gold and antimony. The quantities are small and so far little exploitation has occurred. International interest in the country's minerals is modified by the fact that Burkina is landlocked and has inadequate infrastructure so that exploitation must wait for a better world economic climate. Mineral output (1988) consisted of manganese (15,000mt), phosphates (3,000mt) and gold (3,049 kg) although there is also a substantial illicit gold trade.

Manufacturing

Manufacturing contributes 15.1 per cent of GDP and consists mainly of flour milling, soap and cotton yarn, bicycle and motorcycle tyres, footwear and food products. Manufactures account for 23 per cent of exports.

Infrastructure

There are 620km of narrow gauge single track railway of which 520km consists of the line from Ouagoudou to the Côte d'Ivoire border. There are 16,500km of roads of which 1,300km are paved. There are 38 usable airports, two with permanent surface runways of 2,440 to 3,659m in length. Telecommunications are adequate but little more.

Political considerations

After suffering five coups and military takeovers since independence, Burkina Faso returned to multipartyism in 1991; there was a big increase in international aid in 1993 in recognition of the government's acceptance of a structural adjustment programme (SAP) and return to Western-style economic orthodoxy.

Assessments

Essentially a poor landlocked backwater, in good world economic conditions Burkina Faso might expect to attract some investment for mineral development.

BURUNDI

Area. 10,740 sq. miles (27,816 sq. km).
Population. (1995) 5,936,000.
Capital. Bujumbura (236,334, 1990).
Other major cities. Gitega (20,708).
Language(s). Rundi and French (official), Swahili.
Religion(s). Roman Catholic 65.1 per cent, non-religious 18.6 per cent, Protestant 13.8 per cent, Muslim 1.6 per cent, other 0.9 per cent.
Date of independence. July 1 1962 (from Belgium – as a UN Trusteeship territory).
GNP. (1993) $1,102,000,000, per capita $180.
Land and climate. The country consists mainly of rolling hills and highlands with some plains. The climate is temperate and warm though frost may occur in the highlands.

Introduction

This tiny landlocked country in the centre of Africa lies between Zaire to the west and Tanzania to the east with Rwanda to its north. It is essentially a one-crop economy dependent upon its coffee exports for survival. Politically, it suffers from recurring violence between its historically dominant Tutsi minority and its Hutu majority.

Agriculture

Agriculture accounts for 48.5 per cent of GDP and employs 93 per cent of the workforce. Land use is divided between agricultural and under permanent cultivation 52.2 per cent (one of the highest ratios in Africa or anywhere else), forested 2.6 per cent, meadows and pastures 35.6 per cent, other 9.6 per cent. Coffee is the main crop accounting, on average, for 80 per cent of all exports although this varies according to weather conditions in any one year and overall world demand. Coffee production in 1993 came to 33,000 tonnes and accounted for 76 per cent of exports. Other export crops are tea, animal hides and skins and cotton or cotton fabric. The vast majority of the people are subsistence farmers and the country is just about food self-sufficient. The main long-term problem concerns the relationship of land to population: there is virtually no further available agricultural land, the population at 592.5 persons to the square kilometre is one of the densest in Africa and the doubling time for this population is only 22 years.

Minerals

There are small quantities of a few minerals but these make little contribution to the economy as a whole. Those present include kaolin, lime and gold.

Manufacturing

The manufacturing sector accounts for 12 per cent of GDP but only employs 1.2 per cent of the workforce. Manufactures consist largely of light consumer goods, the assembly of imports, construction and food processing.

Infrastructure

There are 5,900km of highways of which only 400km are paved. Burundi has a substantial coastline on Lake Tanganyika and the port of Bujumbura connects with the transport systems of Zaire and Tanzania. There are four usable airports, one with a runway between 2,440 and 3,659m in length. The telecommunications system is small scale; there is no railway system.

Political considerations

Ever since independence, whether under civilian or military rule, Burundi has lain under the threat of recurring ethnic violence between the Tutsi minority (long in a position of political dominance) and the Hutu majority. Following the disastrous ethnic explosion in neighbouring Rwanda in 1994, the position in Burundi at best appeared thereafter to be exceptionally delicately balanced.

Assessments

At best Burundi will just about survive economically, provided its earnings from coffee are supplemented by international aid. There appears little prospect that it can ever be much more than a precarious subsistence economy.

CAMBODIA

Area. 70,238 sq. miles (181,916 sq. km).
Population. (1995) 9,610,000.
Capital. Phnom Penh (900,000).
Other major cities. Batdambang (45,000), Kampong Cham (33,000).
Language(s). Khmer (official), French.
Religion(s). Buddhist 88.4 per cent, Muslim 2.4 per cent, other 9.2 per cent.
Date of independence. November 9 1953 (from France).
GNP. (1993) $1,580,000,000, per capita $170.
Land and climate. Cambodia consists mainly of low flat plains with mountains in the southwest and north. It has a tropical climate with a rainy monsoon season from May to October and a dry season from December to March with little variation in temperature.

Introduction

A medium-small country in southeast Asia, Cambodia has borders with three neighbours – Laos, Thailand and Vietnam – and a 443km coastline on the Gulf of Thailand. The country has experienced a deeply troubled political history since independence from France in 1953, suffering a civil war, the depredations of the Pol Pot regime which may have been responsible for as many as 3 million deaths, a Vietnam invasion and occupation and more recently, following the Vietnamese withdrawal in 1989, a UN peacekeeping force to supervise a ceasefire while a National Council prepared for elections. King Norodom Sihanouk, one of the world's longest-lasting statesmen, emerged as the leader under these UN arrangements in 1993.

One of the poorest countries in the world whose poverty has been relentlessly exacerbated by continuous violence, war and political uncertainty, Cambodia nonetheless switched to a market economy in 1990 when Soviet aid came to an end. These changes placed further strains upon an already weak economy.

Agriculture

It is a rural economy with 90 per cent of the population directly or indirectly dependent upon agriculture. Rice, sugarcane, bananas, roots and tubers, maize and rubber are the main crops. Agriculture contributes approximately 51 per cent of GDP. Rubber, rice, pepper and roundwood are the main exports. Cambodia is not self-sufficient in food. Land use is divided between forested 75.8 per cent, meadows and pastures 3.3 per cent, agricultural land under permanent cultivation 17.4 per cent, other 3.5 per cent. Development of logging could provide another major source of exports.

Minerals

Minerals only account for a tiny proportion of GDP and consist of fertilizer (phosphates) and salt, although extensive illegal smuggling of gemstones takes place from Khmer Rouge controlled areas on the Thai border. Unless major new mineral discoveries are made there is unlikely to be any international interest in mining in Cambodia. The manufacturing sector is small scale and poorly developed.

Infrastructure

There are 612km of narrow gauge railway (government owned), 13,151km of roads of which 2,622km are paved, and 3,700km of inland waterways. Of nine usable airports five have permanent surface runways and of these two are between 2,440 and 3,659m in length. Telecommunications are just about adequate to service government but not the general public.

Political considerations

After many years of civil strife Cambodia returned to a semblance of ordered government under UN auspices during 1993–4. But the Khmer Rouge still exercise strong influence in parts of the country and their announcement in November 1994 of the execution of three Western tourists taken hostage did nothing to reassure foreigners. King Norodom Sihanouk warned foreigners (November 2 1994) to avoid Cambodia as a country that was 'clearly insecure'.

Assessments

Cambodia is an extremely poor country that looks likely to remain politically volatile and dangerous to foreigners into the foreseeable future.

CAMEROON

Area. 183,569 sq. miles (475,442 sq. km).
Population. (1995) 13,233,000.
Capital. Yaoundé (649,000).
Other major cities. Douala (810,000), Garoua (142,000), Maroua (123,000).
Language(s). French and English (official), 24 major African languages.
Religion(s). Roman Catholic 34.7 per cent, Animist 26 per cent, Muslim 21.8 per cent, Protestant 17.5 per cent.
Date of independence. January 1 1960 (from France but as a UN Trusteeship territory).
GNP. (1995) $9,663,000,000, per capita $770.
Land and climate. A broken, diverse landscape which includes a coastal plain, a dissected central plateau, mountains in the west and further plains in the north. The climate varies from tropical on the coast to hot and semi-arid in the north.

Introduction

Owing to its division for administrative purposes between Britain and France under the League of Nations system of mandates after World War I, Cameroon is the only bilingual (English and French) country in Africa. Situated at the hinge of West Africa with a coastline on the North Atlantic between Nigeria and Equatorial Guinea, Cameroon has six land neighbours – Central African Republic, Chad, Congo, Equatorial Guinea, Gabon and Nigeria – and a coastline of 402km. The discovery and development of offshore oil in the years 1970 to 1985 raised the GNP per capita of Cameroon to place it among the middle-income developing countries. Cameroon possesses one of the more diversified economies of Africa and produces a range of cash crops for export. The manufacturing sector is principally concerned with processing raw materials including imports such as bauxite from Guinea.

Agriculture

Agriculture contributes 23.9 per cent to GDP and engages 74 per cent of the labour force. The main export crops are coffee, cocoa, cotton, and wood and in 1993 these accounted for 39 per cent of all exports. Other export crops are rubber, bananas, oilseed, grains, livestock and root starches. The principal staple food crops are cassava, plantains, vegetables, maize, yams, rice, millet and palm kernels. The national cattle herd stands at 4,867,000 while there are approximately 3.75 million sheep and a similar number of goats. Cameroon is self-sufficient in staple foods. Land use is divided between forested 52.3 per cent, meadows and pastures 17.8 per cent, agricultural land under permanent cultivation 15.1 per cent, other 14.8 per cent.

Minerals

Though only a minor producer, exports of oil from Cameroon accounted for 29.3 per cent of exports in 1993–4; total oil production in 1992 came to 50,565,000 barrels. Oil production began in 1977 and output reached a high point of 9.16m tons in 1985. Output then declined to 7.8m tons in 1990. Exploration in the 1990s has been minimal (due to low world prices) and at present total known reserves which stood at 57.2m tons in 1988 are expected to be depleted during the 1990s. There are reserves of natural gas offshore but so far plans to exploit these have come to nothing due to world over-production and costs. Other major mineral resources include some 1,100m tons of bauxite (as yet untouched), for the Edea smelter only refines bauxite from Guinea. There are significant deposits of iron ore and some 10,000 tons of uranium, both at present unexploited. Mineral production in 1992 included marble, pozzolona, aluminium, limestone and tin ore. Mining contributes 12.9 per cent of GDP but only employs a tiny proportion of the labour force – less than 1 per cent.

Manufacturing

Manufacturing accounts for 13.5 per cent of GDP and employs 4.5 per cent of the labour force. It is principally concerned with food processing, clothing, footwear, import substitution or the processing of Cameroon's raw materials. The country has abundant hydro-electric power and potential.

Infrastructure

There are only 1,000km of railway of which 858km are narrow gauge although the development of the Transcam railway towards the north has opened up new mining possibilities. There are 65,000km of roads of which 2,682km are paved. There are just over 2,000km of inland waterways although their importance is declining. Douala is the main port. There are 51 usable airports, eleven with permanent runways of which six are between 2,440 and 3,659m in length. There is a good general system of telecommunications but only two telephones per one thousand of the population.

Political considerations

Pressures upon the government to become more democratic led to the legalization of opposition parties in 1990 but growing discontent, exacerbated by a declining economy and strikes organized by opposition parties through 1991, heralded a generally troubled start to the 1990s. Even so, Cameroon has maintained one of the more stable political systems of Africa since independence. In 1995 Cameroon's application to join the Commonwealth was accepted.

Assessments

Cameroon is food self-sufficient and a substantial exporter of food commodities as well. Present oil reserves will not last much longer although other reserves may well be discovered. There is unlikely to be much exploration for minerals, however, until the country has a better infrastructure and world economic conditions also improve.

CENTRAL AFRICAN REPUBLIC

Area. 240,324 sq. miles (622,436 sq. km).
Population. (1995) 3,141,000.
Capital. Bangui (451,690).
Other major cities. Berberati (41,891), Bouar (39,676), Bambari (38,633), Bossan-goa (31,502), Carnot (31,324).
Language(s). French (official), Sango, Arabic, Hausa, Swahili.
Religion(s). Protestant 40 per cent, Roman Catholic 28 per cent, traditional 24 per cent, Muslim 8 per cent.
Date of independence. August 13 1960 (from France).
GNP. (1993) $1,267,000,000, per capita $390.
Land and climate. The greater part of the country consists of a vast flat to rolling plain though the landscape is broken by scattered hills in the northeast and southwest. The climate is tropical with hot dry winters and mild to hot wet summers.

Introduction

The most isolated of all Africa's landlocked states, situated very nearly in the exact geographic centre of the continent, the Central African Republic (CAR) is a poor, underpopulated country, mainly dependent upon subsistence agriculture. Its land neighbours are Cameroon, Chad, Congo, Sudan and Zaire and total borders come to 5,203km. Much of the value to the state of its most important mineral resource, diamonds, is lost due to smuggling across the border into Congo. Huge distances by river and rail or road across neighbouring states have to be covered in order for the CAR to gain access to the sea. Heavy dependence upon France for economic aid and the presence in the CAR of a French military base have affected most political decisions since independence.

Agriculture

Agriculture accounts for 53.4 per cent of GDP and employs 80 per cent of the workforce. Including forestry, the sector accounts for about 40 per cent of exports: the principal ones are timber, cotton, tobacco and coffee. The main staples are cassava, yams, bananas, plantains, maize, groundnuts, oranges, pulses, sorghum and rice. The national cattle herd is just under 3 million strong. The CAR is self-sufficient in food except for grains. Land use is divided between 57.4 per cent forested, meadows and pastures account for 4.8 per cent, agricultural land under permanent cultivation 3.2 per cent, and other 34.6 per cent.

Minerals

Mining accounts for 5.8 per cent of GDP and only employs 1.1 per cent of the labour force. Diamonds are the principal (and most valuable) mineral and output in 1994 came to 532,000 carats although a similar quantity is also believed to be smuggled out of the country annually. Diamonds contribute more than 50 per cent of export earnings. Relatively small quantities of gold are also mined. There are an estimated 20,000 tons of uranium resources although these are not at present being exploited.

Manufacturing

The manufacturing sector is small and underdeveloped, accounting for only 7 per cent of GDP and employing only 1.6 per cent of the labour force. It is mainly concerned with processing agricultural products, sawmills, and light industries – breweries, textiles, footwear, the assembly of bicycles and motorcycles.

Infrastructure

The CAR suffers from its remote landlocked position and the long distances that have to be traversed to the Atlantic port of Pointe-Noire (Congo) which is its principal outlet. This route involves 1,800km by river from Bangui to Brazzaville and then a further rail journey from Brazzaville to Pointe Noire. Although the CAR section of the Lagos to Mombasa Trans-Africa Highway was completed in 1984 this in fact has not made much diffference to speed or ease of transport for much of the rest of the highway is still to be completed. There are 22,000km of highways altogether although only 458km are paved. The Oubangui is the principal inland waterway and the country's most important trade route. There are 51 usable airports, three with permanent runways two of which are 2,440 to 3,659m in length. The telecommunications system is poor.

Political considerations

The CAR remains heavily dependent upon France, which maintains an important military base in the country. Over the years since independence political changes, brought about by coups, have been assisted (on one occasion overtly) by French intervention. In August 1993 the military leader, President André Kolingba, was defeated at the polls and the CAR returned to multiparty politics with Ange-Felix Patasse as president.

Assessments

Slow development and continuing poverty are set to continue until the CAR has a far better infrastructure to allow quicker and easier contact with the outside world. Only if major new mineral resources are discovered is this likely to occur.

CHAD

Area. 495,795 sq. miles (1,284,000 sq. km).
Population. (1995) 6,361,000.
Capital. N'djaména (529,555).
Other major cities. Moundou (281,477), Sarh (198,113), Abéché (187,757).
Language(s). Arabic and French (official), Sarn (south), Sango (south) and over 100 languages and dialects.
Religion(s). Muslim 40.4 per cent, Christian 33 per cent, traditional beliefs 26.6 per cent.
Date of independence. August 11 1960 (from France).
GNP. (1993) $1,248,000,000, per capita $200.
Land and climate. The north consists of desert with mountains in the northwest; the centre consists of vast arid plains; the south of lowlands. The climate in the north is desert; this passes into a dry Sahel climate in the centre to become tropical in the south. The north is subject to the dry harmattan wind and the country suffers from locust plagues; the south is affected by droughts and desertification.

Introduction

A vast landlocked country of just under half a million square miles in area, Chad stretches from the southern Sahara in the north through the Sahel zone to a tropical south. It has six land neighbours – Cameroon, Central African Republic, Libya, Niger, Nigeria and Sudan – and a total of 5,968km of boundaries. Chad belongs to that belt of countries across northern Africa which divide between an Arabicized nomadic and Muslim north and a black Christian or Animist south with consequent ethnic and political divisions between the two cultures. The economy is based upon crop farming or nomadic cattle raising and though there are a number of minerals including some unexploited oil, Chad remains one of the poorest countries in the world. The huge Aozou region of 114,000 sq. km (44,000 sq. miles) which lies in the north of the country immediately south of Libya has been claimed by that country for years and the dispute, which has seen a number of Libyan interventions in Chad since 1960 as well as one full-scale war, was formally handed back to Chad by Libya (following an ICJ judgment) in May 1994.

Agriculture

Agriculture is mainly subsistence while cattle herding is carried on in the north and central savannas. Cotton is an important cash crop. Agriculture accounts for 21 per cent of GDP and employs 83 per cent of the labour force. The principal food crops are sugarcane, cassava, yams, millet, maize, sweet potatoes, pulses, rice, dates, mangoes, sesame seeds, potatoes and onions. Cotton is the country's main export and in 1994 raw cotton accounted for 33 per cent of all exports. Groundnuts and gum arabic are also export crops. The national cattle herd stands at 4,621,000 and cattle (or hides and skins) account for 35 per cent of exports. Lake Chad is an important source of fish and a proportion of the catch is exported. Land use is divided between forested 9.8 per cent, meadows and pastures 35 per cent, agricultural land under permanent cultivation 2.5 per cent, other 52.7 per cent. Chad is self-sufficient in food except in drought years.

Minerals

Minerals include clay, natron, tungsten, bauxite and gold. Natron is extracted from an area north of Lake Chad. But mining only accounts for 0.5 per cent of GDP and employs a negligible workforce. There are some petroleum deposits and oil companies are exploring in two regions: north of Lake Chad and in the Doba basin in the south although, as yet, exploitation has not begun.

Manufacturing

Manufacturing accounts for about 5.6 per cent of GDP and covers cotton textile mills (textiles accounted for 5 per cent of exports in 1991), food processing, meat slaughterhouses, brewery, natron (sodium carbonate), soap and cigarettes.

Infrastructure

Chad has a grossly inadequate infrastructure in relation to its remote landlocked position and vast size. There are 31,322km of highways but only 32km are paved; 2,000km of inland waterways; 55 usable airports of which four have runways between 2,440 and 3,659m in length; there are fair telecommunications between cities and a limited television system but telecommunications are subject to frequent breakdowns.

Political considerations

The return of the Aozou Strip to Chad by Libya in May 1994 hopefully brings to an end a long dispute with the country's northern neighbour; this has cost Chad a great deal in both wealth and disruption in the third of a century since independence. In addition, civil war between the north (Arab–Muslim) and south (Black–Christian–Animist) has divided the country over the same period, the two conflicts leading to several French military interventions as well as those by Libya.

Assessments

Great poverty, limited resources, poor communications and infrastructure and huge distances from markets each work against economic growth and quick development. This situation is only likely to change should large-scale deposits of oil or some other valuable mineral be discovered.

CHILE

Area. 292,135 sq. miles (756,626 sq. km).
Population. (1995) 14,210,000.
Capital. Santiago (4,628,320).
Other major cities. Vina del Mar (319,440), Concepción (318,140), Valparaíso (301,677), Temuco (262,624), Talcahuano (257,767).
Language(s). Spanish (official).
Religion(s). Roman Catholic 80.7 per cent, Protestant 6.1 per cent, other 0.4, atheist/non-religious 12.8 per cent.
Date of independence. September 18 1810 (from Spain).
GNP. (1993) $42,454,000,000, per capita $3,070.
Land and climate. A narrow coastal plain and low mountains, a fertile central valley and the rugged Andes mountains which form the natural eastern border of the country. The climate is generally temperate: in the north, however, it is desert and in the south cool to cold and very wet.

Introduction

With a north-to-south Pacific coastline of 6,435km Chile is geographically one of the longest countries in the world. It has three land neighbours – Peru and Bolivia in the north, and Argentina with a boundary of 5,150km that stretches the length of the Andes mountain chain which acts as the natural barrier between the two countries. At its southern extremity Chile shares the island of Tierra del Fuego with Argentina. Chile's Antarctic Territory partially overlaps claims by both Argentina and Britain. The economy is mixed and relatively well balanced although still over-dependent upon mineral exports, particularly copper. Its per capita income places Chile at the upper end of the lower-middle-income group of countries and it is now possible, according to its economic indicators, that in the relatively near future Chile could make the crossover from the status of a developing to that of a developed economy.

Agriculture

Agriculture, including forestry and fisheries, contributes 8 per cent to GDP and employs 15.8 per cent of the labour force. During the 1980s there took place a rapid development of export crops including certain new ones such as the kiwi fruit. The main exports are fruit and vegetables, fish and wood products. Grapes and apples are the most important food exports while Chilean wines have become a significant luxury export. The annual fish catch at about 6 million tonnes is one of the world's largest and fish meal as well as specialist fish such as salmon are major exports. Roundwood production stands at approximately 32 million cu m (1993). Staple crops include sugar beet, wheat, potatoes, tomatoes, maize, onions, oats, rice and barley. Livestock herds include 3,692,000 cattle and 4,649,000 sheep. However, Chile is still a net food importer. Land use is divided between forested 11.8 per cent, meadows and pastures 18.1 per cent, agricultural land under permanent cultivation 5.8 per cent, other 64.3 per cent.

Minerals

Mining accounts for 8.2 per cent of GDP (1993) but only employs 1.8 per cent of the labour force. The main minerals mined are iron ore, copper, zinc, molybdenum, silver and gold, and minerals accounted for 42.9 per cent of all exports in 1993. Of 25 leading minerals, Chile is a world producer for eight of them: see Table 4.1

Copper has long been the most important mineral and Chile became the leading world copper producer in the 1970s and by 1982 (with an output of 1,200,000 tons) accounted for 15 per cent of total world output. At that time copper was equivalent to 45 per cent of Chile's exports. In 1993 copper production exceeded 2 million tonnes. Copper, however, is subject to major world price movements and government policy is to diversify away from over-dependence upon this one mineral. This has been possible because of the wide range of other minerals and the rapid development during the 1980s of the industrial sector. Copper resources are enorm-

Table 4.1 Chile, mineral production, 1992

Mineral	World placing	Output
Copper	1	1,910,000mt
Gold	12	33,300 kg
Iron ore	15	8,500,000mt
Silver	6	1,000kg
Salt	19	1,700,000mt
Elemental sulphur	18	420,000mt
Coal	19	3,200,000mt
Marketed natural gas	15	32 billion cu m

ous. The industry, which is concentrated in the north of the country and at El Teniente in the central valley, was nationalized by the Allende government (1970–73) and is managed by the Corporación Nacional del Cobre de Chile. (CODELCO). Much foreign investment, mainly from the USA, has been channelled into the Chilean mining sector. Chile possesses about 20 per cent of known world molybdenum resources with an output of 14,899 tonnes in 1993. In that year silver production came to 967,551 kg and gold to 33,502 kg. Chile was a founder member of the copper cartel, Intergovernmental Council of Copper Exporting Countries (CIPEC).

In the field of energy Chile is also well endowed. It has a modest oil production though not enough to meet its needs, abundant coal and is a major producer of natural gas. Its hydro-electric capacity is huge: given the country's geography with a large number of short rivers fed by the snows of the Andes and falling through great heights, Chile possesses the highest per caput hydro-electric capacity in the world. Much of this remains unexploited. Oil was first developed in the 1940s from fields in the far south of the country and by the mid-1980s production was equivalent to 50 per cent of requirements. Apart from the Empresa Nacional de Petroleo (ENAP) (the state oil company) a number of US companies have invested heavily in Chile's oil including Atlantic Richfield, Amerada Hess and Phillips Petroleum. Oil output in 1992 came to 5,502,000 barrels, then only equivalent to about 12 per cent of requirements.

Manufacturing

During the 1980s Chile adopted a variety of free-market policies and generally has lower tariffs than its Latin American neighbours and has avoided membership of regional market groups. Manufacturing accounts for 17.4 per cent of GDP and employs 16 per cent of the labour force (1993). All industrial products account for 44.3 per cent of exports with paper and paper products leading with 5.6 per cent of that figure and chemical and petroleum products another 4.8 per cent. Principal manufactures include cement, cellulose, refined sugar, newsprint, noodles, carbonated drinks, tyres, pressed fibre panels and flat glass.

Chile's principal trading partners are Japan, USA, Germany, Britain, Taiwan, Argentina, Brazil and France (for exports) and the USA, Brazil, Japan, Argentina, Germany, Nigeria, France and Italy for imports.

Infrastructure

There are 7,766km of railroads of which 3,974km are wide gauge. There are 79,025km of highways of which 9,913km are paved. Pipelines include 755km for crude oil, 785km for petroleum products and 320km for natural gas. Eight principal ports serve Chile: Antofagasta, Iquique, Puerto Montt, Punta Arenas, Valparaíso, San Antonio, Talcahuano and Arica. Of 351 usable airports 48 have permanent surface runways and thirteen have runways of 2,440 to 3,659m in length. Telecommunications are fair and there is a modern telephone system.

Political considerations

Chile has one of the longest traditions of democracy in Latin America. This was broken by the 1973 military coup which overthrew the Marxist regime of Allende who was replaced as head of state by the military dictator General Pinochet. However, following a plebiscite of 1988 the country returned to democracy with the elections held at the end of 1989; these brought Patricio Aylwin Azócar to power as president. Since 1990 Chile has retained the relatively free-market policies of the Pinochet years and the economy has grown steadily during the decade. In political terms Chile remains one of the most stable countries of South America.

Assessments

Chile stands at the upper end of the lower-middle-income group of countries (as defined by the World Bank) and though over-dependent upon mineral exports (principally copper) also has a rapidly developing manufacturing sector and a broad-based agricultural sector. With sound management (and luck) Chile could well make the leap from developing to developed status during the first quarter of the twenty-first century. Chile's long Pacific coastline as well as its Antarctic Territory put it in an advantageous position for what is likely to be the most important economic development in the next century – the scramble for undersea and Antarctic resources.

COLOMBIA

Area. 440,831 sq. miles (1,141,748 sq. km).
Population. (1995) 35,099,000.
Capital. Bogotá (5,237,635).
Other major cities. Cali (1,718,871), Medellín (1,621,356), Barranquilla (1,064,255), Cartagena (745,689).
Language(s). Spanish (official).

Religion(s). Roman Catholic 93.1 per cent, other 6.9 per cent.
Date of independence. July 20 1810 (from Spain).
GNP. (1993) $50,119,000,000, per capita $1,350.
Land and climate. The country comprises flat coastal lowlands; central highlands; the high Andes mountains which run north–south; and eastern lowland plains. The climate of the coastal lowlands and the eastern plains is tropical; the highlands have much cooler weather. The highlands suffer from periodic volcanic activity; deforestation and droughts affect agricultural performance.

Introduction

Situated at the northwest corner of South America, adjoining the Isthmus of Panama, Colombia is the only South American country with coastlines on both the Pacific Ocean and the Caribbean Sea. It has 7,408km of land boundaries with five neighbours – Brazil, Ecuador, Panama, Peru and Venezuela; 1,760km of Caribbean coastline and 1,448km of Pacific coastline. Colombia is a lower-middle-income country with a reasonably mixed economy which includes a growing minerals sector, a diverse manufacturing sector and the agricultural capacity to meet its domestic needs and provide an export surplus with coffee as the principal export. Colombia also has a reputation for extreme violence between its drug-producing cartels and is the world's leading producer of coca and its cocaine derivatives which provide a substantial (illegal) proportion of total GDP.

Agriculture

Agricultural output is divided between crops (two-thirds) and livestock (one-third). The sector, including forestry and fisheries, accounts for approximately 14 per cent of GDP and employs 28.5 per cent of the labour force. Soil and climate conditions allow a wide range of crops; these include coffee, rice, tobacco, maize, sugarcane, cocoa, oil seeds, fruit and vegetables. Forest products are of increasing importance and in 1993 roundwood output came to 20,903,000cu m. Fish, especially shrimps, are also becoming increasingly important as an export. Coffee, however, has long been Colombia's most profitable commodity and in 1993 accounted for 17.3 per cent of all exports. Output in 1993 came to 1,362,000mt. The coffee sector is vulnerable to international price movements and following the collapse of the International Coffee Agreement's system of export quotas in 1989, which hurt Colombia's earnings, the policy has been to diversify away from over-dependence upon the one crop.

Colombia has become one of the main Latin American exporters of bananas and cut flowers while sugarcane is also another important export commodity. The principal staples are rice, plantains, potatoes, maize and sorghum. The national herd comprises 25,700,000 cattle, 3,708,000 vicuna, 2,635,000 pigs and 2,540,000 sheep. Apart from coffee, forestry and fisheries accounted for 32.4 per cent of exports in 1992, and other food and tobacco exports for a further 4.8 per cent. Land use is divided between forest 48.1 per cent, pasture 39 per cent, agriculture 5.2 per cent, other 7.7 per cent.

Minerals

Mining contributes about 6 per cent of GDP but only employs a fraction of the labour force. The principal mineral resources are petroleum and natural gas, coal, iron ore, nickel, gold, silver, copper and emeralds. Colombia possesses the largest proven reserves of coal in Latin America (3,600 million tons) while potential reserves may be as high as 16,500 million tons. Production of coal began in 1984 and early enthusiasm in the wake of the large discoveries predicted that Colombia might supply 10 per cent of the world market for coal by 1999. By 1991 coal output had reached 24,000,000 tons; Colombia only consumed 6m tons of this, leaving 18m tons for export. There are substantial nickel deposits. Colombia produces 95 per cent of the world's emeralds and has long been a traditional source of gold (667,448 troy ounces' output in 1994) and silver (189,625 troy ounces). There are substantial iron ore deposits and output for 1994 came to 609,615mt.

Although Colombia has considerable oil resources production (due to geological conditions and cautious political attitudes) has not been easy. Proven reserves in the mid-1980s came to 1,117m barrels. From 1985 annual output came to 300,000b/d and rose to 435,000b/d in 1992 while natural gas output came to 4,658,065,000cu m. Petroleum products accounted for 19.2 per cent of exports in 1992. Petroleum will continue as an important export for some years and coal has a long-term future.

Manufacturing

The manufacturing sector, which is increasingly diverse, contributes about 20 per cent to GDP and employs 13 per cent of the labour force. Apart from mining activities, it covers textiles, food processing, oil, clothing and footwear, beverages, chemicals, metal products and cement. Exports of textiles and clothing, chemicals, paper and publishing accounted for 20.4 per cent of all exports in 1992. Colombia's principal trading partners are the USA, Germany, Venezuela and the Netherlands for exports; and the USA, Japan, Venezuela, Germany, Brazil and France for imports.

Colombia is one of the world's leading producers of drugs (cannabis, cocaine and heroin). It has about 37,500 hectares of coca under cultivation and is the largest processor of coca derivatives into cocaine which it supplies to the USA and other markets. A programme to limit the production of drugs (with US assistance) was launched in the mid-1980s though with little long-term effect. Income from illegal drug exports is estimated to be equivalent to the value of all legal exports. The huge violence centring upon the drug cartels does considerable damage to Colombia's international image and almost certainly inhibits inward investment into the economy.

Infrastructure

There are 3,386km of railroads which are narrow gauge and single track. There are 75,450km of highways of which 9,350km are paved; and 14,300km of inland waterways which are navigable by river boats. The pipeline network includes 3,585km for crude oil, 1,350km for petroleum products, 830km for natural gas and 125km for natural gas liquids. The country is served by seven principal ports – Barranquilla, Buenaventura, Cartagena, Covenas, San Andrés (a free port), Santa Marca, Tumaco. There are 1,059 usable airports of which 69 have permanent runways; one has a runway of 3,659m and nine have runways of 2,440 to 3,659m. The telecommunications system is fair.

Political considerations

A democratic republic, Colombia suffers from periodic destabilizing violence, especially in Bogotá, a great deal of drugs-related violence both between the cartels and against the forces of law and order and spasmodic rural insurgency. The hugely profitable but illegal drugs business is central to many other government problems: peasant coca growers do not wish to be prevented from growing a most profitable crop; the drug-distributing cartels are a law to themselves; while US demands for controls exert pressures upon the government without offering a real solution.

Assessments

Colombia can feed its population and has at least two important mineral resources (oil and coal). It also possesses abundant hydro-electric potential. It ought to maintain its position as a lower-middle-income developing country but this is unlikely to alter appreciably unless new mineral discoveries are made and the government is able to control the drugs business.

CONGO

Area. 132,047 sq. miles (342,000 sq. km).
Population. (1995) 2,590,000.
Capital. Brazzaville (937,579, 1992).
Other major cities. Pointe Noire (576,206), Loubomo (83,605).
Language(s). French (official), Lingala, Kikongo.
Religion(s). Roman Catholic 53.9 per cent, Protestant 24.9 per cent, African Christian 14.2 per cent, traditional beliefs 4.8 per cent, other 2.2 per cent.
Date of independence. August 15 1960 (from France).
GNP. (1993) $2,307,000,000, per capita $920.
Land and climate. Apart from a coastal plain, the country divides into three broad regions: a southern basin, a central plateau and a northern basin. The climate is tropical with a rainy season from March to June and a dry season from June to October; temperatures are uniformly high with accompanying high humidity which is generally enervating.

Introduction

A wedge-shaped country on the west coast of Africa which lies astride the equator, Congo has a small Atlantic seaboard of 169km and five land neighbours – Angola (the Cabinda enclave), Cameroon, Central African Republic, Gabon and Zaire. The border with Zaire runs along the Zaire (Congo) river and this stretch of river, including its islands, has never been properly defined. More than half the country is still covered by tropical forest. The port of Pointe Noire also acts as the main outlet for the Central African Republic. Since independence in 1960 Congo has had a troubled political history: after a period of one-party rule it began the move back to multipartyism in 1991. The discovery of oil and its subsequent exploitation transformed the economy during the 1970s and Congo now ranks as a lower-middle-income country with one of Africa's higher per capita incomes.

Agriculture

Until oil supplanted it, forestry provided the main source of export revenues. In 1991 agriculture, including forestry and fisheries, accounted for 14.8 per cent of GDP and employed 59.1 per cent of the workforce. From the early 1970s when oil became the principal motor of the economy, agriculture has suffered from neglect. Much of the sector consists of village-based subsistence agriculture and export crops (except for wood products) only make a small contribution to GDP so that for years the country has been increasing its food imports. In 1993 roundwood output came to 3,561,000 cu m and accounted for about 11.1 per cent of exports while food and live animals accounted for another 1.9 per cent. Export crops consist of peanuts, avocados, palm oil, pineapples, cacao beans and coffee but in generally small quantities. The national cattle herd is only 68,000 strong. The main food staples are cassava, sugarcane, plantains, maize and yams. Congo is not self-sufficient in food and food accounts for more than 10 per cent of all imports. Land use is divided between forested 61.8 per cent, meadows and pastures 29.2 per cent, agricultural land under permanent cultivation 0.5 per cent, other 8.5 per cent.

Minerals

Apart from petroleum, Congo has diamonds, lead, zinc, gold, copper, iron ore, phosphates and bauxite although only small quantities of zinc concentrate, lead and gold were mined in 1990. Prior to 1970 (when oil became important) mining and quarrying accounted for less than 5 per cent of exports. Although there are rich deposits of potassium chloride (at Holle near Pointe Noire) which were mined during the 1960s and 1970s, technical difficulties kept production low and then in 1977 the mines were flooded. No plans exist for their reopening. Prospecting for new deposits of potassium is being carried out along the coast. Deposits of high grade iron ore, phosphates and bauxite exist though they have not yet been exploited. There is a large deposit of 1,000m tons of iron ore in the High Iringo region and an agreement with Gabon for its joint exploitation was signed in 1985, but development awaits external funding and there is, at present, an abundance of more readily available iron ore from elsewhere in the world.

Onshore petroleum deposits were discovered in 1957 but only after 1971 when far larger offshore deposits were found did oil production become the leading industry and foreign exchange earner. In 1972 the Emeraude field went into production; other fields followed and output reached a peak in 1987. By 1992 Congo was producing 180,000b/d, equivalent to 0.3 per cent of world output. Immediately recoverable resources stand at 50,000,000 tons but, for example, the Emeraude field has 600m tons of heavy viscous petroleum that will remain unexploited until a significant rise in oil prices makes recovery economically profitable. There are indications of much more oil but exploitation must await a better economic climate. In 1992 production came to 63,400,000 barrels. There are substantial natural gas deposits but virtually all production, amounting to about 760 million cu m a year, is flared. Production in 1993 came to 4,410,000cu m which was used locally. In 1994 oil and petroleum products accounted for 85 per cent of exports. In 1994 US, Italian and British oil companies agreed to increase oil royalties to the government from 17 per cent to 31 per cent, a move which forced Elf Oil (the principal oil company operating in Congo) to follow suit.

Most of Congo's minerals are present in relatively small quantities and exploitation is costly and in a number of cases, due to inaccessibility or poor infrastructure, exploitation of these minerals is not a viable economic proposition. The indications, however, suggest that Congo may turn out to be a rich storehouse of minerals in the future.

Manufacturing

Manufacturing contributed 9.1 per cent to GDP in 1991 and employed about 6 per cent of the workforce. Most industry is concentrated in Brazzaville and Pointe Noire and is concerned with food processing, wood products, petroleum, cement, brewing, sugar milling, palm oil, soap, cigarettes and footwear. Basic manufactures account for only a small percentage of exports.

Infrastructure

The overall infrastructure is poor. There are 797km of single track 1.067m gauge railroads of which 285km are privately owned. There are only 11,960km of highways of which only 560km are paved. The country's principal highway consists of a 1,120km stretch of the Congo and Oubangui rivers which is suitable for commercial traffic (and also serves the Central African Republic as its main route of transit to the sea). There is a 25km oil pipeline. Of 41 usable airports, five have permanent surface runways and one of these is between 2,440 and 3,659m in length. Telecommunications are adequate for government purposes. There are 18,000 telephones.

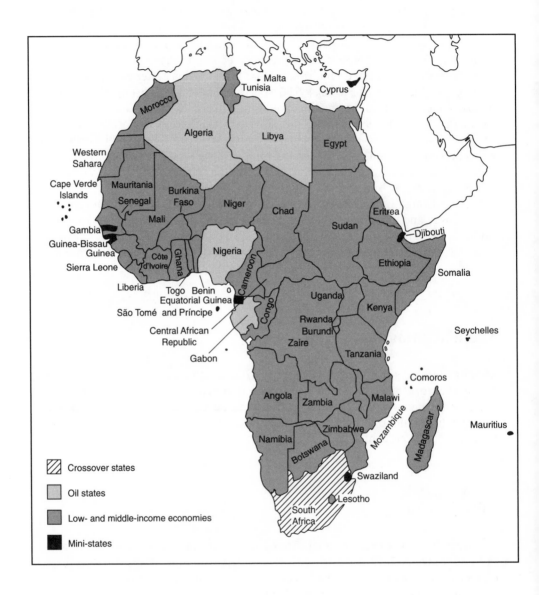

Malta
Tunisia
Cyprus
Morocco
Algeria
Libya
Egypt
Western
Sahara
Cape Verde
Islands
Mauritania
Burkina
Faso
Niger
Chad
Eritrea
Senegal
Mali
Sudan
Djibouti
Gambia
Guinea-Bissau
Guinea
Nigeria
Ethiopia
Somalia
Côte
d'Ivoire
Ghana
Sierra Leone
Liberia
Togo Benin
Cameroon
Equatorial Guinea
Uganda
São Tomé and Príncipe
Congo
Kenya
Central African
Republic
Rwanda
Burundi
Zaire
Seychelles
Gabon
Tanzania
Comoros
Angola
Zambia
Malawi
Madagascar
Mozambique
Mauritius
Zimbabwe
Namibia
Botswana
Swaziland
Lesotho
South
Africa

Crossover states

Oil states

Low- and middle-income economies

Mini-states

Map 6   Africa

Political considerations

Congo has had a troubled political history since independence in 1960 and a period of one-party rule came to an end in 1991 when it began a return to multipartyism. The country was racked by violent clashes in 1994 as opposition groups challenged the 1993 election results. In 1990 Congo abandoned Marxism–Leninism and in 1994 turned again to the IMF for structural adjustment aid.

Assessments

Against a background of difficult terrain, enervating climate, small population and underdeveloped infrastructure Congo is unlikely to make major development strides in the foreseeable future. Rather, it will continue to enjoy a lower-middle-income economy, at least as long as the oil lasts. Substantial new mineral discoveries (which are possible) and a real upturn in world economic conditions that triggers off greater demand for existing minerals could transform this position.

COSTA RICA

Area. 19,730 sq. miles (51,100 sq. km).
Population. (1995) 3,344,000.
Capital. San José (280,613 – canton).
Other major cities. Desamparados (54,668), Limón (50,939), Alajuela (45,442).
Language(s). Spanish (official), English (round Port Limón).
Religion(s). Roman Catholic 81.3 per cent, other 18.7 per cent.
Date of independence. September 15 1821 (from Spain).
GNP. (1993) $7,041,000,000, per capita $2,160.
Land and climate. The two coastal plains are separated by rugged mountains. The climate is tropical: there is a dry season from December to April and a rainy season from May to November. The land is subject to a range of environmental problems: occasional earthquakes, hurricanes along the Caribbean shore, flooding of the lowlands in the rainy season, volcanic action, deforestation and soil erosion.

Introduction

This small country of Central America occupies the broadening isthmus to the north of Panama and south of Nicaragua. It has coastlines on both the North Pacific and the Caribbean Sea. Possessed of few natural resources, the economy depends upon a strong agricultural sector and a relatively sophisticated manufacturing sector. With a per capita income in the region of $2,000 it is ranked as a lower-middle-income country. Costa Rica enjoys one of the longest and most stable democratic traditions in Latin America, broken in the twentieth century only by two short periods of revolt against the democratic process: in 1917–19 and 1948.

Agriculture

Agriculture, including forestry and fisheries, contributes 15.8 per cent to GDP and employs 22.5 per cent of the workforce. Agricultural products are the main export earners. Coffee (10–11 per cent), bananas (27–29 per cent), sugar and pineapples are the most important exports with ornamental plants, leaves and flowers as a new line in exports. Fresh meat is also important as an export commodity. The national cattle herd stands at 2,122,000. The main food staples are rice, plantains, maize, beans and potatoes. Roundwood production stands at 4,306,000cu m. The fish catch includes shrimps for export. Costa Rica is normally self-sufficient in food except for grains. The rapid depletion of forest reserves is leading to a lower output of timber. Land use is divided between forested 32.1 per cent, meadows and pastures 45.4 per cent, agricultural land under permanent cultivation 10.4 per cent, other 12.1 per cent.

Manufacturing and mining

There are no significant mineral resources although limestone is quarried and there is a small gold output – 17,700 troy ounces in 1992. Manufacturing contributes 19.7 per cent to GDP and the sector is relatively sophisticated. The principal manu-factures are textiles (an important export), food processing, clothing, construction materials, fertilizers, plastic products. Hydro-electric energy provides most of the country's needs and the development potential is substantial. There are no other energy sources and oil has to be imported.

Infrastructure

There are 950km of 1.067m gauge railroad of which 260km are electrified. Half the 15,400km of highways are paved. There are 176km of pipeline for refined petroleum products. The country is served by five ports: Puerto Limón, Caldera, Golfito, Moin and Puntarenas. There are 144 usable airports, eight with permanent runways, two of which are 2,440 to 3,659m in length. There is a good domestic telephone service with connections to Central America. Other telecommunications are reasonable.

Political considerations

One of Central America's generally most stable societies, Costa Rica with its long democratic tradition has been able to avoid some of the more violent aspects of politics to be found in neighbouring countries.

Assessments

Apart from hydro-power potential, Costa Rica has few resources. A well-developed agricultural sector and an increasingly diversified manufacturing sector should enable it slowly to improve its lower-middle-income status.

CÔTE D'IVOIRE

Area. 124,856 sq. miles (322,463 sq. km).
Population. (1995) 14,253,000.
Capital. Abidjan (2,168,000) (Yamoussoukro is the capital designate).
Other major cities. Bouaké (329,850), Daloa (121,842), Konhogo (109,445), Yamoussoukro (106,786).
Language(s). French (official), Dioula and some 60 dialects.
Religion(s). Muslim 38.7 per cent, Roman Catholic 20.8 per cent, animist 17 per cent, atheist 13.4 per cent, Protestant 5.3 per cent, other 4.8 per cent.
Date of independence. August 7 1960 (from France).
GNP. (1993) $8,416,000,000, per capita $630.
Land and climate. The country consists of flat and undulating plains with mountains in the northwest (on the Guinea border). The climate on the coast is tropical but it becomes semi-arid in the north. The coast is subject to heavy surf and there are no natural harbours. The country is affected by severe deforestation.

Introduction

Situated in West Africa between Ghana and Liberia, with Burkina Faso, Guinea and Mali to its north, Côte d'Ivoire has a 515km coastline on the Gulf of Guinea. Côte d'Ivoire has one of the better developed economies of Africa although this is heavily dependent upon the agricultural sector; it is one of the continent's major food commodity exporters and is the world's number one cocoa producer and exporter and number three coffee producer and exporter. Politically stable under the long rule of its paternalist leader, Félix Houphouët-Boigny, who dominated the country's politics from before independence to his death in 1993, Côte d'Ivoire returned to multiparty politics at the beginning of the 1990s. In terms of per capita income the country just qualifies for lower-middle-income status.

Agriculture

Since independence Côte d'Ivoire has concentrated upon the agricultural export sector to create one of the most successful cash crop economies in Africa. Agriculture accounts for 34 per cent of GDP and employs 64 per cent of the labour force. The leading cash crops are cocoa beans and coffee; both these crops, however, are subject to seasonal variations of climate and fluctuations in world demand and price. In 1994 production of cacao beans amounted to 809,000mt (Côte d'Ivoire is the world's leading cocoa producer with exports accounting for 33.8 per cent of total exports). In the same year coffee production came to 148,000mt and accounted for 7.3 per cent of exports. Other export crops are fish (3.4 per cent), wood and wood products (9.7 per cent) with a roundwood production in 1993 of 13,694,000cu m, and cotton and cotton cloth accounting for a further 5.2 per cent of exports. Livestock is limited and the national cattle herd is only just over 1 million head. The main food staples are yams, cassava, plantains, rice, maize. Other crops for export include sugarcane, fruit (bananas and coconuts), palm kernel oil and rubber.

The economy was badly affected in 1986 by a collapse of cocoa and coffee prices and it required the balance of the decade to recover. Côte d'Ivoire is not self-sufficient in grains or dairy products. Land use is divided between forested 23.2 per cent, meadows and pastures 40.9 per cent, agricultural land under permanent cultivation 11.6 per cent, other 24.3 per cent.

Minerals and manufacturing

Manufacturing and mining combined account for 16 per cent of GDP. Côte d'Ivoire has few mineral resources and the sector is unimportant except for limited oil production. Diamonds are the only other mineral and output in 1993 came to a mere 20,000 carats. Small-scale offshore oil deposits were discovered in 1977, followed by further modest discoveries in 1980. Production peaked in 1984 with a total output of 1.1m tonnes. Another offshore field was discovered in 1988 but the government tax regime (on royalties) inhibited further exploration. Côte d'Ivoire imports crude oil from Nigeria for processing at the Abidjan refinery for re-export. In 1993 total oil production came to 2,380,000 barrels. Manufacturing is mainly confined to food processing, wood processing, oil refining, automobile assembly, textiles, fertilizers and beverages.

Infrastructure

There is a single railroad of 660km (narrow gauge) from the Burkina Faso border to Abidjan; there are 46,600km of highways of which 3,600km are paved; while 380km of inland waterways comprise rivers, canals and coastal lagoons. The two ports (Abidjan and San Pedro) are artificial. Of 37 usable airports, seven have permanent surface runways and three of these are 2,440 to 3,659m in length. Telecommunications are well developed (in the African context) and operate below capacity.

Political considerations

With the death of its father figure (Houphouët-Boigny) in 1993, Côte d'Ivoire entered upon a more open period of politics with a return to multipartyism. The country has maintained exceptionally close ties with France since independence; it has also become heavily indebted and in 1993 international debts of $10,551,000,000 were equivalent to 120 per cent GNP.

Assessments

Côte d'Ivoire should continue as a major commodity exporter though such a role is subject to wide price variations according to world demand which can have a destabilizing impact upon the economy. Further oil discoveries offshore on the continental shelf are possible although on present knowledge seem unlikely to be on a major scale. Attempts to diversify away from over-dependence upon cash crops and their related processing activities have not so far been very successful.

CUBA

Area. 42,804 sq. miles (112,861 sq. km).
Population. (1995) 11,068,000.
Capital. Havana (2,175,995).
Other major cities. Santiago de Cuba (440,084), Camagüey (293,961), Holguín (242,085), Guantánamo (207,796). (The US naval base at Guantánamo is leased, though the territory remains part of Cuba; the lease can only be terminated by mutual agreement or if the USA abandons the base.)
Language(s). Spanish (official).
Religion(s). Non-religious 48.7 per cent, Roman Catholic 39.6 per cent, atheist 6.4 per cent, Protestant 3.3 per cent, other 2.0 per cent.
Date of independence. May 20 1902 (from Spain) (although Cuba had been administered by the USA from December 10 1898 – following their defeat of the Spanish – until 1902).
GNP. (1991) $17,000,000,000, per capita $1,580.
Land and climate. Flat or rolling plains cover most of the country although there are rugged hills and mountains in the southeast. The climate is tropical but moderated by the trade winds; there are two seasons – dry from November to April and rainy from May to October.

Introduction

The largest island in the Caribbean and located only 90 miles south of Florida, Cuba occupies a dominating strategic position in the region. Its economy or, rather, its economic potential has been distorted ever since the events of 1959–62 which led to US sanctions. Until 1959 when the Batista regime was overthrown by Fidel Castro and his followers, the Cuban economy had been closely tied to that of the USA with American companies controlling the greater part of the island's activities and most Cuban exports going to the USA. Following the Castro revolution and the nationalization of US companies and subsequent loss of the US market (especially for the country's main export sugar), Cuba switched to a state-run economic system modelled on Soviet lines. In 1972, when the Cold War was still at its height, Cuba became a member of the Council for Mutual Economic Assistance (CMEA) which provided it with still firmer links to the Soviet camp so that, for practical purposes, Cuba became an economic and political outcast in the Americas with the USSR accounting for 70 per cent of all its trade and providing fixed amounts of oil in barter exchange for Cuba's sugar exports.

Following the end of the Cold War between 1989 and 1991 Cuba was faced with fundamental economic changes including the need thereafter to pay for its imports from the Soviet bloc in hard currency at world market rates. Cuba is one of the world's leading sugar producers and in the aftermath of the Cold War Russia agreed to import 4,000,000 tonnes of Cuban sugar annually at preferential prices and supply Cuba with 10,000,000 tonnes of oil at market prices. As a result, the economy was forced to contract by approximately one-third between 1989 and 1990 following the loss of an annual $4bn in aid from the USSR.

Agriculture

Agriculture accounts for approximately 16 per cent of GDP and employs 20 per cent of the labour force. Agricultural exports account for more than 80 per cent of the total. Sugar has long been the most important export crop: in 1994 sugarcane production amounted to 39,000,000mt and sugar accounted for 63.4 per cent of all exports. Other principal export crops are tobacco and citrus fruits. Fruit and other agricultural products account for a further 3.4 per cent of exports and tobacco and tobacco products (cigars) for a further 4.1 per cent. The 1993 fish catch was 93,435mt. Roundwood production stands at just over 3,000,000cu m a year. Staple food crops are rice, potatoes, meat and beans; a small amount of coffee is also produced. The national cattle herd stands at 4,500,000 head. Cuba is not self-sufficient in foods. Land use is divided between forested 20.9 per cent, meadows and pastures 27 per cent, agricultural land under permanent cultivation 30.4 per cent, other 21.7 per cent.

Minerals

Mining only contributes 3.9 per cent to GDP. Chromite and nickel are both at present mined and in 1993 chromite output reached 50,000mt and nickel 26,000mt. Minerals and concentrates account for 9 per cent of exports. With 20mt, Cuba has the fourth largest nickel reserves in the world and nickel is the biggest export earner after sugar. There are also huge reserves of chromium ore and the industry has a potential production capacity of 100,000mt a year. Oriente Province alone has an estimated 10 million tons of chromite reserves. Substantial quantities of cobalt are found in association with the nickel. Copper production reached a modest 3,000 tonnes a year in the mid-1980s. There are other resources of iron ore, manganese, lead, zinc, salt and silica although none is currently being exploited. Cuba has some modest offshore oil and natural gas deposits. In 1984 Petroléos Mexicanos (PEMEX) made substantial finds off Cuba's north coast. Agreements for exploitation were entered into with Elf-Aquitaine, Neste Oy and Tricentrol while Cuba had special petroleum exchange arrangements with the USSR and was able to refine Russian oil and re-export it to earn hard currency. Oil production in 1993 came to 6,288,000 barrels (one-sixth of requirements).

Manufacturing

Manufacturing accounts for 39 per cent of GDP and employs about 22 per cent of the workforce. The sector is relatively sophisticated at the secondary level and principal manufactures cover sugar milling and refining, petroleum refining, food processing, tobacco, textiles, chemicals, paper and wood products, metals, cement, fertilizers, consumer goods and agricultural machinery. The manufacturing sector has been badly affected by the end of the Cold War because of a subsequent drastic reduction in the availability of fuel (petroleum) from the USSR. Much industrial production was halted and, for example, 1 million bicycles had to be imported from China for use in Havana to save fuel used for buses.

Infrastructure

There are 12,947km of railroads of which 5,053km are broad gauge (1.435m) while 7,742km are sugar plantation lines. There are 26,477km of highways of which 14,477km are paved. The country is served by five major ports – Cienfuegos, Havana, Mariel, Matanzas, Santiago de Cuba – and 42 secondary or minor ports. There are 166 usable airports of which 73 have permanent surface runways and three have runways of 3,659m length and a further twelve runways between 2,440 and 3,659m. Telecommunications are reasonable.

Political considerations

Cuba's Soviet-style command economy has become increasingly anachronistic in the post-Cold War age and by the mid-1990s there were signs that Castro favoured cautious moves towards adopting a more market-oriented economy. What happens, however, will mainly depend upon new attitudes in the USA. If Washington decides to forget its longstanding quarrel with Cuba so that Cuban–US trade can be resumed and US investment becomes acceptable once more, then the Cuban economy could begin to flourish. Throughout the Castro years Cuba has been one of the most stable countries of Latin America.

Assessments

Cuba has a major agricultural export base in sugar, a reasonable manufacturing sector that is capable of rapid expansion if US restraints upon it were to be removed and some rich mineral resources. In the long term considerably more offshore oil may well be found and exploited. Cuba's per capita income above $1,500 places the country well into the lower-middle-income bracket, an achievement of a state enterprise economy in the face of US sanctions.

DOMINICAN REPUBLIC

Area. 18,704 sq. miles (48,443 sq. km).
Population. (1995) 7,823,000.
Capital. Santo Domingo (2,100,000).
Other major cities. Santiago de los Caballeros (690,000), La Vega (189,000), San Pedro de Macoris (137,000).
Language(s). Spanish (official).
Religion(s). Roman Catholic 91.2 per cent, other 8.8 per cent.

Date of independence. February 27 1844 (from Haiti).
GNP. (1993) $8,039,000,000, per capita $1,080.
Land and climate. It is a country of rugged highland terrain and mountains inter-spersed with fertile valleys. The climate is tropical maritime. It is subject to occasional hurricanes and suffers from deforestation.

Introduction

The Dominican Republic shares the island of Hispaniola in the northern Caribbean with Haiti and enjoys a relatively balanced economy whose principal exports are a mixture of agriculture and minerals. It has experienced a troubled history since it broke away from Haiti in 1844 and in the mid-twentieth century came under the dictatorial control of the Trujillo family. Following civil chaos in 1965, 20,000 US marines landed in the Republic to restore order and subsequently the Organization of American States (OAS) negotiated a settlement between the left and right political factions. The 1970s and 1980s, however, have been a period of multiparty democracy and presidential elections in 1994 returned Joaquín Balaguer for his seventh term of office.

Agriculture

Agriculture accounts for 12.6 per cent of GDP and employs 22 per cent of the labour force. Sugar is the main crop and principal export and raw sugar accounted for 18.2 per cent of exports in 1994. Other export crops are coffee, cotton, cocoa and tobacco and coffee and cocoa accounted for a further 17.8 per cent of exports in 1992. The main staples are rice, maize, potatoes, bananas, plantains and vegetables (beans). Livestock numbers are small though important as a source of food and there is a limited fisheries sector as well as some roundwood production. Agricultural prod-ucts account for 19 per cent of imports and the country is not self-sufficient in food. Land use is divided between forested 12.7 per cent, meadows and pastures 43.2 per cent, agricultural land under permanent cultivation 29.9 per cent, other 14.2 per cent.

Minerals

Minerals consist of nickel, bauxite, gold and silver. Ferronickel production in 1994 came to 30,757mt and ferronickel accounted for 28.4 per cent of exports. Gold alloy came to 51,400 troy ounces and accounts for 4 per cent of exports. Bauxite production, once substantial, was abandoned in the mid-1980s. Although govern-ment policy is to expand the mineral sector, international companies such as Canada's Falconbridge entered into fierce arguments with the government over taxes and then withdrew.

Petroleum deposits at Charco Largo are estimated to be able to produce 20,000b/d but as yet no exploitation has taken place. The country has good hydro-electric potential.

Manufacturing

The manufacturing sector now accounts for 18.4 per cent of GDP and employs 11.7 per cent of the labour force. The principal activities are processing agricultural products, especially sugar, oil refining, chemicals. The creation and rapid growth of free trade zones has boosted manufacturing and in particular wearing apparel. There are, in addition, a number of light industries while tourism is of increasing import-ance and yielded more than $1bn in receipts in 1994.

The Dominican Republic has become a transit country for drugs from South America to the USA. Per capita income which is just above $1,000 places the republic in the ranks of the lower-middle-income countries.

Infrastructure

There are 1,655km of varying gauge railtracks; 12,000km of roads of which 5,800km are paved; 96km of oil pipeline; four ports serve the country; of 30 usable airports, four have runways between 2,440 and 3,659m in length. Telecommunications are relatively efficient.

Political considerations

Although prone to periodic violence the country has adhered to multiparty democ-racy since the passing of the Trujillo era in 1961. There exists considerable suspicion about the Dominican Republic on the part of the English-speaking Caribbean countries and in 1990, for example, its application for full membership of CAR-ICOM was turned down though it enjoys observer status. It is an ACP country and benefits from agricultural export quotas to Europe.

Assessments

It is a middle level economy that is unlikely to change significantly; the prospects of major mineral discoveries are remote.

ECUADOR

Area. 105,037 sq. miles (272,045 sq. km).
Population. (1995) 11,460,000.
Capital. Quito (1,100,847).
Other major cities. Guayaquil (1,508,844), Cuenca (194,981), Machala (144,197), Portoviejo (132,937).
Language(s). Spanish (official), Quechua (and other Indian languages).
Religion(s). Roman Catholic 93 per cent, other 7 per cent.

Date of independence. May 24 1822 (from Spain).
GNP. (1993) $13,217,000,000, per capita $1,170.
Land and climate. There is a coastal plain and a region of interior-Andean central highlands; flat to rolling jungle country occupies the eastern part of Ecuador. The climate is tropical along the coast but cooler in the highland region. Ecuador is subject to frequent earthquakes, landslides, volcanic activity; and the land is deteriorating as a result of deforestation, desertification, soil erosion and periodic drought.

Introduction

One of the smaller countries of South America, Ecuador is sandwiched between Colombia to the north and Peru to the south and has a 2,237km coastline on the Pacific Ocean. The country is a multiparty democracy with a reasonable economy which achieves a fair balance between agriculture (there are rich land resources), mining (oil), and a growing manufacturing sector. Unfortunately, Ecuador has run up substantial international debts and by 1993 these were equivalent to 75 per cent of GNP. However, in 1993 the government entered into restructuring agreements for $7.6bn of commercial debts and issued bonds to cover interest (not paid since 1987) to the value of $2.5bn. The per capita GNP at just over $1,100 places Ecuador in the lower-middle-income group of countries.

Agriculture

There are rich agricultural areas and agriculture, including forestry and fisheries, contributes 17.2 per cent to GDP and employs 30.8 per cent of the workforce. The principal export crops are bananas, shrimps, coffee and cocoa. Balsa wood is also an important export. In recent years banana exports have been adversely affected by EU quota restrictions and banana blight. Ecuador is a member of the Union of Banana Exporting Countries. The collapse in 1989 of the International Coffee Agreement helped depress coffee prices. Fisheries have become an increasingly important export and Ecuador has a long coastline on the Pacific seaboard. The national cattle herd is slightly over 4.5 million head. Plantains, rice, maize, potatoes and soybeans are the main food staples. Land use is divided between forested 38.3 per cent, meadows and pastures 18.7 per cent, agricultural land under permanent cultivation 9.9 per cent, other 33.1 per cent.

Minerals

The mineral sector accounts for 17.8 per cent of GDP but employs only 0.6 per cent of the workforce. Limestone is quarried and there is a limited output of gold but in real terms minerals means oil. Petroleum output in 1992 came to 119 million barrels. Ecuador's proved reserves are equivalent to 0.2 per cent of world reserves and at present rates of extraction will last another ten years. In world terms Ecuador has negligible resources of natural gas and in 1992 produced 100,000,000cu m which was consumed locally. Petroleum exports accounted for 42.3 per cent of all exports in 1993. It was the completion in 1972 of the Trans-Andean pipeline which enabled Ecuador to export petroleum and in 1973 the country joined OPEC although leaving it in 1985 over quota restrictions. Ecuador is well endowed with hydro-electric power and potential.

Manufacturing

The manufacturing sector has become increasingly diverse and accounts for 11 per cent of GDP and employs 11 per cent of the workforce. The sector covers food and beverages, textiles, chemical products, metal products, paper and wood, and plastics. Ecuador has a generally favourable balance of payments. Most imports require licences. The government of Sixto Durán-Ballén, elected in 1994, relaxed investment regulations to make Ecuador more attractive to foreign companies. Ecuador has trade agreements with the Andean Group of countries – Colombia, Peru, Bolivia and Venezuela. Since 1992 it has moved towards a policy favouring market forces. The USA takes just under half Ecuador's exports.

Infrastructure

There are 965km of single track 1.067m gauge railways; 28,000km of highways of which 3,600km are paved; and 1,500km of inland waterways. Pipelines include 800km for crude oil and 1,358km for petroleum products. Ecuador is served by four principal ports: Guayaquil, Manta, Puerto Bolivar and Esmeraldas. There are 173 usable airports of which 52 have permanent surface runways, one over 3,659m in length and six with 2,440 to 3,659m runways. Telecommunications facilities are generally adequate.

Political considerations

A border dispute with Peru that has persisted since the Ecuador–Peru war which ended in 1942 when Peru obtained substantial territory at Ecuador's expense flared up early in 1995. The country is a democracy although it has experienced a generally troubled political history with 35 presidents between 1931 and 1981 and fairly frequent military interventions. Since the passing of the 1979 Constitution presidential elections have been held every four years.

Assessments

A moderately well-off, middle-level economy whose long-term future is more likely to depend upon agriculture and manufactures than oil unless major new discoveries are made.

EGYPT

Area. 385,229 sq. miles (997,739 sq. km).
Population. (1995) 59,690,000.
Capital. Cairo (6,849,000).
Other major cities. Alexandria (3,382,000), al-Jizah (2,096,000).
Language(s). Arabic (official), English, French.
Religion(s). Sunni Muslim 90 per cent, Christian 10 per cent.
Date of independence. February 28 1922 (from Britain).
GNP. (1993) $36,674,000,000, per capita $660.
Land and climate. Egypt consists of a huge desert plateau bisected by the Nile Valley which flows the length of the land from south to north to end in its great delta on the Mediterranean. It has a desert climate of hot dry summers with moderate winters.

Introduction

Egypt's geographic position has enabled it to play a unique role on two continents since earliest times. Occupying the northeast corner of Africa – the hinge of the continent – that connects it to Asia, Egypt even at its weakest has been in an especially influential position between the African and Arab worlds. It has land borders with Libya (1,150km) and Sudan (1,273km) in Africa, while on the eastern extremity of the Sinai Peninsula it has a tiny border of 11km with the Gaza Strip and a 255km border with Israel. Egypt also has 2,450km of coastlines split between the Mediterranean in the north and the Red Sea to the east. The country is divided by the Valley of the Nile, the world's longest river which flows into the Mediterranean through its huge delta. Ninety per cent of the population live along the Nile Valley and since ancient times Egypt has regarded itself as the 'gift of the Nile'; it is the fertility of the Nile Valley that has made possible the growth of such a huge population in the middle of the Sahara Desert for the rest of the country consists simply of desert.

Egypt controls the Suez Canal and has the most sophisticated and complex economy on the African continent after that of South Africa. Egypt became a petroleum exporting country in 1976, an event which made a significant difference to the economy. Even so, the huge rate of population growth means that most economic advances are swallowed up by the demands of increased numbers. Economic development and survival are heavily dependent upon international aid (especially from the USA) but Egypt is also a heavily indebted country, with total international debts in 1993 amounting to $36,603,000,000, equivalent to 100 per cent of GNP.

Agriculture

Agriculture depends upon irrigation, using the Nile waters whose annual flooding gave rise to the 'legend' that Egypt was the 'gift of the Nile'; the Aswan High Dam whose construction with Russian aid followed the Anglo-French Suez débâcle of 1956 was intended to bring enough extra land under irrigation to enable Egypt to feed a million more people. By the time this was possible the expected population increase had already passed the numbers the Dam was destined to care for and that goes to the nub of Egypt's food problem. Egypt is not self-sufficient in food and seems unlikely ever to achieve such a status given the rate of population increase and the land available for irrigation.

Agriculture accounts for 16.5 per cent of GDP and employs 39.5 per cent of the workforce. Egypt is now the world's sixth largest producer of cotton (a major export) and cotton lint in 1993 came to 314,000mt; cotton yarn, textiles and fabrics accounted for 13.2 per cent of exports. The other main crops are rice, maize, wheat, beans, fruit and vegetables. Livestock make an important contribution to diet as does an annual fish catch of 300,000mt. Food production, however, does not keep pace with population and food imports account for about 18 per cent of total imports. Land use is divided between agricultural 2.7 per cent; other (virtually all desert) 97.3 per cent.

Minerals

Minerals (which means petroleum) account for 10 per cent of GDP although only employing a negligible 0.3 per cent of the workforce. Egypt became a petroleum surplus country in 1976 and by 1980 production was at the rate of 600,000b/d. Rising home consumption then suggested that Egypt would be a net importer once more by 1995 but new finds led to a substantial increase in production so that output for 1993 came to 333,200,000 barrels while consumption at 178,300,000 barrels was just over half this, leaving the balance for export. Egypt's proven reserves at the end of 1992 stood at 6,200,000,000 barrels or 0.6 per cent of world reserves with an estimated life (at current rates of extraction) of 18.6 years. All natural gas produced is consumed locally. Petroleum accounted for 48.9 per cent of exports in 1993–4. Iron ore, salt and clay are also mined.

Manufacturing

The manufacturing sector accounts for 16.7 per cent of GDP and employs 12.2 per cent of the workforce. It is one of the most diverse and sophisticated in the Third World. Principal manufactures are cement, nitrate fertilizer, reinforcing iron, sugar, phosphates fertilizer, cotton yarn, refrigerators and automobiles. Food processing is of major importance. There is a growing arms industry which was already earning $500,000,000 a year in the mid-1980s. Egypt is one of Africa's most important tourist destinations and tourism earned $1,332,000,000 in 1993 (less than half the earnings of the previous year). However, the tourist trade suffers during depression periods and is subject to political uncertainty as a result of deliberate attacks upon tourists by anti-Western fundamentalists. In recent years Egypt has developed as a transit country for (illegal) drugs moving from the golden triangle and golden crescent to markets in Europe and the USA.

Infrastructure

There are 5,110km of railroads of which 4,763km are standard 1.435m gauge; and 51,925km of highways, 17,900km of which are paved. The Nile has been a highway since time immemorial; there are 3,500km of waterways including the Nile, Lake Nasser (formed by the Aswan High Dam), the Alexandria–Cairo Waterway and many canals connecting the branches of the delta. The Suez Canal is 193.5km long and can be used by ocean-going vessels with a draught up to 16.1 metres; it is perhaps the most famous waterway in the world. Oil pipelines include 1,171km for crude oil, 596km for petroleum products and 460km for natural gas. Alexandria, Port Said, Suez, Bur Safajah and Damietta are the country's main ports. There are 82 usable airports of which 66 have permanent surface runways and of these two have runways of 3,659m length and 44 runways of 2,440 to 3,659m length. Although telecommunications are diverse and relatively good by Third World standards they are always behind requirements as the demands of the economy constantly increase.

Political considerations

Egypt's pivotal role in the Arab world became crucial in the 1970s when President Sadat broke the Arab–Israeli deadlock at the time of the Camp David Accords by recognizing Israel's right to exist. Three basic restraints now operate in Egypt. The first is the geographic fact that 95 per cent of the land is desert so that the huge population is confined to the Nile Valley and Delta while greater Cairo is one of the fastest growing metropolitan areas in the world. The second is the fact that the population is increasing at a rate of more than 1 million a year, always ahead of economic advances. Third, a new phenomenon, Egypt is coming more and more under the threat of fundamentalist activity which is part of a process that is now infecting the whole Muslim world. The ability of the government to contain fundamentalist challenges to its authority on the one hand, and to satisfy the ever-growing demands for better living standards of its expanding population on the other will be the most important tests in the years ahead.

Assessments

Egypt is unlikely ever to join the ranks of wealthy nations for its problems of poverty and numbers are simply too great. But its manufacturing base represents the best chance of improving its overall living standards in the future. Egypt is heavily dependent upon international aid. Its per capita income puts it at the top end of the low-income economies.

EL SALVADOR

Area. 8,124 sq. miles (21,041 sq. km).
Population. (1995) 5,768,000.
Capital. San Salvador (422,570 – metropolitan area 1,522,126).
Other major cities. Soyapango (251,811), Santa Ana (202,337), San Miguel (182,817), Mejicanos (145,000).
Language(s). Spanish (official), Nahua.
Religion(s). Roman Catholic 75 per cent, other 25 per cent.
Date of independence. September 15 1821 (from Spain).
GNP. (1993) $7,230,000,000, per capita $1,320.
Land and climate. The country is mountainous with a narrow coastal plain and central plateau. The climate is tropical with a rainy season from May to October and a dry season from November to April. El Salvador is subject to frequent earthquakes, deforestation and erosion.

Introduction

A tiny country of Central America, El Salvador is wedged between Guatemala and Honduras to the north and east and has a 307km coastline on the North Pacific. The economy is divided between agriculture, with coffee as the principal crop and export commodity, and manufacturing. There are virtually no minerals.

Agriculture

Agriculture accounts for 8.6 per cent of GDP and employs 34 per cent of the labour force. Coffee is the main commercial crop and in 1993 accounted for just over 31 per cent of export earnings. The prices received for coffee fluctuate substantially, especially since 1989 when the International Coffee Agreement collapsed. Other commercial crops such as sugar, cotton and tobacco were badly disrupted during the civil war of the 1980s when guerrillas attacked plantations. In 1993 sugar accounted for 4.3 per cent of exports and shrimps for a further 3.3 per cent (1992). The main staples are maize, rice, beans, oilseeds, beef and dairy products. The national cattle herd stands at 1,256,000. El Salvador is not self-sufficient in food. Land use is divided between forested 5 per cent, meadows and pastures 29.5 per cent, agricultural land under permanent cultivation 35.2 per cent, other 30.3 per cent.

Mining and manufacturing

The only mining activity is quarrying limestone. Prior to 1980 El Salvador was the most industrialized country in the Central American Common Market (CACM) but the civil war of the 1980s retarded economic growth as it damaged agriculture. There was a flight of capital from the country and, as a result of the 'Soccer War' with Honduras, no trade with that country over the years 1969 to 1982. In 1993 manufacturing accounted for 19 per cent of GDP and employed 13.9 per cent of the labour force. Principal products are food and beverages, textiles, petroleum products, chemicals, non-metallic mineral products, clothing, footwear, tobacco. The economy appeared to be recovering during the first years of the 1990s. Import licences are required for coffee seeds, sugar, leather and cotton. There was a major reduction of import tariffs in 1989.

Infrastructure

The country only has 602km of single track narrow gauge railway and 10,000km of highways of which 1,500km are paved. Acajutla and Cutuco are the main ports. There are 74 usable airports, five with permanent surface runways of which one has a runway over 2,440m in length. Telecommunications are adequate.

Political considerations

Hopefully the 1994 presidential elections signalled a new political phase. The twelve-year civil war between government forces and leftwing guerrillas had ended at the beginning of 1992 when the guerrillas signed an agreement with the government, although in 1994 the government was accused of not implementing its side of the agreement. The peace appeared precarious.

Assessments

Although it is in the ranks of the lower-middle-income economies, El Salvador has no minerals and an agriculture that is over-dependent upon the one crop (coffee) while the land is subject to a number of environmental hazards. It is unlikely that El Salvador will alter its economic standing or performance significantly in the foreseeable future.

ERITREA

Area. 45,300 sq. miles (117,400 sq. km).
Population. (1995) 3,531,000.
Capital. Asmara (400,000).
Other major cities. Assab (50,000), Keren (40,000), Massawa (40,000).
Language(s). No official language; Tigre, Kenama, Cushitic dialects, Arabic.
Religion(s). Muslim 50 per cent, Christian 50 per cent (of believers).
Date of independence. April 27 1993 (from Ethiopia).
GNP. (1993) $393,415, per capita $115.
Land and climate. A mountainous country which descends to a coastal plain in the east. Along the Red Sea coast it has a hot dry desert climate which becomes cooler and wetter in the highlands. The country is subject to frequent droughts and famine as well as deforestation and soil erosion.

Introduction

After 30 years of warfare against the government in Addis Ababa which had tried since 1950 to incorporate Eritrea fully into Ethiopia, the fall of Mengistu and collapse of his regime heralded the immediate possibility of Eritrean independence. A provisional government in Eritrea was set up on May 29 1991 under Issaias Afewerke (secretary-general of the Eritrean People's Liberation Front, EPLF) and two years later on April 23–25 1993 the people voted overwhelmingly in a referendum for independence and this followed on April 27 1993. Desperately poor, with infrastructure and economy in ruins after long years of bitter and destructive fighting, Eritrea faces a difficult economic future. The country has three land neighbours: Sudan, Ethiopia and Djibouti and a Red Sea coastline of 1,151km. Its position effectively makes Ethiopia landlocked.

Agriculture

A majority of the population depends upon subsistence farming. The national cattle herd is only 1,550,000 strong with similar numbers of sheep and goats. Staple foods consist of tubers, cereals, sorghum, vegetables, melons, pulses. (NB accurate statistics are not yet available.)

Mining and manufacturing

Salt and sand are at present exploited; there are unexploited deposits of copper, zinc, mica, gold, iron, manganese, nickel and lead. The total value of all manufactures in the mid-1980s came to about $57,000,000 at current prices.

Infrastructure

There are 307km of railroads and 3,845km of highways of which 807km are paved. Assab and Massawa are the country's ports. There are five usable airports two with runways between 2,440 and 3,659m in length. Telecommunications at present are minimal.

Political considerations

Given its extreme poverty and the expectations that must follow independence after 30 years of warfare, Eritrea faces a daunting task of building an economy virtually from scratch.

Assessments

A major source of finance consists of remittances from overseas Eritreans. With its long coastline on the Red Sea, Eritrea has three encouraging prospects: the possibility of offshore oil finds; the development of a tourist industry; and an expanding fisheries industry. In addition, it will receive revenues from the use of its ports by Ethiopia.

ETHIOPIA

Area. 437,794 sq. miles (1,133,882 sq. km).
Population. (1995) 55,053,000.
Capital. Addis Ababa (1,673,000).
Other major cities. Dire Dawa (117,734), Gonder (95,000), Nazret (90,975).
Language(s). Amharic (official), Tigrinya, Orominga, Guaraginga, Somali, Arabic, English.
Religion(s). Ethiopian Orthodox 52.5 per cent, Muslim 31.4 per cent, traditional beliefs 11.4 per cent, other 4.7 per cent.
Date of independence. Oldest independent country in Africa (2,000 years or more).
GNP. (1993) $5,329,000,000, per capita $100.
Land and climate. Most of the country consists of a high plateau with a central mountain range which is divided by the Great Rift Valley. The climate is tropical monsoon with wide variations according to altitude. Parts of the country are subject to periodic and extensive droughts. The Great Rift Valley is susceptible to earthquakes and volcanic action. Ethiopia suffers from a wide range of environmental problems including deforestation, over-grazing and soil erosion, desertification, drought and consequent famine.

Introduction

After 30 years of constant civil and military strife from 1962 to 1991, Ethiopia desperately needs a period of peace in which to rebuild what in any case is one of the poorest and least developed economies in the world. This 30-year period of conflict witnessed the war of liberation waged by breakaway Eritrea, the revolt of Tigre province, periodic uprisings among the Oromo of the south, the revolution of 1974–5 that overthrew the Emperor Haile Selassie and brought Mengistu Haile-Mariam and his Marxist regime to power, and the war with Somalia of 1977. The overthrow of Mengistu and his regime by the Ethiopian People's Revolutionary Democratic Front (EPRDF) in May 1991 brought this long period of fighting to an end. Independence for Eritrea in April 1993, by depriving Ethiopia of its direct access to the Red Sea, made it Africa's fifteenth landlocked state. Ethiopia has more than 5,000km of borders with five land neighbours – Sudan, Kenya, Somalia, Djibouti and Eritrea. The economy is almost entirely agricultural and with a per capita income of only $100 Ethiopia in recent years has vied with Mozambique for the dubious distinction of being rated the world's poorest country.

Agriculture

Agriculture is by far the most important economic activity even though drought, famine and inadequate agricultural practices mean that output is far below potential. Half agricultural production is at the subsistence level. State farms are responsible for a considerable part of cash crop output – that is, coffee and oilseeds. Agriculture accounts for 54.4 per cent of GDP and employs 74 per cent of the workforce. The main staples are maize, sorghum, barley, wheat, pulses, potatoes, millet, yams. The national cattle herd of 29,450,000 head is one of the largest in Africa; there are 21,700,000 sheep and 16,700,000 goats, 8,500,000 horses and 1 million camels.

Coffee has long been Ethiopia's most important export and production in 1994 came to 198,000mt while coffee accounted for 67.1 per cent of all exports. Hides account for another 16.4 per cent of exports. Cotton and oilseeds are also important cash crops. In the 1970s and 1980s Ethiopia suffered from major famines, partly the result of war, partly from drought and inadequate farming practices. Whether in conditions of peace and with greatly improved farming methods Ethiopia could meet her requirements in staple foods remains to be seen. In 2010 on present trends the population will have passed the 85 million mark. Land use is divided between forested 24.4 per cent, pasture 40.7 per cent, agriculture 12.7 per cent, other 22.2 per cent.

Minerals

The mining sector is very small; its basic components are cement, salt and limestone. The only highly valuable mineral (in small quantities) is gold. There is also a very small amount of platinum. Gold output in 1993 came to 128,603 troy ounces. The output of platinum was 48 troy ounces. There is some copper and potash, at present unexploited.

Manufacturing

Over 90 per cent of industry is state run though the successor government to the Mengistu regime is considering returning much of this to the private sector. Manufacturing contributes about 8 per cent to GDP and principal manufactures are food and beverages, textiles, leather goods and shoes, cigarettes and chemicals. Debts at more than $4.5bn are equivalent to 80 per cent of GNP.

Infrastructure

There is a total of 781km of railroads of which the most important stretch consists of 307km of 0.950m gauge line that runs from Addis Ababa to the port of Djibouti on the Red Sea; control of this line is shared between Ethiopia and Djibouti. There are 39,150km of highways of which only 2,776km are paved. Ethiopia is now landlocked and its two principal ports of entry are Massawa in Eritrea and the port of Djibouti.

There are 82 usable airports of which only nine have permanent surface runways; one of these has a runway above 3,659m and thirteen have runways between 2,440 and 3,659m in length. Telecommunications are adequate for government use.

Political considerations

In 1994 only Mozambique had a lower per capita GNP (worldwide) than did Ethiopia and given its poverty, the rapid increase taking place in an already large population and the legacy of 30 years of internecine warfare, the main political problem (with an extremely poor economic base upon which to build) is to maintain stability and peace between the widely varying ethnic groups that make up the population. In May 1994 the draft constitution for the Federal Democratic Republic of Ethiopia was approved by the transitional Council of Representatives. This constitution lays down a doctrine of ethnic federalism and grants each 'nation' which makes up Ethiopia the right to self-determination. Whether the constitution holds is the key political question.

Assessments

One of the world's poorest countries with minimal resources and a large population, Ethiopia faces a long hard haul simply to improve a standard of living rated among the lowest in the world.

GEORGIA

Area. 26,900 sq. miles (69,700 sq. km).
Population. (1995) 5,514,000.
Capital. T'bilisi (1,270,000).
Other major cities. K'ut'aisi (240,200), Rust'ari (158,000), Bat'umi (137,000), Sukhumi (112,000).
Language(s). Georgian (official), Armenian, Azerbaijani, Russian.
Religion(s). Georgian Orthodox 65 per cent, Muslim 11 per cent, Russian Orthodox 10 per cent, Armenian Orthodox 8 per cent.
Date of independence. April 9 1991 (from the USSR).
GNP. (1993) $3,055,000,000, per capita $560.
Land and climate. The country is predominantly mountainous with the Great Caucasus Mountains in the north and the Lesser Caucasus Mountains in the south; lowlands open on to the Black Sea. There are good soils in the river valley flood plains. The Black Sea enjoys a Mediterranean climate.

Introduction

The once prosperous Georgian SSR, which formerly accounted for 97 per cent of USSR citrus fruit and 93 per cent of its tea while also offering a notable Black Sea tourist industry, has been reduced by destructive internecine fighting, since the break-up of the USSR, to the level of a low-income economy in which half its productive capacity has simply collapsed. The major mineral resource is manganese. Georgia has four neighbours: Turkey, Russia, Armenia and Azerbaijan, the latter two countries having also become independent from the former USSR during the course of 1991. Georgia has a 310km coastline on the Black Sea.

Agriculture

In 1992 agriculture accounted for 52 per cent of GDP and employed 33 per cent of the labour force. The main products are fruit, vegetables, grapes, maize and potatoes, with relatively small amounts of wheat and barley. Livestock includes 1,050,000 head of cattle and a similar number of sheep and goats. Food products accounted for 19 per cent of exports in 1992. The subsequent fighting in 1992–4 as Abkhazia sought to break away and further internal dissent threatened growing civil war led to the collapse of normal production. Citrus fruits and tea should remain major export crops to Russia and other ex-Soviet countries once political normality has been restored. Land use is divided between forested 38.7 per cent, pastures 28.7 per cent, agriculture 14.8 per cent, other 17.8 per cent.

Mining

Georgia is one of the world's principal sources of manganese and ranks eighth as a world producer with an output in 1993 of 250,000mt. Other minerals include iron ore and copper and there are small coal and oil deposits. There are also resources of molybdenum, arsenic, tungsten and mercury. Fuel is largely imported from neighbouring republics.

Manufacturing

During 1994, as a result of factionalism and civil war, Georgia registered a drop of 42 per cent in industrial production, a situation that was made worse by the non-delivery of natural gas from Turkmenistan due to the Georgian government's inability to pay $500m of debts. The main industrial products (1991) were crude steel, rolled ferrous metals, rolled steel, cast iron, steel tubes, canned food, mineral fertilizers, meat and sausage, synthetic resins and plastics, synthetic fibres, soap, bricks, cement tiles, footwear, knitwear, colour television, machine tools, prefabricated concrete structures, ceramic tiles, silk fabrics, cotton fabrics, wool fabrics, carpets, wine, beer, cognac, vodka and liqueurs. It has, therefore, the industrial potential for a developed economy. In 1992 light industrial products accounted for 7.6 per cent of exports, machinery and metal-working equipment for another 16.9 per cent. Virtually all exports (about 98 per cent) go to former Soviet republics.

Infrastructure

There are 1,570km of railroads (excluding industrial lines), 33,900km of roads of which 29,500km are hard surfaced, 370km of pipeline for crude oil, 300km for refined products and 440km for natural gas. Georgia is served by three ports on the Black Sea – Batumi, Poti and Sukhumi. There are 26 usable airports, nineteen with permanent surface runways, ten of which are 2,440 to 3,659m in length. Telecommunications are inadequate to poor.

Political considerations

Since its independence in 1991 Georgia has been devastated by three conflicts: the breakaway of Abkhazia; the secessionist efforts of South Ossetia (where the hard-line secessionists were still in the ascendant in 1995); and major opposition in Georgia itself to the government of Eduard Shevardnadze especially following his (necessary) rapprochement with Moscow in 1993 when Georgia agreed to join the Commonwealth of Independent States (CIS). In April 1994 an agreement was reached between Abkhazia, Russia, Georgia and the UN whereby Georgians in Abkhazia would be repatriated although subsequently Abkhazia showed reluctance to keep its side of the agreement. The result of these divisions has been a state of ongoing civil war which has done great damage to the economy while an estimated 1 million Georgians have emigrated to Russia. Until these questions have been fully settled, especially the relationship with Russia, Georgia cannot expect to enjoy any long-term stability.

Assessments

Georgia has a reasonable mineral base, excellent agricultural potential for export crops and a widely developed industrial structure. It should become a prosperous middle-income economy with better long-term prospects but only when the current divisive and destructive differences have been resolved.

GHANA

Area. 92,098 sq. miles (238,533 sq. km).
Population. (1995) 16,472,000.
Capital. Accra (949,100).
Other major cities. Kumasi (385,200), Tamale (151,100), Tema (110,000), Sekondi-Takoradi (103,600).
Language(s). English (official), Akan, Moshi-Dagomba, Ewe, Ga.
Religion(s). Christian 62.6 per cent, traditional beliefs 21.4 per cent, Muslim 15.7 per cent, other 0.3 per cent.
Date of independence. March 6 1957 (from Britain).
GNP. (1993) $6,992,000,000, per capita $430.

Land and climate. The country consists mainly of low plains and dissected plateau in the south-central region; the climate is tropical, and hot and dry in the north which is subject to the Harmattan (desert) wind. Drought, deforestation, over-grazing and soil erosion affect the land.

Introduction

When the Gold Coast became independent as Ghana in 1957 it had a sound all-round economy with a strong agricultural sector, was the world's leading producer of cocoa and looked forward to apparently major new industrial possibilities with the completion of the Akosombo Dam and the consequent creation of the world's largest manmade lake, Lake Volta. In the succeeding quarter of a century, however, a great deal went wrong with the economy and many of the high hopes at independence were dashed, especially during the 1970s which were a period of economic collapse under military rule. An economic rebuilding programme (with substantial international aid) was launched in 1983 but though many advances have been made since that date, the economy is still too dependent upon cocoa and timber exports from the agricultural sector, and gold, which is the principal mineral earner. A stock exchange was opened in 1990. Ghana has three land neighbours: Côte d'Ivoire to the west, Burkina Faso to the north and Togo to the east; and a 539km Atlantic coastline on the Gulf of Guinea.

Agriculture

Agriculture accounts for 47.8 per cent of GDP and employs 59.4 per cent of the workforce – about 3,300,000. The main cash crop is cocoa. Ghana was the leading cocoa producer in the world in the 1960s but production declined disastrously in the 1970s (due to political and economic mismanagement). Today, after a period of painful rehabilitation, cocoa production is rising again. In 1994 cocoa output was 270,000mt and cocoa accounted for 26.1 per cent of exports. Other cash crops are coffee, bananas, palm kernels, copra, limes, kola and shea nuts. Staple food crops are cassava, yams, maize, sorghum, millet, rice, groundnuts, sugarcane, coconuts and a range of fruits. Timber production is of major importance and roundwood output in 1993 came to 17,192,000cu m and timber accounted for 13.5 per cent of exports. The fisheries sector is strong and in 1993 the fish catch came to 371,227mt of which anchovies (an export item) accounted for 81,350mt. The national cattle herd, however, is quite small (1,680,000 head). Ghana is normally self-sufficient in food although it is subject to periodic droughts which affect marginal agricultural activities.

Mining

Ghana is a leading world producer of three minerals: bauxite (and aluminium), manganese and gold. In 1994 bauxite output came to 451,802mt; manganese to 238,429mt; and gold to 44,505kg. Gold accounted for 44.7 per cent of exports.

Mining, however, only accounts for 1.9 per cent of GDP and only employs 0.5 per cent of the workforce. Industrial diamonds (739,961 carats in 1994) accounted for 1.7 per cent of exports. There are substantial manganese deposits and huge bauxite deposits although there is a surfeit of bauxite worldwide. Small offshore oil fields were brought on stream in 1978 but low world prices subsequently made their exploitation unviable. In 1986 a mineral code was enacted which specifies that mining operations must be self-financing in foreign exchange.

Manufacturing

Manufacturing achieved a high point in the 1960s when it accounted for 22 per cent of GDP. In 1993, however, it accounted for only 9.1 per cent of GDP and employed 10.5 per cent of the workforce. Nonetheless, the sector is reasonably diversified and covers cement, petroleum products, flour, soap, iron rods, cocoa (cake, butter and liquor), edible fats and oils, toothpaste, textiles, soft drinks, beer, evaporated milk, ice cream, cigarettes, paper, and chemicals. A high proportion of food processing activity is for exports such as cocoa.

Infrastructure

Major renovation is being undertaken on Ghana's 953km of 1.067m gauge railways. There are 32,250km of highways of which 6,084km are hard surfaced. There are 168km of inland waterways on the Volta, Ankobra and Tano rivers while Lake Volta provides an additional 1,125km of arterial feeder waterways. The country is served by two ports: Tema and Takoradi. There are nine usable airports, five with permanent surface runways of which two are between 2,440 and 3,659m in length. Telecommunications are poor or inadequate.

Political considerations

Since independence Ghana has suffered from wasteful civilian regimes and incompetent military ones. Since 1983 the Rawlings government has been working on an economic rebuilding programme that, broadly, has accepted the application of greater market forces and has gradually relaxed government controls. Ghana has received substantial international aid for its economic rebuilding programme; in 1994 total external debts were equivalent to 39 per cent of GNP.

Assessments

A rich agricultural country that is self-sufficient in food and well endowed with minerals, Ghana has reasonable prospects of moving up into the lower-middle-income group of economies. Pressures of growing population, however, present major problems for the future; the estimated population doubling time is only 23 years.

GUATEMALA

Area. 42,042 sq. miles (108,889 sq. km).
Population. (1995) 10,621,000.
Capital. Guatemala City (1,167,495).
Other major cities. Mixco (436,668), Villa Nueva (165,567), Chinautla (61,335).
Language(s). Spanish (official), Indian languages.
Religion(s). Roman Catholic 75 per cent, Protestant (fundamentalist) 25 per cent.
Date of independence. September 15 1821 (from Spain).
GNP. (1993) $11,123,000,000, per capita $1,110.
Land and climate. Guatemala is a mainly mountainous country with narrow coastal plains and a rolling limestone plateau. The climate is tropical with hot humid lowlands and cooler highlands. It is a volcanic region and subject to frequent earthquakes. The Caribbean coast suffers from hurricanes; the land is deteriorating as a result of deforestation and soil erosion.

Introduction

The politics of this Central American country have long been troubled with constant left–right violence, military intervention and return to civilian control, and near dictatorship. In January 1994 the government and the Guatemala National Revolutionary Unity resumed peace negotiations which had been broken off in May 1993. But 1994 was, nonetheless, a year of continuing violence. Guatemala has four land neighbours: Mexico, Belize, Honduras and El Salvador; a 400km coastline on the Pacific; and a short coastline on the Caribbean. It is a predominantly agricultural economy.

Agriculture

Agriculture accounts for just under 25 per cent of GDP and employs 58 per cent of the labour force. The sector divides between family and corporate agriculture. The principal export crops are coffee, sugar, bananas and cardamom. Fishing is also of growing importance as a source of exports and in 1993 these between them accounted for 55 per cent of all exports. Cotton and cotton seed is another cash crop. The main staples are maize, tomatoes, beans, sorghum, plantains. The national cattle herd is just over 2 million head. Roundwood production in 1993 came to 11,263,000cu m and is another source of foreign exchange earnings. Guatemala is not self-sufficient in food. Land use is divided between forested 33.8 per cent, meadows and pastures 13 per cent, agricultural land under permanent cultivation 17.4 per cent, other 35.8 per cent.

Mining

Mining contributes only 0.3 per cent to GDP and employs only 0.1 per cent of the labour force. Gypsum, iron ore and antimony are mined and there are small petroleum deposits which yielded 2,206,000 barrels of oil in 1992.

Manufacturing

By pursuing a policy of high tariffs and import substitution Guatemala has managed to create the largest local industrial sector of Central America and directed a significant 25 per cent of its trade to the Central American Common Market (CACM) countries. But the 1980s were a period of political instability and recession and Guatemala suffered an adverse trade balance during the decade. Manufacturing accounts for 14.3 per cent of GDP and employs 13.6 per cent of the workforce. The main manufactures are food and beverages, clothing and footwear, textiles and metal products, furniture, rubber, petroleum and chemicals. Tourism contributes about $250m a year to foreign exchange earnings, most visitors coming from the USA. Efforts at trade liberalization at the end of the 1980s were reversed in the early 1990s but in 1992 new moves towards liberalization led to a growth of trade.

Infrastructure

There are 1,019km of 0.914m gauge railways of which 102km are privately owned; 26,429km of highways of which 2,868km are paved; and 260km of inland waterways navigable year round. There is a 275km pipeline for crude oil. The country is served by three Pacific ports: Puerto Barrios, Puerto Quetzal and Santo Tomás de Castilla. There are 418 usable airports, eleven with permanent surface runways of which three are between 2,440 and 3,659m in length. The telecommunications system is reasonable.

Political considerations

Guatemala has experienced a deeply troubled, violent history ever since the 1954 invasion from Honduras (backed by the USA) to 'prevent' the country from turning to communism. The period 1954 to 1966 was one of political instability and rising violence; during the 1970s left–right violence developed into civil war and the 1980s were a period of permanent civil war. Moves towards an accommodation between the government and the left began to look promising in 1993 to 1995.

Assessments

Guatemala ranks as a lower-middle-income country and has a mixed economy with a reasonable agricultural base and considerable potential for growth in the manufacturing sector. It is not a mineral-rich country.

GUINEA

Area. 94,926 sq. miles (245,857 sq. km).
Population. (1995) 6,700,000.
Capital. Conakry (705,280).
Other major cities. Kankan (88,760), Labé (65,439), Kindia (55,904).
Language(s). French (official), a number of tribal languages.
Religion(s). Muslim 85 per cent, traditional beliefs 5 per cent, other 10 per cent.
Date of independence. October 2 1958 (from France).
GNP. (1993) $3,260,000,000, per capita $520.
Land and climate. A flat coastal plain extends inland to hilly and then mountainous country: the Futa Djallon Mountains in the northeast are a major watershed for West Africa. The climate is hot and humid; there is a monsoon season (June to November) with southwesterly winds; and a dry season (December to May) with the northeasterly harmattan wind.

Introduction

Under a National Recovery Council put in place by the military in 1989 on the death of Sekou Touré, the new military president promised a return to civilian multiparty democracy by the mid-1990s. Guinea has one of the strongest mineral sectors in Africa but remains a predominantly agricultural society while its manufacturing remains very small. Guinea has six neighbours: Guinea-Bissau, Senegal, Mali, Côte d'Ivoire, Liberia and Sierra Leone; and a 320km Atlantic seaboard.

Agriculture

Most agricultural activity consists of subsistence farming, and agriculture, including forestry and fisheries, accounts for 24 per cent of GDP and employs 78 per cent of the workforce. The principal staples are cassava, yams, rice, plantains, vegetables and melons, sugarcane, maize, pineapples, pulses, palm kernels and palm oil. The country is not self-sufficient in grains. There is a substantial roundwood production – 4,549,000cu m in 1993. The national cattle herd is 1,650,000 strong. Coffee and fish are important exports; in 1993 coffee accounted for 6 per cent of exports, fish for a further 2.7 per cent. Land use is divided between forested 58.8 per cent, meadows and pastures 22.4 per cent, agricultural land under permanent cultivation 3 per cent, other 15.8 per cent.

Mining

Guinea ranks second to Australia in world terms as a producer of bauxite and is estimated to possess about one-third of the world's high-grade bauxite resources. In 1993 bauxite production came to 16,259,000mt and bauxite accounted for 53.3 per cent of exports while alumina accounted for a further 17.9 per cent. There are huge iron ore deposits including an estimated 1,000 million tons of high-grade ore at the one site of Mount Nimba near the border with Liberia. Exploitation of this ore, however, depends upon transport through Liberia and so awaits a resolution of the civil war chaos in that country.

The mining of diamonds has had a chequered history since the 1960s when it became important to the economy. During the 1970s output reached 80,000 carats a year but theft and smuggling became so prevalent that the government suspended all diamond production in the late 1970s to curtail these activities. Diamond mining was resumed by private companies in 1980 and diamond output in 1993 came to 100,000 carats and accounted for 11.5 per cent of exports. Gold mining is small scale, done by individuals as well as industrially, and output is subject to substantial fluctuations. In 1993 gold output came to only 500 kg. A search for oil which has so far yielded nothing nonetheless continues. Guinea is blessed with very substantial hydro-electric potential. In 1993 mining contributed 19.5 per cent to GDP but only employed 0.7 per cent of the workforce.

Manufacturing

The manufacturing sector is small and underdeveloped, accounting for only 4.6 per cent of GDP and employing a mere 0.6 per cent of the workforce. The principal manufactures are corrugated and sheet iron, plastics, tobacco products, cement, printed matter, fruit juice, beer and matches.

Infrastructure

There are 1,045km of railroads of which 239km are standard gauge 1.435m and 806km are 1.000m gauge. Of 30,100km of highways only 1,145km are paved. There are 1,295km of inland waterways navigable by shallow-draft craft. Conakry and Kamsan are the country's two ports. There are fifteen usable airports, four with permanent surface runways of which three are between 2,440 and 3,659m in length. Telecommunications are poor to fair.

Political considerations

President Sekou Touré, who became head of state at independence in 1958, was to exercise dictatorial powers for thirty years. He moved the country to the left, partly from ideological conviction and partly in response to France's virtual boycott following Guinea's 'no' vote to association with France in 1958. However, an economic stabilization programme with IMF backing was launched in 1986 while a rapprochement with France and adherence to the EU Lomé Conventions brought Guinea back into closer economic association with Europe.

Assessments

Huge mineral exports ensure a positive balance of payments while Guinea's debt, equivalent to 55 per cent of GNP in 1992, is more manageable than in the 1980s. Even so, the country remains a very poor low-income economy. There are considerable prospects for increasing agricultural output while capital injection would allow an adequate proportion of the huge bauxite output to be turned into alumina prior to export.

HAITI

Area. 10,695 sq. miles (27,700 sq. km).
Population. (1995) 6,589,000.
Capital. Port-au-Prince (752,600 – metropolitan area 1,255,078).
Other major cities. Carrefour (241,223), Delmas (200,251), Cap Haïtien (92,122).
Language(s). French (official), Haitian Creole.
Religion(s). Roman Catholic 80.3 per cent, Protestant 15.8 per cent, non-religious/other 3.9 per cent.
Date of independence. January 1 1804 (from France).
GNP. (1992) $2,479,000,000, per capita $370.
Land and climate. Mostly rough mountainous country with a tropical climate. The east is semi-arid where mountains cut off the trade winds.

Introduction

Abject poverty and lack of basic amenities – the majority of the people do not have access to safe drinking water, proper medical care or adequate food – have made Haiti a two-tier society split between its poor masses and the rich right-wing oligarchy that normally controls the country. The elections of December 1990 which brought the popular left-wing priest, Jean-Bertrand Aristide, to power were countered in September 1991 by a right-wing coup to oust him. This, in turn, led to eventual US intervention in September 1994 when 20,000 US troops were landed in Haiti to restore President Aristide to power. Haiti shares the island of Hispaniola in the northern Caribbean (the western half) with the Dominican Republic.

Agriculture

Most agricultural activity consists of small-scale subsistence farming. Commercial crops are coffee, mangoes, sugarcane and wood. The food staples are rice, maize, sorghum. Haiti is not self-sufficient in food, especially wheat. Agriculture accounts for 39 per cent of GDP and employs 57 per cent of the workforce. Crop production in 1994 included sugarcane 2,250,000mt, plantains 272,000mt, mangoes 230,000mt, bananas 230,000mt, maize 210,000mt. Coffee production came to 34,000mt and accounted for 9 per cent of exports. Roundwood production (in 1993) came to 6,171,000cu m and timber, sisal and twine and sisal handicrafts combined accounted for 10.1 per cent of exports. The national cattle herd is 800,000 strong. Land use is divided between forested 1.3 per cent, meadows and pastures 18 per cent, agricultural land under permanent cultivation 33 per cent, other 47.7 per cent.

Mining and manufacturing

Mining only contributes 0.1 per cent to GDP and employs 0.9 per cent of the workforce. Mining activity consists of quarrying for limestone and marble. Manufacturing accounts for 12.9 per cent of GDP and employs 5.6 per cent of the workforce. The manufacturing sector is principally concerned with the assembly of components or producing garments for the US market and US companies have located in Haiti because of the low wage structure. Most light industries have been established in the industrial zone outside Port-au-Prince. Principal manufactures are cement, essential oils (amyris, neroli, vetiver), cigarettes and beer. Articles for re-export include garments, sports equipment, toys, electronic components, luggage and handbags. Manufactures account for 68.5 per cent of exports.

Infrastructure

There is only one 40km stretch of privately owned narrow gauge industrial rail track. There are 4,000km of highways of which 950km are paved. Port-au-Prince and Cap Haïtien are the country's two ports. Of ten usable airports, three have permanent surface runways, one with a length between 2,440 and 3,659m. Telecommunications are only just adequate.

Political considerations

Following the US intervention (with UN approval) in Haiti in 1994, the government of President Aristide came back to precarious control once more. The question for the future must be: what happens when the USA withdraws its forces?

Assessments

One of the two poorest countries (the other is Guyana) of the Central American region in terms of resources, rate of population increase (doubling time 33 years), poverty and long-standing divisions between rich and poor, Haiti seems likely to remain at the lower end of the poverty scale into the foreseeable future.

HONDURAS

Area. 43,277 sq. miles (112,088 sq. km).
Population. (1995) 5,512,800.
Capital. Tegucigalpa (738,500).
Other major cities. San Pedro Sula (353,800), La Ceiba (82,900), El Progreso (77,300), Choluteca (66,200).
Language(s). Spanish (official), Indian dialects.
Religion(s). Roman Catholic 85 per cent, Protestant 10 per cent, other 5 per cent.
Date of independence. September 15 1821 (from Spain).
GNP. (1993) $3,220,000,000, per capita $580.
Land and climate. The interior is mountainous but there are narrow coastal plains. The climate is subtropical in the lowlands and temperate in the highlands.

Introduction

During the 1980s Honduras became an unwilling host to Contra bases as the civil war in Nicaragua escalated; at least, in compensation it received $1bn of aid over the period from the USA. Honduras is one of the poorest countries of Central America, its economy heavily tied to the USA as its principal export market and main source of imports. Bananas and coffee are the main export crops. Honduras has boundaries with three neighbours – Guatemala, El Salvador and Nicaragua – and a total coastline of 820km, mainly on the Caribbean but with a short Pacific coast on the Gulf of Fonseca.

Agriculture

This is the most important sector of the economy, accounting for 20 per cent of GDP and employing 45 per cent of the labour force. It also accounts for more than 70 per cent of exports. The most important cash crops are bananas, coffee, timber, beef, citrus fruits and shrimps. The banana crop in 1993 was 930,000mt and accounted for 28.3 per cent of exports; coffee at 128,000mt accounted for 15.3 per cent of exports; shrimps and lobsters for 16.5 per cent and frozen meats for 4.8 per cent. Although roundwood production is in excess of 6,000,000cu m a year, in 1994 Honduras introduced a moratorium on logging while it formulated a new policy to control state forests and the rate of depletion and defined the role of the private sector in this field. The government was alarmed at the rate of deforestation which was causing soil erosion. The national cattle herd is 2,286,000 head. The principal staples are maize, plantains, sorghum, beans and rice. Honduras is an importer of wheat. Land use is divided between forested 28.4 per cent, meadows and pastures 23 per cent, agricultural land under permanent cultivation 16.5 per cent, other 32.1 per cent.

Mining

Mineral resources include gold, silver, copper, lead, zinc, iron ore, antimony and coal, but not all are currently being exploited. Mining contributes 2 per cent to GDP but only employs 0.3 per cent of the workforce. The principal mineral exports are lead and zinc: in 1991 zinc production came to 32,000mt and lead to 9,000mt. Combined they accounted for 3.4 per cent of exports. There are small petroleum deposits but Honduras still has to import part of its oil requirements.

Manufacturing

Manufacturing accounts for 18 per cent of GDP and employs 11.8 per cent of the workforce. Most industry is in its early stages. Principal manufactures are cement, raw sugar, flour, beer, cigarettes. Following the 'Soccer War' with El Salvador in 1969, Honduras stopped all trade with that country until 1982 which had an adverse effect upon its industrial growth.

Infrastructure

There are 785km of railroad of which 508km are 1.067m gauge. Of 8,950km of roads, 1,700km are paved. There are 465km of inland waterways open to small craft. Puerto Castillo, Puerto Cortés and San Lorenzo are the main ports. There are 137 usable airports of which eleven have permanent surface runways, four of them between 2,440 and 3,659m in length. Telecommunications are generally inadequate.

Political considerations

An economic reform programme was initiated in 1990 by President Callejas. A Liberal President, Carlos Roberto Reina, came to office in January 1994 and pledged the government to promote economic growth.

Assessments

A low-income economy with few natural resources, Honduras faces a number of problems which inhibit economic development including rapid population growth, high unemployment and over-dependence upon two export crops, bananas and coffee, which are subject to world price fluctuations. Little alteration of this situation appears likely to take place in the foreseeable future.

JAMAICA

Area. 4,244 sq. miles (10,991 sq. km).
Population. (1995) 2,520,000.
Capital. Kingston (103,721 – metropolitan area 587,798).
Other major cities. Spanish Town (92,383), Portmore (90,138), Montego Bay (83,446).
Language(s). English (official), Creole.
Religion(s). Protestant (various sects) 55.9 per cent, Roman Catholic 5 per cent, non-religious, atheist, unstated 28.9 per cent, other 10.2 per cent of which Rastafarian 5 per cent.
Date of independence. August 6 1962 (from Britain).
GNP. (1993) $3,927,000,000, per capita $1,190.
Land and climate. A mountainous island with narrow, broken coastal plains, Jamaica has a tropical climate which is hot and humid though temperate in the hills. The island is subject to hurricanes, deforestation and water pollution.

Introduction

Lying 160 miles south of Cuba in the northern Caribbean, Jamaica is one of the largest of the West Indian islands. A British colony for more than 300 years, Jamaica's population is mostly of African descent from former slaves brought over to work the sugar plantations. Although politics can sometimes be violent there is a firm democratic tradition. Since independence Jamaica has struggled to overcome problems of poverty in an island whose economy is dominated by three activities – bauxite production, sugar and tourism.

Agriculture

Agriculture accounts for 9.7 per cent of GDP and employs 20 per cent of the labour force; agricultural products account for 17 per cent of exports. The most important export crops (1994) are raw sugar (5.6 per cent), bananas (3.7 per cent), rum (1.7 per cent) and coffee (1.3 per cent). Jamaica's Blue Mountain coffee is famous. Other commercial crops include citrus fruits, potatoes and vegetables. The livestock sector is small and Jamaica is not self-sufficient in meat or dairy products and also has to import grains. Land use is divided between forested 17 per cent, meadows and pastures 17.5 per cent, agricultural land, under permanent cultivation 25 per cent, other 40.5 per cent.

Mining

Mining contributes 7 per cent to GDP but employs less than 1 per cent of the labour force. The sector is dominated by bauxite (Jamaica is the world's third largest producer of bauxite and has extensive deposits of the mineral). In 1994 a total of

3,628,000mt of bauxite was produced and 3,221,000mt of alumina and alumina accounted for 44.1 per cent of exports, bauxite for a further 5.9 per cent. The bauxite industry in which the government has a 51 per cent stake is otherwise controlled by US and Canadian companies. The only other mineral of any importance mined is gypsum. Jamaica has neither oil nor coal and is a net importer of power.

Manufacturing

Apart from mining activities, principal manufactures consist of textiles, food processing and light industries. The sector contributes 19.7 per cent to GDP and employs 9 per cent of the workforce. Tourism is of major importance (most visitors come from North America) and in 1994 receipts from tourism came to $915,000,000. The illegal production and export of drugs (marijuana) may be equal in value to legitimate exports.

Infrastructure

There is a 294km 1.435m standard gauge single track railway; of 18,200km of roads 12,600km are paved. Kingston, Montego Bay and Port Antonio are the island's three ports. There are 23 usable airports, ten with permanent surface runways of which two are between 2,440 and 3,659m in length. The telecommunications network is reasonable, the domestic telephone system is fully automatic.

Political considerations

Politics are volatile and in 1994, for example, the opposition Jamaica Labour Party (JLP) refused to participate in elections so enabling the People's National Party (PNP) to retain its hold on power in by-elections. The JLP claimed the 1993 elections had been unfair and insisted upon reform of the electoral system. Poverty and unemployment (officially running at 16 per cent) are the main political–social problems. The government stated in 1994 that it saw the existing IMF Extended Fund Facility due to end in 1995 as the last since the economy was improving (Jamaica had been receiving IMF loans since 1977). International debts are slightly less than the GNP and Jamaica is a recipient of US and EU aid.

Assessments

A lower-middle-income economy, Jamaica is unlikely greatly to alter its economic status in the foreseeable future; its three basic foreign exchange earners – bauxite, sugar and tourism – are especially subject to world economic variations.

JORDAN

Area. 34,342 sq. miles (88,946 sq. km).
Population. (1995) 4,187,000.
Capital. Amman (963,000).
Other major cities. ar-Zarqa (344,524), Irbid (208,201), as-Salt (187,014), ar-Rusayfah (131,130), al-Mafraq (109,841).
Language(s). Arabic (official), English.
Religion(s). Islam, Sunni Muslim 93 per cent (official), Christian 4.9 per cent, other 2.1 per cent.
Date of independence. May 25 1946 (from Britain which held the League of Nations mandate).
GNP. (1993) $4,881,000,000, per capita $1,190.
Land and climate. Jordan consists mainly of a desert plateau with a highland area in the west. The Great Rift Valley separates the East and West Banks of the Jordan River. The climate is arid desert, although there is a rainy season in the west from November to April. The country suffers from over-grazing, soil erosion and increasing desertification.

Introduction

Created as the British Protectorate of Trans-Jordan in 1923 when it was separated from Palestine (as a kingdom for Britain's Hashemite allies from World War I) Jordan became fully independent in 1946 and has been ruled as a constitutional monarchy (more or less) since 1953 by King Hussein, by far the most enduring and longest lasting of Arab leaders in the Middle East. Open desert country with no easily definable borders, without oil (except very small shale possibilities) and wedged between Israel on the one hand and the far more powerful Arab states of Syria, Iraq and Saudi Arabia on the other, Jordan's political survival has always been problematic. Virtually landlocked and very much a transit country, it does have a 26km coastline on the strategic Gulf of Aqaba where Aqaba is its only port. The country derives about 65 per cent of its GDP (one of the highest such figures in the world) from service industries.

Jordan has always been heavily dependent upon foreign aid and relies on Iraq for oil supplies as well as revenues for trans-shipment of that country's imports and exports. Jordan was adversely affected by the events of 1990–91 (the Gulf War against Iraq) when by force of circumstances it was largely obliged to support Iraq and, as a consequence, was subsequently penalized by UN sanctions which led to a heavy drop in Iraq's transit trade, a cut-back in trade with Saudi Arabia and the return home of Jordanians who formerly had remitted currency. Jordan's rapprochement with Israel in 1994 when the two countries signed a bilateral peace treaty (October 26) represented a major step towards greater security. But Israel's recognition of Jordan's 'custodian' role over Islamic holy sites in Jerusalem led to worsening Jordanian relations with the Palestinian Arabs.

Agriculture

Formerly, Jordan's best agricultural land was found in the West Bank. Today, though it produces a range of foodstuffs including wheat, barley, citrus fruit, tomatoes, melons and olives, Jordan is a huge net importer of foodstuffs, particularly grains, and in 1994 food accounted for 17.3 per cent of all imports. Nonetheless, fruits and vegetables account for 8.2 per cent of exports, dairy products and eggs for another 5 per cent. The most important product in both quantity and exports is tomatoes (550,000mt output in 1994). Agriculture accounts for 8 per cent of GDP and employs 6.4 per cent of the workforce. Jordan is unlikely to be food self-sufficient in the foreseeable future. Land use is divided between forested 0.8 per cent, meadows and pastures 8.9 per cent, agricultural land, under permanent cultivation 4.5 per cent, other (mainly desert) 85.8 per cent.

Mining

Mineral resources include phosphates, potash and small deposits of shale oil and mining accounts for 3.1 per cent of GDP. Mining output in 1994 included 4,218,000mt of phosphate ore and 1,550,000mt of potash. Phosphate fertilizers accounted for 12.6 per cent of exports in 1994, potash for a further 11.7 per cent and fertilizers for another 11.2 per cent. Jordan is the world's third largest exporter of phosphate and potash. A significant find of natural gas was made in 1989 though it awaits exploitation. The oil refinery at Zarqa has an annual capacity of 4,200,000mt. The Tapline from Saudi Arabia to the Mediterranean crosses Jordan.

Manufacturing

Manufacturing accounts for 14.4 per cent of GDP and employs 10.6 per cent of the workforce. The principal manufactures are chemicals, non-metallic mineral products, tobacco, food products, petroleum refining, basic metal products, beverages, paper and paper products, fabricated metal products, plastics, clothing, printing and publishing, non-electrical machinery, electrical machinery. The sector is heavily dependent on Iraq as a market so was badly affected by the Gulf War of 1991 and its aftermath. A large proportion of the transit trade through the port of Aqaba is for Iraq. Pharmaceuticals, soap and detergents account for about 15 per cent of exports, cement for another 2.5 per cent.

Infrastructure

There are 789km of single track 1.050m gauge railroad; 7,500km of highways of which 5,500km are paved; and 209km of pipeline for crude oil. The country has only one outlet to the sea at the port of Aqaba. There are fifteen usable airports, one with a runway of 3,659m and thirteen with runways between 2,440m and 3,659m in length. The home telephone system is reasonable and regional and international tele-communications are fair to good.

Political considerations

Jordan was an artificial state created out of the former Ottoman Empire at the end of World War I. Its position between far more powerful (and potentially predatory) Arab states as well as facing Israel has always meant that its international standing has been precarious. Under the remarkable leadership of King Hussein since 1953 Jordan has survived repeated threats to its existence. Despite its minerals and a reasonable manufacturing base it remains very much a service country, dependent upon aid, and as a transit country both for the Saudi Tapline to the Mediterranean and for the passage of goods to Iraq. As a frontline Arab state facing Israel, Jordan has always been obliged to perform a political balancing act. Since the 1994 peace treaty with Israel it faces new problems in relation to the Israeli–Palestinian peace process.

Assessments

There are light restrictions on foreign currency transactions but non-residents may transfer 70 per cent of salaries abroad. Generally, Jordan seeks and welcomes foreign investment. All foreign exchange earnings from phosphate and potash exports have to be surrendered to the Central Bank. Jordan's long-term future, apart from possible mineral discoveries, will best be served if it continues to act as a transit and service country for its larger neighbours with Amman as a major banking centre for much of the Middle East.

KENYA

Area. 224,961 sq. miles (582,646 sq. km).
Population. (1995) 28,626,000.
Capital. Nairobi (1,504,900).
Other major cities. Mombasa (465,000), Kisumu (185,100), Nakuru (162,800), Machakos (92,300).
Language(s). Swahili (official), English, many indigenous African languages.
Religion(s). Christian (a mixture of Roman Catholic, Protestant and African indigenous) 73 per cent, traditional beliefs 19 per cent, Muslim 6 per cent, other 2 per cent.
Date of independence. December 12 1963 (from Britain).
GNP. (1993) $6,743,000,000, per capita $270.
Land and climate. Low coastal plains rise to central highlands which are bisected by

the Great Rift Valley. There is a fertile plateau region in the west. The climate is tropical on the coast but arid in parts of the interior.

Introduction

This East African former colony of Britain has created one of the better, more diversified economies of Africa based, first and foremost, upon agriculture. The port of Mombasa is one of the busiest on the continent and besides serving Kenya is also a port of entry for Uganda, Burundi, Rwanda and southern Sudan. Two attempts to make an East African Economic Community work foundered, in part, and iron-ically, upon the fact that the economy was more advanced than those of its neighbours, arousing jealousies that Kenya would dominate the community. Kenya has land borders with Ethiopia, Somalia, Sudan, Tanzania and Uganda, an import-ant shoreline on Lake Victoria and an Indian Ocean coastline of 586km.

Agriculture

Kenya's agricultural sector is one of the most developed and diversified in Africa and agriculture contributes just under 29 per cent to GDP while employing 18.6 per cent of the labour force. The principal export crops are tea and coffee, for both of which Kenya has a high reputation (and with India and Sri Lanka is one of the world's leading tea exporters), fruit, vegetables, flowers (Kenya is also one of the world's leading flower exporters) and sisal, although world markets for this com-modity have been much depressed in recent years. Although plantation (company) agriculture is important, a high proportion of all output comes from small-scale farmers.

Agricultural products account for 65 per cent of exports and in 1993 tea accounted for 26.2 per cent of exports, coffee for 15.5 per cent and fruits and vegetables for another 11 per cent. Other major crops are sugarcane, maize, cassava, sweet potatoes, plantains, pineapples, potatoes, bananas, pulses, wheat, sorghum, millet, coconuts, barley, seed cotton, cashew nuts and sunflower seeds. The national cattle herd is 11,000,000 strong and meat and dairy products are substantial and contribute to exports. Roundwood output at 38,000,000cu m is also important. The huge annual increase of the population means that agricultural output is no longer keeping pace with consumption and crop production, increasingly, is being extended into marginal lands. Land use is divided between forested 4 per cent, meadows and pastures 66.9 per cent, agricultural land, under permanent cultivation 4.3 per cent, other 24.8 per cent.

Mining

The mining sector is small and only soda ash is important as an export mineral, accounting in 1993 for 1.7 per cent of exports. Other minerals extracted include fluorite, salt, limestone, and garnet. There is a small trade in semi-precious stones.

The sector only contributes 0.3 per cent to GDP and employs the same percentage of the labour force.

Manufacturing

Manufacturing contributes just over 10 per cent to GDP and employs 13 per cent of the labour force. Kenya is the most industrialized country of East Africa. Most industries are import substitution oriented although, increasingly, Kenya is aiming at regional export markets for its industrial products. The principal manufactures are cement, sugar, wheat flour, beer, mineral water, paint, alcoholic beverages, food processing. Tourism has long made a significant contribution to the economy and earns Kenya somewhat above $400,000,000 a year. Although possessing no oil of its own, Kenya imports crude oil and refines it for re-export, petroleum products accounting for over 9 per cent of exports.

Infrastructure

Kenya (Nairobi) has become a regional centre for East Africa. The international airport is a major jumping-off place for other parts of Africa, for Asia and Europe. The city is also host to a number of UN organizations including Habitat, UNEP and the regional offices of UNESCO. The city is especially well equipped with first-class hotels. There are 2,040km of 1.000m gauge railways; 64,500km of highways of which 7,000km are paved; part of Lake Victoria is within the Kenya boundaries and acts as an important inland waterway. There are three principal ports: Mombasa and Lamu on the coast, and Kisumu on Lake Victoria. There are 208 usable airports, eighteen with permanent surface runways of which two are over 3,659m and three between 2,440 and 3,659m in length. Telecommunications are among the best in Africa.

Political considerations

At the beginning of the 1990s leading donor countries withheld aid to Kenya in an effort to force the government of President Daniel arap Moi to introduce a more democratic form of government. The ban was lifted in November 1993, following elections the previous year which Moi had in any case won. The quarrel with the aid donors illustrates a major Kenya problem: its continuing dependence upon substantial regular aid inputs to balance its economy. These are all the more important because of the rate of population increase which, at about 3.5 per cent, is one of the highest in the world so that the population is expected to double in 21 years.

Assessments

The twin pillars of the economy are agriculture and tourism. The best chance of improving overall development prospects lies in the expansion of the manufacturing sector and in this respect Kenya's good infrastructure represents a substantial bonus. Kenya will require major inputs of development investment for years to come.

NORTH KOREA

Area. 47,399 sq. miles (122,762 sq. km).
Population. (1995) 23,487,000.
Capital. Pyongyang (2,355,000).
Other major cities. Hamhung (701,000), Ch'ongjin (520,000), Namp'o (370,000), Sanch'ou (356,000).
Language(s). Korean.
Religion(s). Atheist, non-religious 67.9 per cent, traditional beliefs 15.6 per cent, Ch'ondogyo 13.9 per cent, Buddhist 1.7 per cent, Christian 0.9 per cent.
Date of independence. September 9 1948 (but liberation from Japan took place on August 15 1945).
GNP. (1992) $22,000,000,000, per capita $990.
Land and climate. A country of hills and mountains separated by deep valleys. There is a wide coastal plain in the west and a broken coastal plain in the east. The climate is temperate with wet summers.

Introduction

The northern half of the Korean peninsula was part of the Japanese Korean colony from 1911 to 1945 when Japan was defeated and the country was partitioned along the 38th parallel. In September 1948 the Communist Democratic People's Republic of North Korea came into being. Today, North Korea is one of the most extreme command (state-controlled) economies in the world. This Stalinist state was ruled by Kim Il Sung from 1948 until his death in July 1994. North Korea is rich in minerals and under the Communist regime concentrated upon the build-up of heavy industries and mining. Yet, comparison with South Korea which followed a capitalist path of development shows a startling difference in economic achievement after the disastrous Korean War of 1950–53. Thus, in 1993, while North Korea had a per capita income of $990, South Korea had a per capita income of $7,679. North Korea has land boundaries with China and South Korea.

Agriculture

Agricultural land is collectivized. The principal crops are rice, maize, potatoes, soybeans, pulses, cabbage, sweet potatoes, wheat, fruit, barley, tobacco and millet. However, despite an extensive system of irrigation canals that make possible two rice harvests a year, North Korea is not self-sufficient in grains and these are a major import item. The national cattle herd is only 1,300,000 head but meat, especially pork and chickens, and dairy products are important, while the annual fish catch comes to about 1,700,000mt a year. Roundwood output is 4,783,000cu m a year.

Agriculture accounts for about 25 per cent of GDP and employs 44 per cent of the workforce. Land use is divided between forested 74.5 per cent, meadows and pastures 0.4 per cent, agricultural land, under permanent cultivation 16.7 per cent, other 8.4 per cent.

Mining

North Korea is rich in minerals which include iron ore, magnesite, phosphates, sulphur, zinc, lead, fluorspar, graphite, copper, gold, silver, tungsten, molybdenum. It has no oil or natural gas but does possess major hydro-power potential. The leading minerals produced in 1992 were coal 91,000,000mt, iron ore 10,500,000mt, magnesite 1,800,000mt, phosphate rock 510,000mt, sulphur 240,000mt and zinc 200,000mt.

Of 26 major minerals North Korea is a leading producer for 7 as shown in Table 4.2. Minerals form a substantial part of total exports.

Table 4.2 North Korea, mineral production, 1992

Mineral	World placing	Output
Iron ore	13	10,500,000mt
Crude steel	22	8,100,000mt
Lead	10	75,000mt
Zinc	9	200,000mt
Hydraulic cement	19	17,000,000mt
Sulphur	23	240,000mt
Coal	12	91,000,000mt

Manufacturing

In this sector concentration has been upon heavy industry, especially steel making and ship building. Much of the light industry has been automated. Major manufactures in 1993 were cement, crude steel, pig iron, steel semi-manufactures, coke, chemical fertilizers, gasoline, textile fabrics, foodstuffs. North Korea's principal trading partners are China, Japan, Russia and Hong Kong. State-owned industry produces 95 per cent of all manufactured goods.

Infrastructure

There are 4,915km of railroad of which 4,250km are 1.435m standard gauge and 665km are 0.762m narrow gauge. Of 30,000km of roads only 7.5 per cent are paved.

Although there are 2,253km of inland waterways most of these are only navigable by small craft. There is a 37km oil pipeline. The country is served by twelve ports of which Ch'ongjin, Hamhung, Najin, Namp'o and Wonsan are primary while Haeju, Kimchaek, Kosong, Sinuijin, Songnim, Sonbong and Ungesang are secondary. There are 55 usable airports of which 30 have permanent surface runways, five over 3,659m and twenty between 2,440 and 3,659m in length. Telecommunications are fair; there are 3,500,000 radio receivers.

Political considerations

The death of Kim Il Sung in 1994 ended an era and might have signalled an opening up of the economy. During the year North Korea had been in conflict with the International Atomic Energy Agency (IAEA) which suspected that it was diverting plutonium to build nuclear weapons. The dispute involved the USA and was only resolved when, in October, Washington agreed to arrange finance and construction of two light water reactors for electrical power production at a cost of $4bn in return for which North Korea would halt the construction of two other reactors and abide by the Nuclear Non-proliferation Treaty. Political decisions in the aftermath of Kim Il Sung's long reign and the question of whether his son Kim Jong Il would last as head of state will have a great bearing on the future political–economic direction that the country takes.

Assessments

North Korea has the mineral resources and manufacturing base to develop the economy until it becomes one of the middle rank with reasonable prospects of long-term prosperity. Whether such a development takes place, however, must in part depend upon the extent to which North Korea maintains its state-controlled structure or opens up the economy to at least some degree of market-oriented forces.

KYRGYZSTAN

Area. 76,600 sq. miles (198,500 sq. km).
Population. (1995) 4,483,000.
Capital. Bishkek (631,300).
Other major cities. Osh (218,700), Dzhalal-Abad (74,200), Tokmak (71,200), Przhevalsk (64,300).
Language(s). Kyrgyz and Russian (official).
Religion(s). Believers are mainly Sunni Muslims.
Date of independence. August 31 1991 (from USSR).
GNP. (1993) $3,745,000,000, per capita $830.
Land and climate. The Tien Shan mountains rise to more than 7,000m and the

country is enclosed in a series of valleys and basins. The climate is dry continental, polar in the high mountains and subtropical in the Ferzana Valley in the south.

Introduction

Situated in central-south Asia between Kazakstan and China, Kyrgyzstan also has borders with Tajikistan and Uzbekistan though not with Russia. It only came into being as an independent state in 1991 from the former USSR. It is landlocked and much of the country consists of the high Tien Shan mountains. It possesses only modest resources and its economy, formerly, contributed less than 1 per cent to that of the USSR.

Agriculture

Agriculture contributes 37.2 per cent of GDP and employs 38 per cent of the workforce. It is, by far, the most important sector of the economy. The main products are grains, vegetables, potatoes, fruit, seed cotton and grapes; the national cattle herd is just 1 million head but there are also 9 million sheep and goats and wool is an important product. Kyrgyzstan with its small population is largely food self-sufficient and food products account for about 7 per cent of exports. Land use is divided between forested 3.5 per cent, meadows and pastures 45.3 per cent, agricultural land, under permanent cultivation 6.7 per cent, other 44.5 per cent.

Mining and manufacturing

Mining, manufacturing and public utilities combined contribute 35 per cent to GDP and employ 16 per cent of the workforce. Antimony, gold and mercury are mined as well as small amounts of oil which provide a surplus to needs for export. There are also mineral resources of coal, natural gas, nepheline, rare earth metals, bismuth, lead and zinc. The country has substantial hydro-electric capacity.

The principal manufactures are cement, light bulbs, roofing tiles, knitted fabrics, electrical engines, washing machines, centrifugal pumps, trucks, hay-baling machines, metal-cutting machines, forge press machines, textiles, rugs, window glass. Manufactures account for the bulk of exports which go almost entirely to territories of the former USSR.

Infrastructure

There are 370km of railroad plus some industrial lines; 30,300km of roads of which 22,600km are paved or gravelled; and 200km of pipelines for natural gas. There are 27 usable airports, twelve with permanent surface runways of which one is over 3,659m and four between 2,440m and 3,659m in length. Telecommunications are generally poor.

Political considerations/assessments

Kyrgyzstan has had an uneasy political history since independence from the USSR despite its reputation as the most democratic state of Central Asia. Its tiny economy and remote landlocked situation suggest it will take a long time for it substantially to improve its standard of living or development prospects.

LAOS

Area. 91,429 sq. miles (236,800 sq. km).
Population. (1995) 4,887,000.
Capital. Vientiane (178,203).
Other major cities. Savannakhet (96,652), Louangphrabang (68,399), Pakxe (47,323).
Language(s). Lao (official), French, English.
Religion(s). Buddhist 57.8 per cent, tribal religions 33.6 per cent, Christian 1.8 per cent, other/none 6.8 per cent.
Date of independence. July 19 1949 (from France).
GNP. (1993) $1,308,000,000, per capita $290.
Land and climate. Rugged mountains, plains and plateaux with a tropical monsoon climate; the rainy season lasts from May to November, the dry season from December to April.

Introduction

This small, desperately poor South East Asian country, which for many years has been locked into the communist politics of its more powerful neighbours, began slowly in the 1990s to relax the state controls that still dominate its economic system. Symbolic in this respect was the opening in April 1994 of the Thai–Laos Friendship Bridge which now links the two countries across the Mekong River, opening Laos up to the influence of its only non-communist or left-wing neighbour. The bridge had been built with US and Australian aid. In practice, if not in theory, by 1994 Laos had shed many of its socialist economic principles even if it remained politically a communist state. An important investment law was passed in March 1994 which codified rules for joint ventures and foreign-owned companies. Poverty, however, is the country's overriding problem. Laos is landlocked with five neighbours: Burma (Myanmar), China, Vietnam, Cambodia and Thailand.

Agriculture

Agriculture accounts for 56 per cent of GDP and employs 72 per cent of the labour force. The main crop is rice with an annual output of approximately 1,653,000mt (1994). Other important crops are sweet potatoes, sugarcane, cassava, maize, onions, potatoes, pineapples, melons, oranges, bananas. The national cattle herd is just over 1 million head; pigs and chickens are important. Roundwood production in 1993 came to 4,906,000mt and wood accounted for 33 per cent of the year's exports. Most agricultural production comes from subsistence farming and 80 per cent of cultivated land produces rice. Coffee is a small but significant export item. Laos is normally food self-sufficient (except in drought years). Illicit drugs however form a major part of the economy; Laos is the world's third producer of opium and is part of the so-called 'golden triangle'. Land use is divided between forested 54.2 per cent, meadows and pastures 3.5 per cent, agricultural land, under permanent cultivation 3.5 per cent, other 38.8 per cent.

Mining and manufacturing

The mining sector is very small and accounts for only 0.2 per cent of GDP; it consists of gypsum and rock salt mining with the production of some gemstones (sapphires). Tin is also mined and is the most valuable export. Laos has surplus hydro-power capacity and electricity is the second largest export (after wood products) accounting for nearly 24 per cent of exports in 1993. There are unexploited deposits of high grade iron ore and potash. The manufacturing sector accounts for 12.8 per cent of GDP. The principal manufactures are detergents, soap, plastic products, nails, clothing, cigarettes, plywood, electrical wire, soft drinks and beer.

Infrastructure

There is no railroad and of 27,527km of roads only 1,856km are paved. There are 5,487km of inland waterways, mainly the Mekong River and its tributaries. There is a 136km pipeline for petroleum products. Of 41 usable airports, eight have permanent surface runways of which only one is between 2,440m and 3,659m in length. Telecommunications are either non-existent or erratic (government).

Political considerations/assessments

With the end of the communist era Laos is readjusting to a market-oriented world which it is ill-equipped to face either in terms of resources and wealth or economic structures. Soviet and other bloc aid has been drastically reduced and into the foreseeable future it must rely upon help from other sources. Although, in the new climate of the 1990s, interest in investment has been expressed by a number of foreign nations, in real terms this is unlikely to amount to much unless some new and important minerals are discovered. Laos seems set to remain in the less developed band of countries into the foreseeable future.

LEBANON

Area. 3,950 sq. miles (10,230 sq. km).
Population. (1995) 3,009,000.
Capital. Beirut (1,100,000, 1990).
Other major cities. Tripoli (240,000), Juniyah (100,000), Zahlah (45,000), Sidon (38,000).
Language(s). Arabic (official), French, Armenian, English.
Religion(s). No official data have been collected since the census of 1932 gave the Christians a slight national majority; estimates suggest that the Muslims – Shi'a and Sunni – are now in a majority; Christians include Maronites, Greek Orthodox, Greek Catholic, Armenian Christian and Druze.
Date of independence. November 22 1943 (from France which held the League of Nations mandate).
GNP. (1994) $15,800,000,000, per capita $4,360.
Land and climate. There is a narrow coastal plain and then rugged mountains (the Lebanon and Anti-Lebanon Mountains) separated by the fertile Bekaa Valley. The climate is Mediterranean with mild cool wet winters and hot dry summers. The mountains have heavy winter snows.

Introduction

A part of the Ottoman Empire which was made a mandate of the League of Nations under France after World War I, Lebanon became independent in 1943. An agreement based upon the population structure of the 1930s and 1940s divided political power in favour of the Christian majority so that the president should always be a Christian and the prime minister a Muslim. From the late 1960s onwards an influx of Palestinian refugees upset this delicate balance and the country descended into civil war in 1975; this lasted for the next sixteen years. The war also involved Syria which, in any case, has a claim to Lebanon as part of Greater Syria; the PLO whose presence in the country became an excuse for Israeli interventions; and Israel which saw control of southern Lebanon as a key to its own security. At the height of the civil war, apart from the Lebanon National Army (LNA), forces from Syria and Israel, as well as the UN, there were an estimated 35 separate independent militias operating on behalf of particular factions.

Prior to the civil war Lebanon had become a prosperous entrepôt nation and banking centre for much of the Middle East. Under the Ta'if accord of October 1990 Lebanon, hopefully, brought the civil war to an end and began rebuilding its national institutions. Since the end of 1990 Lebanon has held its first elections in twenty years and weakened and disbanded most of the militias while the central government has gradually extended its authority over more and more of the country, although both Syria and Israel have continued to intervene in its affairs. Facing huge tasks of reconstruction, Lebanon has a long way to go before it can expect to regain the prosperity it enjoyed prior to 1975. Lebanon, which is tiny, is situated at the eastern end of the Mediterranean, wedged between Syria to the north and east and Israel to the south, with a 225km coastline on the Mediterranean.

Agriculture

Agriculture accounts for about 9 per cent of GDP and employs 19 per cent of the labour force. The principal products are grapes, potatoes, oranges, tomatoes, apples, cucumbers, lemons, limes, olives and onions. Livestock consists mainly of sheep, goats and chickens. Lebanon also produces opium poppies and marijuana though these were supposedly eradicated in 1993. The country is not self-sufficient in grains. Land use is divided between forested 7.8 per cent, meadows and pastures 1 per cent, agricultural land, under permanent cultivation 29.9 per cent, other 61.3 per cent.

Mining and manufacturing

Mining makes little contribution to the economy although there are deposits of limestone, iron ore, salt and gypsum; small quantities of lime, salt and gypsum are mined. Lebanon, however, is a water surplus country in a region of water shortage. Manufacturing contributes 12.6 per cent to GDP and employs 18 per cent of the labour force. Principal manufactures are cement, paper, cigarettes, refined petroleum products, dairy products, leather goods, flour milling. Lebanon has long been a centre for jewel setting and jewellery, clothing, pharmaceutical products and metal products between them account for 25 per cent of exports. Tourism, which used to be a major source of income, has been drastically curtailed as a result of decades of violence. As of the mid-1990s, family remittances, banking and the drugs business were substantial sources of foreign exchange apart from farming and manufacturing.

Infrastructure

The railway system has broken down. Of 7,300km of highways, 6,200km are paved. No pipelines are currently in operation. The country is served by nine ports: Beirut, Tripoli, Ra'Sil'ata, Janiyah, Sidon, Az Zahrani, Tyre, Jubayl, Shikka Jadidah. There are eight usable airports, six with permanent surface runways of which three are between 2,440 and 3,659m in length. Telecommunications were severely damaged during the years of civil war and invasions and rebuilding is under way.

Political considerations/assessments

If Lebanon can rebuild its badly damaged infrastructure and maintain the precarious post-civil war peace, then it should be able, slowly, to regain its former position as an entrepôt country for the region since, with few resources, that is where its best future lies. Much will depend upon the Israeli–Arab peace process which is largely outside Lebanon's control.

225

LESOTHO

Area. 11,720 sq. miles (30,355 sq. km).
Population. (1995) 2,057,000.
Capital. Maseru (109,382).
Other major cities. Maputsoe (20,000), Teyateyaneng (14,251), Mafeteng (12,667).
Language(s). Sesotho and English (official), Zulu, Xhosa.
Religion(s). Roman Catholic 43.5 per cent, Protestant 29.8 per cent, Anglican 11.5 per cent, other Christian 8 per cent, traditional beliefs 6.2 per cent, other 1 per cent.
Date of independence. October 4 1966 (from Britain).
GNP. (1993) $1,254,000,000, per capita $660.
Land and climate. It is a highland country which includes some of the highest mountains in southern Africa and a high plateau which make it, in aggregate, the loftiest country on the whole continent. The climate is temperate with cool to cold winters and hot wet summers.

Introduction

The Kingdom of Lesotho was formed in the mid-nineteenth century and was to become a British Protectorate for a hundred years. Since independence in 1966 it has had a troubled political history: partly due to a continuing power struggle between the King and the politicians with the former aiming to achieve greater power than that allotted to him as a constitutional monarch; and partly between the politicians and the military. Fighting between rival military factions broke out in 1994 with one military faction opposed to the Basotho Congress Party (BCP) which had won the 1993 elections, taking all seats. The possibility of a coup receded, however, when South Africa warned it would close the borders should one be mounted. Lesotho is situated in southern Africa, entirely surrounded by the territory of its much greater neighbour, South Africa.

Agriculture

Agriculture is entirely subsistence and the land is deteriorating as a result of soil erosion and the absence (as migrant labour) of a high proportion of the adult male population. Agriculture contributes just under 12 per cent to GDP and employs 66 per cent of the labour force. The principal crops are maize, wheat, pulses, sorghum and barley. The national cattle herd is 663,000 strong and there are 1,691,000 sheep and 1,010,000 goats. Wool is an important product and Lesotho's blankets are famous and a valuable export item. Mohair and wool account for 6.2 per cent of exports. Lesotho is not self-sufficient in food which together with live animals accounts for 19 per cent of imports. Land use is divided between meadows and pastures 65.9 per cent, agricultural land, under permanent cultivation 10.5 per cent, other 23.6 per cent.

Mining

Mining makes an insignificant contribution to GDP. The small diamond mine at Letseng-la-Terai at over 10,000 ft was worked out in the early 1980s although there are a few alluvial diamonds. The only quarrying at present consists of sand and gravel for construction purposes. Lesotho, however, does possess one vital resource in abundance: water from its high mountains. At the end of 1991 the government signed an agreement with European banks for $525m to fund the first phase of its Highlands Water Project which will harness and store water for hydro-electric purposes and for use by South Africa. It is one of the biggest civil engineering projects in the world and will cost $3bn by 2020 when the whole project is expected to be completed. The first phase (the Muela hydro-electric project) is due for completion in 1996 and will save Lesotho $10m a year in electricity imports from South Africa. When complete the project should earn Lesotho $60m a month from South Africa.

Manufacturing

Manufacturing contributes 13.7 per cent to GDP and employs about 3 per cent of the labour force. Most industries are small scale, aimed at re-export and designed to be labour intensive to provide maximum employment. Manufacturing consists mainly of food processing, milling, canning, leather and jute, textiles, clothing, chemicals, publishing, iron and steel products, furniture and fixtures. Manufactured goods account for 87.5 per cent of all exports.

Infrastructure

There is a 2.6km stretch of South African Railways from the border to Maseru. Of 7,215km of roads, 572km are paved. There are 28 usable airports of which three have permanent surface runways and only one is between 2,440 and 3,659m in length. The telecommunications system is rudimentary.

Political considerations/assessments

Lesotho is entirely surounded by the territory of South Africa and therefore subject to political pressures from that country; these were often applied during the apartheid era, the blockade at the beginning of 1986 leading to the downfall of Prime Minister Jonathan. Since 1994 and the elections which brought Nelson Mandela to power in South Africa relations with that powerful neighbour have become easier. Nonetheless, Mandela like his predecessors has exerted pressure upon Lesotho, as he did in 1994 when he insisted that the King should stand by the 1993 election results which he wished to put aside. A long-term question, now apartheid has passed, is whether Lesotho will eventually become a part of South Africa, perhaps in some federal structure.

Meanwhile, Lesotho's long-term economic prospects are not encouraging, especially as the population doubling time is only 24 years. Apart from the Highlands Water Project, Lesotho's principal sources of income are remittances from migrant labour in South Africa (an estimated 100,000 or more adult male Basotho are working in the Republic at any given time); revenues from its membership of the Customs Union of Southern Africa (CUSA); and international aid. These three sources of revenue seem set to continue as the mainstay of the economy into the foreseeable future.

LIBERIA

Area. 38,250 sq. miles (99,067 sq. km).
Population. (1995) 2,380,000 (including an estimated 700,000–750,000 refugees in surrounding countries).
Capital. Monrovia (400,000, 1985).
Other major cities. Harbel (60,000), Buchanan (25,000).
Language(s). English (official), about twenty local Niger–Congo group of languages.
Religion(s). Christian 67.7 per cent, Muslim 13.8 per cent, traditional beliefs, other 18.5 per cent.
Date of independence. July 26 1847 (the country was 'created' by philanthropists for the repatriation to Africa from the USA of former slaves).
GNP. (1990) $1,178,000,000, per capita $498. (NB this figure by 1995 would have been much reduced as a result of the breakdown of the economy due to the civil war.)
Land and climate. Flat and rolling coastal plains rise to a plateau and low hills in the northeast. The climate is tropical, hot and humid. Winters are dry with hot days and cool nights; summers are wet with frequent heavy rain showers.

Introduction

Comparatively well endowed for such a small country, with a range of minerals, forests and good agricultural potential, Liberia has been in a state of chaos and misery since the outbreak of civil war in 1990. Much of the economy and the infrastructure round Monrovia, the capital, has been destroyed as a result of the civil war and many businessmen and members of the élite have fled, taking both capital and expertise with them. The Liberian economy depended largely upon the export of a range of raw materials – both mineral and agricultural – while its manufacturing base remained small. About 750,000 Liberians have become refugees in neighbouring countries and in 1995 there was what appeared to be a 'stand-off' between the interim government which is backed by ECOMOG (the peacekeeping force of the Economic Community of West African States, ECOWAS) and the forces of the main rebel leader, Charles Taylor. Liberia is situated on the southern coast of the great bulge of West Africa and has boundaries with three neighbours – Côte d'Ivoire, Guinea and Sierra Leone – and an Atlantic coastline of 579km.

Agriculture

Agriculture accounts for 34.4 per cent of GDP (1989) and employs 68 per cent of the labour force. The principal crops are rubber, timber, coffee, cocoa, rice, cassava, palm oil, sugarcane and bananas. In 1990 rubber accounted for 28 per cent of exports, logs and timber for 8.4 per cent, coffee for another 1.5 per cent. Liberia, however, is not self-sufficient in staples and about 25 per cent of its rice requirements have to be imported. Land use is divided between forested 17.6 per cent, meadows and pastures 58.9 per cent, agricultural land, under permanent cultivation 3.9 per cent, other 19.6 per cent.

Mining

Mining accounts for 10 per cent of GDP and employs 2.5 per cent of the labour force. Minerals include iron ore, diamonds and gold and in 1988 iron ore accounted for 55 per cent of exports; diamonds for 2.1 per cent; gold for 1.8 per cent. Iron ore production, prior to the civil war, was equivalent to 6,500,000mt a year, diamonds up to 200,000 carats, and gold to 22,000 troy ounces. Iron ore extraction began in 1961 and Liberia had soon become a major exporter of this mineral which replaced timber as the country's leading foreign exchange earner. Deposits are extensive, over 1,000m tonnes, and much of it high grade. Other minerals include bauxite, copper, columbite-tantalite, corundum, lead, manganese, tin and zinc. Exploration for oil has not so far revealed any deposits worth working.

Manufacturing

Manufacturing contributed under 7 per cent to GDP on the eve of the civil war and most manufactures are concerned with rubber processing, food processing, palm oil processing, construction materials, furniture and the mining sector (iron ore).

Infrastructure

There are 480km of railroads of which 328km are 1.435m standard gauge; railways are single track and operated by foreign steel and financial interests in co-operation with the government. There are 10,087km of roads of which 603km are paved. The country is served by four ports: Monrovia, Buchanan, Greenville and Harper. Liberia operates a shipping flag of convenience and its 1,618 registered ships are all foreign owned: 16 per cent are US owned, 14 per cent Japanese owned, 11 per cent Norwegian owned and 9 per cent Hong Kong owned. There are 41 usable airports of which two have permanent surface runways and one of these has a length between 2,440 and 3,659m. Telecommunications have largely broken down as a result of the civil war.

Political considerations

Until peace, followed by a genuine, equitable solution to the civil war has been implemented the political outlook must remain both bleak and threatening.

Assessments

Given an end to the civil war and an acceptable political system, Liberia has the resources at least to guarantee a passable lifestyle for its people.

MADAGASCAR

Area. 226,658 sq. miles (587,041 sq. km).
Population. (1995) 14,763,000.
Capital. Antananarivo (1,052,835).
Other major cities. Toamasina (127,441), Antsirabe (120,239), Mahajanga (100,807), Fianarantsoa (99,005).
Language(s). Malagasy (official), French.
Religion(s). Christian 51 per cent, traditional beliefs 47 per cent, Muslim 1.7 per cent, other 0.3 per cent.
Date of independence. June 26 1960 (from France).
GNP. (1993) $3,055,000,000, per capita $240.
Land and climate. The centre of this huge island consists of mountains and high plateaux; there are narrow coastal plains. The coastal climate is tropical; inland it is temperate but arid in the south. Apart from periodic cyclones, the land suffers from deforestation, over-grazing, soil erosion and desertification.

Introduction

The fourth largest island in the world and a French colony from 1890 to 1960, Madagascar is one of the world's poorest countries. It has both a unique ecology and an unusual racial mix with people of South Asian–Pacific origin – the Merina and Betsileo – as well as Arabs and Africans. Poverty and a relatively large population have produced extensive degradation of the land with over-grazing and deforestation by slash and burn agriculture. Plans by the transnational mining company RTZ to mine titanium dioxide and other minerals on the scenic coastline in southern Madagascar near Tolanaro led, in 1995, to a major internationl row with fierce opposition to the project by 'greens' who argued that the mining operations would do irreparable damage to the ecology. The former president, Didier Ratsiraka, who finally lost power in the elections of 1993, is accused of having done great damage to the economy during his long tenure of office with his doctrinaire Marxist policies with the result that the country's production is estimated to have been halved under his rule.

Situated in the western Indian Ocean, Madagascar lies 430km east of Mozambique; the seas round it are rich in fish. Although regarded as an African country, its isolation as an island as well as the unusual ethnic make-up of its people have meant, in practice, that it has not become involved in many aspects of continental African politics.

Agriculture

Agriculture contributes over 32 per cent to GDP and employs 86 per cent of the workforce. Cash crops include coffee, vanilla, sugarcane, cloves and cocoa and in 1994 coffee accounted for 18 per cent of exports, vanilla for 16.7 per cent, cloves and clove oil for 2.6 per cent and sugar for 2.2 per cent. Seed cotton is also important and cotton fabrics accounted for another 2.9 per cent of exports. Although the fish catch is relatively small (115,000mt) shrimps are a major export and accounted for 13.2 per cent of the total in 1992. The main food crops are rice, cassava, beans, bananas, peanuts. Madagascar is almost self-sufficient in its first staple, rice. The national cattle herd is over 10,000,000 head and cattle raising is widespread round the island. Roundwood production is at the rate of approximately 8,500,000cu m a year. The emphasis of the 1986 Five Year Plan was to achieve self-sufficiency in food. Land use is divided between forested 26.6 per cent, meadows and pastures 58.5 per cent, agricultural land, under permanent cultivation 5.3 per cent, other 9.6 per cent.

Mining

The mining sector only contributes 0.3 per cent to GDP. The principal minerals worked in 1994 were chromite concentrate, salt, graphite, mica and gold but in modest or small quantities. A wide variety of semi-precious stones and gemstones (topaz, garnet, amethyst) are also produced. However, a wide range of minerals is known to exist and these also include bauxite, ilmenite (titanium ore), zircon, rutile, nickel and platinum. Madagascar has extensive offshore oil shale and its eventual exploitation could transform the country's energy situation. The proposal by Qit, a subsidiary of RTZ, to invest $350m to mine titanium dioxide and other minerals along the coast of southern Madagascar raised, in acute form during 1995, questions about possible damage to the ecology and the willingness of the company to restore the land when the mining operations come to an end on the one hand, and the desperate need to inject finances and to promote development in one of the world's poorest countries on the other. Some 200,000 local people would be affected by such a mining project.

Manufacturing

Manufacturing accounts for just under 12 per cent of GDP and employs about 1 per cent of the workforce. The majority of industries are concerned with food processing, textiles, cement, soap, palm oil, paint, cigarettes and beer.

Infrastructure

There are 1,020km of 1.000m gauge railway, 40,000km of roads of which 4,694km are paved. The main ports are Toamasina, Antsiranana, Mahajanga and Tolara. There are 103 usable airports of which 30 have permanent surface runways and of these three are between 2,440 and 3,659m in length. Telecommunictions are above average and include a submarine cable to Bahrain.

Political considerations

The end of the Ratsiraka era in 1993 led to a more open system of politics with some 30 political parties operating although the new constitution whose main object is to prevent dictatorship has also had the effect of dissipating power and making strong government unlikely. In 1994 the government under President Albert Zafy adopted a series of IMF/World Bank measures including a wage freeze and a reduction of the civil service and seemed determined to tackle problems of economic development without being doctrinaire.

Assessments

With one of the world's lowest per capita incomes ($240) and a doubling time for its 14 million population of only 22 years, Madagascar faces formidable problems. Many of its minerals are in remote geographic locations that make profitable exploitation doubtful, at least in the near future, and though agriculture is mainly subsistence it will remain the backbone of the economy accounting for the greater part of all exports. Madagascar remains heavily aid dependent and total external debts in 1993 at $3,920,000,000 were equivalent to 120 per cent of GNP. Madagascar is ranked thirteenth from the bottom among the world's low-income economies.

MALAWI

Area. 45,747 sq. miles (118,484 sq. km).
Population. (1995) 9,939,000.
Capital. Lilongwe (395,500).
Other major cities. Blantyre (446,800), Mzuzu (62,700).
Language(s). English and Chichewa (official).
Religion(s). Christian 64.5 per cent, traditional beliefs 19 per cent, Muslim 16.2 per cent, other 0.3 per cent.
Date of independence. July 6 1964 (from Britain).
GNP. (1993) $2,034,000,000, per capita $230.
Land and climate. The country consists of a narrow elongated plateau of rolling plains and hills; Lake Malawi (formerly Nyasa) and the southern Shire Valley are an extension of the Great Rift Valley. The climate is tropical with a rainy season from November to May and a dry season from May to November.

Introduction

One of Africa's fifteen landlocked countries and among the world's poorest, Malawi is situated in southern Central Africa; it was formerly a British colony and then a member of the ill-fated Central African Federation (CAF) with the two Rhodesias before achieving independence in 1964. For 30 years thereafter it was ruled more or less autocratically by its first President, Kamuzu Hastings Banda, until he was first stripped of his title of Life President in 1993 and then defeated in the elections of 1994. The economy depends, overwhelmingly, upon agriculture.

In the period after independence Malawi found itself in the position of a frontline state in relation to Rhodesia which had declared unilateral independence (UDI) under Ian Smith in 1965 and in relation to apartheid South Africa although in neither case was it prepared to apply sanctions to those countries. Malawi was also adversely affected by the civil war in Mozambique whose two northern 'butterfly' wings enclose the southern half of Malawi which, at one time in the 1980s, was host to 650,000 Mozambican refugees. Malawi has three neighbours – Mozambique, Tanzania and Zambia – and is in dispute with Tanzania over the boundaries of Lake Malawi all of whose waters it claims.

Agriculture

Ninety per cent of the population live in rural areas and agriculture accounts for 31 per cent of GDP, employs just under 86 per cent of the workforce and earns almost all the country's foreign exchange. The principal cash crops are tobacco, sugar, tea and cotton and in 1994 tobacco accounted for 70.5 per cent of exports, tea for 7.5 per cent, sugar for 7.4 per cent and cotton for 0.5 per cent. Other exports include confectionary grade goundnuts, coffee, cassava, rice and sunflower seeds. A high proportion of export crops are produced by smallholders whose products are marketed by the Agricultural Development and Marketing Corporation (ADMARC). Concentration upon smallholder agriculture in Malawi has paid dividends and attracted a great deal of international aid from the IDA, IFAD, the EU and individual donor countries.

Malawi is the second largest producer of tobacco (after Zimbabwe) in Africa and the only important producer of burley tobacco. There are about 6,500 tobacco estates as well as 66,000 tenant smallholders producing tobacco. The tobacco is exported to some 50 countries although Britain is the main customer. After Kenya, Malawi is the largest tea producer in Africa; 90 per cent of tea production comes from large estates. Malawi is not a cattle country and the national herd numbers less than a million head. Roundwood production is at the rate of 10,000,000cu m a year. The freshwater fish catch averages 65,000mt. Land use is divided between forested 36.2 per cent, meadows and pastures 19.6 per cent, agricultural land, under permanent cultivation 18.1 per cent, other 26.1 per cent.

Mining

Mining contributes virtually nothing to GDP and consists mainly of limestone quarrying. However, there are unexploited resources of uranium, coal, bauxite, asbestos, vermiculite and graphite. A brief attempt to mine coal was abandoned as uneconomic in 1984 after only a year. There are also gemstones. The huge deposits of bauxite at Mlanje Mountain in the extreme south of the country are estimated to amount to some 29 million metric tons of ore but exploitation is at present uneconomic due to the remote location of the deposits and the high cost of transporting it to the coast.

Manufacturing

Manufacturing contributes just under 14 per cent to GDP but only employs 2.8 per cent of the workforce. Most manufactures are concerned with food processing, cement or import substitution light industries.

Infrastructure

There are 789km of 1.067m gauge railway and, as a landlocked country, Malawi depends upon rail routes through Mozambique to Nacala or south to Beira and Maputo. The war in Mozambique during the 1980s disrupted this system so that much of Malawi's traffic had to go much farther south through South Africa. There are 13,135km of highways of which 2,364km are paved; Lake Malawi acts as a major inland waterway and is served by four ports: Chipoka, Monkey Bay, Nkhata Bay and Nkotakota; 144km of the Shire River are also navigable. There are 41 usable airports, five with permanent surface runways of which one is between 2,440 and 3,659m in length. The telecommunications system is fair.

Political considerations

Throughout the Banda years (1964–94) Malawi adhered to economic practices that broadly earned sympathetic support from the World Bank and IMF as well as the main Western donors. The country stands to gain from the opening up of Southern Africa as a result of the end of the civil war in Mozambique and the end of apartheid in South Africa.

Assessments

Malawi is ranked as the ninth lowest of the world's low-income economies, with a population of 10 million which is due to double in just 20 years. This gives Malawi little capacity to do other than keep pace with the essential demands of its people. Agriculture will remain the backbone of the economy into the foreseeable future.

MALI

Area. 482,077 sq. miles (1,248,574 sq. km).
Population. (1995) 9,008,000.
Capital. Bamako (646,163).
Other major cities. Ségou (88,877), Mopti (73,979), Sikasso (73,050), Gao (54,874).
Language(s). French (official), Bambara, numerous African languages.
Religion(s). Muslim 90 per cent, traditional beliefs 9 per cent, Christian 1 per cent.
Date of independence. September 22 1960 (from France).
GNP. (1993) $2,744,000,000, per capita $300.
Land and climate. Most of the country consists of flat to rolling plains, desert in the north, savanna in the centre. There are rugged hills in the northeast and the River Niger valley in the south where most agriculture and commercial activity is to be found. Climate varies from desert through savanna to subtropical in the south. The dry harmattan wind is common in the dry season. The country is subject to continuing desertification.

Introduction

This huge landlocked country of northwestern Africa covers just under half a million square miles and stretches from the Sahara in the north through the dry Sahel region to the subtropical valley of the River Niger in the south. One of the world's poorest countries which largely consists of desert or arid semi-desert, the economy depends overwhelmingly upon agriculture and though it possesses a range of mineral resources few of these have been exploited because of Mali's landlocked remoteness and poor infrastructure. After independence in 1960 Mali first experienced a left-wing government under Modibo Keita (to 1968), then a period of military rule to 1979 when, under Moussa Traore, it reverted to civilian government although under one-party rule. Traore was overthrown in 1991 and the country returned to parliamentary, multiparty democracy. Mali has seven neighbours: Algeria, Burkina Faso, Guinea, Côte d'Ivoire, Mauritania, Niger and Senegal.

Agriculture

Agriculture contributes 42 per cent to GDP and employs 82 per cent of the workforce. Most agriculture is concentrated along the valley of the Niger where fishing is also an important occupation. A majority of agricultural production comes from subsistence farming. About 10 per cent of the population are nomads for whom cattle, sheep and goats are the economic mainstay. Nearly 70 per cent of all exports consist of cotton and cotton products and live animals to neighbouring countries. The main staples are sorghum, millet, rice, maize, groundnuts, cassava, sweet potatoes. The national cattle herd is 5,500,000 strong and there are more than 13,000,000 sheep and goats. Land use is divided between forested 5.7 per cent, meadows and pastures 24.6 per cent, agricultural land, under permanent cultivation 1.8 per cent, other 67.9 per cent.

Mining

Mining contributes 2.2 per cent to GDP and, currently, gold accounts for 18 per cent of exports. Otherwise, small quantities of limestone, marble and phosphates are also mined. However, there are known deposits of varying size and quality of bauxite, copper, iron ore, nickel, manganese, kaolin, salt, tin, uranium and phosphates which have not been exploited mainly for reasons of geographic remoteness, poor infrastructure and the fact that Mali is landlocked. Prospecting is under way for petroleum, uranium, tungsten, diamonds and gold. New gold deposits in the south were discovered in 1995.

Manufacturing

The manufacturing sector is very small, accounting for 8.9 per cent of GDP and employing only 5.5 per cent of the workforce. Most manufacturing is concerned with local consumer goods, food processing, construction, the mining industry or fishing.

Infrastructure

There is a 642km 1.000m gauge railway that connects with the system in Senegal; about 15,700km of roads of which 1,670km are paved; and 1,815km of navigable inland waterways (the Niger). Of 27 usable airports, eight have permanent surface runways, five between 2,440 and 3,659m in length. Telecommunications are poor though efforts are under way to improve them.

Political considerations

A new constitution was adopted following a referendum in January 1992 and elections for a National Assembly and President were held in March and April that year as the country turned from authoritarian to multiparty politics. During 1994 there were massive student demonstrations against the government which resulted in considerable violence. In June 1994 the government signed an agreement with the Tuareg Unified Movements and Fronts of Azaouad (MFUA) in a move to end the Tuareg rebellion in the north which had gone on for a number of years although some fighting continued to take place.

Assessments

Poverty and remoteness make any rapid economic change unlikely; something like 86 per cent of the population over six years of age have received no formal education. Mali has substantial mineral resources but capital for their exploitation

must depend upon the development of infrastructure and this will not be forthcoming while more accessible resources are available elsewhere. International debts
are equivalent to 80 per cent of GNP.

MAURITANIA

Area. 398,000 sq. miles (1,030,700 sq. km).
Population. (1995) 2,274,000.
Capital. Nouakchott (480,408).
Other major cities. Noâdhibou (72,305), Kaédi (35,241), Kiffa (29,292), Rosso
(27,783).
Language(s). Arabic (official), Fulani, Soyinke and Wolof (national languages).
Religion(s). Islam (official) 99.4 per cent, Christian 0.4 per cent, other 0.2 per
cent.
Date of independence. November 28 1960 (from France).
GNP. (1993) $947,000,000, per capita $438.
Land and climate. Most of the country consists of barren flat Saharan desert plains;
there are some hills in the centre. The climate is desert, hot, dry and dusty.

Introduction

This large country of West Africa with a coastline on the Atlantic stretches from the
Sahel zone in the south to the Sahara Desert in the north; most of Mauritania is
desert. The population splits between the Moors of the north, many of whom are
nomads, who comprise 70 per cent of the whole, and the remaining 30 per cent
blacks in the south. The people are virtually 100 per cent Muslim. The discovery and
exploitation of huge iron ore deposits during the 1960s raised Mauritania from
among the poorest countries in Africa into the second rank.

Mauritania's claim to part of Western Sahara (formerly Spanish Sahara or Rio de
Oro) which it advanced between 1975 and 1978 involved the country in a crippling
conflict with the Polisario liberation movement that put the economy, and especially
the iron ore developments, at risk. However, following a coup which overthrew Ould
Daddah in 1978, Mauritania withdrew its claim and the exploitation of the iron ore
was able to proceed once more, unhindered by guerrilla warfare. The other major
source of wealth lies in Mauritania's rich offshore fisheries. Multiparty politics were
legalized in July 1991 under a new Constitution. Mauritania has four neighbours –
Algeria, Mali, Senegal and Western Sahara – and a 754km Atlantic seaboard.

Agriculture

Agriculture, including fisheries, accounts for 24 per cent of GDP and employs 38 per
cent of the workforce. Farming is divided between subsistence activity and nomadic

Map 7 Latin America

cattle and sheep herding and most farming activity is along the Senegal river valley in the south. Mauritania is subject to droughts and when these occur faces major deficits of staple crops. Droughts during the 1970s and 1980s altered the pattern of life, forcing many nomads as well as subsistence farmers to move into the cities. The main crops are sorghum, pulses, rice, dates, vegetables, melons, sweet potatoes, yams, millet and maize. The numbers of sheep, goats and cattle were greatly reduced as a result of the droughts in the 1970s and 1980s. The fish catch in 1994 came to 296,627mt and fish accounts for 55 per cent of exports. Land use is divided between forested 4.2 per cent, meadows and pastures 38.3 per cent, agricultural land, under permanent cultivation 0.2 per cent, other 57.3 per cent.

Mining

Mauritania possesses a range of minerals, most still awaiting exploitation, although iron ore at present is the only mineral produced in quantity to make a significant contribution to the economy. There are between 5,000m and 6,000m tons of iron ore reserves in the Guelbs region and development began under French auspices in 1959 with predominantly French but also British and West German interests putting up the capital. Mauritania nationalized these holdings in 1974 when the iron ore production came under the state mining corporation Société nationale industrielle et minière (SNIM). The development of the mines included the construction of a 670km railway and a mineral port. During the first years production averaged between 11m and 7m tons a year. Recession in the 1980s led to a cutback in production but this was increased again to 12.1m tons in 1989. In 1994 iron ore output came to 10,342,000mt. Iron ore exports in 1993 accounted for 39.8 per cent of all exports. Given the rail and port infrastructure to serve the Guelbs region there is no reason why Mauritania should not maintain this level of output and exports indefinitely. The African Development Bank, the European Investment Bank and the French government have each put up finances for further development of the iron ore deposits.

A small amount of gypsum was also mined in 1994 but this did not reflect reserves. Production of copper at Akjouit (with estimated reserves of 32m tons) began in 1970 and a peak output of more than 28,000 tons was reached in 1973; but production was stopped in 1978 because of the low grades of the deposits and plans to reopen the mine await adequate investment finance. There are also gold deposits at Akjouit.

Although gypsum production is at present small scale (4,230mt in 1994) this is due to technical problems since total reserves are estimated at 4,000m tons, making these deposits among the largest in the world.

SNIM was partially opened to private participation in 1978 and became SNIM – SEM (Société d'économie mixte) with Arab governments and institutions holding a 29 per cent stake. The company is prospecting for tungsten, iron ore, petroleum, phosphates and uranium. So far, phosphates reserves of between 95m and 150m tons have been located in the south of the country at Bofal. Offshore drilling has yet to reveal any oil but it continues. Mining which really only means iron ore at present contributes 9.1 per cent to GDP though only employing 1.1 per cent of the workforce. On present evidence, however, there is every reason to suppose that Mauritania will prove to be a storehouse of minerals. The exploitation of the iron ore alone since 1960 has doubled per caput income.

Manufacturing

Manufacturing contributes slightly over 11 per cent to GDP but employs only 1 per cent of the workforce. It is concerned almost entirely with fish and other food processing – dairy products, especially cheese, meat, hides and skins. Otherwise, there is little industrial development apart from mining. Efforts to create other industries were attempted in the 1970s and 1980s and included a petroleum refinery, a sugar refinery and a steel mill – but these proved costly failures.

Infrastructure

There is a single 690km 1.435m gauge railway operated by the government mining company to move the iron ore to the mineral port at Nouadhibou. The country's other port is also the capital, Nouakchott. There are 7,525km of roads of which 1,685km are paved. Ferry traffic uses the Senegal River. There are 29 usable airports of which nine have permanent surface runways and of these one is over 3,659m and five are between 2,440 and 3,659m in length. Telecommunications are generally poor though improvements are under way.

Political considerations

A return to multipartyism in the 1990s has opened up the political system though parties tend to be based upon tribes. Border conflict with Senegal has been a continuing problem for years and has not been resolved. Over-dependence upon mining and a tiny manufacturing sector make the non-agricultural economy very lopsided. Mauritania, moreover, incurred large debts to finance the original exploitation of its iron ore and pay for the infrastructure so that in 1994 total debts of $2,500,000,000 were equivalent to 250 per cent of GNP. With a very high rate of population growth (it is expected to double in 22 years) Mauritania faces acute problems of unemployment as large numbers of young people come on to the labour market each year and an estimated 50 per cent of the economically active population was deemed to be unemployed at the end of the 1980s.

Assessments

The minerals exist and more are likely to be discovered. The most effective way to tackle long-term development needs must be to create local industries that add value to the minerals which are mined before these are exported. Finding the capital for such ventures, however, will be far more difficult than obtaining further capital simply to extract minerals from the ground for immediate export.

MONGOLIA

Area. 604,800 sq. miles (1,566,500 sq. km).
Population. (1995) 2,307,000.
Capital. Ulan Bator (680,600).
Other major cities. Darhan (85,800), Erdenet (63,500).
Language(s). Khalkha Mongolia (official), Turkic, Russian, Chinese.
Religion(s). Formal freedom of worship exists but there are no reliable statistics of religious adherence.
Date of independence. March 13 1921 (from China).
GNP. (1993) $984,800,000, per capita $400.
Land and climate. The greater part of the country consists of a vast semi-desert or desert plain, merging into the Gobi Desert in the southeast. There are mountains in the west and southwest. The climate is a desert one of continental extremes.

Introduction

This huge landlocked country in Central Asia, the original heartland of the Mongol 'hordes' of Genghis Khan, is one of the poorest as well as one of the most remote countries in the world. On achieving independence from China in 1921 it became the second country in the world, after Russia, to embrace communism and until the collapse of the USSR, at the beginning of the 1990s, was heavily dependent upon the Soviet Union as its principal trading partner and source of aid.

With a tiny scattered population in relation to its vast land area, Mongolia has poor infrastructure and until recently an economy largely based upon agriculture and the breeding of livestock. The discovery and exploitation of a range of minerals in the two decades prior to the collapse of the USSR opened up new prospects for the economy although Mongolia still has a long way to go to transform itself from a low-income economy to the next lower-middle-income group of countries. Although, until 1990, all power lay in the hands of the Mongolian People's Revolutionary Party (MPRP), in that year, moving with the spirit of perestroika, multiparty elections were held and the country embarked upon a post-communist democratic path. Mongolia also announced at this time a policy of privatization for 70 per cent of the economy. The country is sandwiched between China and Russia and its boundaries with these two countries are 4,673km and 3,441km respectively.

Agriculture

Agriculture and livestock breeding are the traditional occupations. Agriculture contributed 15 per cent of GDP and employed 35.5 per cent of the workforce in 1993. The raising of livestock predominates with sheep (13,779,000), goats (7,239,000) the most important animals, followed by cattle (3,003,000) and horses (2,408,400). The main crops are wheat, potatoes, vegetables. Land use is divided between forested 8.9 per cent, meadows and pastures 79.7 per cent, agricultural land, under permanent cultivation 0.9 per cent, other 10.5 per cent.

Mining

Mongolia has a range of minerals including oil, coal, copper, molybdenum, tungsten, phosphates, tin, nickel, zinc, wolfram, fluorspar, gold. Joint Soviet–Mongolian exploitation of minerals in the 1970s and 1980s included the opening up of copper and molybdenum deposits at Erdenet in Bulgan province and the development of gold and fluorspar deposits. By the 1990s the mining and processing of coal, copper, molybdenum, tin, tungsten and gold accounted for the greater part of industrial production. Mining output in 1994 included fluorspar (383,200mt), copper (343,300mt), molybdenum, silver and gold. Mongolia is more than self-sufficient in coal and produced 7,425,000mt in 1993. In 1991 the government passed legislation to allow foreign companies to explore and assist in the recovery of the country's estimated 400,000,000 tonnes (3,000,000,000 barrels) of oil reserves.

Manufacturing

Manufacturing (with mining) contributes 27 per cent to GDP and employs 14.7 per cent of the workforce although by the end of 1992 the economy was close to collapse as a result of shortfalls in energy production as well as the virtual termination of Soviet aid while, at the same time, the government was moving away from central planning towards privatization. Principal products include processed foods, textiles, leather and hides, construction materials, clothing and apparel, wood products, chemicals, printing and publishing, glass and ceramics.

Infrastructure

There are 1,750km of 1.524m broad gauge railway, 46,700km of roads of which only 1,000km are hard surfaced, and 31 usable airports of which eleven have permanent surface runways and of these five have runways of 3,659m and about twenty are between 2,440 and 3,659m in length. Telecommunications are underdeveloped and, for example, repeat Russian TV shows.

Political considerations/assessments

Mongolia is in the process of reforming its system away from state control to privatization. It has substantial mineral resources but small population and remoteness make any rapid economic development unlikely in the near future.

MOROCCO

Area. 177,117 sq. miles (458,730 sq. km).
Population. (1995) 26,980,000.
Capital. Rabat (1,229,000).
Other major cities. Casablanca (2,943,000), Fes (564,823).
Language(s). Arabic (official), Berber dialects, French.
Religion(s). Islam (official) 98.7 per cent (Sunni), Christian 1.1 per cent.
Date of independence. March 2 1956 (from France).
GNP. (1993) $27,645,000,000, per capita $1,030.
Land and climate. A mountainous country that includes the western end of the great Atlas chain across the north of Africa, with rich coastal plains and a Mediterranean climate that becomes dryer and more extreme into the interior towards the Sahara Desert.

Introduction

One of the most sophisticated economies of the African continent, poised somewhat uneasily on the periphery of the European Union with which the bulk of its trade, both imports and exports, is conducted, Morocco has worked with the other Maghreb countries to achieve an Arab Maghreb Union that would integrate their joint economies. Although it is still an agriculture-oriented economy, Morocco is also one of the world's leading producers of phosphates which account for 10 per cent of exports, has a well-developed, diversified manufacturing sector and an important tourist industry. The Moroccan claim to Western Sahara (the former Spanish colony of Rio de Oro) has involved it ever since 1975 in the occupation of the territory, fighting with the Sahrawi liberation organization, Polisario, and conflict with both the OAU and the UN. The issue had still to be resolved in 1996 although Morocco remains in occupation and has made clear that it will not withdraw. Morocco has land boundaries with Algeria and Western Sahara but also, if its occupation of Western Sahara is taken into account, with Mauritania; and coastlines on the Atlantic and Mediterranean.

Agriculture

Agriculture accounts for just over 14 per cent of GDP and employs 40 per cent of the workforce. Once food self-sufficient, Morocco is now a substantial food importer with food and beverages accounting for 15 per cent of all imports though a part of these is to service the needs of tourists. Exports of citrus fruits, vegetables and wines earn valuable foreign exchange and food, apart from fish, accounts for 26 per cent of exports. The principal crops are sugar beet, wheat, barley, sugarcane, tomatoes, potatoes, oranges, olives and dates. Sheep are the most important livestock (16m head), followed by goats and then cattle (2,431,000). Morocco is an important fishing nation, the catch for 1993 totalling 607,000mt and fish (fresh, canned and frozen) account for over 14 per cent of all exports. Rising population, the development of industry and tourism suggest that Morocco will become more dependent upon imported food in the future. Land use is divided between forested 17.7 per cent, meadows and pastures 46.8 per cent, agricultural land, under permanent cultivation 22.1 per cent, other 13.4 per cent.

Mining

Morocco possesses a range of minerals including phosphates, coal, iron ore, manganese, lead, zinc, salt, copper, cobalt, fluorspar, barite, silver, antimony although by far the most important of these is phosphates. The majority of the minerals have either not been exploited or, so far, have only been exploited at modest levels. Morocco possesses roughly two-thirds of the world's known phosphates resources with proved reserves of 10,600 million tonnes and probable total reserves of 57,200 million tonnes. Substantial investment has gone into the downstream phosphates industry so as to add value to the mineral by producing fertilizers, phosphoric acid and sulphuric acid prior to export. In 1994 minerals accounted for 10.2 per cent of exports and phosphates for 7 per cent of this. Other minerals mined include zinc, copper, lead, manganese, fluorspar, barite and iron ore.

Morocco has very small sources of oil and produced 83,600 barrels in 1992 against consumption of 47,500,000 barrels. The country consumes all the natural gas it produces. Mining contributes 2 per cent to GDP and employs 1.1 per cent of the workforce.

Manufacturing

Morocco has one of Africa and the Middle East's most developed manufacturing sectors which accounts for 18 per cent of GDP and employs 15.5 per cent of the workforce. Much of the sector is concerned with phosphate production followed by petroleum refining, sugar and cement production, textiles, olive oil, wine, passenger and commercial vehicles, and leather goods. Clothing accounts for nearly 12 per cent of exports. Morocco is one of the leading tourist destinations in Africa and income from visitors came to $1,267,000,000 in 1994.

Infrastructure

There are 1,893km of 1.435m standard gauge railway (246km double track and 976km electrified); 59,198km of roads of which nearly half (27,740km) are paved; and 362km of pipelines for oil, and 241km for natural gas. The main ports are Agadir, Casablanca, El Jorf Lasfar, Kénitra, Mohammedia, Hadar, Safi, Tangier. (There are also the two Spanish enclaves of Ceuta and Melilla.) Of 65 usable airports, 26 have permanent surface runways of which two are over 3,659m and thirteen between 2,440 and 3,659m in length. The telecommunications system is generally good.

Political considerations

King Hassan II of Morocco, who came to the throne in 1961, is the longest-surviving African head of state. The country is a constitutional monarchy with some fifteen political parties operating although the elections due in 1984 were postponed to the 1990s and King Hassan is far more than simply a constitutional monarch. The fact that the UN referendum on the future of Western Sahara has been repeatedly postponed at Morocco's insistence is an indication of the government's determination to keep control of the territory. Morocco, generally, is moderate in its policies in the Arab/Islamic world and maintains good relations with the West (the USA and the EU).

Assessments

Morocco is a lower-middle-income country; its debts in 1993 at $20,310,000,000 were equivalent to 71 per cent of GNP. Phosphates and other minerals will provide an important source of exports into the foreseeable future while various foods, wines, mineral waters and fish another. Concentration upon increasing and diversifying the manufacturing base offers the best means of expanding the economy in the future. An investment code of 1983 allows full foreign ownership of companies registered in Morocco; terms for the repatriation of profits are reasonable.

MOZAMBIQUE

Area. 313,661 sq. miles (812,379 sq. km).
Population. (1995) 17,889,000.
Capital. Maputo (931,951).
Other major cities. Beira (298,847), Nampula (250,473).
Language(s). Portuguese (official), indigenous dialects.
Religion(s). Traditional beliefs 47.8 per cent, Christian 38.9 per cent (of which Roman Catholic 31.4 per cent), Muslim 13 per cent, other 0.3 per cent.
Date of independence. June 25 1975 (from Portugal).
GNP. (1993) $1,375,000,000, per capita $70.
Land and climate. Coastal lowlands the length of the country rise to interior uplands and plateaux, with high plateaux in the northwest and mountains in the west. The climate is tropical to subtropical.

Introduction

After 30 years of brutal warfare, first as a liberation struggle against the Portuguese from 1961 to 1975 and then as a civil war between the Frelimo government and the National Resistance Movement (Renamo) rebels, Mozambique entered the 1990s with a per capita income of only $80 to make it the poorest country in the world. Yet it has the potential to be a reasonably prosperous society: it has rich agricultural land

and should be able to feed its population; it possesses some of the richest offshore fisheries of the African continent; it is a storehouse of minerals (mainly untouched or neglected as a result of warfare); it has vast hydro-electric capacity; and its strategic position makes it the natural transit country for Zambia, Zimbabwe, Malawi, Swaziland and parts of South Africa. Hopefully, 1994 was a turning-point: after many false starts it finally appeared that the ceasefire in the civil war was holding and that the two sides (the government and Renamo) were prepared to accept UN-monitored elections in October. These were won convincingly by President Joaquin Chissano and the Mozambique Liberation Front (Frelimo) and Afonso Dhlakama of Renamo agreed to accept the results and co-operate with the government. Offers of aid to assist the process of reconciliation were made during the year, especially by Britain and the World Food programme.

In the north Mozambique has boundaries with Tanzania and Malawi; in the west with Zambia and Zimbabwe; in the southwest and south with South Africa and Swaziland; while it has a 2,470km coastline on the Mozambique Channel facing Madagascar.

Agriculture

Much of the land that formerly was productive has fallen into disuse after years of shifting warfare but the long-term agricultural potential is good. In 1993 agriculture accounted for 31 per cent of GDP and employed 84 per cent of the workforce. The main cash crops are cotton, cashew nuts, sugarcane, tea and shrimps and these provide the bulk of all exports; in 1994 shrimps accounted for 42.3 per cent of exports, cotton for 12.6 per cent, sugar 7.4 per cent, cashew nuts 2.2 per cent. The production of export crops could probably at least be doubled if peace becomes permanent and neglected areas are brought back under cultivation.

Livestock is relatively unimportant in the agricultural sector and the national cattle herd is only 1,250,000 strong with other livestock on a comparably small scale. The fish catch at 24,000mt could be considerably increased although there are dangers that the Mozambique Channel will be over-fished. The principal staples are cassava, maize, coconuts, sorghum, bananas. Mozambique is not self-sufficient in food though it could be; in 1994 food imports accounted for 28.9 per cent of all imports. Land use is divided between forested 17.9 per cent, meadows and pastures 56.1 per cent, agricultural land, under permanent cultivation 4.1 per cent, other 21.9 per cent.

Mining

In 1993 mining only contributed 0.4 per cent to GDP and employed 1.3 per cent of the workforce. Mining output (1994) is very small scale: salt 40,000mt, bauxite 9,620mt, copper 133mt, garnet 3,000 kg, gemstones 6,865 carats, coal 40,000mt. These figures do not remotely represent potential. If the years of unrest have really come to an end the possibility exists for substantial and immediate mineral development. There are huge coal reserves, a confirmed 6,000m tons, and the Moatize mine near Tete has a capacity for 600,000 tons' output a year (a figure almost achieved in 1975) while prior to independence coal exports came to 100,000 tons a year though in the 1990s they were down to 7,000 a year. Plans to revive the industry include increasing the capacity of the port at Beira to handle exports of 1.2m tons a year as opposed to its present capacity of 400,000 tons. Mozambique is examining various mineral development possibilities which would include the repayment of loans in the form of coal.

There are deposits of ilmenite north of the Zambezi mouth, zircon, titano-magnetite, rutile and monazite. Mozambique began mining iron ore in the 1950s and production reached 6 million tons a year by the early 1970s but then ceased (1975–84) as a result of the civil war. The mines are at Cassinga and a resumption of mining depends upon rehabilitating the railway to the coast (this was also a war casualty). There are huge deposits of iron ore – an estimated 360m tons – in Moçambique province near Namapa. Other mineral deposits nationwide include manganese, graphite, fluorite, platinum, nickel, uranium, asbestos, further iron ore, diamonds.

Although a search has so far failed to reveal any oil, Mozambique has confirmed reserves of 60,000m cu m of natural gas. There are gold deposits in Manica province and an agreement to mine has been concluded with the multinational Lonrho. Agreement with South Africa in 1992 to extract and export natural gas to the Republic from the Pande field in Inhambane province which has estimated reserves of 40,000m cu m will depend upon the construction of a 900km pipeline. Mozambique also has huge hydro potential: both from the giant Cabora Bassa Dam which has only been operating at minimal capacity due to war conditions and the frequent cutting of power lines to South Africa but should provide Mozambique with substantial annual income from sales to the Republic; and from the number of rivers that fall from the inland plateaux to the coastal plains. These and other developments of the mineral sector depend upon permanent peace, followed by new injections of capital and the rehabilitation of infrastructure, especially the railways.

Manufacturing

Manufacturing contributes 28 per cent to GDP and employs 5 per cent of the workforce. Most manufactures are related to food processing and the principal ones are wheat flour, sugar, cement, cotton threads, beer, soap, cigarettes, poplin.

Infrastructure

There are 3,288km of railroads of which 3,140km are 1.067m gauge. The three main railways each connect the landlocked countries or regions of the interior with Mozambique's main ports: Malawi to Nacala in the north; Malawi and Zimbabwe to Beira in the centre; and Zimbabwe to Maputo in the south. Prior to independence up to 40 per cent of government revenues came from transit fees for these landlocked countries but the civil war reduced the transit traffic almost to a standstill as the various railway lines were attacked or cut by the insurgents. There are 26,498km of highways of which 4,593km are paved; and there are 3,750km of inland waterways. The oil pipeline from Zimbabwe to Beira is no longer operating though it could be rehabilitated.

There are three ports: Nacala, which is one of the largest natural harbours in Africa; Beira, which with European aid has been updated to become one of the world's most advanced container (RoRo) ports; and Maputo. There are 131 usable airports, 25 with permanent surface runways, one of which is over 3,659m and four which are between 2,440 and 3,659m in length. The telecommunications system is fair.

Political considerations

As of 1995 everything really depended upon whether the peace between the warring factions of the long civil war would hold and the new multiparty system work. If so, economic rehabilitation can follow and Mozambique could begin to obtain new investment. Much will also depend upon the continuing progress in neighbouring South Africa.

Assessments

In 1993 external debts were equivalent to more than 400 per cent of GNP while Mozambique's ability to repay was almost non-existent; the country is listed according to World Bank criteria as the poorest in the world. But Mozambique has major economic potential: the development of its minerals could be followed by a rapid expansion of its manufacturing sector while its agriculture is capable of returning to food self-sufficiency. But 30 years of warfare have produced two generations most of whose children either received no schooling or only a few years of interrupted primary education. Other statistics for health, nutrition and adult literacy show that as a whole the population suffers from a depressingly low general standard of living and that sustained efforts over a long period will be needed to make any substantial changes to such a state of affairs. Nonetheless, Mozambique has the resource potential to rise above its present miserable poverty.

MYANMAR (BURMA)

Area. 261,228 sq. miles (676,577 sq. km).
Population. (1995) 46,527,000.
Capital. Rangoon (2,513,023).
Other major cities. Mandalay (532,949), Moulmein (219,961), Pegu (150,528), Bassein (144,096).
Language(s). Burmese (official), minority ethnic group languages (e.g. Karen).

Religion(s). Buddhist 89.1 per cent, Christian 4.9 per cent, Muslim 3.8 per cent, other 2.2 per cent.
Date of independence. January 4 1948 (from Britain).
GNP. (1993) $30,707,000,000, per capita $700.
Land and climate. Central lowlands are ringed by rugged mountains; the climate is tropical monsoon with cloudy rainy hot humid summers (June to September) and milder less cloudy winters (December to April).

Introduction

Since 1948 when it became independent Myanmar (then Burma) has pursued a policy of isolation from mainstream Third World politics, remaining both neutral and non-aligned and refusing Western aid for its development. Although it is a country rich in resources, it remains poor in the general standard of living of its people. It was effectively ruled from 1962 to 1988 by General Ne Win and the Burman Socialist Programme Party (BSPP) but in the latter year the army took control to establish a State Law and Order Restoration Council (SLORC) and while multiparty elections were held in 1990 SLORC did not subsequently permit the results (a win by the National League for Democracy) to be implemented and the leader of this party, Aung San Suu Kyi (a Nobel laureate), has been kept in detention. Ever since the 1940s Myanmar has faced a series of insurrections by a variety of insurgent groups representing a range of minorities; in 1994 the twelfth such rebel group to do so, the Kayan New Land Party, formally brought its insurgency to an end to leave only two other rebel groups, representing the Mon and Karen minorities, still operating in the field against the government.

Myanmar is the world's largest producer of illicit opium poppy (as well as producing some cannabis) for the international drug market and with its neighbours, Laos and Thailand, forms part of the 'golden triangle' of drug-producing countries. Myanmar has five neighbours – Bangladesh, China, India, Laos and Thailand – and a coastline of 1,930km on the Bay of Bengal and the Andaman Sea.

Agriculture

Agriculture including forestry and fisheries contributes just over 60 per cent to GDP and employs 69 per cent of the workforce. Myanmar has long been one of the world's major rice producers and exporters and in 1994 the rice crop amounted to 19,057,000mt. In recent years, however, there has been a drop in world rice prices as well as a fall-off in demand so that teak has replaced rice as the number one export. Roundwood production in 1993 came to 22,544,000cu m. Myanmar possesses the world's largest stand of hardwood trees. Rice and teak combined account for about 55 per cent of all exports. Other major crops are maize, oilseed, sugarcane, pulses, fruits and vegetables. Tobacco and jute are also produced in modest quantities. The national cattle herd is 9,691,000 head. Myanmar is self-sufficient in food. Land use is divided between forested 49.3 per cent, meadows and pastures 0.5 per cent, agricultural land, under permanent cultivation 15.3 per cent, other 34.9 per cent.

Mining

Mining contributes only 0.6 per cent to GDP and employs only 0.5 per cent of the workforce, yet the country possesses a range of minerals including petroleum which has been produced for decades if only in small quantities. Minerals, apart from oil, include tin, antimony, zinc, copper, tungsten, lead, coal, gypsum, marble, limestone, precious stones and natural gas. In 1993 quantities of gypsum, copper, lead, tin, jade and silver were mined. A total of 71,000mt of coal (slightly less than consumption) was mined and 5,100,000 barrels of oil were produced (consumption was somewhat more at 5,285,000 barrels). Myanmar consumes all the natural gas it produces (approximately 973,000,000cu m a year).

Manufacturing

Manufacturing accounts for 7.5 per cent of GDP and employs 7.3 per cent of the workforce. The principal manufactures concern food processing, textiles, footwear, wood and wood products, construction materials, pharmaceuticals, fertilizer and industries connected with mining. Although in recent years Myanmar has eased its isolationist stance in an effort to attract foreign investment so far it has had little success. Tourism is unimportant. The illicit production and trade in drugs is a major source of wealth – much of the resistance by dissident groups over the years has been funded by drugs – although precise estimates of its contribution to the economy are not possible.

Infrastructure

There are 3,991km of government-owned railway of which 3,878km are 1.000m gauge; 27,000km of roads with 3,200km paved; and 12,800km of inland waterways of which 3,200km are open to navigation by large commercial vessels. There are 1,343km of oil pipelines and a further 330km of natural gas pipelines. Rangoon, Moulmein and Bassein are the country's main ports. Of 78 usable airports, 26 have permanent surface runways of which three are between 2,440 and 3,659m in length. Internal telecommunications meet minimal requirements for government and business; international telecommunications are of good standard.

Political considerations

Myanmar's deliberate isolation and the dictatorial nature of its regime under the military do not make it an attractive country in which to invest and there are few indications that this image will change much in the foreseeable future. At least one beneficial result has been the accumulation of only minimal international debts which were equivalent to 16 per cent of GNP in 1993.

Assessments

Able to feed itself and possessed of a range of natural resources, Myanmar is now at the upper end of the low-income economies. It is unlikely that this position will alter very much in the foreseeable future.

NAMIBIA

Area. 318,580 sq. miles (825,118 sq. km).
Population. (1995) 1,651,000.
Capital. Windhoek (125,000).
Other major cities. Swakopmund (15,500), Rundu (15,000), Rehoboth (15,000), Keetmanshoop (14,000).
Language(s). English (official), Afrikaans, German, indigenous African (Ovambo, Kavango, Herero, Damara, Nama).
Religion(s). Lutheran 51.2 per cent, Roman Catholic 19.8 per cent, Dutch Reformed 6.1 per cent, Anglican 5 per cent, other 17.9 per cent.
Date of independence. March 21 1990 (from South Africa which controlled the mandate).
GNP. (1993) $2,598,000,000, per capita $1,660.
Land and climate. Most of Namibia consists of a high plateau with the Namib Desert along the coast and the Kalahari Desert in the east. The northern boundary with Angola (along the Cunene) and the Caprivi Strip enjoy subtropical to tropical climates but overall the climate is desert – hot and dry – with sparse rainfall.

Introduction

This vast underpopulated country of Southern Africa, which includes the extreme Namib Desert on its Atlantic seaboard, is a storehouse of minerals, especially diamonds (gemstones) and uranium, and is the fourth largest exporter of non-fuel minerals in Africa. Colonized during the scramble for Africa by Germany to become German South West Africa, it was occupied by troops from South Africa in 1915 and was made a mandate of the newly formed League of Nations immediately after World War I when the mandate was given to South Africa to administer. When, in 1946, the mandatory powers of the old League of Nations agreed that their mandates should be turned into Trusteeship Territories under the United Nations, South Africa refused to recognize UN authority in South West Africa (as the territory was still called) and over the succeeding 44 years was to be in dispute with the UN. At one point South Africa virtually incorporated Namibia into the republic, treating it as a fifth province. Finally, after years of pressure and 23 years of guerrilla warfare against the South West Africa People's Organization (SWAPO), South Africa agreed to UN-supervised multiparty elections in 1989 which gave SWAPO a clear majority under its leader Sam Nujoma who became Namibia's first president at independence in March 1990. In 1994 Namibia held its first post-independence elections to return Nujoma and SWAPO to power for a further term.

Namibia has land boundaries with Angola and Zambia in the north; it meets Zambia, Zimbabwe and Botswana at the only quadripoint in the world where the Chobe River enters the Zambezi at the end of the Caprivi Strip; and it has boundaries with Botswana to the east and South Africa to the east and south; and a coastline on the South Atlantic of 1489km.

Agriculture

Most agriculture is in the form of subsistence farming although livestock raising is a source of cash income as are sheep for the karikul pelts. Agriculture contributes just under 14 per cent to GDP and employs 38 per cent of the labour force. The principal crops are millet, maize, sorghum, fruits, vegetables, melons and pulses. The national sheep flock is 2,620,000, cattle 2,036,000 and goats 1,639,000. Cattle account for 11 per cent of exports, karakul pelts for a further 0.9 per cent. Namibia's offshore waters are one of Africa's richest fishing grounds. They were grossly over-fished during the last decade of South African rule and since independence the policy has been to under-fish in order to allow restocking to take place. Nonetheless, the fish catch in 1993 was 329,790mt although the potential is in the region of 1 million mt a year. Namibia is not self-sufficient in food and food products account for 17 per cent of imports.

Mining

Mining accounts for 15.9 per cent of GDP and employs 3 per cent of the workforce. Mineral resources include diamonds, copper, uranium, gold, lead, tin, lithium, cadmium, zinc, salt, vanadium, natural gas, coal and iron ore. Mining output in 1994 included diamonds 1,316,000 carats (mainly gemstones), zinc 64,600mt, copper 29,800mt, lead 23,800mt, uranium 2,242mt, silver 1,993,300 troy ounces, gold 78,607 troy ounces. Namibia is the world's eighth producer of uranium and the sixth of diamonds (and the leader in gem quality diamonds). It possesses the world's largest uranium mine and some of the world's largest reserves of tin and lithium. It is the second producer in Africa of lead, the third of cadmium and the fourth of zinc and copper.

During the years of South African control Namibia was a magnet for multi-national mining corporations (which remained after independence) and include Consolidated Diamond Mines (CDM), a subsidiary of De Beers which operates the great diamond mine at Oranjemund and has a near monopoly of the diamond market; Rio Tinto Zinc (RTZ) which operates the huge Rossing uranium mine; and the Tsumeb Corporation which operates four base metal mines for copper, lead and zinc. Government policy is to diversify the mining sector and a number of other minerals are mined on a small scale. There is optimism that prospecting along the coast may reveal offshore oil fields. In 1994 minerals accounted for 50.2 per cent of exports and of these diamonds accounted for 31.4 per cent.

Manufacturing

The manufacturing sector is minuscule, accounting for 9.3 per cent of GDP and employing only 4.6 per cent of the workforce. The great majority of manufactures are imported, principally from South Africa. The most important manufacturing activities cover mining – diamond cutting, copper and lead refining; fur products (karakul pelts), processed foods (fish, dairy products and meat), textiles and carved wood products.

Infrastructure

Walvis Bay, the only deep water port on the Namibian coast which had been held by South Africa after independence, was handed over to Namibia in February 1994 to bring to an end the only important post-independence boundary/land dispute and provide the new country with its own deep water outlet. Walvis Bay is the centre of the fishing industry where all canning and processing takes place. There are 2,341km of 1.067m gauge single track railway (part of the South African network) linking Walvis Bay through Windhoek into South Africa and down to the Cape which is still the principal route for the country's imports and exports. There are 54,500km of roads of which 4,079km are paved. Luderitz is the only port apart from Walvis Bay. Of 112 usable airports, 21 have permanent surface runways, one is over 3,659m and four are between 2,440 and 3,659m in length. Telecommunications are good in the urban areas and fair in rural areas with reasonable international links.

Political considerations

Since independence in 1990 Namibia has remained a stable multiparty democracy and maintained a low political profile. Its principal political problem relates to unemployment, the gap between the rich élite minority (including the 5 per cent of whites in the population) and the poor majority whose post-independence expectations have still largely to be met. The rate of population increase means a doubling time of only 23 years.

Assessments

Namibia is unlikely ever to be able to feed itself. Its mineral resources and offshore fisheries represent the two main sources of wealth while manufacturing must always be overshadowed by the vastly greater production of South Africa. In many respects it remains overwhelmingly dependent upon South Africa as a source of imports and exports as well as skills. The Republic is the main transit country for inward and outward goods of all kinds. A primary consideration of government is to lessen dependence upon South Africa. On his visit to Namibia in 1994 President Mandela of South Africa indicated that his country might cancel the $1,330,000,000 of Namibian debts to the Republic. Total international debts (including those to

South Africa) amounted to $3,180,000,000 in 1993 as opposed to a GNP of $2,598,000,000.

NEPAL

Area. 56,827 sq. miles (147,181 sq. km).
Population. (1995) 20,093,000.
Capital. Kathmandu (419,073).
Other major cities. Biratnagar (130,129), Lalitpur (117,203), Pokhara (95,311), Birganj (68,764).
Language(s). Nepali (official), twenty other languages/dialects.
Religion(s). Hindu (official) 90 per cent, Buddhist 5 per cent, Muslim 3 per cent, other 2 per cent (it is the only official Hindu state in the world).
Date of independence. 1768 (unification under Prithvi Narayan Shah).
GNP. (1993) $3,174,000,000, per capita $160.
Land and climate. The land divides into three regions: the southern river plain of the Ganges; the central hills; and the rugged Himalayas of the north. The climate varies between cool summers and severe winters in the Himalayas to subtropical summers and mild winters in the south.

Introduction

Unified in 1768, Nepal has remained one of the world's most remote and inaccessible states until modern times. Landlocked between Asia's two giants, India and China, it is inevitably subject to their pressures and in real terms, though it has good relations with both, is mainly an economic appendage of India. Some minerals, subsistence agriculture, huge hydro-electric potential and scenic beauty to attract tourists (it contains eight out of the world's ten highest peaks) are its principal resources. It is a constitutional monarchy and in 1990 adopted a democratic form of government; elections were last held in 1994.

Agriculture

The great majority of the people depend upon agriculture, usually at the subsistence level, for their livelihood and in 1993 agriculture accounted for just under 41 per cent of GDP and employed 81 per cent of the workforce. The main crops are rice, sugarcane, maize, wheat, potatoes, millet, pulses, barley, with jute and tobacco as cash crops. The national cattle herd is just over 6,000,000 head but buffaloes (3,058,000) are a major source of meat. Roundwood production at slightly above 19,000,000cu m is an important contributor to the economy. The country is not self-sufficient in food and is also subject to droughts, soil erosion, water pollution and deforestation. Land use is divided forested 18.1 per cent, meadows and pastures 14.6

per cent, agricultural land, under permanent cultivation 19.4 per cent, other 47.9 per cent.

Mining

The contribution of mining to the economy is negligible although limestone, magnesite, talc and garnet are quarried or mined. There are also deposits of quartz, lignite, copper, cobalt and iron ore.

Manufacturing

Manufacturing contributes 8.7 per cent to GDP but only employs 2 per cent of the workforce. The main manufactures are concerned with food or agricultural processing (rice, jute, sugar, oilseed mills), cigarettes, clothing and textiles, carpets, cement and bricks. Tourism, relying upon Nepal's spectacular scenery, has become increasingly important in recent years and receipts from tourism in 1992 came to $110,000,000.

Infrastructure

There are 52km of 0.762m narrow gauge railroad close to the Indian border; and 7,080km of roads of which 2,898km are paved. Of 37 usable airports, five have permanent surface runways of which one is between 2,440 and 3,659m in length. Telecommunications are poor to fair.

Political considerations

After three decades of mounting pressures the monarchy accepted a constitutional democratic system at the beginning of the 1990s. The crucial political concern remains India which dominates the economy and is the source of nearly half Nepal's imports and the destination for 40 per cent of its exports. When Nepal opted to buy arms from China in 1988 India imposed a partial blockade (1989–90) which forced the government to abandon part of the deal. Imports other than from India require licences.

Assessments

With its limited resources and high population Nepal has few prospects of major economic improvements in the foreseeable future. It is among the world's poorest countries and will double its population in 28 years. Remote, backward and underdeveloped, it seems unlikely to be able to attract much foreign investment.

NICARAGUA

Area. 50,838 sq. miles (131,670 sq. km).
Population. (1995) 4,340,000.
Capital. Managua (973,759).
Other major cities. Léon (172,042), Masaya (101,878), Chinandega (101,605), Matagalpa (95,268), Granada (91,929).
Language(s). Spanish (official), English, Indian minority languages on Caribbean coast.
Religion(s). Roman Catholic 89.3 per cent, other 10.7 per cent.
Date of independence. September 15 1821 (from Spain).
GNP. (1993) $1,421,000,000, per capita $360.
Land and climate. There are extensive plains on the Atlantic (Caribbean) seaboard which rise to interior mountains; and a narrow Pacific plain made irregular by volcanoes. The climate is tropical in the lowlands and cooler in the uplands.

Introduction

This small Central American country has had a deeply troubled political history. Following the overthrow of the Somoza family dictatorship in 1979 Nicaragua was to experience a decade of civil war. Although the Sandinista revolution was widely based and popular, US opposition to a left-wing government and Washington's subsequent support for the Contras ensured escalating violence throughout the 1980s which culminated (for the USA) in the Irangate Scandal. The Contra war finally came to an end in 1989, by which time an estimated 25,000 people had been killed while many more had been maimed for life and the economy had been ruined. In the elections of 1990 the Sandinistas were defeated by the National Opposition Union (UNO) led by Violetta Chamorro although subsequently, during the 1990s, UNO required the support of the Sandinistas to carry out national programmes. Continuing violence in the rural areas was a feature of the post-civil war era. The economy of Nicaragua is a mixture and there are some minerals but the principal exports are agricultural. Nicaragua has land boundaries with Honduras and Costa Rica and coastlines on the Caribbean and Pacific.

Agriculture

The majority of Nicaraguan exports are agricultural – coffee, cotton, bananas, sugar and meat. In 1993 coffee accounted for 12 per cent of exports, fresh and frozen meat for 22.8 per cent, sugar 6.5 per cent. Cotton, bananas and sesame are also important exports. The principal food staples are rice, maize, cassava, citrus fruits, beans and a variety of meat products including beef, pork, veal, poultry and dairy products. The national cattle herd is 1,650,000 strong. Nicaragua is normally self-sufficient in food. Agriculture accounts for just over 30 per cent of GDP and employs 30 per cent of the workforce. Land use is divided between forested 27 per cent, meadows and pastures 46.3 per cent, agricultural land, under permanent cultivation 10.7 per cent, other 16 per cent.

Mining

Mining accounts for only 0.7 per cent of GDP and employs only 0.6 per cent of the workforce. Minerals include gold, silver, copper, tungsten, lead and zinc. During the 1970s a number of oil companies carried out exploration work on both coasts and 43 offshore concessions had been granted by 1979. This work was suspended during the 1980s when the country was involved in the Contra war. During 1993, 39,900 troy ounces of gold were mined.

Manufacturing

Manufacturing accounts for 17 per cent of GDP and employs 13.6 per cent of the labour force. Under the Chamorro government from 1990 a number of firms have been privatized so that by 1993 less than 50 per cent of the total were state owned. Industrial output in the first years of the 1990s has remained below the pre-1979 figure. The principal manufactures are food products, beverages, tobacco, cement, bricks, tiles, rubber products and textiles.

Infrastructure

Although there are 373km of 1.067m gauge railway, most of it is not operational. There are 25,930km of roads of which 4,000km are paved. The 2,200km of inland waterways include two large lakes. There are 56km of oil pipelines. Corinto, El Bluff, Puerto Cabezas, Puerto Sandino and Rama are the principal ports. Of 151 usable airports eleven have permanent surface runways and of these two are between 2,440 and 3,659m in length. The telecommunications system is poor though in the process of being expanded.

Political considerations

The destabilizing tactics of the USA through the 1980s on behalf of the right-wing Contras indicate the international political parameters that affect Nicaraguan decisions. The USA made plain by its actions that it would not permit a political regime antithetical to its interests to survive except under enormous pressures; this will continue to be a prime factor of political life.

Assessments

At least Nicaragua is able to feed itself. Should offshore oil be discovered this would boost both industry and the general standard of living. Meanwhile, with a per capita income below $400 Nicaragua remains among the world's poorest economies, a status that seems unlikely to change in the foreseeable future.

NIGER

Area. 458,075 sq. miles (1,186,408 sq. km).
Population. (1995) 9,151,000.
Capital. Niamey (392,169).
Other major cities. Zinder (119,838), Maradi (104,386), Tahoua (49,948), Agadez (49,361).
Language(s). French (official), Hausa, Djerma.
Religion(s). Muslim (mainly Sunni) 98.6 per cent, other 1.4 per cent.
Date of independence. August 3 1960 (from France).
GNP. (1993) $2,279,000,000, per capita $270.
Land and climate. A country of desert plains and sand dunes, flat to rolling in the south, more hilly in the north. The climate is desert – hot, dry and dusty – but tropical in the extreme south.

Introduction

A vast landlocked country of northwestern Africa, Niger returned to a democratically elected form of government in 1993 after a long period of military/one-party rule. The economy really depends upon agriculture which accounts for about 40 per cent of GDP, and the mining of uranium which is the principal export. With a per capita income of only $270 Niger is among the world's poorest nations. A rebellion of Tuaregs in northern Niger was resolved in 1994 when the Tuareg Coordination of Armed Resistance (CAR) and the government signed a peace accord (October 9 1994). An area in the north of the country has been granted limited autonomy for an estimated 750,000 Tuaregs. Niger has a total of 5,697km of land boundaries with seven neighbours – Algeria, Benin, Burkina Faso, Chad, Libya, Mali and Nigeria.

Agriculture

Agriculture accounts for 37.1 per cent of GDP and employs 76.2 per cent of the workforce. Most of the sedentary agriculture is located in the extreme south of the country along the Niger valley. Livestock rearing covers goats (5,900,000), sheep (3,700,000) and cattle (1,986,000). The main cash crops are tobacco, cowpeas, cotton and peanuts. In 1993 live animals accounted for 10.5 per cent of exports. Food staples are millet, sorghum, cassava and rice. The country is normally self-sufficient in food except during drought years. Land use is divided between forested 1.5 per cent, meadows and pastures 6.9 per cent, agricultural land, under permanent cultivation 2.8 per cent, other (desert) 88.8 per cent.

Mining

Mining accounts for 5.6 per cent of GDP and this, effectively, means uranium which accounted for 45.7 per cent of exports in 1993. Production of uranium began in 1971 with an output of 410 tons of metal; output rose to 1,982 tons in 1980, went still higher in the middle of the decade before falling back as a result of the depression in the uranium market. Output began to rise again in the 1990s and reached 2,914 tons in 1993. Proven uranium reserves stand at 280,000 tons. High mining costs and geographic remoteness (output has to be transported to Cotonou, Benin, for shipment to Niger's principal European customers – France, Germany and Spain or to Japan) threaten to make Niger uncompetitive with other African suppliers such as Namibia and South Africa.

Niger possesses a number of other minerals although as yet exploitation has either been on a small scale or awaits further finance and better infrastructure. Resources include cassiterite, iron ore (including an estimated 650m tons at Say), calcium phosphates which were mined at Tahoua until 1984, though there are far larger deposits including an estimated 207m tons at Tapoa. There are also deposits of gypsum, salt (a mine is being developed at Tidekelt), gold and coal. Small deposits of petroleum have been located in the southwest but so far have not been considered worth exploiting although in 1991 the government introduced new legislation to attract foreign oil companies to prospect further: Elf and Exxon undertook evaluations.

Manufacturing

Manufacturing accounts for slightly less than 7 per cent of GDP and is mainly concerned with food processing, the mining sector and some import substitution. The leading manufactures are processed meat, cement, butter, peanut oil, beer, cotton fabrics.

Infrastructure

Niger has no railroad. There are 39,970km of roads of which 3,170km are paved. The Niger river in the south is navigable from mid-December to the end of March for 300km from Niamey to the Benin border at Gaya. There are 26 usable airports of which nine have permanent surface runways two of which are between 2,440 and 3,659m in length. The small telecommunications system is concentrated in the south of the country.

Political considerations/assessments

Despite its vast size, Niger is a small poor country in economic terms, mainly dependent upon agriculture and its one major mineral export of uranium. Its remoteness suggests that new developments will be slow and funding difficult unless major new discoveries of oil or some other valuable mineral are made. The country returned to multiparty politics in the 1990s.

PAKISTAN

Area. 307,374 sq. miles (796,095 sq. km).
Population. (1995) 140,497,000.
Capital. Islamabad (204,364).
Other major cities. Karachi (5,208,132), Lahore (2,552,689), Faisalabad (1,104,209), Rawalpindi (794,843).
Language(s). Urdu (official), English, Punjabi, Sindhi, Pashtu, Balochi.
Religion(s). Islam (official) 96.7 per cent, Christian 1.6 per cent, Hindu 1.5 per cent, other 0.2 per cent.
Date of independence. August 14 1947 (from Britain).
GNP. (1993) $54,045,000,000, per capita $440.
Land and climate. The country divides into three broad regions: the Indus plain in the east; the Balochistan plateau in the west; and mountains in the north and northwest. The climate ranges from hot dry desert in the south through temperate in the northwest to arctic in the high mountains of the north.

Introduction

Created from the partition of British India in 1947, Pakistan began life as a Dominion in the Commonwealth. It became an Islamic republic in 1956; in 1971 its eastern half seceded to form the state of Bangladesh. Politically, since independence, Pakistan has alternated between civilian and military rule. It reverted to civilian rule in the 1980s and in 1988 the elections were won by Benazir Bhutto, its first woman Prime Minister. Pakistan's relations with its neighbour, India, have always been troubled and sometimes violent, including three wars, and an ongoing dispute over the territory of Jammu and Kashmir which both states claim. Pakistan is among the world's poorest countries although, as a result of international tensions, has always maintained a large military establishment.

The country is not rich in minerals and remains a predominantly agricultural economy. It has the world's largest integrated irrigation system and its main crop and export is cotton. Pakistan has four neighbours – Afghanistan, China, India and Iran – and 1,000km coastline on the Indian Ocean (the Arabian Sea).

Agriculture

Agriculture contributes 22.3 per cent of GDP and employs 44.5 per cent of the workforce. Virtually all agriculture is in private hands. The sector dominates the economy as a whole: it produces the major export commodities and provides the main occupation and support for the rural population as well as being the main source of raw materials for industry. The irrigation system for the Indus is the largest integrated system in the world and a key to successful agricultural production.

Cotton is the most important crop and output in 1993 came to 9,054,000 bales. Cotton dominates exports with textile fabrics accounting (1993–4) for 53.6 per cent, readymade garments for 22 per cent, and cotton for 2.1 per cent. Other agricultural exports include rice 3.6 per cent, leather and leather goods 3.5 per cent and fresh fish

2.3 per cent. The main food crops are sugarcane 44,427,000mt, wheat 15,114,000mt, rice 3,995,000mt, maize 1,215,000mt. The national herds consist of 41,340,000 goats, 28,975,000 sheep, 18,887,000 buffalo, 18,146,000 cattle and 1,121,000 camels. Round-wood production exceeds 27,000,000cu m and the annual fish catch is well above 600,000mt. Pakistan is self-sufficient in staple foods. The country is a major producer of illicit drugs – opium and hashish – for the international drug trade and the government has had limited success in its eradication programme. Land use is divided between forested 5.3 per cent, meadows and pastures 6.5 per cent, agricultural land, under permanent cultivation 27.4 per cent, other 60.8 per cent.

Mining

Mining only contributes 0.6 per cent to GDP. Pakistan possesses extensive natural gas reserves although at present exploitation is solely for the home market (14,240,000,000cu m in 1993). There are some small oil fields but total output at approximately 22,000,000 barrels a year is only equivalent to half the country's consumption. Other minerals include coal (inferior quality), iron ore, copper, limestone, rock salt, gypsum, silica and chromite although only moderate quantities of these minerals are mined.

Manufacturing

Manufacturing accounts for 15.5 per cent of GDP and, with mining, employs 11.6 per cent of the workforce. The principal manufactures are cement, chemical fertilizers, refined sugar, cotton yarn, chemicals, vegetable products, jute textiles, paper and paper board, cotton textiles, cigarettes, motor vehicle tyres and bicycles. An important export consists of professional instruments. During the 1990s Pakistan has denationalized a number of state-owned firms and attracted a certain amount of new investment as a consequence.

Infrastructure

There are 8,773km of railways of which 7,718km are broad gauge. Of 101,315km of highways 40,155km are paved. There are 250km of piplines for crude oil, 4,044km for natural gas and 885km for petroleum products. The country is served by three main ports: Gwadar, Karachi and Port Muhammad bin Qasim. Of 104 usable airports 75 have permanent surface runways, one over 3,659m and 31 between 2,440 and 3,659m in length. There is a fair system of international telecommunications although at home, while adequate for government and business, it is otherwise poor.

Political considerations

A multiparty democracy, heavily influenced by Islam which is the state religion, Pakistan is a country of often volatile political tensions that are greatly exacerbated by problems of poverty at home and conflicts with its neighbours: in the west the civil war in Afghanistan has resulted in a major influx of refugees into Pakistan; in the east a near permanent state of confrontation with India has been greatly heightened during the 1990s by the escalating conflict in Kashmir over whose status the two countries have been in dispute (and sometimes at war) ever since independence.

Assessments

Rated among the world's poorest countries, Pakistan depends upon large annual inputs of aid to sustain its economy. Total external debts in 1993 stood at $20,306,000,000, equivalent to 37 per cent of GNP. Pakistan began a major programme of economic liberalization in 1990 whose object was to boost foreign and domestic private investment so as to lower dependence upon foreign aid. According to present demographic projections the population of 140,000,000 will double in only 24 years and that represents the country's most urgent political/economic problem. With limited mineral resources but agricultural self-sufficiency as well as plenty of available land, the greatest hope for future development lies in increased industrialization.

PANAMA

Area. 29,157 sq. miles (75,517 sq. km).
Population. (1995) 2,631,000.
Capital. Panama City (450,668).
Other major cities. Miguelito (293,564), David (65,763), Colón (54,654).
Language(s). Spanish (official), English.
Religion(s). Roman Catholic 80 per cent, Protestant 10 per cent, Muslim 5 per cent, other 5 per cent.
Date of independence. November 28 1821 (from Spain; Panama began its independent existence as part of Greater Colombia but broke away – with US encouragement – to become the state of Panama on November 3 1903).
GNP. (1993) $6,621,000,000, per capita $2,610.
Land and climate. The interior of Panama consists of rugged mountains and high plains; the coastal regions are divided between plains and rolling hills. The climate is tropical hot, humid and cloudy with a long rainy season from May through to January.

Introduction

This small Central American country occupies the strategic isthmus that connects the land masses of North and South America. Much of Panama's history since its independence from Colombia in 1903 has been synonymous with the history of the Panama Canal: its construction and opening in 1914; its operation and American insistence upon control of what Washington has always regarded as a highway of strategic importance to the USA. There is a US military force stationed permanently in the Canal Zone; whether this will be withdrawn at the end of the century as promised remains to be seen.

Panama operates a flag of convenience for an international fleet of more than 3,000 vessels which is a major source of income. The country is also, by virtue of its geographic position, a natural trans-shipment point for drugs en route from South to North America as well as being a drug money laundering centre. Growing American opposition to the role of General Manuel Noriega in the drugs business led the USA to send an invading force of marines into Panama at the end of 1989 and Noriega was subsequently taken to the USA where he was tried on various drugs-related charges and sentenced to a long prison term. Panama is a multiparty democracy with separate presidential and legislative assembly elections. The country has two land neighbours, Costa Rica and Colombia, and two coastlines – on the Caribbean to the north and the North Pacific to the south. The Panama Canal is the world's second most strategic highway after the Suez Canal.

Agriculture

Agriculture accounts for just over 10 per cent of GDP and employs 20.5 per cent of the workforce. Bananas, shrimps, other fish products and raw sugar together account for 60 per cent of exports. The main staple crops are rice and maize. Coffee and tobacco are also produced in small quantities. The national cattle herd is 1,400,000 strong. About 1,000,000cu m of roundwood are produced annually. Panama is not self-sufficient in food and imports grains and vegetables. Land use is divided between forested 42.9 per cent, meadows and pastures 20.7 per cent, agricultural land, under permanent cultivation 8.6 per cent, other 27.8 per cent.

Mining

Mining plays an insignificant role in the economy and contributes a mere 0.2 per cent to GDP, employing only 0.3 per cent of the workforce. Limestone is quarried and a small amount of gold is mined (8,000 troy ounces in 1992). There are some copper deposits.

Manufacturing

The principal manufacturing activities consist of petroleum refining, brewing, cement, other construction materials, sugar milling, textiles, food and beverage processing, tobacco products, paints, soaps and pharmaceuticals. Clothing accounts for nearly 5 per cent of exports. Tourism earns slightly more than $200,000,000 a year. Manufacturing contributes just over 9 per cent to GDP and employs just under 10 per cent of the workforce.

Infrastructure

There are 238km of railroads of which 78km are 1.524m broad gauge; 8,530km of highways of which 2,745km are paved; and 800km of inland waterways (suitable for shallow draft vessels) and the 82km Panama Canal. There is an 130km crude oil pipeline. The country is served by three ports: Cristóbal, Balboa, Bahia las Minas. The merchant marine of 3,244 registerd vessels (1993) of 1,000 GRT or more all fly the Panamanian flag of convenience; the top owners are Japan, Greece, Hong Kong and Taiwan (57 per cent). There are 104 usable airports, 39 with permanent surface runways two of which are between 2,440 and 3,659m in length. Panama has a well-developed system of telcommunications, both domestic and international.

Political considerations

The application of sanctions to Panama by the USA in 1988 and the subsequent invasion by US forces in December 1989 which brought about the downfall of General Manuel Noriega were a potent reminder (added to the permanent presence of US troops in the Canal Zone) of just how vulnerable is Panama to pressures from the northern superpower. International debts at $3,709,000,000 (1993) cost $900m a year to service.

Assessments

Approximately 70 per cent of GDP is derived from service activities: financial services, flag of convenience dues, and the Colón Free Zone which is the second largest in the world after Hong Kong with an annual turnover in excess of $6bn. In addition, but unquantifiable, the drug transit and money laundering business seems unlikely to diminish and Panama's role, generally, will continue as that of an entrepôt servicing country rather than as a producer, although its agricultural exports will remain important.

PAPUA NEW GUINEA

Area. 178,704 sq. miles (462,840 sq. km).
Population. (1995) 4,302,000.
Capital. Port Moresby (193,242).
Other major cities. Lae (80,655), Madang (27,057), Wewak (23,224).
Language(s). English (official), Tok Pisin, Motu (there are a total of 715 indigenous languages).
Religion(s). Roman Catholic 22 per cent, Protestant (various sects) 44 per cent, indigenous beliefs 34 per cent.
Date of independence. September 16 1975 (from Australia which administered the UN Trusteeship).
GNP. (1993) $4,646,000,000, per capita $1,120.

Land and climate. Coastal lowlands give way to rolling foothills and an interior of high, rugged mountains. The climate is tropical and the country is subject to the northwest monsoon (December to March) and the southeast monsoon (May to October).

Introduction

Formerly part of the German colonial empire and subsequently administered first as a League of Nations and then as a United Nations Trusteeship by Australia, Papua New Guinea became independent in 1975. A country of jungle and mountains that appeared until recently to have been bypassed and forgotten by the modern world, Papua New Guinea probably has many minerals still undiscovered. It is a constitutional monarchy in the Commonwealth. A separatist group in the island of Bougainville (which possesses huge copper deposits), aiming to break away from Papua New Guinea, is a source of ongoing opposition and violence to government. The territory has one land neighbour, Indonesia, which controls Irian Jaya, the other half of the island of New Guinea.

Agriculture

Agriculture accounts for nearly 26 per cent of GDP and employs 77 per cent of the workforce. Most output is at the subsistence level and fertile soils permit the cultivation of a wide variety of commodity crops for export. These include palm oil, copra, palm kernels, coffee, cocoa, pineapples and tea. Palm oil, copra, coffee and cocoa beans between them account for 20 per cent of exports. Other foods include sugarcane, yams, cassava. Pigs are the most important livestock. Roundwood production is at the level of 8,000,000cu m a year and timber (including plywood) accounts for 18 per cent of exports. The country is basically self-sufficient in food although imports are required to meet the needs of the urban areas. Land use is divided between forested 84.4 per cent, agricultural land, under permanent cultivation 0.9 per cent, meadows and pastures 0.2 per cent, other 14.5 per cent.

Mining

Mining accounts for 29 per cent of GDP although only employing 0.6 per cent of the workforce. The country is richly endowed with minerals and there are almost certainly more to be discovered. Exploitation, however, has been slow due to lack of infrastructure and the rugged nature of the interior. The main minerals are gold, copper, silver and natural gas. There are oil deposits but their extent has yet to be established. In 1994 copper output from the island of Bougainville where there are huge deposits came to 206,329mt, silver 75,025kg, and gold 57,751kg. Papua New Guinea is now seen to be the world's third largest source of gold after South Africa and Russia and is among the world's top producers of copper as well. Minerals (gold and copper) account for 40 per cent of exports.

Manufacturing

Manufacturing accounts for under 9 per cent of GDP and employs 1.9 per cent of the workforce. The principal manufactures concern foods, beverages, tobacco, mining, metals and metal products, machinery and equipment and wood products.

Infrastructure

There are no railways. Of 19,200km of roads 640km are paved. There are 10,940km of inland waterways and the country is served by five main ports: Anewa Bay, Lae, Madang, Port Moresby, Rabaul. Of 457 usable aiports, eighteen have permanent surface runways and only one is between 2,440 and 3,659m in length. Telecommunications are adequate.

Political considerations

A high proportion of the population is isolated in the centre of the country, living by subsistence farming, and little affected by modern economic developments. The opening up of minerals in these regions could bring changes and consequent political problems. The secessionist rebellion on the island of Bougainville from 1989 to 1994 led to a temporary closure of the Panguna copper mine to deprive the country of 40 per cent of its export earnings. Growing political awareness is likely to produce similar problems in the future.

Assessments

Rich mineral resources and the likelihood of more discoveries to come could transform Papua New Guinea's economy. However, exploitation is hampered by the nature of the rugged terrain and the lack of infrastructure. Papua New Guinea ought to be able to feed itself without difficulty.

PARAGUAY

Area. 157,048 sq. miles (406,752 sq. km).
Population. (1995) 4,828,000.
Capital. Asunción (502,426).
Other major cities. Ciudad del Este (133,893), San Lorenzo (133,311), Lambare (99,681), Fernando de la Mora (95,287) .
Language(s). Guaraní (official), Spanish.

Religion(s). Roman Catholic 93.1 per cent, other 6.9 per cent.
Date of independence. May 14 1811 (from Spain).
GNP. (1993) $6,995,000,000, per capita $1,500.
Land and climate. A mixture of grassy plains and wooded hills to the east while west of the Paraguay river lies the Gran Chaco region of low marshy plain, dry forest and scrub. The climate ranges from temperate in the east to semi-arid in the west.

Introduction

One of South America's only two landlocked countries, Paraguay is not richly endowed with resources except for hydro-power although it is a relatively rich agricultural country and agriculture is by far the most important sector of the economy. The country was ruled by the military dictator, Gen. Alfedo Stroessner, from 1954 until 1989 when he was overthrown in a coup led by Gen. Andres Rodriguez who subsequently became president. In 1993, the country returned to a civilian elected government. Paraguay has three neighbours: Argentina to the south and southwest, Bolivia to the northwest and Brazil to the northeast and east.

Agriculture

Agriculture, which contributes 25 per cent to GDP and employs 43 per cent of the workforce, is by far the most important sector of the economy and accounts for about 90 per cent of all exports. The principal cash crops are cotton, sugar and soybeans. Meat products and wood are important exports. In 1994 soybean flour led exports at 27.2 per cent, while cotton fibres accounted for another 20.9 per cent, timber for 9.6 per cent, hides and skins 7.7 per cent, vegetable oil 7.7 per cent, processed meat 6.9 per cent, followed by oilseed cake, perfume oils and tobacco. The main staple crops are maize, wheat, cassava, fruits and vegetables. The national cattle herd is 8,000,000 strong. Roundwood output is somewhat above 8,000,000cu m a year. Paraguay is basically self-sufficient in foods. Cannabis is produced illegally for the international drug market and Paraguay also acts as a trans-shipment point for Bolivian cocaine *en route* for the USA. Land use is divided between forested 33.3 per cent, meadows and pastures 53.9 per cent, agricultural land, under permanent cultivation 5.6 per cent, other 7.2 per cent.

Mining

Paraguay possesses few mineral resources and no oil though it does have major hydro-power which it has developed on the Paraná River at Itaipú and Yacyretá; these two developments are joint ventures with Brazil and Argentina respectively and the heavy investment means that Paraguay can meet all its own electricity requirements and export the surplus to her two large neighbours. Otherwise, mineral resources are limited to iron ore, manganese, limestone, kaolin and gypsum.

Manufacturing

Manufacturing contributes 16.5 per cent to GDP and employs 12 per cent of the workforce. The main manufacturing activities are meat packing, oilseed crushing, milling, brewing, textiles, cement, other construction materials and a range of light industries.

Infrastructure

There are 970km of railroads of which 440km are 1.435m broad gauge. There are 21,960km of roads of which only 1,788km are paved; and 3,100km of inland waterways with three river ports: Asunción, Villeta and Ciudad del Este. Of 719 usable airports only seven have permanent surface runways and of these four are between 2,440 and 3,659m in length. Asunción has good telecommunications with reasonable links to other cities.

Political considerations/assessments

Now a multiparty civilian government (after the long dictatorship of Stroessner), Paraguay is a lower-middle-income country whose real economic base is and will remain agriculture. The country's remoteness, landlocked position and lack of minerals mean it is unlikely to change its economic status in any significant way in the foreseeable future.

PERU

Area. 496,225 sq. miles (1,285,216 sq. km).
Population. (1995) 23,489,000.
Capital. Lima (5,706,127).
Other major cities. Arequipa (619,156), Callao (615,046), Trujillo (509,312), Chiclayo (411,536).
Language(s). Spanish, Quechua, Aymara (official).
Religion(s). Roman Catholic 92.5 per cent, Protestant 5.5 per cent, other 2 per cent.
Date of independence. July 28 1821 (from Spain).
GNP. (1993) $33,973,000,000, per capita $1,490.
Land and climate. There are three main geographic divisions: the western coastal plain, the High Andes of the centre and the eastern lowlands of the Amazon Basin (jungle). The climate ranges from tropical in the east through mountain temperate to desert in the west.

Introduction

A huge country of just under half a million square miles with a 1,500-mile coastline on the South Pacific Ocean and incorporating a long stretch of the High Andes, Peru was formerly the centre of the ancient Inca Empire before becoming part of Spain's Latin American empire. Today it has a mixed economy with a strong mining sector as well as the doubtful distinction of being the world's largest producer of coca, the base for cocaine. Throughout the 1980s and to the mid-1990s the country has faced the bitter insurgency of the Shining Path (Sendero Luminoso) guerrillas, one of the world's more extreme Marxist groups. Apart from its long Pacific coastline Peru has five land neighbours: Bolivia, Brazil, Chile, Colombia and Ecuador.

Agriculture

Agriculture accounts for just over 14 per cent of GDP and employs 33 per cent of the workforce. Cash crops for export include coffee, cotton, sugar and fish products. The main food staples are rice, maize, potatoes, plantains and cassava. The national herd includes 11,600,000 sheep and 4,000,000 cattle. Peru is one of the world's leading fishing nations and the catch for 1993 came to 8,450,600mt while fish flour contibuted 16.3 per cent to exports. Roundwood production is just over 8,000,000cu m a year. Wool is an important product and export. Peru, however, is not self-sufficient in grains or vegetable oils. Something like 121,000 hectares of land are used to grow coca leaf (more than 85 per cent of it illegally) for the world drug market and most of the crop is shipped to dealers in Colombia where it is processed into cocaine. During the 1980s the Shining Path guerrillas financed much of their activity with money derived from the coca business. Land use is divided between forested 53.1 per cent, meadows and pastures 21.2 per cent, agricultural land, under permanent cultivation 2.9 per cent, other 22.8 per cent.

Mining

Mining accounts for just under 10 per cent of GDP and employs 2.4 per cent of the workforce. Peru is a major producer, in world terms, of copper, lead, silver, tin and zinc and is also a substantial producer of iron ore. In 1993 copper accounted for 17.4 per cent of exports with production running at 375,000mt; zinc (664,600mt) accounted for 7.9 per cent of exports, gold for 6.2 per cent, lead for 2.8 per cent and silver for 2.2 per cent. As a leading world producer Peru is a member of the Inter-governmental Council of Copper Exporting Countries (CIPEC).

Peru has been a moderate oil producer since the end of the nineteenth century and petroleum and its derivatives account for 4.3 per cent of exports. In 1992 crude oil output came to 42,000,000 barrels (less than domestic consumption) while natural gas at 1,314,000,000cu m was more than double domestic requirements. Altogether, minerals contribute more than 50 per cent of exports. With the decline in activity of the Shining Path guerrillas, geologists and miners are showing renewed interest in prospecting in the Andean region and joint ventures with foreign investors are giving a boost to gold and copper extraction. The mid-1990s have also witnessed renewed interest in oil and gas prospects.

Manufacturing

Manufacturing accounts for 26.6 per cent of GDP and employs 10.4 per cent of the workforce. The main products are processed foods, base metal products, beverages, tobacco, textiles, chemicals (mainly industrial), wearing apparel and wood products. The manufacturing sector generally offers considerable possibilities for expansion. Moves towards privatization in the 1990s and a programme to encourage Peruvians to invest in companies by buying stocks and shares has encouraged new growth in the sector and in 1994 the rate of economic growth was 8.5 per cent while the rate of inflation fell. Tourism yields about $230m income a year and could be considerably expanded.

Infrastructure

There are 1,801km of railroads of which 1,501km are 1.435m gauge; 69,942km of roads of which 7,459km are paved; and 8,600km of navigable waterways (tributaries of the Amazon) as well as 200km on Lake Titicaca; 800km of oil pipelines and 64km of natural gas and gas liquids pipelines. Peru's chief ports are Callao, Ilo, Iquitos, Matarani and Talara. There are 199 usable airports of which 37 have permanent surface runways, two of which are over 3,659m and 23 between 2,440 and 3,659m in length. The system of telecommunications, both domestic and international, is fair.

Political considerations

When the Fujimori government took office in 1990 it instituted an austerity pro-gramme as well as moves towards creating a more market-oriented economy (as opposed to the generally state-directed economy of the 1980s). Huge debt arrears in the 1980s had led the World Bank and IMF to cut off support. However, by 1994 major lending agencies had returned to Peru. International debts at $16,123,000,000 in 1993 were just under 50 per cent of GNP.

Assessments

Peru faces major problems of poverty and unemployment and has still to resolve the 15-year-old war against the Shining Path guerrillas, although their capacity to inflict damage appeared to be in sharp decline in the 1990s. The illicit trade in coca (the largest in the world) contributes a great deal to the hidden or black economy and will almost certainly continue as a major factor into the foreseeable future. Peru has a rich mineral base and a reasonable agricultural one as well despite its shortfall in grains. The greatest room for improvement lies in the manufacturing sector. Peru is rated among the lower-middle-income group of countries.

PHILIPPINES

Area. 115,860 sq. miles (300,076 sq. km).
Population. (1995) 70,011,000.
Capital. Manila (1,894,667).
Other major cities. Quezon City (1,627,890), Davao (867,779), Cebu (641,042), Caloocan (629,473), Zamboanga (453,214).
Language(s). Pilipino and English (official).
Religion(s). Roman Catholic 84.1 per cent, Aglipayan 6.2 per cent, Muslim 4.3 per cent, Protestant 3.9 per cent, other 1.5 per cent.
Date of independence. July 4 1946 (from USA).
GNP. (1993) $54,593,000,000, per capita $830.
Land and climate. The islands are mainly mountainous with coastal plains that vary between narrow and extensive. It is a tropical marine climate, subject to the northeast monsoon from November to April and the southwest monsoon from May to October. Apart from cyclones, the country is subject to landslides, earthquakes, volcanic action, deforestation, soil erosion and water pollution.

Introduction

This large cluster of islands in Southeast Asia between Indonesia and China lies astride the typhoon belt. The people are Malay and the Philippines were long part of the Spanish Empire until they were ceded to the USA by Spain following its disastrous war with that country in 1898. Although it possesses a relatively diverse manufacturing sector the Philippines remains a predominantly agricultural economy. After the long and corrupt dictatorship of Ferdinand Marcos, the country began to open up both politically and economically under the presidency of Corazón Aquino who came to power in 1986 when Marcos was forced to flee the country. Since that time the emphasis has been upon investment rather than consumption. The Philippines claims Sabah, the Malaysian province which occupies the northern extremity of the neighbouring island of Borneo.

Agriculture

Agriculture contributes 22 per cent to GDP and employs 42 per cent of the workforce. In 1994 food, live animals, animal and vegetable oils and fats together accounted for 17 per cent of exports. The principal crops are rice, coconuts, maize, sugarcane, bananas, pineapples, mangoes, cassava, tobacco, coffee. Pigs are the most important livestock followed by buffalo and goats; the national cattle herd is

1,658,000 strong. Roundwood production at 38,000,000cu m a year makes a substantial contribution to the economy. The annual fish catch is about 25,000mt. Land use is divided between forested 33.5 per cent, meadows and pastures 4.3 per cent, agricultural land, under permanent cultivation 30.8 per cent, other 31.4 per cent.

Minerals

Mining contributes just over 1 per cent to GDP and employs only 0.5 per cent of the workforce. Small quantities of gold, silver, copper concentrate, cobalt, salt, coal, and nickel ore are produced. There are limited oil fields with an output of approximately 3,000,000 barrels of oil a year but this represents only a fraction of home consumption.

Manufacturing

Manufacturing contributes 24 per cent to GDP and employs 9 per cent of the workforce. Electronics and garments are the two leading manufactures and the sector is the main source of export earnings. The principal manufactures are food products, petroleum and coal products, industrial chemicals, footwear and wearing apparel, beverages, electrical machinery and non-metallic mineral products. Tourism is a major industry and earned $2,122,000,000 in 1993.

Infrastructure

There are 378km of railway on Luzon Island; 157,450km of roads of which 22,400km are paved; 3,219km of inland waterways limited to shallow draft vessels; and 357km of pipelines for petroleum products. The principal ports are Cagayan de Oro, Cebu, Davao, Guimaras, Iloilo, Legaspi, Manila, Subic Bay. The Philippines operates a merchant marine flag of convenience. There are 238 usable airports of which 73 have permanent surface runways and of these nine are between 2,440 and 3,659m in length. There are good international telecommunications while domestic and inter-island services are fair.

Political considerations

Always strongly influenced by its relations with the USA for whom it provided massive base facilities until the 1990s, the Philippines faces many of the problems of a country which has made some significant development strides but has yet to achieve real breakthroughs. Its population of 70 million is due to double in 30 years.

The Philippines has been troubled for decades by the activities of a variety of insurgent groups – left-wing, communist and religious.

Assessments

Only just in the lower-middle-income group of countries, the Philippines must remain a predominantly agricultural country into the foreseeable future. A moderate recipient of aid, the Philippines nonetheless has international debts (1993) of $27,471,000,000, equivalent to half GNP.

RWANDA

Area. 9,757 sq. miles (25,271 sq. km).
Population. (1995) 6,700,000 (perhaps up to 2 million were refugees in mid-1995).
Capital. Kigali (237,782).
Other major cities. Ruhengeri (29,578), Butare (28,645), Gisenyi (21,578).
Language(s). Rwandan and French (official), Kiswahili.
Religion(s). Roman Catholic 65 per cent, traditional beliefs 17 per cent, Protestant 9 per cent, Muslim 9 per cent.
Date of independence. July 1 1962 (from Belgium which administered the UN Trusteeship).
GNP. (1993) $1,499,000,000, per capita $200.
Land and climate. A land of grassy uplands and hills rising to mountains in the west; the climate, moderated by altitude, is temperate with two rainy seasons from February to April and November to January. Frost and snow are possible in the mountains. The land is subject to deforestation, soil erosion and periodic droughts.

Introduction

Between April and August 1994 the country experienced the worst genocide and mass slaughter in modern Africa's history when perhaps 1 million Rwandans were killed while similar numbers became refugees. Extreme Hutu militants, armed by the government, had launched the massacres on the death of President Juvenal Habyarimana who was killed in an aircrash on April 6. The UN, which then had a presence in the country, first reduced this but later increased its strength to 5,500 men although the European powers and the USA refused to send troops. In any case the troops, when they came, were too late to prevent the massacres. The Rwandan Patriotic Front which is dominated by Tutsis (the minority tribe) had been waging a civil war against the government since 1990; it now succeeded (August) in taking the capital, in the wake of the massacres, and establishing a precarious government although its Hutu opponents, many then in refugee camps in neighbouring countries, were planning a return so that 1995 was a year of continuing tensions with nothing resolved. Rwanda is a tiny landlocked country in the centre of equatorial Africa with four neighbours: Burundi, Tanzania, Uganda and Zaire.

Agriculture

Agriculture accounts for 42 per cent of GDP and employs 90 per cent of the workforce. Although the land is fertile it is over-used and under constant pressure from too large a population. Coffee and tea are the principal export crops with coffee accounting for 60 per cent of exports and tea for a further 23.5 per cent. Pyrethrum for insecticides is another export crop as well as small quantities of tobacco. The main food crops are bananas, plantains, beans, sorghum and potatoes. Stock raising for meat and dairy products includes small herds of cattle, goats and sheep. The annual fish catch from Lake Kivu is about 3,500mt. Although formerly self-sufficient in food, Rwanda is becoming a food importer since agricultural production is not keeping pace with an annual growth of population at 3.8 per cent. Land use is divided between forested 22.3 per cent, meadows and pastures 18.3 per cent, agricultural land, under permanent cultivation 47.4 per cent, other 12 per cent.

Minerals

The mineral sector is very small, contributing a mere 0.2 per cent to GDP and employing a similar percentage of the workforce. Small quantities of cassiterite, wolframite and gold are mined. Limited production of natural gas is consumed at home. There are, however, large resources of natural gas under Lake Kivu (which is shared with Zaire) but a market has yet to be found for this resource.

Manufacturing

Manufacturing contributes 12.3 per cent to GDP although only employing 1.4 per cent of the workforce. Most manufactures are concerned with food processing and the main divisions of this sector are: cement, lye soap, sugar, beer, soft drinks, footwear, blankets, matches.

Infrastructure

There are 4,885km of roads of which 460km are paved; Lake Kivu is navigable by shallow draft barges. There are seven usable airports of which two have runways betwen 2,440 and 3,659m in length. The telecommunications system is fair.

Political considerations/assessments

The ethnic explosion of 1994 which caused 1 million deaths and created twice as many refugees will affect the politics and economic and social life of the country for years to come. Apart from this legacy of tribal hatred, Rwanda is essentially an agricultural country which has to maximize its land use. Overcrowding and a rate of growth that will double the population in 21 years together put enormous pressure upon this land resource. Debts are equivalent to just over half the GNP.

SENEGAL

Area. 75,551 sq. miles (196,712 sq. km).
Population. (1995) 8,312,000.
Capital. Dakar (1,729,823).
Other major cities. Thiès (201,350), Kaolack (179,894), Ziguinchor (148,831), Saint-Louis (125,717).
Language(s). French (official), Wolof, Pulaar, Diola, Mandingo.
Religion(s). Sunni Muslim 94 per cent, Christian 4.9 per cent, other 1.1 per cent.
Date of independence. August 20 1960 (from France).
GNP. (1993) $5,867,000,000, per capita $740.
Land and climate. The land mainly consists of undulating plains with low hills in the southeast. The climate is tropical, hot and humid with a rainy season from December to April. The dry season is characterized by the harmattan wind from the north. The lowlands suffer from flooding and the country is subject to over-grazing, soil erosion, deforestation and desertification.

Introduction

During the French colonial era Senegal was developed to service the whole of French West Africa and though, following independence, the other Francophone countries went their own ways, Senegal still possesses one of the better infrastructures of the region and one of its more developed economies. A multiparty democracy, Senegal experienced a year of anti-government violence during 1994, sparked off by the devaluation of the CFA franc at the beginning of the year which caused considerable hardship; this violence damaged the country's reputation for democracy and tolerance. The tiny Anglophone state of The Gambia is entirely surrounded by the territory of Senegal except for its 80km coastline on the Atlantic and in 1981 The Gambia and Senegal entered upon a loose confederal arrangement – Senegambia – but the arrangement did not work satisfactorily and was formally ended in September 1989. Senegal has five neighbours: The Gambia, Guinea, Guinea-Bissau, Mali and Mauritania; and an Atlantic coastline of 531km.

Agriculture

Agriculture contributes 22 per cent to GDP and employs 65 per cent of the workforce. The principal crops are sugarcane, millet, groundnuts, rice, maize, sorghum and seed cotton. About 40 per cent of cultivated land produces groundnuts which form the most important agricultural export. Cotton is also an important export crop, accounting for 4 per cent of exports. The national livestock herd includes 4,600,000 sheep, 3,200,000 goats and 2,800,000 cattle. The Atlantic fish catch makes a major contribution to exports and the 1993 catch was 377,676 tonnes, with fish and fish products accounting for 27 per cent of all exports. Senegal is about two-thirds self-sufficient in food production. Land use is divided between forested 54.3 per cent, meadows and pastures 16.1 per cent, agricultural land, under permanent cultivation 12.2 per cent, other 17.4 per cent.

Minerals

Mining activities contribute less than 1 per cent to GDP. The principal natural resources are phosphates and iron ore, and calcium phosphate production in 1992 came to 1,663,100mt with phosphates contributing 8.2 per cent of exports. Aluminium phosphate mining was important prior to 1989 when it was discontinued. Calcium phosphates reserves stand at 100m tonnes; aluminium phosphates at 50m–70m tonnes. Senegal accounts for 1.5 per cent of world phosphate output and 3 per cent of world exports. There are an estimated 330m tonnes of high-grade iron ore at Falémé in east Senegal but exploitation requires new sources of electric power (which are being developed). In any case, the world is currently over-supplied with iron ore although production from Falémé has been scheduled to begin in 1996. There are considerable deposits of heavy oil off the Casamance coast – an estimated 52–58m tonnes – and also small deposits of natural gas. Offshore prospecting for oil is continuing.

Manufacturing

Senegal has the second most sophisticated manufacturing sector of Francophone Africa after Côte d'Ivoire. The majority of enterprises consist of light industries concerned with food processing or import substitution. Principal manufactures include sugar, oil mills, fish canning, flour mills, drinks, dairy products and tobacco. Between them these account for 40 per cent of value added. Extractive industries related to phosphates form the second tier of manufactures followed by textiles, leather goods, chemicals, paper and packaging. The textile industry is the most developed in Francophone Africa. Refined petroleum is another major source of export earnings, refined products accounting for 12 per cent of all exports. Senegal has one of the more balanced economies of West Africa and enjoys a greater degree of trade with her neighbours than do most African countries, with more than 12 per cent of her exports going to other West African countries. Tourism is of growing importance, earning $173,000,000 in 1993.

Infrastructure

There are 1,034km of 1.000m gauge railway, all single track except for the 70km Dakar to Thiès stretch; 14,007km of highways of which 3,777km are paved; 897km of inland waterways on the Senegal (785km) and Saloum (112km) rivers. The country is served by four ports – Dakar, Kaolock, Foundiougue and Zinguinchor. There are nineteen usable airports, ten with permanent surface runways of which one is between 2,440 and 3,659m in length. Telecommunications are reasonable – above average for the region.

Political considerations/assessments

Although 1994 witnessed some violent challenges to the government, Senegal has a generally tolerant reputation and has not experienced any major political upheavals since independence in 1960. Pursuing right-of-centre policies and open to investment, Senegal has achieved a relatively balanced economy and a stable political system and should continue with steady development into the foreseeable future.

SIERRA LEONE

Area. 27,699 sq. miles (71,740 sq. km).
Population. (1995) 4,509,000.
Capital. Freetown (469,776).
Other major cities. Koidu-New Sembehun (80,000), Bo (26,000).
Language(s). English (official), Mende, Temne, Krio.
Religion(s). Sunni Muslim 60 per cent, traditional beliefs 30 per cent, Christian 10 per cent.
Date of independence. April 27 1961 (from Britain).
GNP. (1993) $625,500,000, per capita $140.
Land and climate. A coastal belt of mangrove swamps gives way to wooded hill country and then an upland plateau with mountains in the east. The climate is tropical, hot and humid, with a rainy season from May to December and a dry season from December to April. Deforestation and soil degradation are taking place.

Introduction

A small country on the southern edge of the bulge of West Africa, Sierra Leone has experienced a troubled history since its independence from Britain in 1961, including several coups and military interventions, culminating in a civil war during the 1990s which started as a result of interventions from neighbouring Liberia which was also in the throes of a civil war. By August 1995 the survival of the government and protection from the rebels of the capital, Freetown, was largely dependent upon mercenaries. The country is one of the poorest in Africa and though it has a number of minerals their extraction has brought comparatively little wealth to the people. Most agriculture is of the subsistence variety. Sierra Leone has two neighbours (Guinea and Liberia) with which for a time it attempted to operate an economic union – the Mano River Union, now defunct – and a 402km Atlantic seaboard.

Agriculture

Subsistence agriculture dominates the sector – and the activity of the majority of the population – and in 1994 agriculture contributed 41 per cent to GDP and employed 62 per cent of the workforce. The main agricultural products are rice, cassava, sugarcane, pulses, palm kernels, plantains, millet, sorghum, tomatoes, groundnuts, sweet potatoes and maize. Cocoa and coffee are important export crops (formerly accounting for the greater part of foreign exchange earnings) but in 1993 only accounting for 5 per cent of exports. The national livestock herd includes 362,000 cattle, 302,000 sheep and 168,000 goats. Roundwood production at more than 3,000,000cu m a year is another export earner. The annual fish catch is in the region of 65,000mt. Land use is divided between forested 28.5 per cent, meadows and pastures 30.8 per cent, agricultural land, under permanent cultivation 7.5 per cent, other 33.2 per cent.

Minerals

Mining contributes 7 per cent to GDP and employs just over 8 per cent of the workforce. The three major minerals exported in 1995 were rutile and ilmenite (36.2 per cent), diamonds (26.6 per cent) and bauxite (12.6 per cent) which between them earned the bulk of the country's foreign exchange. Small quantities of gold are also produced. Diamonds are potentially the most valuable mineral but there is a major illicit diamond trafficking business so that probably less than half the value of the diamonds mined accrues to the formal economy. Sierra Leone has large iron ore deposits and these were mined from 1933 into the 1970s when the mines were closed as uneconomic. An effort to resuscitate iron ore mining was attempted in the 1980s but did not succeed. Rutile, essential for paint pigments, became the lead mineral in the 1990s and accounts for over a third of the country's foreign exchange earnings. Large investment in the sector is required to make it more profitable but this is not going to take place until Sierra Leone has ended its civil war and achieved political stability.

Manufactures

Despite a promising start in 1960 under the Development Ordinance to encourage industrial development and the creation of new industries aiming at import substitution or food processing, the sector declined sharply in the 1970s as a result of foreign exchange shortages and infrastructure problems. Most manufacturing is small scale and related to beverages, textiles, cigarettes, footwear and (on a limited scale) refined petroleum products. Manufacturing contributed 11 per cent to GDP in 1994 and employed just over 12 per cent of the workforce.

Infrastructure

There is a single 84km stretch of 1.067m gauge railway (now closed) which was constructed for transport of minerals from Marampa. There are 7,400km of roads of which 1,150km are paved and 800km of inland waterways of which 600km are navigable all year. The country is served by three ports: Freetown, Pepel and Bonthe. Of seven usable airports, four have permanent surface runways of which one is between 2,440 and 3,659m in length. Telecommunications are poor and in part unserviceable as a result of civil disturbances.

Political considerations/assessments

An uneasy tradition of alternate elected governments and military takeovers since independence has combined with a much older tradition of distrust between the coastal Creoles (resettled slaves) and interior ethnic groups to produce developing political instability that finally deteriorated into full-scale and very brutal civil war in the 1990s. Until a permanent resolution of this civil war can be achieved there is no prospect of external investment or further development of what in any case is a very poor economy.

SOMALIA

Area. 246,000 sq. miles (637,000 sq. km).
Population. (1995) 6,734,000.
Capital. Mogadishu (570,000, 1984).
Other major cities. Hargeisa (90,000), Kismayo (86,000), Berbera (83,000) (figures for 1984).
Language(s). Somala (official), Arabic, Italian, English.
Religion(s). Islam (Sunni Muslim) 99.8 per cent, other 0.2 per cent.
Date of independence. July 1 1960 (from Britain – British Somaliland became independent June 26 1960; and Italy – the Italian-administered UN Trusteeship became independent on July 1 1960. The two territories then combined to form the Somali Republic).
GNP. (1990) $946,000,000, per capita $150.
Land and climate. Most of the land consists of flat or undulating plateaux with hills in the north. It has a desert climate affected by the northeast monsoon (December to February) and the southwest (cooler) monsoon (May to October). Rainfall is irregular and there are hot humid periods between the monsoons. The land is subject to droughts and dust storms in the eastern plains during the summer. Over-use of the land is leading to deforestation, soil erosion and desertification.

Introduction

Situated on the Horn of Africa with its long coastline of 3,025km partly facing the Red Sea in the north and partly the Indian Ocean to the east, Somalia has three land neighbours: Djibouti, Ethiopia and Kenya. The majority of the population has always been nomadic and historically they have long moved over an area which includes territory in Somalia's neighbouring states. Since 1960 this has led to a series of confrontations with its neighbours, principally Ethiopia, and to an influx into Somalia of large numbers of refugees from that country.

Civil strife escalated steadily through the 1980s to end in the downfall of President Siyad Barre and his government early in 1991. Since then Somalia has been engulfed in civil war: northern Somalia, the former British territory, has proclaimed itself as independent Somaliland although it has not received any international recognition. A massive US military intervention in 1992 failed to solve anything and in March 1994 the UN military presence in the country was reduced from 29,000 troops to 19,000 when the remaining US and EU forces were withdrawn by their respective governments. A UN presence (UNOSOM) which attempted to maintain the peace and allow the distribution of food was withdrawn in March 1995. Efforts to bring the main warring factions together have continued since that time. Somalia is one of the poorest and least developed countries in the world although the nomadic nature of the people makes assessments of their true wealth very difficult. Livestock are the mainstay of economic activities.

Agriculture

Agriculture accounts for about 65 per cent of GDP and employs over 70 per cent of the labour force. Over half the population consist of nomads and semi-nomads who depend upon livestock for their survival. The national herd consists of 13,000,000 sheep, 12,000,000 goats, 6,000,000 camels and 5,000,000 cattle. Principal exports from livestock consist of live sheep and goats (about 23 per cent of all exports), live camels (7 per cent), live cattle (6.4 per cent). Bananas are also a major export crop accounting for a further 6 per cent of exports while fisheries account for another 10 per cent. The main crops for home consumption are fruits, sugarcane, sorghum, maize, sesame, rice, beans, dates and cotton. Forest products include the traditional ancient exports of frankincense and myrrh and the drug qat which is regarded as an essential part of Somali life. There has been widespread famine and malnutrition as a result of the civil war. Land use is divided between forested 14.4 per cent, meadows and pastures 68.5 per cent, agricultural land, under permanent cultivation 1.7 per cent, other 15.4 per cent.

Mining and manufacturing

Mining contributes a tiny 0.2 per cent to GDP in the form of sepiolite. The possibility of offshore oil has attracted oil companies for years but so far without any important finds. The manufacturing sector, which contributes about 4 per cent to GDP, covers food processing, cigarettes and matches, hides and skins, paper and printing, plastics, chemicals and beverages. Much of this in any case small sector has been devastated by the civil war.

Infrastructure

There are 22,500km of roads of which 2,700km are paved; and a 15km oil pipeline. The country is served by four ports: Mogadishu, Berbera, Kismayo and Benden Cassim. There are 48 usable airports of which eight have permanent surface runways, two of 3,659m and six with runways between 2,440 and 3,659m in length. The civil war destroyed the telecommunications system and both UNOSOM and the various relief agencies rely upon their own systems.

Political considerations/assessments

Until a long-term solution to the ethnic divisions including the attempted breakaway of the northern region, Somaliland, has been achieved there are few prospects of any meaningful development taking place. Meanwhile, the country has a number of 'presences' in the form of various NGOs responsible for famine relief services. International debts (1993) at $1,897,000,000 are double GNP.

SRI LANKA

Area. 25,332 sq. miles (65,610 sq. km).
Population. (1995) 18,090,000 (over 400,000 Tamils have fled the country to escape the civil war and are in refugee camps in southern India or elsewhere).
Capitals. Colombo (administrative) (615,000), Sri Jayewardenepura Kotte (legislative) (109,000).
Other major cities. Dehiwala-Mount Lavinia (196,000), Moratuwa (170,000), Jaffna (129,000).
Language(s). Sinhala and Tamil (official), English.
Religion(s). Buddhist 69.3 per cent, Hindu 15.5 per cent, Muslim 7.6 per cent, Christian 7.5 per cent, other 0.1 per cent.
Date of independence. February 4 1948 (from Britain).
GNP. (1993) $10,573,000,000, per capita $600.
Land and climate. Most of Sri Lanka consists of low, flat or rolling plains; there are mountains in the south-central interior. The climate is tropical monsoon. There are occasional cyclones and tornadoes and the land is subject to deforestation and soil erosion.

Introduction

The island of Sri Lanka, formerly Ceylon, lies 29km southeast of the Indian subcontinent across the Palk Strait. Part of the British Asian Empire for a century and a half, Ceylon became independent in 1948 to pursue a non-aligned, left-of-centre development course until, in the mid-1980s, the demands of the Tamils for a separate Tamil state in the Northern and Eastern provinces led the country into a brutal civil war. India attempted mediation in the late 1980s but without success although it deployed substantial numbers of troops in Sri Lanka for several years. By 1994,

281

34,000 people had been killed in the fighting and although a change of government raised hopes that a new political approach would bring the civil war to an end the fighting continued through 1995 into 1996.

The economy is mainly based upon agriculture although tourism is important (it has been adversely affected by the civil violence) and there is a developing diamond cutting and jewellery manufacturing industry. Sri Lanka occupies a strategic location close to major Indian Ocean sea lanes.

Agriculture

Agriculture contributes about 21 per cent to GDP and employs 40 per cent of the labour force. The most important staple crop is rice and Sri Lanka is no longer self-sufficient in its production. Other staples are sugarcane, cassava and sweet potatoes. Livestock includes 1,600,000 cattle, 870,000 buffalo, 500,000 goats. Roundwood production is above 9,000,000cu m a year and the fish catch is close to 200,000mt. The main exports are tea (for which Sri Lanka has long been famous) contributing about 16 per cent to exports, rubber and coconut oil and desiccated coconut. Other minor export crops are cocoa, pepper, cloves, nutmegs, cardamom, cinnamon and citronella. Land use is divided between forested 32.5 per cent, meadows and pastures 6.8 per cent, agricultural land, under permanent cultivation 29.5 per cent, other 31.2 per cent.

Minerals

Mining contributes just over 1 per cent to GDP and employs just under 1 per cent of the labour force. Principal minerals extracted are quartz stone, limestone, titanium, graphite and gemstones. There are also phosphate deposits. The gemstone industry is of growing importance.

Manufactures

Manufacturing accounts for 17 per cent of GDP and employs just under 11 per cent of the workforce. The principal manufactures are textiles which account for nearly 50 per cent of exports, food and tobacco processing, petrochemical products (Sri Lanka imports crude oil for refining and re-export). The export of gems is controlled by a state corporation and the diamond (and other precious stone) cutting industry and related manufacture of jewellery is making a growing contribution to the export trade. Industrial production in the 1990s has been increasing at the rate of 7 per cent a year.

Infrastructure

There are 1,948km of 1.868m broad gauge railway; 75,749km of roads of which 27,637km are paved; 430km of inland waterways suitable for shallow draft craft; and

62km of pipelines for crude oil and petroleum products. Colombo and Trincomalee are the ports. There are thirteen usable airports, twelve with permanent surface runways and one with a runway between 2,440 and 3,659m in length. Domestic telecommunications are inadequate, international telecommunications are of good standard.

Political considerations

The civil war is about Sinhalese dominance (they represent 74 per cent of the population while the Tamils only account for 18 per cent) and Tamil resistance to a majority that has tended to treat their group as second-class citizens; until this conflict has been resolved economic development will be disrupted or held back. Otherwise, Sri Lanka has no international disputes.

Assessments

With a sound agricultural base although it is not self-sufficient in its staple food, rice, and a growing industrial sector Sri Lanka ought to be able to provide a slowly improving standard of living for its people although gains will have to be offset against a relatively high rate of population increase. International debts at $5,936,000,000 (1993) are equivalent to 60 per cent GNP.

SUDAN

Area. 966,757 sq. miles (2,503,890 sq. km).
Population. (1995) 28,098,000.
Capitals. Khartoum (executive) (476,218), Omdurman (legislative) (526,287).
Other major cities. Khartoum North (341,146), Port Sudan (215,000), Wad Madani (145,000).
Language(s). Arabic (official), Nubian, Ta Bedawie, Nilotic (various dialects), Nilo-Hamitic, Sudanic, English.
Religion(s). Sunni Muslim 74.7 per cent, traditional beliefs 17.1 per cent, Christian 8.2 per cent.
Date of independence. January 1 1956 (from Britain and Egypt).
GNP. (1992) $8,176,000,000, per capita $300.
Land and climate. The land consists mainly of a flat plain with mountains in the east and west. The climate varies between tropical in the south to desert in the north with a rainy season from April to October. The country is subject to a high rate of desertification.

Introduction

This huge country of just under 1 million sq. miles is the largest in Africa and the tenth largest in the world but its great potential has been repeatedly held back by political divisions and civil war. The country is bisected from south to north by the Nile, Africa's longest river, and divided between the Muslim, Arabicized northern two-thirds of the population who dominate the political agenda and the black Christian or animist people of the south who have been waging a civil war against the north, especially because of their refusal to accept the imposition of Muslim Sharia law.

Agriculture is the basis of the economy and during the 1970s the hope was expressed that Sudan could become the 'breadbasket' of the Middle East, a possibility arising from its extensive rich soils. There is some oil though its proposed exploitation in the 1980s was curtailed by the escalation of the civil war. Since the military coup of 1989 Sudan has followed a militant, fundamentalist Islamic path. The country has eight neighbours – the Central African Republic, Chad, Egypt, Eritrea, Ethiopia, Kenya, Uganda and Zaire – and an 853km coastline on the Red Sea.

Agriculture

Agriculture accounts for about 36 per cent of GDP and employs 63.5 per cent of the workforce while agricultural products make up more than two-thirds of exports. Cotton is the lead crop and export and Sudan has long been renowned for the quality of its cotton (the Gezira cotton scheme created under the British administration was, for a time, a model of its kind). Cotton (1994) accounted for 19 per cent of exports. Other export crops are sesame seeds, gum arabic and roselle. The livestock herd includes 22,870,000 sheep, 21,751,000 cattle, 16,449,000 goats and 2,856,000 camels. Sheep and lambs are a major export as are hides and skins. Staple crops include sugarcane, sorghum, wheat, groundnuts, millet, yams. There is an annual round-wood production of about 24,000,000cu m. The fish catch is only 33,000mt year.

Two-thirds of the land is suitable for raising crops or livestock and the triangle of land contained between the Blue and White Niles to the south of Khartoum is judged to contain some of the richest soils in the world; it was this large region that led optimists to advance the idea that Sudan could become the 'breadbasket' of the Middle East. Sudan is self-sufficient in foods. Land use is divided between forested 18.8 per cent, meadows and pastures 46.3 per cent, agricultural land, under permanent cultivation 5.4 per cent, other (mainly desert) 29.5 per cent.

Minerals and mining

Mining only contributes 0.2 per cent to GDP and employs 1 per cent of the workforce. Sudan has moderate oil resources and quite substantial resources of iron ore, copper, chromium ore, zinc, tungsten, mica, silver, salt and gold which is being mined in the Red Sea Hills. Exploring in southwestern Sudan, Chevron found oil deposits with a yield potential of 190,000b/d but after a deal had been struck with Royal Dutch Shell early in 1984 (under which the latter purchased a 25 per cent interest in the find) operations had to be suspended due to the escalating civil war and in 1996 they had not been resumed. In 1987 confirmed oil resources came to 2,000m barrels of which 500m were then estimated to be recoverable. There is a medium-size natural gas field in the Red Sea off Suakin.

Sudan's gold in the Red Sea Hills has been known since ancient times. There are an estimated 500m tons of iron ore. The seabed of the Red Sea is rich in minerals but these like most of the others onshore await exploitation. Although Sudan is not a major mineral resource country it does possess a considerable variety of minerals which, fully exploited, would add substantially to the national wealth.

Manufacturing

The manufacturing sector contributed 10.5 per cent to GDP in 1993 and employed 4.2 per cent of the workforce. Principal manufactures are cotton ginning and the processing of other agricultural products: wheat flour, refined sugar, cattle and horse hides, calfskins, goatskins, sheepskins, cigarettes, cement, shoes, soap, petroleum refining and textiles. Most industries are small scale, geared to import substitution.

Infrastructure

There are 4,800km of 1.067m gauge railway and a further 716km of 1.609m broad gauge railways serving plantations; 20,703km of roads of which 2,000km are paved; 5,310km of inland waterways; and 815km of pipeline for refined products. The country is served by two ports on the Red Sea: Port Sudan and Suakin. There are 56 usable airports, ten with permanent surface runways of which six have runways between 2,440 and 3,659m in length. There is a substantial but poorly maintained telecommunications system.

Political considerations

The move to adopt Islamic fundamentalism which followed the 1989 coup has placed Sudan among a minority of Arab–Islamic countries whose policies are feared by their neighbours. The longstanding civil war between north and south which is both racial and religious in its motivations has brought most development to a standstill. Even apart from these two considerations, Sudan has a history of political instability. The economy is dominated by parastatals that absorb 70 per cent of investment. In 1990 the IMF declared Sudan to be non-co-operative because of its non-payment of arrears.

Assessments

The economic potential of the country is substantial; political considerations and civil violence are holding back development. Sudan could become a substantial food exporter and, in addition, has modest yet important mineral deposits. But real development, as well as the ability to attract external capital on the scale required, is unlikely to occur until the civil war which has divided Sudan since independence in 1956 (though with a ten-year break under Nimeiri from 1973 to 1983) has been resolved and the political climate becomes more stable. International debts in 1993 at $8,994,000,000 were $800,000,000 in excess of GNP at $8,176,000,000.

SYRIA

Area. 71,498 sq. miles (185,180 sq. km).
Population. (1995) 14,313,000.
Capital. Damascus (1,549,932).
Other major cities. Aleppo (1,591,400), Homs (644,204), Latakia (306,535), Hamah (229,000).
Language(s). Arabic (official), Kurdish, Armenian, Aramaic, Circassian, French.
Religion(s). Muslim (mainly Sunni) 89.6 per cent, Christian 8.9 per cent, other 1.5 per cent.
Date of independence. April 17 1946 (from the French administered Mandate of the League of Nations).
GNP. (1991) $16,204,000,000, per capita $1,170.
Land and climate. The land consists mainly of a desert plateau with a narrow coastal plain and mountains in the west. The climate is desert, with sunny summers and mild rainy winters on the coast.

Introduction

Politically one of the most important countries in the Middle East, Syria for many years has been the principal opponent and brake upon Israel, constantly confronting that state in Lebanon. No peace agreement in the Middle East will stand up unless Syria is a full party to it. The country has been ruled by President Hafiz Al Assad and the moderate wing of the Ba'ath Party since 1970 when he came to power as the result of a coup. Assad has usually followed an independent line including close economic ties with the Soviet bloc during the 1970s and most of the 1980s. Syria has maintained troops in the north of Lebanon since 1976 and has disputes with Israel (which still occupies the Golan Heights), Turkey over the Hatay border region, and both Turkey and Iraq over the Tigris–Euphrates water rights. It appeared through 1994 and into 1995 that Syria and Israel (equally reluctantly) were nonetheless coming together to work out a general peace for the region. Syria has five neighbours – Iraq, Israel, Jordan, Lebanon and Turkey – and a Mediterranean coastline of 193km. The country is moderately well endowed with minerals (including oil) and has a reasonable agricultural base and a growing industrial sector.

Agriculture

Agriculture accounts for 18 per cent of GDP and employs 26 per cent of the workforce. Fresh vegetables and fruits, raw cotton, live animals and meats between them account for about 18 per cent of exports. Wheat, barley, seed cotton, tomatoes, grapes, apples, eggplants, lentils and chick peas are the main crops and they are grown on rain-watered land so that there are wide annual variations in harvests. The livestock herd includes 12,000,000 sheep, 1,200,000 goats and 770,000 cattle. Neither roundwood nor fish production is important. Syria is not self-sufficient in grains. Land use is divided between forested 3.6 per cent, meadows (steppe) and pastures 43.8 per cent, cultivable land 32.1 per cent, other 20.5 per cent.

Mining

Mining contributes 33 per cent to GDP but only employs 0.2 per cent of the workforce. Although not a traditional oil-producing country, discoveries of oil in the 1970s and 1980s gave a major boost to the Syrian economy and in 1993 oil output stood at 222,997,000 barrels of which more than half went for export; crude oil and refined products together account for about 67 per cent of exports by value. At the end of 1992 Syria had an estimated 1,700,000,000 barrels of oil reserves, equivalent to 0.2 per cent of world oil resources. Phosphates was a major export before the discovery of oil and remains the most important mineral apart from it with a 1992 output of 930,000mt. Apart from oil and phosphates, Syria possesses chrome, manganese, asphalt, iron ore, rock salt, marble and gypsum.

Manufacturing

Manufactures (there has been a decline in this sector) only account for 6 per cent of GDP while employing 13 per cent of the workforce. During the 1990s the government has taken some deregulation measures and in 1992 gave economic development a boost by loosening controls on domestic and foreign investment. Syria received $5bn in aid from Arab, European and Japanese donors at the time of the 1991 Gulf War and this provided a further boost to the economy together with increased oil prices. Even so, the industrial sector remains top heavy with parastatals whose performance is usually poor. Principal manufactures are cement, flour, refined sugar, nitrogenous fertilizers, olive oil, silk and other textiles, rugs, soap. Tourism earns $700,000,000 a year.

Infrastructure

There are 1,998km of railways of which 1,766km are standard gauge and 232km narrow 1.050m gauge; 29,000km of roads of which 22,680km are paved; 870km of inland waterways (not much used); and 1,304km of pipelines for crude oil and 515km for petroleum products. The country is served by four ports: Tartus, Latakia, Baniyas and Jablah. There are 100 usable airports, 24 with permanent surface runways of which 21 are between 2,440 and 3,659m in length. The telecommunications system is reasonable and is undergoing general upgrading.

Political considerations

The future stability of Syria and the region depend upon the achievement of a permanent peace being established between Israel and her neighbours; this must include the return of the Golan Heights to Syria. Only then would Syria be able to withdraw from northern Lebanon. Syria's strategic position, substantial population, powerful military forces and reasonably developed economy, as well as its flexible approach to Middle East politics, make it one of the most important countries in the region. Syria holds the key to finding a lasting peace with Israel. Internally the Ba'ath regime under Assad has stood up remarkably well to a quarter of a century's rule.

Assessments

In the long term Syria needs either to privatize or drastically reorganize its poorly performing parastatals if it is to maximize its economic potential. Exports of certain crops and crude petroleum are government monopolies and trade generally (imports and exports) is subject to extensive government intervention even though a number of incentives are on offer to attract foreign investment, especially into agro-industries and tourism. These include tax exemptions over the initial period of investment. Syria has entered into a number of investment agreements with countries such as Germany and the USA. The country is ranked in the lower-middle-income group of nations. International debts (1993) at $16,234,000,000 were equivalent to GNP.

TAJIKISTAN

Area. 55,300 sq. miles (143,000 sq. km).
Population. (1995) 5,832,000.
Capital. Dushanbe (582,400).
Other major cities. Khudzhand (164,500), Kulyab (79,300), Kurgan-Tyube (58,400).
Language(s). Tajik (official), Russian.
Religion(s). Sunni Muslim 80 per cent, other 20 per cent.
Date of independence. September 9 1991 (from Soviet Union).
GNP. (1993) $2,671,500,000, per capita $470.
Land and climate. The land is dominated by the Pamir and Altay mountains while great valleys – the Fergana Valley in the north and the Kafirnigan and Uaksh valleys in the south – are important geographic features. The climate is continental, affected by altitude, and ranges from semi-arid to polar in the high Pamirs.

Introduction

A republic of the USSR until its break-up in 1991, Tajikistan emerged as an independent state in September of that year to be plunged at once into civil strife between its pro-Russian old guard who clung to communist ways and the Islamic opposition who obtained support from Afghanistan. Civil war at various levels of intensity continued through 1995 with Russia supplying the government with troops to police the border with Afghanistan which Moscow regards as its frontline against militant Islam. Russia, however, refused to become involved in the civil conflict although it has made repeated efforts to persuade the two sides in the civil war to make peace. Presidential elections held in November 1994 under a newly approved constitution saw Imomali Rakhmonov declared victor despite charges of fraud and intimidation; the Islamic opposition did not recognize his legitimacy. Tajikistan, the poorest of the successor states to the USSR, depends upon Russia for economic support as well as for its troops to protect the border against Afghan incursions. The country is landlocked in the centre of the Asian landmass and has four neighbours: Afghanistan, China, Kyrgyzstan and Uzbekistan.

Agriculture

Agriculture contributes 5.2 per cent to GDP and employs 46.7 per cent of the workforce. The main crops are cotton (important as an export), vegetables, potatoes, fruits, wheat, grapes, barley, maize and rice. Livestock includes 2,845,000 sheep and goats and 1,250,000 cattle. Land use is divided between forested 2.9 per cent, pastures 24.7 per cent, agricultural land, under permanent cultivation 7 per cent, other 65.4 per cent.

Minerals

Statistical information is unreliable. Tajikistan has limited resources of both oil and gas and produced 733,000 barrels of oil and 99,900,000cu m of natural gas in 1992. Other minerals which are mined include antimony, mercury and molybdenum. There are also resources of uranium, coal, lead, zinc and tungsten.

Manufacturing

The manufacturing sector was developed so that Tajikistan could supply other parts of the former USSR and the future of its industries must largely depend upon keeping those markets. The sector has been badly disrupted by the civil war. The main activities are hydro-power production, processing alumina, machine tools, refrigerators and freezers, cement, mineral fertilizers, vegetable oil and leather footwear. The principal exports, which go to Russia, Kazakstan, Ukraine and Uzbekistan, are alumina, cotton, fruit and vegetables and textiles.

Infrastructure

There are 480km of railtrack apart from industrial lines; 29,900km of roads of which 21,400km are paved; 400km of pipelines for natural gas. There are 30 usable airports of which twelve have permanent surface runways and four have runways between 2,440 and 3,659m in length. Telecommunications are poorly developed and there are approximately 100 telephones to every 1,000 people; Tajikistan is linked to the other CIS republics.

Political considerations

The immediate descent into civil war after independence highlighted the country's main problem: how to reconcile the Islamic hardliners, who are supported by Afghanistan, with the rest of the population and government. Although attempts to bring about a lasting peace were made through 1994 and 1995, as yet no permanent settlement appears to be in sight. The second problem concerns Tajikistan's relationship with Russia. In 1994 Tajikistan adopted the Russian rouble and hopes for complete economic integration with Russia (a monetary union) but Russia is less keen on such a link and sees Tajikistan as a potential burden rather than economic asset. In any case Tajikistan is separated from Russia by the neighbouring territories of Kyrgyzstan and Uzbekistan.

Assessments

The poorest of the successor states to the USSR, Tajikistan faces a bleak economic future with limited mineral resources and an economy geared to supplying its neighbours which may now suffer should they change their economic policies.

TANZANIA

Area. 364,017 sq. miles (942,799 sq. km).
Population. (1995) 28,072,000.
Capital. Dar es Salaam (1,360,850), Dodoma (203,833) (the capital designate).
Other major cities. Mwanza (223,013), Tanga (187,634), Zanzibar (157,634).
Language(s). Swahili and English (official), a range of local languages.
Religion(s). Muslim 35 per cent, animist 35 per cent, Christian 30 per cent.
Date of independence. Tanganyika, December 9 1961 (from Britain), Zanzibar, December 19 1963 (from Britain); April 26 1964 Tanganyika and Zanzibar united to form the United Republic of Tanzania.
GNP. (1995) $2,521,000,000, per capita $100.
Land and climate. The land divides between coastal plains, central plateaux and highlands in the north and south. The Great Rift Valley runs north–south down the western border and includes Lake Tanganyika. Mount Kilimanjaro in the north is the highest mountain in Africa. The climate is tropical along the coast but temperate in the highlands. Agriculture is limited by lack of water and the tsetse fly.

Introduction

Formerly German East Africa and then a British League of Nations Mandate, Tanganyika became independent in 1961 and changed its name to the United Republic of Tanzania in 1964 following its union with the offshore island of Zanzibar. From independence to 1985 when he resigned as President, the politics of Tanzania were dominated by Julius Nyerere whose socialist ideas had influence far beyond his own country. Experiments in socialism and most notably *ujamaa*, or self-help collective villages, were not popular and from 1985, under Nyerere's successor President Hassan Mwinyi, the country reverted to more orthodox economic policies, so much so as to earn the praise of the World Bank in 1994 as being second only to Ghana in carrying out its economic reform programme. The economy, over-whelmingly, is based upon agriculture. Tanzania is located in eastern Africa with a 1,424km coastline on the Indian Ocean. Its land neighbours are Burundi, Kenya, Malawi, Mozambique, Rwanda, Uganda and Zambia while Lake Tanganyika acts as the border with Zaire.

Agriculture

Agriculture contributes 58 per cent to GDP, employs 80 per cent of the workforce and accounts for the greater part of all exports. Even so, most agriculture is subsistence and less than 5 per cent of the land is suitable for cultivation. The two main export crops are coffee and cotton and in 1993 they accounted for 25.9 per cent and 23.6 per cent of exports respectively. Sisal, which used to be the major export crop, has suffered from diminishing world demand and now only accounts for about 1.4 per cent of exports. Other export crops include tea, pyrethrum, cashews, tobacco and cloves (from Zanzibar). The main food crops are cassava, maize, sugarcane, bananas, plantains, sorghum, rice, coconuts, sweet potatoes, millet and potatoes. Livestock includes 13,376,000 cattle, 9,682,000 goats and 3,955,000 sheep. Large areas of Tanzania are unsuitable for cattle because of the tsetse fly. Roundwood production runs at approximately 36,000,000cu m a year while the fish catch at 345,000mt (1993) makes a major contribution to the economy. Tanzania is not self-sufficient in grains. Land use is divided between forested 46.1 per cent, meadows and pastures 40.7 per cent, agricultural land, under permanent cultivation 3.9 per cent, other 9.3 per cent.

Minerals

Mining contributes 1.1 per cent to GDP. Salt, gold and diamonds are mined in limited quantities. Other minerals include tin, phosphates, iron ore, coal, gemstones (including the largest ruby mine in the world), natural gas and nickel. At present the sector is small scale when related to the spread of resources though none of these is to be found in major quantities. The most valuable mineral is diamonds with an output of 40,847 carats in 1993 although this production is very small compared with an output of nearly 1 million carats in the 1960s.

Manufacturing

Manufacturing only contributes 5 per cent to GDP and consists mainly of cement production, food processing, textiles and small import substitution activities. Tanzania possesses some of the finest tourist attractions in Africa but the sector has been given low development priority and receipts from visitors in 1993 only came to $147,000,000. Large capital injections into tourist infrastructure will be needed before the sector can achieve its potential.

Infrastructure

There are 3,555km of railroads of which 960km are 1.067m gauge and 2,595km 1.000m gauge. The Tanzam Railway, which links Dar es Salaam to Kapiri Mposhi in Zambia, was built by the Chinese in the 1970s and opened in 1976; it raised great expectations that trade which traditionally went southwards could be diverted to the north but the railway never lived up to expectations and has suffered from breakdowns and maintenance problems. There are 81,900km of roads of which 3,600km are paved; 982km of pipeline for crude oil (through to Zambia). The main ports are Dar es Salaam, Mtwara, Tanga and Zanzibar on the Indian Ocean, Mwanza on Lake Victoria and Kigoma on Lake Tanganyika. There are 92 usable airports, of which twelve have permanent surface runways, four with runways between 2,440 and 3,549m in length. The telecommunications system is reasonable.

Political considerations

Tanzania has avoided some of the harsher politics which have affected much of Africa in the post-independence era. Its greatest problem is poverty and how to deal with it. In addition, the relationship of mainland Tanganyika with the island of Zanzibar whose population is overwhelmingly Muslim has always been delicate and has sometimes come close to disintegration although it still holds. When 250,000 refugees fled into Tanzania from the massacres in Rwanda during 1994 the country did not have the resources to cope with them without immediate international assistance.

Assessments

With a per capita income of only $100 Tanzania is one of the poorest countries in the world. Dependent almost entirely upon its agricultural base, its long-term prospects, at best, offer only a slow increase in living standards.

TOGO

Area. 21,925 sq. miles (56,785 sq. km).
Population. (1995) 4,138,000.
Capital. Lomé (366,476).
Other major cities. Sokodé (48,098), Kpalimé (27,669).
Language(s). French (official), Ewe, Mina, Dagomba, Kabye.
Religion(s). Traditional beliefs 58.9 per cent, Roman Catholic 21.5 per cent, Muslim 12.1 per cent, Protestant 6.8 per cent, other 0.7 per cent.
Date of independence. April 27 1960 (from France which exercised the UN Trusteeship).
GNP. (1993) $1,329,000,000, per capita $330 .
Land and climate. There is rolling savanna in the north, hills in the centre, a southern plateau and a low coastal plain with lagoons and marshes. The climate is tropical – hot and humid in the south and semi-arid in the north which is affected by the dry harmattan wind.

Introduction

This small West African country was formerly German Togoland and then a French Mandate under the League of Nations. It became independent in 1960 with a reasonably prosperous little economy. This, however, had declined substantially by the 1990s which the country entered with heavy debts. It is now listed among the world's least developed nations. In 1990 a period of political unrest followed demonstrations in October of that year demanding an end to one-party rule under President Gnassingbé Eyadéma. Multiparty politics were introduced in 1991 but 1994 witnessed constant challenges to the government which President Eyadéma still hoped to control. The economy is mainly agricultural although Togo possesses the richest phosphates deposits in the world. Togo is wedged between Ghana and Benin and has a border with Burkina Faso to the north and a tiny 56km coastline on the Bight of Benin in the south.

Agriculture

Agriculture contributes 48.6 per cent to GDP and employs 70 per cent of the workforce. Cotton, coffee and cocoa are the principal cash crops and in 1990 ginned cotton accounted for 19.3 per cent of exports, with coffee and cocoa also important exports. The main staples are yams, cassava, maize, sorghum, millet, pulses, groundnuts, rice, bananas, coconuts, palm oil, oranges, tomatoes, palm kernels. Livestock includes 2,044,000 goats, 1,250,000 sheep and 250,000 cattle. Most agriculture is subsistence. Togo is self-sufficient in foods in a normal (drought free) year. Land use is divided between forested 26.6 per cent, meadows and pastures 32.9 per cent, agricultural land, under permanent cultivation 12.3 per cent, other 28.2 per cent.

Minerals

Mining contributes 3.9 per cent to GDP and, basically, that means phosphate rock. Exports of calcium phosphates in 1994 came to 31.3 per cent of total exports. Togo ranks fifth in world terms as a producer of calcium phosphates. Phosphates were discovered in 1952 and are considered to be the richest in the world with an 81 per cent mineral content. There are 260m tons of first-grade ore reserves and a further 1,000m tons of carbon phosphates. There is also an estimated 200m tons of limestone reserves. Exploration for oil is under way though as yet no commercial reserves have been discovered.

Manufacturing

Manufacturing enterprises are small scale and account for 7 per cent of GDP. Cement, wheat flour, beer, soft drinks, footwear, textiles and handicrafts are the main products and they are all geared to the home market. A number of ambitious projects, including an oil refinery, were launched in the more prosperous 1970s but subsequently had to be closed down.

Infrastructure

Infrastructure, generally, requires upgrading. There are 570km of 1.000m gauge railway; 6,462km of roads of which 1,762km are paved; and 50km of navigable waterway on the Mono river. Lomé is the principal port, Kpalimé the phosphate port. There are nine usable airports, two with permanent surface runways which are also between 2,440 and 3,659m in length. Telecommunications are reasonable.

Political considerations/assessments

The continuing (1995) political unrest over the issue of multiparty politics has an inevitable impact upon development. Lomé gave its name to the conventions which link the EU and the ACP countries and in the 1970s Togo's economic future looked considerably brighter than in 1995 when it has come to be ranked among the least developed nations. With a small population and limited market Togo must look to its agricultural base and phosphates for surplus resources to channel into development and the economy is unlikely to grow very fast.

TRINIDAD AND TOBAGO

Area. 1,980.1 sq. miles (5,128.4 sq. km).
Population. (1995) 1,265,000.
Capital. Port of Spain (50,878).
Other major cities. Chaguanas (56,601), San Fernando (30,092), Arima (29,695), Port Fontin (20,025), Scarborough (Tobago) (3,000).

Language(s). English (official), Hindi, French, Spanish.
Religion(s). Roman Catholic 29.4 per cent, Hindu 23.8 per cent, Anglican 10.9 per cent, Muslim 5.8 per cent, other 30.1 per cent.
Date of independence. August 31 1962 (from Britain).
GNP. (1993) $4,776,000,000, per capita $3,730.
Land and climate. The islands consist mainly of plains though with some hills and mountains; the climate is tropical with a rainy season from June to December.

Introduction

The most prosperous of the larger British Caribbean islands, Trinidad and Tobago became independent in 1962 and has maintained a system of multiparty democracy ever since. In 1990 Black Muslim extremists were responsible for a coup attempt when, for a time, they held the Prime Minister hostage. Although Trinidad has a relatively diversified economy, its base depends upon the production and refining of oil. With a per capita income close to $4,000 Trinidad and Tobago is in the upper-middle-income group of countries.

Agriculture

Agriculture accounts for only 2.4 per cent of GDP and employs just over 10 per cent of the workforce. Food exports are important, however, and are led by sugar, the traditional crop. The 1994 sugarcane crop came to 1,422,000mt and raw sugar accounts for about 2 per cent of exports. Other export crops include cocoa, bananas, coffee and citrus fruits. Some sugarcane acreage is now being turned over to the production of rice, fruit or vegetables. Sugar qualifies for preferential prices under both EU and US quota systems although Trinidad has not always been able to meet its full quotas. Staple crops include small quantities of maize and a moderate 10,000mt a year fish catch while poultry is important as a source of protein. Trinidad imports a large proportion of its food requirements. Land use is divided between forested 42.7 per cent, meadows and pastures 2.1 per cent, agricultural land, under permanent cultivation 23.4 per cent, other 31.8 per cent.

Minerals

Mining contributes 26.6 per cent to GDP and employs 3.7 per cent of the workforce. Trinidad has produced crude oil since the 1930s and constructed two refineries so that it also imports crude oil to refine and re-export. It has substantial reserves of natural gas. In 1993 crude oil production came to 45,203,000 barrels (5,000,000 surplus to consumption needs) while natural gas production came to 7,038,000,000cu m (more than 2bn cu m above requirements). Mineral fuel lubricants account for 64 per cent of exports. Asphalt from the natural pitch lake at La Brea is the other important mineral resource with production running at 16,700mt a year. The oil industry has picked up during the 1990s after the recession of the 1980s.

Manufacturing

Manufacturing accounts for 8.7 per cent of GDP and employs 10 per cent of the workforce. Much of the sector is oil related and principal manufactures are: anhydrous ammonia and urea (nitrogenous fertilizers), cement, methanol, steel billets, steel wire rods, sugar, beer, rum. Chemicals and chemical products contribute 15 per cent to exports. Tourism produced $80,000,000 in 1993. The USA is, by far, Trinidad's largest trading partner for both imports and exports.

Infrastructure

The infrastructure as a whole requires rehabilitation. There is a minor agricultural railway at San Fernando. There are 8,000km of roads of which 4,000km are paved; 1,032km of pipelines for crude oil, 19km for petroleum products and 904km for natural gas. Port of Spain and Pointe-à-Pierre are the ports for Trindad, Scarborough for Tobago. There are five usable airports, two with permanent surface runways between 2,440 and 3,659m in length. Trinidad has a first-class system of international telecommunications and a reasonable domestic system.

Political considerations/assessments

Trinidad has maintained its democratic system since independence without any serious threat although it faces challenges from extremist groups from time to time. The most pressing economic/political problem concerns the high level of unemployment – about 20 per cent of the economically active are unemployed. On the other hand, Trinidad possesses a broader-based economy than most of the Caribbean islands and enjoys one of the region's higher general standards of living.

TUNISIA

Area. 63,378 sq. miles (164,150 sq. km).
Population. (1995) 8,896,000.
Capital. Tunis (674,100).
Other major cities. Safaqis (230,900), Aryanah (152,700), Ettadhama (149,200), Susah (125,000).
Language(s). Arabic (official), French.
Religion(s). Sunni Muslim (official) 99.4 per cent, other 0.6 per cent.
Date of independence. March 20 1956 (from France).
GNP. (1993) $15,332,000,000, per capita $1,780.
Land and climate. The north of the country is mountainous, the centre consists of a dry plain and the south is semi-arid, merging into the Sahara. The climate is

temperate in the north with Mediterranean wet winters and dry summers; the south is desert.

Introduction

A former French protectorate, Tunisia became independent in 1956 and has pursued a moderate policy in the Arab–Islamic world since that time. It is a multiparty democracy though with a strong authoritarian bias and in the elections of 1994 the ruling Constitutional Democratic Party won all but nineteen of the 163 seats for the assembly while the president, Gen. Zine al-Abidine Ba Ali, won the presidential election with 99.9 per cent of votes cast in a 95 per cent turn-out. The Tunisian economy is one of the most sophisticated and developed on the African continent with petroleum, phosphates, textiles, tourism and agricultural products as its main foreign exchange earners. The country is a member of the Maghreb Arab Union with Algeria, Libya and Morocco, while its trade is geared to the European market. Tunisia is located on the North African coast 144km from Italy across the Strait of Sicily and has Algeria and Libya as neighbours and a Mediterranean coastline of 1,148km.

Agriculture

Agriculture contributes 13 per cent to GDP and employs 23 per cent of the workforce. Olives, dates, oranges, almonds and wine are the principal export crops with olive oil accounting for 6.5 per cent of export earnings. Agricultural output is subject to severe weather fluctuations resulting from periodic droughts. The main staples are wheat, barley, tomatoes, watermelons, sugarbeet, potatoes, alfafa. The livestock herd includes 7,100,000 sheep, 1,420,000 goats and 660,000 cattle. The fish catch averages 85,000mt a year. Tunisia is not self-sufficient in food. Land use is divided between forested 4.3 per cent, meadows and pastures 27.9 per cent, agricultural land, under permanent cultivation 31.4 per cent, other 36.4 per cent.

Minerals

Mining contributes 4.4 per cent to GDP. The discovery of oil at El Borma in 1964 transformed the sector and oil became the lead export during the 1970s. Tunisia is only a minor producer but output is well in excess of requirements to provide a surplus for export. Production in 1993 came to 35,754,000 barrels while home consumption was only 12,687,000 barrels. In 1994 petroleum and petroleum products accounted for 9.4 per cent of exports. Known reserves of oil are about 1,300 million barrels. Natural gas reserves are far larger, estimated at 85,000,000,000cu m. Tunisia is the world's fourth largest source of calcium phosphates and phosphates production in 1994 came to 5,564,000mt; exports of phosphates earned 2.8 per cent of foreign exchange with phosphoric acid accounting for an additional 3.2 per cent (1993). Iron ore production, which has declined since the 1970s, came to 235,000mt, zinc 23,400mt. There are lead and salt deposits.

Manufacturing

Manufacturing accounts for 17.7 per cent of GDP and employs 17.9 per cent of the workforce. Apart from mining-related industries and chemicals, the principal manufactures are cement, textiles, flour, crude steel and food processing. In 1994 clothing and accessories accounted for 43.3 per cent of exports. Vehicle assembly is also important. Strong emphasis is placed upon import substitution industries. Tunisia is a leading African tourist destination and receipts from visitors in 1993 came to $1,114,000,000. Like the other Maghreb Arab Union countries, Tunisia gears its trade (about 75 per cent) to the EU and in consequence has to pay careful attention to EU economic policies.

Infrastructure

There are 2,115km of railroad of which 465km are 1.435m standard gauge and 1,650m 1.000m gauge; 17,700km of roads of which 9,100km are paved; 797km of pipeline for crude oil, 86km for petroleum products and 742km for natural gas. Seven ports serve the country: Bizerta, Gabès, Safaqis, Susah, Tunis, La Goulette and Zarzis. There are 26 usable airports, thirteen with permanent surface runways of which seven are between 2,440 and 3,659m in length. The telecommunications system is reasonable and better than the average for the African continent.

Political considerations

Unemployment of more than 13 per cent had adversely affected the popularity of the government, forcing it to slow down its economic reforms. Tunisia, a moderate in Arab–Islamic affairs, is fearful of the growth of Islamic fundamentalism which it sees as a real threat to its stability.

Assessments

A reasonably balanced economy has allowed Tunisia to join the ranks of the lower-middle-income countries and now it has a sufficiently diverse economic base to allow it to make steady advances in the future. Much, however, will depend upon the future cohesion of the Maghreb Arab Union and its relations with the EU. International debts at $7,627,000,000 are just under half GNP.

TURKMENISTAN

Area. 188,500 sq. miles (488,000 sq. km).
Population. (1995) 4,081,000.
Capital. Ashkhabad (416,400).
Other major cities. Chardzhou (166,400), Dashovus (117,000), Mariy (94,900), Nebit-Dag (89,000).

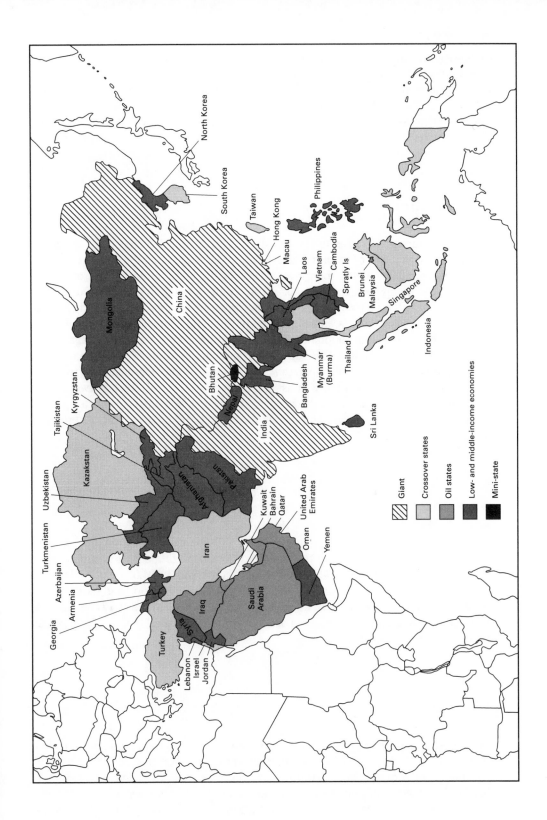

Map 8   Asia

Language(s). Turkmen (official), Russian, Uzbek.
Religion(s). The majority are Sunni Muslims.
Date of independence. October 27 1991 (from the Soviet Union).
GNP. (1993) $4,898,390,000, per capita $1,270.
Land and climate. It is mainly a land of flat to rolling sandy desert broken by dunes. The climate is subtropical desert.

Introduction

One of the successor states to the USSR, Turkmenistan became independent in October 1991; in terms of resources and development it seemed the best equipped of the Islamic republics to stand on its own. Possessing large natural gas reserves and some oil, there was exaggerated talk of the country becoming a new Kuwait but performance in the years since 1991 has not been promising and has included the accumulation of large debts, the rapid growth of corruption and large expenditures upon extravagant white elephants such as a presidential palace or huge hotel complex, the loss of skilled Russian labour and the creation of a personality cult round Presient Saparmurad Niyazovz, the leader of the Democratic (formerly Communist) Party. Turkmenistan is landlocked in Central Asia between four neighbours: Afghanistan, Iran, Kazakstan and Uzbekistan. It also has a 1,768km shoreline on the Caspian Sea and needs to negotiate boundaries with Azerbaijan, Iran and Kazakstan.

Agriculture

Agriculture contributes 11.9 per cent to GDP (1993) and employs 44.2 per cent of the workforce. The principal crops are seed cotton, vegetables, grains, and fruit. Livestock herds include 6,314,000 sheep and goats and 1,104,000 cattle. The fish catch is 37,000mt (1993). Turkmenistan is not self-sufficient in food and food imports are equivalent to 17 per cent of all imports. Land use is divided between forested 35.4 per cent, meadows and pastures 62.3 per cent, agricultural land, under permanent cultivation 2.3 per cent.

Minerals

In 1992 crude petroleum output came to 35,184,000 barrels (less than consumption) but natural gas output at 60,107,000,000cu m was nearly six times local consumption. Turkmenistan has proved natural gas reserves (at the end of 1992) of 2,500,000,000,000cu m representing 1.8 per cent of world reserves. There is more to be exploited. In an agreement with Iran, Turkmenistan is to ship natural gas across Iran to Turkey and Western Europe by pipeline. Other minerals include coal, sulphur and salt.

Manufacturing

The major problem facing the manufacturing sector is to readjust the economy from the role of supplying the Soviet Union 'to order' to a more flexible one of greater choices and outlets. Prior to 1991 Turkmenistan was responsible for 11 per cent of the USSR's gas supplies and 1 per cent of its oil while it was the second producer of cotton in the Union. It is now searching for new markets (as opposed to these rigid if assured ones) and has to decide the degree to which it will switch to a private enterprise system – so far only very limited moves have been made in this direction. The principal manufactures are cement, cotton fibre, mineral fertilizers, centrifugal pumps and rugs. Principal exports are fuels and lubricants, manufactured items and chemicals.

Infrastructure

There are 2,120km of railroads apart from industrial lines; 23,000km of highways of which 18,300km are hard surfaced; 250km of crude oil pipelines and 4,400km of natural gas pipelines. Krasnovodsk is the country's only port on the Caspian Sea. There are seven usable airports, four with permanent surface runways and these are each between 1,220 and 2,439m in length. Telecommunications are poor with only 65 telephones per 1,000 of the population and cable links to other CIS member countries.

Political considerations/assessments

Turkmenistan's major political problem is to determine the kind of state and economy it wishes to become in its post-Soviet independence. Its chief international problem, especially as a landlocked state, is to determine its relations with its neighbouring CIS states and Russia on the one hand, and the Islamic world on the other. Its insistence upon the payment of debts for gas supplies to its former Soviet partners has caused both hardship to them and resentment. There has been a general decline in economic production since 1991. In May 1994 Turkmenistan joined NATO's Partnership for Peace, being the first CIS country to do so.

UGANDA

Area. 93,070 sq. miles (241,040 sq. km).
Population. (1995) 18,659,000.
Capital. Kampala (773,000).
Other major cities. Jinja (61,000), Mbale (54,000).
Language(s). English (official), Swahili, Luganda, Nilotic and Bantu languages.
Religion(s). Roman Catholic 49.6 per cent, Protestant 28.7 per cent, Muslim 6.6 per cent, other 15.1 per cent.
Date of independence. October 9 1962 (from Britain).

GNP. (1993) $3,425,000,000, per capita $190.

Land and climate. The main feature is a central plateau including part of Lake Victoria in the southest surrounded by a rim of mountains. The climate is tropical and wet with dry seasons from December to February and June to August. The north is semi-arid.

Introduction

Once described by Winston Churchill as the pearl of Africa, Uganda passed through such a destructive period of civil war during the 1970s and 1980s that it came close to ruining a sound and balanced economy. The country possesses some of the most productive soil in Africa as well as a range of minerals and ought to have one of the better developed economies on the continent. Only when Yoweri Museveni emerged as President of Uganda in 1986 did the country begin to recover as he restored law and order after more than a decade of chaos which included an estimated 800,000 deaths. By 1994 Museveni's government felt able to hold elections for a single assembly on a non-party basis while the draft constitution proposed the suspension of party politics for five years.

Uganda has rich agricultural possibilities (its coffee is some of the finest in the world) and a range of minerals, as well as magnificent tourist attractions. The standard of living, however, has been so reduced by civil troubles that it is now numbered among the poorest countries in the world with a per capita GNP under $200. Uganda is landlocked in east-central Africa straddling the equator and has five neighbours: Kenya, Rwanda, Sudan, Tanzania and Zaire.

Agriculture

Agriculture contributes 49 per cent to GDP and employs 80 per cent of the workforce. It is mainly subsistence but there is a range of cash crops including coffee, cotton and tea. Coffee is by far the most important cash crop and even during the most troubled times sufficient has been produced to fund government expenditure. In 1994 unroasted coffee accounted for 67.9 per cent of exports and cotton and tea accounted for a further 5 per cent. Principal food crops are bananas and plantains, cassava, sweet potatoes, cane sugar, maize, millet, beans, sorghum and groundnuts. Livestock includes 4,900,000 cattle, 5,400,000 goats and 1,300,000 sheep. Roundwood production stands at 15,000,000cu m a year and the freshwater fish catch is approximately 200,000mt a year. Uganda is self-sufficient in food and with a period of peace should greatly increase the level of her cash crop exports. Land use is divided between forested 27.6 per cent, meadows and pastures 9 per cent, agricultural land, under permanent cultivation 33.9 per cent, other 29.5 per cent.

Minerals

Although Uganda possesses a range of minerals their exploitation virtually collapsed during the years of civil strife. Tungsten, tin and gold are being mined on a small scale. Uganda has substantial copper resources but production ceased in the 1970s and 1980s though both copper and cobalt production is now being rehabilitated. Other minerals include apatite, beryl, columbo-tantalite, bismuth, phosphates, limestone and tin. There are an estimated 220 to 225 million mt of phosphates deposits in the Sakulu hills and there are plans to produce 80,000mt of phosphates a year. Only gold (57,900 troy ounces in 1993) makes a significant contribution to exports at the present time, accounting for just under 5 per cent of the total.

Manufacturing

Manufacturing contributes only 6.8 per cent to GDP and the principal manufactures are soap, sugar, animal feed, cement, metal products, footwear, fabrics, cigarettes and beer. Most industries concentrate upon import substitution products except for food processing for export. The tourist potential of Uganda is substantial – Lake Victoria, the Mountains of the Moon, the Nile and game parks – but civil war as well as the unsettled state of its neighbours have virtually brought the industry to a standstill, at any rate for the time being.

Infrastructure

There are 1,300km of 1.000m gauge railway; 26,200km of roads of which 1,970km are paved. Uganda has major inland waterways on Lakes Victoria, Albert, Kigoga, George and Edward as well as the Victoria and Jinja Niles. Jinja and Port Bell on Lake Victoria are the principal inland water ports. There are 23 usable airports, five with permanent surface runways, one of which is over 3,659m while three are between 2,440 and 3,649m in length. The telecommunications system is reasonable. Uganda's principal trade outlet is through Kenya's port of Mombasa.

Political considerations

Uganda requires a long period of peace to restore confidence so that the economy can revive. A slow return to democracy probably makes more sense than too swift a departure from the authoritarian rule of President Museveni. The younger generation in Uganda has been brought up under conditions of civil war.

Assessments

The country is self-sufficient in food and can produce a range of cash crops for export. It has mineral resources. The greatest immediate areas for growth are in the manufacturing sector and tourism both of which could sustain a level of growth that could alter the present low standard of living. Debts are equivalent to 60 per cent of GNP. Uganda ought to be one of the more balanced economies of Africa.

URUGUAY

Area. 68,037 sq. miles (176,215 sq. km).
Population. (1995) 3,186,000.
Capital. Montevideo (1,311,976).
Other major cities. Salto (80,823), Paysandú (76,191), Las Piedras (58,288), Rivera (57,316).
Language(s). Spanish (official) .
Religion(s). Roman Catholic 66 per cent, Protestant 2 per cent, Jewish 0.8 per cent, non-religious, atheist 31.2 per cent.
Date of independence. August 25 1828 (from Brazil).
GNP. (1993) $12,314,000,000, per capita $3,910.
Land and climate. A country of rolling plains and low hills with fertile coastal lowlands, Uruguay enjoys a temperate warm climate.

Introduction

Sandwiched between Argentina and Brazil, South America's two giants, Uruguay, which by contrast is one of the continent's smallest countries, finds inevitably that it is dominated by its two neighbours and policies must always take this fact into account. Although Uruguay has been a traditional agricultural producer and exporter, since the 1970s it has managed a successful programme of industrialization. More than 40 per cent of imports and exports go to Argentina and Brazil. In 1991 Uruguay joined Argentina, Brazil and Paraguay to form the Southern Cone Common Market (Mercosur) (the Treaty of Asunción, March 26 1991) and though subsequently in 1994 opposition parties and the Chamber of Commerce expressed fears that Mercosur would damage Uruguay's interests and that there should be a five-year pause in implementation, the government resisted these pressures. Possessing a relatively well-balanced economy and normally enjoying a trade surplus, Uruguay is in the upper-middle-income group of countries with a per capita income approaching $4,000. Apart from its borders with Argentina and Brazil it has a 660km coastline on the South Atlantic.

Agriculture

Traditionally an agricultural country whose principal exports were cattle, meat, hides and wool, Uruguay did much to change its economic base (to manufacturing) during the 1970s and 1980s: in the mid-1970s meat and wool exports accounted for 80 per cent of the total; by the late 1980s they had dropped to 35 per cent though they were to increase again at the end of the decade. Agriculture (1994) accounts for 8.3 per cent of GDP and employs 4.5 per cent of the workforce. The principal crops are rice, sugarcane, barley, sugar beets, maize and wheat. But livestock is the key to the sector. The national herd consists of 25,702,000 sheep, 10,093,000 cattle and 477,000 horses. Live animals and live animal products (wool) account for 25.6 per cent of exports, vegetable products for 13 per cent, hides and skins for 11.1 per cent. Large areas of Uruguay are devoted to livestock raising. The annual fish catch comes to about 120,000mt. The country is self-sufficient in food and one of the largest producers of wool in the world. Land use is divided between forested 3.8 per cent, meadows and pastures 77.3 per cent, agricultural land, under permanent cultivation 7.5 per cent, other 11.4 per cent.

Minerals

Uruguay is not well endowed with minerals although it has large hydro-power potential. Apart from hydraulic cement, the principal mineral produced is gypsum (145,000mt in 1994). There is no coal, oil or natural gas.

Manufacturing

Manufacturing contributes 17.5 per cent to GDP and employs 20.7 per cent of the workforce. Principal manufactures include food processing, petroleum products (from imported crude oil), chemicals and chemical products, textiles, beverages, transport equipment, tobacco, leather products, paper and paper products. Textiles account for 20.5 per cent of exports, synthetic plastics, resins, rubber and mineral products for another 3.3 per cent. Tourism yields about $450,000,000 a year in receipts.

Infrastructure

There are 3,000km of railroads of 1.435m standard gauge (government owned); 49,900km of roads of which 6,700km are paved; 1,600km of inland waterways (suitable for coastal and shallow draft craft). Montevideo, Punta del Este and Colonia are the three main ports. There are 81 usable airports of which sixteen have permanent surface runways, two of which are between 2,440 and 3,659m in length. The telecommunications system is reasonable and Montevideo possesses the most modern of its facilities.

Political considerations

The economy is closely linked with those of Argentina and Brazil and, given the disparities in size, Uruguay has always to pay careful attention to the policies of its neighbours. Most tourists come from Argentina and there is a large illegal cross-border trade with that country. A substantial proportion of industry is government controlled and major privatizing legislation of President Lacalle in 1992 was over-turned by a national referendum.

Assessments

Uruguay has achieved a reasonable balance between agriculture and manufacturing and usually has a trade surplus. With its small population and relatively high per capita GNP it should continue to improve the overall living standards of its population. Debts at $4,629,000,000 in 1993 were equivalent to 35 per cent of GNP.

UZBEKISTAN

Area. 172,700 sq. miles (447,400 sq. km).
Population. (1995) 22,886,000.
Capital. Tashkent (2,119,900).
Other major cities. Samarkand (372,000), Namangan (333,000), Andizhan (302,000), Bukhara (235,000).
Language(s). Uzbek (official), Russian, others.
Religion(s). Believers are mainly Sunni Muslims.
Date of independence. August 31 1991 (from Soviet Union).
GNP. (1993) $21,030,000,000, per capita $960.
Land and climate. The land consists mainly of flat to rolling desert with sand dunes; the Fergana Valley in the east is surrounded by the mountains of Tajikistan and Kyrgyzstan. The Aral Sea in the west is drying up. The country has a desert climate with semi-arid grasslands in the east.

Introduction

A former republic of the USSR, Uzbekistan obtained its independence in 1991; the ruling Communist Party continued in control, changing its name to the People's Democratic Party (PDP). It has repressed the opposition and in 1994 arrested a number of opposition leaders and put activists on trial. In the parliamentary elections of December 25 1994 all genuine opposition groups were excluded from voting and the PDP and its allies took 205 of 250 seats. However, in moves designed to attract both Chinese and Japanese trading partners, the government of President Islam Karimov embarked upon a policy of privatization. As with the other former members of the USSR, Uzbekistan is uneasily coming to terms with a new political and economic situation without any longer possessing the guaranteed markets for its prescribed products which it enjoyed when it was a member of the USSR. The country is landlocked in central Asia between five neighbours: Afghanistan, Kazakstan, Kyrgyzstan, Tajikistan and Turkmenistan. It shares the Aral Sea with Kazakstan; the sea is drying up as a result of disastrous (ecological) irrigation policies.

Agriculture

Agriculture contributes 25 per cent to GDP and employs 43 per cent of the workforce. Cotton is the key to these figures and prior to the break-up of the USSR, Uzbekistan produced two-thirds of its total cotton requirements. It remains the fourth largest producer in the world. However, to achieve this position it was obliged to irrigate ever larger tracts of land and it was this irrigation programme which deprived the Aral Sea of its regular sources of water and led to the drying-up process that is now taking place. This was accompanied by the over-use of fertilizers which resulted in widespread pollution and health problems.

Uzbekistan is trying to encourage food production to replace some of the cotton output yet, despite moves by the central Asian countries to reverse the drying up of the Aral Sea, Uzbekistan remains economically too dependent upon cotton exports to cut them back significantly and so resists any major reduction of its irrigation programme. Textiles in 1991 came to 20.6 per cent of all exports. Apart from seed cotton, the main staples are vegetables, fruit, rice, grapes, potatoes, maize, barley, rye. The livestock herd includes 9,400,000 sheep and 5,300,000 cattle. Uzbekistan is broadly self-sufficient in food. Land use is divided between forested 3 per cent, meadows and pastures 51.1 per cent, agricultural land, under permanent cultivation 10.8 per cent, other 35.1 per cent.

Minerals

Uzbekistan has a range of minerals including natural gas, petroleum, coal, gold, uranium, silver, copper, lead, zinc, tungsten, molybdenum. Formerly it supplied 30 per cent of the USSR's gold. Copper and lead were mined in 1992 and gold production at 85,000kg put Uzbekistan in eighth place as a world producer. Coal output is under 4,000,000mt and is consumed locally; similarly, the small oil output is equivalent to only a fifth of local needs; natural gas production is consumed locally.

Manufacturing

Mining, manufacturing and public utilities combined account for 30 per cent of GDP and employ just under 14 per cent of the workforce. The industrial sector concentrates upon agricultural machinery, mineral fertilizers, vegetable oil and bridge cranes. Other manufactures include cement, cotton fibre, rolled metals, plastic synthetic fibre, textiles, refrigerators, compressors, tractors, television receivers, footwear. As with other Soviet republics Uzbekistan was geared to supply the rest of the Union with a quota of heavy manufactured goods.

Infrastructure

There are 3,640km of railroad apart from industrial lines; 78,400km of roads of which 67,000km are hard surfaced; 250km of pipeline for crude oil, 40km for petroleum products and 810km for natural gas. There are 74 usable airports, 30 with permanent surface runways of which two are over 3,659m and twenty between 2,440 and 3,659m in length. Telecommunications are generally poor and sparsely available.

Political considerations

Uzbekistan is still in the immediate post-independence phase and though it did not collapse into civil war as did several of the other former Soviet republics, the ruling People's Democratic Party (formerly Communist) has yet to come to terms with open democracy. Economically Uzbekistan has to reorient its system to a wider import/export pattern than that which existed (almost entirely with the other Soviet republics) at the time of independence.

Assessments

First, Uzbekistan needs to break its dependence upon cotton if it is to avert a total ecological disaster in the Aral Sea. It is able broadly to feed itself and also possesses a reasonable industrial/manufacturing base as well as a range of minerals which should allow it to achieve steady economic growth. So far, in the period since 1991, the government has avoided embarking upon real economic reforms though it has passed some land reforms.

VIETNAM

Area. 127,816 sq. miles (331,041 sq. km).
Population. (1995) 74,545,000.
Capital. Hanoi (2,154,600).
Other major cities. Ho Chi Minh City (4,322,300).
Language(s). Vietnamese (official), French, Chinese, English, Khmer.
Religion(s). Buddhist 67 per cent (e), Roman Catholic 8 per cent (e).
Date of independence. September 2 1945 (from France); the union of North and South Vietnam as the Socialist Republic of Vietnam took place on July 2 1976.
GNP. (1993) $11,997,000,000, per capita $170.
Land and climate. There are low flat deltas in the south and north, central highlands, and hilly mountains in the north and northwest. The climate is tropical; the north is affected by monsoon weather with a rainy season from May to September and a warm dry season from October to May.

Introduction

After years of devastating wars, first the war of nationalist liberation against the French from 1945 to 1954; and then the ideological contest between the communist North and the US-backed South which saw a massive US military involvement, the two Vietnams finally united to become a single country on July 2 1976 as the Socialist Republic of Vietnam. For the next fifteen years, however, apart from its communist links, Vietnam was largely isolated from the West at US insistence.

A land of considerable potential and resources and one of the world's great rice-producing regions, Vietnam has to face vast problems of post-war rehabilitation including a slow regeneration of huge land areas that were defoliated by US chemical warfare. Since 1990 and the collapse of the USSR, Vietnam has made cautious moves away from a centrally planned to a more market-oriented economy. The process accelerated after February 1994 when the USA lifted its trade embargo and increased contacts with the West, including the arrival of US companies and entrepreneurs seeking investment opportunities. The Communist Party of Vietnam approached economic reforms with care but by 1995, when most prices had been fully decontrolled and the currency floated at world market rates, it appeared readier to adopt significant market changes. Vietnam occupies the eastern half of the Indo-China Peninsula and has three neighbours – Cambodia, China and Laos – and a coastline of 3,444km on the South China Sea.

Agriculture

Agriculture accounts for 30 per cent of GDP and employs 73 per cent of the workforce. The main crop is rice (22,500,000mt in 1994) and rice accounts for 12 per cent of exports (Vietnam is the third largest rice exporter in the world). Other main crops are sugarcane, cassava, coconuts and maize; commercial crops include rubber, soybeans, coffee, tea and bananas. Vietnam is a major fishing nation with a fish catch in 1993 of 1,100,000mt. Livestock includes 15,043,000 pigs, 3,438,000 cattle and 3,009,000 buffalo. Roundwood output is significant at 3,000,000cu m a year. Apart from rice, agricultural and forestry products account for 13 per cent of exports (1994) and fish and fish products for another 13 per cent. Land use is divided between forested 29.2 per cent, pastures 1 per cent, agricultural land 20.6 per cent, other 48.8 per cent.

Minerals

Vietnam is moderately endowed with minerals which include phosphates, coal, manganese, bauxite, chromite and offshore oil deposits. Mineral extraction in 1993 included phosphate rock (250,000mt) and gold (10,000 kg). Offshore oil production has provided Vietnam with its largest source of export earnings (24 per cent in 1994). Production is running at 38,880,000 barrels a year of which Vietnam currently uses less than 300,000 barrels. Mining and manufacturing including oil contribute 30 per cent to GDP and employ 10.7 per cent of the workforce.

Manufacturing

The principal manufactures are cement, sugar, steel, fish sauce. Laws have been introduced to give legal recognition to private business but as yet industrial production is stagnant, most of it still controlled by state-owned enterprises. There is a small but growing tourist industry. With the lifting of the US trade embargo in 1994, Vietnam faced a period of rapid change as outside interests began to come in and test both trading and investment opportunities.

Infrastructure

There are 3,059km of railways of which 2,454km are 1.000m gauge; 85,000km of roads of which 9,400km are paved; 17,702km of inland waterways of which 5,149km are navigable year round by vessels with up to 1.8m draft; 150km of pipelines for petroleum products. The principal ports are Da Nang, Haiphong and Ho Chi Minh City. There are 100 usable airports, 50 with permanent surface runways of which ten have runways between 2,440 and 3,659m in length. The telecommunications system is outdated and inadequate with poor internal contacts while its shortcomings restrict Vietnam's newly developing international relations.

Political considerations

The resumption of trade with the USA in 1994 signalled Vietnam's return to open relations with the West as it began also to embrace a market-oriented approach to development. Given the long bitter history of the period between 1945 and 1990 and the fact that it remains a communist state, changes are likely to be both painful and slow.

Assessments

Vietnam possesses the agricultural potential to feed its large population and a highly industrious people. It has limited but important mineral resources including some oil and needs to concentrate upon industrialization to widen its economic base. The population is growing rapidly and will reach an estimated 97 million in 2010 so that the most pressing political–economic problem must be to increase employment opportunities. The tiny GNP in relation to the population places Vietnam near the bottom of the table of least developed countries. International debts at $24,700,000,000 are more than double GNP.

YEMEN

Area. 182,278 sq. miles (472,089 sq. km).
Population. (1995) 13,058,000.
Capital. Sana'a (427,150).
Other major cities. Aden (318,000), Ta'izz (178,043), al-Hudaydah (155,110).
Language(s). Arabic (official).
Religion(s). Islam (official) 99.9 per cent (divided between Sunni 53 per cent and Shi'a 46.9 per cent), other 0.1 per cent.

Date of independence. May 22 1990 (the merger of North and South Yemen).
GNP. (1993) $6,864,000,000, per capita $520.
Land and climate. There are narrow coastal plains behind which rise flat-topped hills and then rugged mountains. The upland desert plains extend into the great desert of the Arabian Peninsula. The climate is mainly desert and in the east this is exceptionally hot, harsh and dry. The west coast, which is affected by the seasonal monsoon, is hot and humid.

Introduction

In 1990 the two Yemens, the Yemen Arab Republic or North Yemen and the People's Democratic Republic of Yemen or South Yemen, merged to form the Republic of Yemen. North Yemen had become independent from the Ottoman Empire in 1914 and until the 1960s had remained one of the least known countries in the world but then, during a long civil war between royalists (traditionalists) and republicans (modernizers), the country gradually came to terms with the modern world. South Yemen or Aden had been a British colony from 1839 to 1967 and achieved independence in the latter year after a particularly bitter war against the British that resulted in the emergence of a radicalized Marxist government in 1967. Relations between the two Yemens were uneasy through the 1970s and 1980s and included a border war or series of wars but finally they agreed to merge as a single state and this was accomplished in 1990. Differences between the two component parts led to a brief civil war in 1994 when secessionists from the south attempted, unsuccessfully, to break up the new state. The preponderance of power and population lay with the north and following the crushing of the revolt in which 5,000 people were killed and the flight of its leaders the government tried to heal the wounds. The state is a multiparty democracy. Yemen occupies the southwest corner of the Arabian Peninsula and has borders with Saudi Arabia and Oman and a coastline of 1,906km facing the Red Sea in the west and the Indian Ocean (Gulf of Aden) to the south.

Agriculture

Agriculture contributes 20 per cent to GDP and employs more than 56 per cent of the workforce. North Yemen was formerly self-sufficient in food but civil war, the exit of large numbers to work in Saudi Arabia or the Gulf and the turnover of land to grow the drug qat in place of foodstuffs mean that Yemen is now a food importer. (South Yemen was not self-sufficient in food.) Food and live animals account for 24 per cent of all imports. The principal crops are sorghum, potatoes, tomatoes, wheat, grapes, watermelons, bananas, onions, millet and papayas. Fish are the most important export (65 per cent in 1991) followed by coffee (6 per cent). Cotton used to be an important export but in recent years production has declined though it could be revitalized. Livestock includes 3,715,000 sheep, 3,232,000 goats, 1,128,000 cattle, 500,000 asses and 173,000 camels. The fish catch averages 85,000mt a year. Land use is divided between forested 3.8 per cent, meadows and pastures 30.4 per cent, agricultural land, under permanent cultivation 2.8 per cent, other 63 per cent.

Minerals

Mining contributes 5.5 per cent to GDP though only employing 0.6 per cent of the workforce. The discovery and exploitation of oil in the 1980s – Yemen became an oil exporter in 1987 – and the subsequent finds of important resources of natural gas have transformed the country's economic prospects. Much of the oil lies along the old border area between the former North and South Yemen. In 1993 oil production came to 87,497,000 barrels and 50 per cent of this was available for export. At the end of 1992 Yemen's oil reserves stood at 4,000,000,000 barrels, equivalent to 0.4 per cent of world reserves with an estimated lifespan of 60 years. The refinery at Aden enables Yemen to produce about 5.5mt of refined products a year, half of which is available for export. Other minerals include rock salt, gypsum, marble, and small deposits of coal, gold, lead, nickel and copper. Salt and gypsum were mined in 1992.

Manufacturing

Manufacturing contributes just under 10 per cent of GDP and employs 4.6 per cent of the workforce. Principal manufactures consist of processed foods, cotton lint, foam rubber, textiles, cigarettes (a substantial export), biscuits, and leather goods (also a major export). There is a small tourist sector though the potential for expansion is considerable. Aden with its port facilities and refinery is the commercial and economic capital of the newly united country.

Infrastructure

There are 15,000km of roads of which 4,000km are paved; 644km of pipelines for crude oil and 32km for petroleum products. The main ports are Aden, Al Hudaydah, Al Khalif, Al Mukalla, Mocha, Nishtun, Ra's Kathib, Salif. There are 39 usable airports, ten with permanent surface runways and eighteen with runways between 2,440 and 3,659m in length. Since the unification of the two Yemens a programme to modernize and unify the telecommunications systems of the two former countries has been started.

Political considerations

The union of the two Yemens in 1990 was a delicate political operation as the brief civil war of 1994 demonstrated. The republican tradition in the North was in any case of recent origin and had been imposed on a royalist–traditionalist society while the South, at least in Aden colony, was extremely radical. The ending of Soviet aid as the USSR broke up helped to persuade the South to join the North. If the two elements that make up the new state of Yemen can overcome these and other differences the country has sufficient economic capacity to improve its living standards quite substantially over the coming decades.

Assessments

Oil, which should last for 60 or more years, will provide the means whereby Yemen can develop and improve the other main sectors of the economy – agriculture and manufacturing. The country could be self-sufficient in food and has the capacity to produce a number of export commodities (Mocka coffee has long been famous). However, diversification is essential and the largest potential for growth lies with an improved manufacturing sector. Debts in 1993 at $8,198,000 were equivalent to 120 per cent of GNP. Yemen is ranked at the upper end of the least developed group of countries. The economy is also heavily dependent upon remittances from Yemenis living and working abroad.

ZAIRE

Area. 905,354 sq. miles (2,344,858 sq. km).
Population. (1995) 43,901,000.
Capital. Kinshasa (4,655,313).
Other major cities. Lubumbashi (851,382), Mbaji-Mayi (806,475), Kisangani (417,517), Kananga (393,030).
Language(s). French (official), Lingala, Swahili, Kingwana, Kikongo, Tshiluba.
Religion(s). Roman Catholic 48.4 per cent, Protestant 29 per cent, indigenous Christian 17.1 per cent, traditional beliefs 3.4 per cent, Muslim 1.4 per cent, other 0.7 per cent.
Date of independence. June 30 1960 (from Belgium).
GNP. (1991) $8,123,000,000, per capita $220.
Land and climate. Most of Zaire consists of a vast low lying central basin or plateau, much of it covered by tropical rainforest; there are mountains in the east. The climate is tropical, hot and humid in the huge Congo (Zaire) river basin; cooler and dryer in the southern highlands, and cooler and wetter in the eastern highlands. Lying across the equator, the wet season varies: north of the equator it runs from April to October and south of the equator from November to March.

Introduction

This huge country in the geographic centre of Africa has had a deeply troubled political history: first as the Congo Free State (the personal colonial 'fief' of Leopold II of the Belgians), then as the Belgian Congo which achieved independence in 1960 only to be plunged immediately into chaos (1960–65) so that the name Congo became synonymous with breakdown of law and order in Africa.

From 1965 onwards the country, which changed its name to Zaire in 1970, came under the rule of the strongman Mobutu Sese Sheko. Against a background of mounting unrest Mobutu announced political reforms in April 1990 which would return the country to a system of multiparty politics, although in reality he then manipulated the system to ensure that ultimate power remained in his hands. During the 1990s, while Mobutu clung on to huge personal power at the expense of almost any kind of national order, the formal economy largely collapsed and hyper-inflation destroyed stable living standards for ordinary people who were forced to survive on subsistence agriculture and bartering. The situation was made worse by the arrival in eastern Zaire during 1994 of 1 million refugees from the genocidal massacres then taking place in Rwanda.

Zaire is Africa's third largest country and has eight neighbours: Angola, Burundi, the Central African Republic, Congo, Rwanda, Sudan, Uganda and Zambia. The Congo (Zaire) River is Africa's second river in length (after the Nile) but the first in volume of its waters. Zaire has a 37km outlet on to the Atlantic where the river reaches the sea. Potentially, Zaire is one of the world's richest countries in terms of its natural resources, both agricultural and mineral.

Agriculture

The agricultural potential of Zaire is very great and the country has the capacity to produce a wide range of cash crops including coffee, palm oil, rubber (natural), quinine and cotton – as well as many staples. These include cassava, plantains, sugarcane, maize, groundnuts, rice, bananas, sweet potatoes, yams, mangoes, papayas, oranges, beans, peas, avocados, tomatoes, onions, cabbages. In 1995, with the virtual breakdown of any meaningful political or economic control, most people survived by returning to some form of subsistence agriculture and bartering. The livestock herds are limited (due to climate). Roundwood production in 1992 came to 44,532,000cu m and the fish catch to 147,250mt. Agriculture is estimated to contribute about 31 per cent to GDP and employs 65 per cent of the workforce. Land use is divided between forested 76.7 per cent, meadows and pastures 6.6 per cent, agricultural land, under permanent cultivation 3.5 per cent, other 13.2 per cent.

Minerals

Mining contributes 24 per cent to GDP. Zaire has a huge range of minerals including cobalt, copper, cadmium, petroleum, industrial and gem diamonds, gold, silver, zinc, manganese, tin, germanium, uranium, radium, bauxite, iron ore, coal. It also possesses an estimated 13 per cent of the world's hydro-power capacity. There is an abundance of most of the above minerals but the most important are copper, cobalt, diamonds and zinc. Although production of copper was at the level of 500,000mt a year in the mid-1980s it had fallen drastically by the 1990s and in 1994 was a mere 37,725mt. Zinc output in 1993 was 2,515mt, cobalt 3,631mt and diamonds 16,252,000 carats. Cassiterite and gold are also mined. In 1990 copper accounted for 47.6 per cent of exports, diamonds for 11.4 per cent and crude petroleum for 10.8 per cent. Zaire has only limited reserves of oil (about 140,000,000 barrels of heavy crude) which covers its own needs and not a great deal more though it has to be exported for refining. The country's known mineral resources are huge and even in a situation approaching political breakdown they remain the principal source of government revenues. Under a stable political regime mineral production could be widely increased to provide the wealth upon which to diversify and build up the rest of the economy.

Manufacturing

The manufacturing sector contributed a tiny 1.4 per cent to GDP in 1991 despite a far greater output capacity. Principal manufactures are cement, sulphuric acid, sugar, soap, animal feeds, explosives, plastics, iron and steel products, paint, medicines, printed fabrics, cigarettes, tyres, bicycles, automobiles, beer, other beverages, leather shoes (statistics are unreliable).

Infrastructure

There are 5,254km of railways of which 3,968km are 1.067m gauge; 146,500km of roads of which only 2,800km are paved; 15,000km of inland waterways (the Congo and its tributaries and various lakes); and 390km of pipelines. The country is served by three ports – Matadi, Boma and Banana. There are 235 usable airports, 25 with permanent surface runways of which one is over 3,659m in length and six are between 2,440 and 3,659m in length. The telecommunications system is inadequate.

Political considerations

By the 1990s the politics of Zaire had resolved themselves into a complicated power struggle between Mobutu and various political and other interest groups; Mobutu, a master at such activities, was succeeding in holding on to supreme power despite promises to return the country to multiparty rule. There would seem to be little prospect of political, economic or social improvement until the present system has been swept away.

Assessments

In terms of its agricultural potential, mineral wealth and hydro-power potential, Zaire ought to be one of the leading economies on the African continent. Development, however, must await political reform. The nominal per capita income (1991) at $220 places Zaire in the ranks of the least developed nations; it ought not to be so low rated more than 35 years after independence. Debts at $8,769,000,000 (1993) were $646,000,000 in excess of GNP.

ZAMBIA

Area. 290,586 sq. miles (752,614 sq. km).
Population. (1995) 9,456,000.
Capital. Lusaka (982,362).
Other major cities. Ndola (376,311), Kitwe (348,571), Mufulira (175,025).
Language(s). English (official), about 70 indigenous languages.
Religion(s). Christian 72 per cent, traditional beliefs 27 per cent, Muslim 0.3 per cent, other 0.7 per cent.
Date of independence. October 24 1964 (from Britain).
GNP. (1993) $3,155,000,000, per capita $370.
Land and climate. The country consists of a high plateau bordered in the south by the Zambezi valley, with some hills and mountains. The climate is tropical modified by altitude with a rainy season from October to April.

Introduction

Formerly the British colony of Northern Rhodesia and then a part of the Central African Federation (1953–63), Zambia became independent in 1964 and for the next ten years, boosted by high world copper prices, the economy did well and Zambia was able to expand the manufacturing sector rapidly, to create a number of new industries. Responding to the Unilateral Declaration of Independence (UDI) in neighbouring Rhodesia (Zimbabwe), in 1965 Zambia applied UN sanctions to its neighbour at great cost to its own economy in the years between 1965 and 1980. In 1973 the price of copper, Zambia's major foreign exchange earner, collapsed and over the succeeding ten years the government borrowed heavily with the result that Zambia entered the 1980s as one of the most indebted countries in the world (on a per capita basis). Subsequently, mismanagement as well as poor economic policies made a bad economic position worse. Zambia had become a one-party state under President Kenneth Kaunda in 1973 but the deep unpopularity of his government by the beginning of the 1990s forced him to adopt political reforms and the country returned to multiparty politics in 1991. Copper, though a declining asset, remains the cornerstone of the economy. Zambia is landlocked in central Africa and has eight neighbours: Angola, Botswana, Malawi, Mozambique, Namibia, Tanzania, Zaire and Zimbabwe.

Agriculture

Agriculture contributes 13 per cent to GDP and employs 69 per cent of the workforce. The main staple is maize and in a good (drought-free) year Zambia is largely self-sufficient in food. Other staples are sugarcane, cassava, fruit and vegetables, wheat, sweet potatoes, groundnuts, millet, sorghum, soybeans, sunflower seeds. Tobacco is the principal export crop. There are a number of large commercial farms (expatriate) and since independence these farmers have been joined by a growing number of indigenous commercial farmers although the bulk of agricultural output still comes from subsistence farmers. Apart from tobacco, cash crops are sugar, fruit, vegetables, cotton, groundnuts, sunflower seeds and coffee. Land use comprises forested 38.6 per cent, meadows and pastures 40.4 per cent, agricultural land, under permanent cultivation 7.1 per cent, other 13.9 per cent.

Minerals

Mining contributes 15.5 per cent to GDP although only employing 2 per cent of the workforce. Mineral resources include copper, cobalt, zinc, lead, coal, emeralds, gold, silver and uranium. Copper, however, has always been the key to the economy, accounting for 85 per cent of exports, up to 50 per cent of government expenditure and, formerly, more than 25 per cent of GDP though that figure has now dropped to about 15 per cent. Copper output, which reached 700,000mt a year in the mid-1970s, declined thereafter. Output in 1994 came to 510,606mt and accounted for 86.4 per cent of exports. Zambia is the world's fourth-ranking copper producer. Other minerals include cobalt, lead, silver and gold. Zambia produces about 12 per cent of the world's cobalt. On current estimates copper reserves will be exhausted early in the twenty-first century when the economy will require radical restructuring. Unfortunately, Zambia has persistently relied too much upon copper to the detriment of other sectors of the economy. There is neither oil nor natural gas; limited reserves of coal were developed and mined in the 1970s but the operation was abandoned in the 1980s as too costly though in 1995 coal was being reappraised for possible new mining operations. The country has extensive hydro-power capacity.

Manufacturing

Manufacturing contributes 28 per cent to GDP although only employing 1.9 per cent of the workforce. During the period of high copper prices after independence (1963–73) Zambia started a number of ambitious new industries although in the depressed conditions of the later 1970s and 1980s some of these ventures had to be curtailed or abandoned. At the beginning of the 1990s industrial production was declining at a rate of 2 per cent a year. Principal manufactures include refined copper, cement, sulphuric acid, sugar, refined zinc, refined lead, processed foods and cigarettes.

Infrastructure

There are 1,266km of 1.067m gauge railway lines; 36,370km of roads of which 6,500km are paved; 2,250km of inland waterways (the Zambezi and Luapula rivers and Lake Tanganyika); and 1,724km of pipelines for crude oil. Mpulunga is a substantial port on Lake Tanganyika. There are 104 usable airports, thirteen with permanent surface runways of which one is over 3,659m and four are between 2,440 and 3,659m in length. Zambia possesses one of the best systems of telecommunications in sub-Saharan Africa. Zambia shares the Tanzam railway with Tanzania in the north.

Political considerations

During the period between 1965 and 1980 Zambia's development was hindered by the confrontation with Rhodesia following that country's UDI in 1965. Subsequently, under Kenneth Kaunda, Zambia played a leading role as a frontline state in the wider confrontation with apartheid South Africa that only came to an end in 1990. Zambia's central, landlocked position made it very difficult for it to avoid this frontline role. Internal developments, unfortunately and in part as a result, were often subordinated to external considerations and economic decline led to persistent and growing demands for reform which forced the government of President Kaunda to return the country to multipartyism at the beginning of the 1990s; in elections of 1992 Kaunda was defeated for the presidency by Frederick Chiluba.

Assessments

The economy declined through the 1980s and into the 1990s, both as a result of depressed world copper prices and of ill-conceived economic policies. Over-reliance upon copper ever since independence has created a lopsided economy. In terms of land resources Zambia ought to be able both to feed itself and produce a surplus of food commodities for export. Its most urgent task is to diversify the economy before the copper reserves are exhausted as they will be early in the twenty-first century.

ZIMBABWE

Area. 150,872 sq. miles (390,757 sq. km).
Population. (1995) 11,261,000.
Capital. Harare (1,184,109).
Other major cities. Bulawayo (620,936), Chitungwiza (274,035), Mutare (131,808), Gweru (124,735).
Language(s). English (official), Shona, Sindebele.
Religion(s). Christian 44.8 per cent, animist 40.4 per cent, other 14.8 per cent.
Date of independence. April 18 1980 (from Britain).
GNP. (1993) $5,756,000,000, per capita $540.
Land and climate. Most of the country consists of a high plateau with an uplifted central plateau and mountains in the east. The climate is tropical moderated by altitude with a rainy season from November to March.

Introduction

When the white minority government of the British colony of Southern Rhodesia made a Unilateral Declaration of Independence (UDI) in 1965 in an attempt to maintain white minority control indefinitely, it sparked off a regional crisis. During fifteen years of UDI (1965–80) when UN sanctions were applied to Rhodesia, the economy though beleaguered was able to survive (with South African help in sanction breaking) while great efforts were made to build up an import substitution manufacturing sector. UDI came to an end after fifteen years of mounting guerrilla warfare when a settlement was implemented following the 1979 Commonwealth Heads of Government meeting held in Lusaka, Zambia. As a result an independent Zimbabwe emerged in 1980 following universal franchise elections. The 1980s then witnessed the 'dissidents' war between the government of the ruling ZANU (PF) party under Robert Mugabe and the opposition ZAPU of Joshua Nkomo. However, 'unity' was achieved in 1987 when Nkomo and other ZAPU leaders joined the government and ZAPU was dissolved. Zimbabwe is a single-chamber multiparty government. The country is richly endowed with both agricultural potential and mineral resources. Zimbabwe has five neighbours: Botswana, Mozambique, Namibia (where four nations meet at the quadripoint of the Caprivi Strip), South Africa and Zambia.

Agriculture

Zimbabwe possesses a strong agricultural economy with an especially important commercial sector much of which remains in the hands of white farmers. The sector accounts for 10 per cent of GDP and employs 26 per cent of the workforce (although a far larger proportion of the population is wholly or partially dependent upon subsistence agriculture). There are about 4,500 large commercial farms (40 per cent of the land) while communal lands account for another 42 per cent. Tobacco is the lead cash crop, accounting for 24.3 per cent of exports in 1993. Zimbabwe is normally an exporter of maize (except in drought years); other export crops are cotton, coffee and sugar. The principal staples (apart from the above) are wheat, vegetables, sorghum, soybeans, groundnuts. Livestock includes 4,500,000 cattle, 2,530,000 goats and 550,000 sheep. Roundwood production and the fresh water fish catch are relatively small scale. The country is self-sufficient in food and a net exporter.

Minerals

Zimbabwe possesses a range of minerals (about 40 are mined) and mining accounts for 6.9 per cent of GDP and employs 4 per cent of the workforce. The most important minerals are gold, asbestos, coal, nickel, copper and chrome. Gold (18,000 kg) accounted for 11.4 per cent of exports in 1992, ferroalloys (chromite 560,000mt) for 7.9 per cent, nickel for 5 per cent, asbestos 3.9 per cent, copper 1.4 per cent. Other minerals produced include iron ore, tin, silver, graphite, lithium and cobalt. Value added to minerals is a significant factor in overall manufacturing output.

Manufacturing

Manufacturing accounts for 41 per cent of GDP and employs just over 15 per cent of the workforce. Zimbabwe has one of the most sophisticated manufacturing sectors in sub-Saharan Africa and its principal manufactures include metals and metal products, foodstuffs, chemicals and petroleum products, textiles, beverages, tobacco, clothing, footwear, paper, printing and publishing, transport equipment, wood and furniture, non-metallic mineral products as well as a range of other manufactures. The base for a good tourist industry exists and this should expand rapidly now that South African visitors are welcome.

Infrastructure

There are 2,745km of 1.067m gauge railways; 85,237km of roads of which 15,800km are paved; 212km of petroleum pipelines. Lake Kariba, which Zimbabwe shares with Zambia, is a potential inland waterway of significance. There are 403 usable airports, 22 with permanent surface runways of which two are over 3,659m and three between 2,440 and 3,659m in length. The telecommunications system, which formerly was very good, has deteriorated as a result of poor maintenance. Generally, however, Zimbabwe offers one of the best overall infrastructures for business in Africa.

Political considerations

The end of apartheid and international rehabilitation of South Africa, ironically, has posed a new threat to Zimbabwe which sees its hard-won position as the most advanced and rounded economy of the SADC countries now threatened by the far greater economy of its southern neighbour. As South Africa feels its economic strength and begins to invest and trade to its north, Zimbabwe may well find itself adopting a defensive role so as to safeguard its trading advantages in the region. It will not be easy. At home the most pressing problem concerns the rapid growth of population (the estimated doubling time is only 23 years) and the consequent need to create new employment. This problem is exacerbated by a growing land hunger among small subsistence farmers.

Assessments

Zimbabwe possesses one of the best developed and most rounded economies in Africa and ought to be able to move from the least developed to the middle-income group of countries in the near future. There are, however, huge disparities in income and standards of living between the small white minority and the majority of the population. Debts at $3,021,000,000 in 1993 were equivalent to slightly over 50 per cent of GDP.

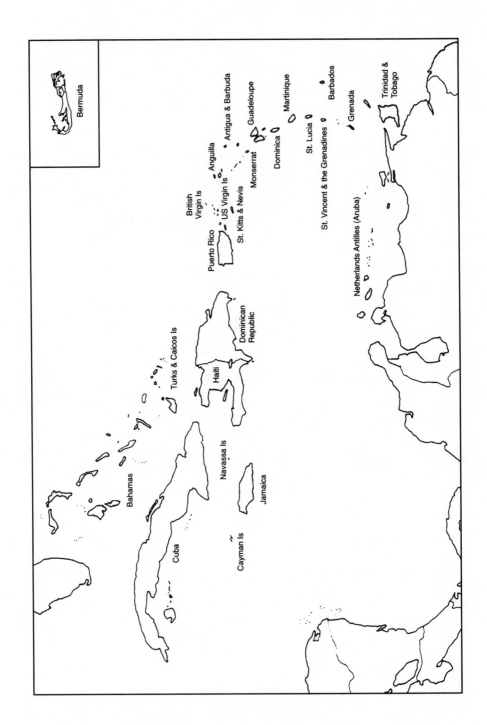

Map 9 The Caribbean

5 THE MINI-STATES

INTRODUCTION

Thirty-five small countries, the great majority of them islands, are included in this section as mini-states. There is considerable range in terms of their economic development and some of them, such as Bahamas or Barbados, have relatively high per capita incomes and enjoy reasonable standards of living which place them at the upper end of the middle-income group of countries. Seychelles is an excellent example of a mini-state that has managed to maximize its limited resources – fisheries, tourist attractions and an oil refinery for re-export – to provide at least a tolerable standard of living for its 75,000 inhabitants. What these states have in common is an absolute limitation of size and resources that makes any major change of economic status in the future, except in one or two possible cases, extremely unlikely. Almost all the states included here have populations of less than 1 million – the cut-off point for a mini-state – although there are one or two borderline cases. Guyana, for example, has a population of 770,000 but a land mass as large as Britain (most of it uninhabited). The mini-state is also characterized by its actual or potential political vulnerability to the pressures of larger neighbours and in a majority of cases is and will remain dependent upon aid into the foreseeable future.

ANTIGUA AND BARBUDA

Area. 170.5 sq. miles (441.6 sq. km).
Population. (1995) 63,900.
Capital. St John's (21,514).
Language(s). English (official), dialects.
Religion(s). Christian (predominantly Anglican).
Date of independence. November 1 1981 (from Britain).
GNP. (1993) $425,000,000, per capita $6,390.
Land and climate. Low-lying with coral islands and some higher volcanic areas. The climate is tropical.

Introduction

These two tiny eastern Caribbean islands are devoid of resources and rely for their livelihood upon tourism, a little light industry and a continuing input of international aid. Antigua and Barbuda is a member of the Commonwealth.

Economy

There are negligible resources although the climate is inducive to tourism. Exports consist mainly of light manufactures; imports are equivalent to ten times exports. Tourism is the principal means of livelihood.

Assessments

This tiny country will continue to be tourist and aid dependent into the foreseeable future.

BAHAMAS

Area. 5,382 sq. miles (13,939 sq. km).
Population. (1995) 279,000.
Capital. Nassau (172,196).
Other major cities. Freeport/Lucaya (26,574).
Language(s). English (official), Creole.
Religion(s). Protestant (non-Anglican) 55.2 per cent, Anglican 20.1 per cent, Roman Catholic 18.8 per cent, other 5.9 per cent.
Date of independence. July 10 1973 (from Britain).
GNP. (1993) $3,059,000,000, per capita $11,500.
Land and climate. A series of islands of which the principal ones are New Providence, Grand Bahama, Andros, Eleuthera and Grand Abaco while another 24 islands are inhabited.

Introduction

A group of islands in the North Atlantic lying southeast of Florida and northwest of Cuba, the Bahamas lack natural resources although climate and scenery make them an ideal centre for tourism which is the principal source of both income and employment. The majority of the people, 85 per cent, are black, the remaining 15 per cent are white. Bahamas is a middle-income developing country.

Economy

The economy of the Bahamas is minuscule by world standards and largely dependent upon tourism, offshore banking and petroleum refining. Agriculture consists of fisheries products such as crayfish, fruit and vegetables and only accounts for 5 per cent of GDP; Bahamas is a large net importer of foodstuffs. There is a tiny mining industry, mainly salt. Tourism, which is preponderantly dependent upon visitors from the USA, is the principal occupation and accounts for 50 per cent or more of GDP and employs about 40 per cent of the workforce. Offshore banking is a second important source of income but this is an activity dependent upon a variety of international political factors over which the country has no control. There are a number of industries dependent upon imports in the first place of which petroleum refining involving the import and export of petroleum products is by far the most important.

Assessments

Bahamas is a relatively well-off, stable society whose long-term prosperity, however, depends upon being seen as a haven for holidaymakers, offshore bankers and one or two other industries whose inputs all come from outside the islands.

BARBADOS

Area. 186 sq. miles (430 sq. km).
Population. (1995) 265,000.
Capital. Bridgetown (6,070 – urban area 85,000).
Language(s). English.
Religion(s). Anglican 39.7 per cent, other Protestant 26.6 per cent, Roman Catholic 4.4 per cent, other 12.8 per cent.
Date of independence. November 30 1966 (from Britain).
GNP. (1993) $1,620,000,000, per capita $6,240.
Land and climate. The climate is tropical with a single rainy season (June to October). The land is generally flat with a moderate central highland region.

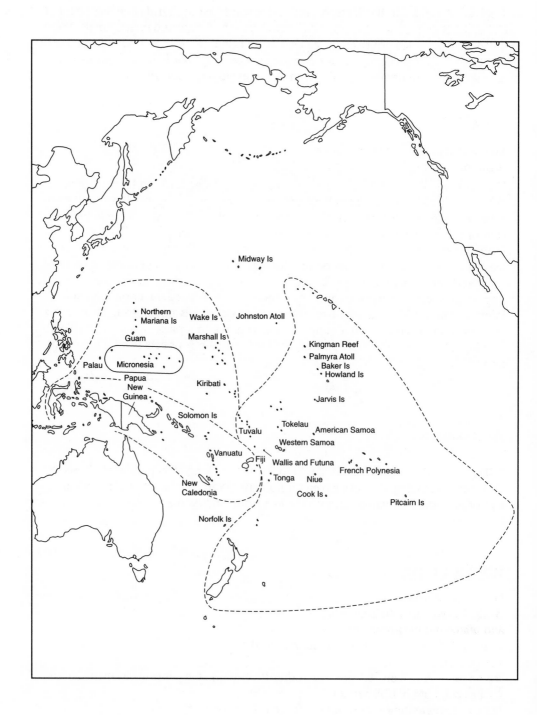

Map 10 The Pacific Ocean

Introduction

Situated in the eastern Caribbean only 375km northeast of Venezuela, Barbados possesses one of the better, more rounded economies of the Caribbean islands. British since the seventeenth century, its economy was based upon sugar. More recently, since independence, tourism has become its leading industry.

Agriculture

The principal crop is sugar though this is of far less importance than formerly. Raw sugar production in 1994 came to 50,700mt. Other crops consist of a range of vegetables such as sweet potatoes and yams, and some cotton. Barbados is not self-sufficient in food and beverages and food account for 18 per cent of all imports. There are 33,000 cattle and 66,000 sheep. Fishing is of growing importance. Agriculture and fishing contribute only 4.3 per cent of GDP and employ only 4.6 per cent of the labour force.

Minerals

Moderate finds of offshore oil and natural gas have assisted the economy in recent years but otherwise Barbados does not possess any exploitable minerals.

Manufacturing

Tourism is now the chief industry and caters especially for the North American market; receipts from tourism in 1993 came to $502,000,000. Other mainly light industries include sugar, component assembly for export, petroleum. Manufacturing contributes approximately 6.0 per cent of GDP, tourism 30 per cent.

Infrastructure

For its size Barbados has a good infrastructure: 1,475km of paved roads, one airport. Bridgetown is the only seaport. There is an island-wide automatic telephone system and telecommunications links to Trinidad and St Lucia.

Political considerations

Enjoying one of the highest standards of living in the Caribbean, Barbados has been ruled by the Democratic Labour Party since independence and is generally conservative in its politics.

Assessments

There is little prospect of much change in the economic fortunes of Barbados in the foreseeable future.

BELIZE

Area. 8,867 sq. miles (22,965 sq. km).
Population. (1995) 216,000.
Capital. Belmopan (3,852).
Other major cities. Belize City (47,723, 1993), the capital until struck by a severe hurricane in 1961 when plans were made to move the capital to Belmopan; Orange Walk (11,922), San Ignacio/Santa Elena (9,702).
Language(s). English (official), Spanish, Maya, Garifuna.
Religion(s). Roman Catholic 57.7 per cent, Protestant (various denominations) 28.5 per cent, other Christian 2.3 per cent, Hindu 2.5 per cent, non-religious, other 9 per cent.
Date of independence. September 21 1981 (from Britain).
GNP. (1993) $499,000,000, per capita $2,440.
Land and climate. Belize is mainly low lying and much of the coastal region consists of a swampy plain; there are low mountains in the south. The climate is hot, humid tropical and subject to frequent hurricanes and coastal flooding. The country is also subject to deforestation.

Introduction

The smallest country on mainland Central America and the only one without a Pacific seaboard, Belize is overwhelmingly dependent upon agriculture. Its principal economic thrust is to diversify away from sugar production which has long been its main activity. Guatemala has laid claim to Belize since the nineteenth century.

Agriculture

Agriculture, including forestry and fisheries, accounts for just under 20 per cent of GDP and employs 17.6 per cent of the labour force. Approximately 44 per cent of the land is forest, 2.1 per cent meadows and pastures and 2.5 per cent under permanent cultivation. The principal crop is sugarcane, followed by oranges, grapefruit and bananas. Maize and rice are the staples. The national cattle herd is only 59,000. Lumber and shrimps are important exports. A programme to diversify away from dependence upon sugar is being assisted by the USA. Belize, however, is a net importer of basic food requirements and likely to remain so.

Minerals and manufacturing

There are no mineral resources of any value. Mining and manufacturing between them contribute 4.6 per cent of GDP. There is a growing industrial sector concerned with garments and food processing while tourism is of increasing importance.

Infrastructure

There are 500km of paved roads and 1,600km of gravel roads. Belize City is the principal port. There are 32 usable airports, three with permanent surface runways. Telecommunications are of reasonable standard.

Political considerations

Belize is generally politically stable and in 1993 Britain announced it was withdrawing the garrison, which had been based in the country for 45 years to counter the Guatemalan claim to Belize, as a result of better Belize–Guatemalan relations since 1991. However, the United Democratic Party (UDP) government which won the June 1993 elections announced it would suspend all agreements with Guatemala until a final agreement was signed to end Guatemala's claims. There is illegal cultivation and export of marijuana.

Assessments

The economy of Belize, which is small and weak, will continue to require aid to meet its annual trade deficit into the foreseeable future. A majority of goods may be imported on open general licence.

BHUTAN

Area. 18,150 sq. miles (47,000 sq. km).
Population. (1995) 816,000.
Capital. Thimphu (30,340).
Other major cities. Phuntsholing (10,000).
Language(s). Dzongkla (official), Tibetan and Nepalese dialects.
Religion(s). Buddhist 69.6 per cent, Hindu 24.6 per cent, Muslim 5 per cent, other 0.8 per cent.
Date of independence. August 8 1949 (from India).
GNP. (1993) $253,000,000, per capita $310.
Land and climate. A mountainous country with fertile valleys and savanna. The southern plains have a tropical climate; the central valleys have cool winters and hot summers; the Himalaya mountains have severe winters and cool summers.

Introduction

This tiny landlocked country lies between India and China in the Himalayas. Its population is almost entirely dependent upon agriculture and forestry and its people are amongst the least skilled and poorest in the world. The one major resource is water with the possibility of producing hydro-electric power. It is closely linked with India which provides most of its imports and takes almost all its exports.

Agriculture

Agriculture accounts for about 41 per cent of GDP and provides employment for 90 per cent of the population. It produces a range of fruit, vegetables, rice, maize, dairy products and eggs. It is self-sufficient in foodstuffs except for grains, part of which have to be imported. Timber and wood products account for 17 per cent of exports, fruit and vegetables for 11 per cent.

Minerals and manufacturing

Limestone, dolomite and gypsum are mined. However, hydro-electric power is Bhutan's main source of export earnings and electricity accounts for 29 per cent of all exports. Almost all imports and exports are to and from India. There is an important cement industry which accounts for another 10 per cent of exports. Bhutan is potentially very attractive as a tourist destination but the government limits tourists to 3,000 a year to minimize foreign influence.

Infrastructure

There are 2,165km of roads of which 1,703km are surfaced. Two airports are out of commission. Telecommunications are generally poor; there is a telegraph service via India.

Political considerations

A conservative society where the King, Council of Ministers, National Assembly and priesthood share power, Bhutan is effectively in India's absolute sphere of influence.

Assessments

Bhutan is likely to remain a poor, under-developed state dependent upon the goodwill of India and international aid into the foreseeable future.

CAPE VERDE

Area. 1,557 sq. miles (4,033 sq. km).
Population. (1995) 392,000.
Capital. Praia (61,644, 1990).
Other major cities. Mindelo (47,109), São Felipe (5,616).
Language(s). Portuguese (official), Crioulo (Portuguese and West African).
Religion(s). Roman Catholic 93.2 per cent, other 6.8 per cent.
Date of independence. July 5 1975 (from Portugal).
GNP. (1993) $347,000,000, per capita $870.
Land and climate. The islands, which are volcanic, are steep, rugged and rocky. The climate is temperate with warm dry summers; rainfall is very erratic and they are subject to recurrent droughts and affected by the dry harmattan wind. They suffer from deforestation and over-grazing and remain volcanically active.

Introduction

The Cape Verde Islands lie 500km due west of Senegal in the Atlantic. The group's location is on or near the major north–south shipping route from Europe to the Cape which gives it a strategic importance of value that is enhanced by its communications station and the fact that it also acts as an air refuelling station. The archipelago is in rich fishing grounds and fish are its main natural resource. Otherwise the islands have few resources and are mainly dependent upon food aid and financial aid for survival.

Agriculture

Agriculture including fisheries accounts for 21 per cent of GDP. Farming is mainly subsistence although bananas and plantains are an export crop accounting for 11.7 per cent of exports in 1993. The staple crops are maize, beans, sweet potatoes, potatoes and cassava. Goats, pigs and a small cattle herd of 18,000 head make up the livestock resource. The fish catch of approximately 7,000 tons (mainly tuna and lobster) provides both a principal occupation and the major export (62.6 per cent of all exports in 1993); fisheries offer considerable development and expansion possibilities which have yet to be adequately realized. However, Cape Verde only produces 10 per cent of its actual food requirements and must import 90 per cent of its basic needs. It depends upon food aid for its survival.

Minerals and manufacturing

There are no important minerals. Small quantities of salt (about 4,000 tons) are mined annually. Manufacturing accounts for 6 per cent of GDP and is principally concerned with fish processing, clothing, ship repair, food and beverages, and construction materials. A small tourist industry is being developed. A proportion of export earnings come from petroleum and petroleum products (imported mainly for refuelling purposes) for airlines and shipping using Cape Verde as a staging post.

Infrastructure

Mindelo and Praia are the seaports. There are six usable airports with permanent runways of which two have runways of 2,440 to 3,659m length. Telecommunications are good. Cape Verde's strategic position in mid-Atlantic on sea and air routes constitutes a major resource whose potential has still to be fully exploited.

Political considerations

Cape Verde abandoned a one-party political system (maintained since independence) and adopted multiparty politics in 1990, holding its first multiparty elections in 1991.

Assessments

There are an estimated 600,000 Cape Verdeans living abroad, mainly in the USA, and their remittances home are a principal source of finance. International aid is the other major source and without these two regular inputs the economy would collapse.

COMOROS

Area. 719 sq. miles (1,862 sq. km).
Population. (1995) 545,000.
Capital. Moroni (24,000).
Other major cities. Matsamudu (15,000), Domoni (8,000), Fomboni (5,000), Mitsaniouli (4,200).
Language(s). Arabic, French, Comoran (a mixture of Swahili and Arabic) (official).
Religion(s). Sunni Muslim 99.4 per cent, Roman Catholic 0.6 per cent.
Date of independence. July 6 1975 (from France).
GNP. (1993) $272,000,000, per capita $520.
Land and climate. A series of volcanic islands, the land varies between steep mountains and low hills. There is a tropical marine climate with a rainy season from November to May.

Introduction

This tiny country consists of a group of islands lying in the north of the Mozambique Channel two-thirds of the distance between Mozambique and Madagascar. A former French possession, three of the four main islands – Grand Comore, Anjouan and Mohéli – broke away from France with a unilateral declaration of independence (UDI) in 1975 while the fourth, Mayotte, elected to remain a dependency of France. They form a Federal Islamic Republic. Desperately poor and dependent on aid, the Comoros's economy consists almost entirely of agricultural activities including fishing.

Economy

An agricultural-based economy whose principal exports are vanilla (59 per cent), ylang-ylang (20 per cent) and cloves (11 per cent). Small quantities of coffee, cinnamon and tobacco are also exported. There is a developing fisheries industry based upon tuna and a small forest industry. The staple food is rice which also accounts for 12 per cent of imports. The islands will never be self-sufficient in food and must remain heavily dependent upon aid inputs into the indefinite future. Efforts are being made to develop a tourist industry. The manufacturing sector, which is minuscule, contributes only 4.5 per cent to GDP. The position of the islands in the mouth of the Mozambique Channel has potential strategic value.

Infrastructure

There are 750km of roads of which 210km are paved. Two ports – Mutsamudu and Moroni – serve the islands which have four airports, one with a runway of 2,440 to 3,659m length. Telecommunications are sparse and inadequate.

Political considerations and assessments

A low level of education, restricted economic activity, high unemployment and heavy aid dependence give little promise that Comoros will be able to alter its status in the future from that of an economically dependent mini-state.

CYPRUS

Introduction

The island of Cyprus lies at the eastern end of the Mediterranean, 64km south of Turkey. A British colony to 1960 and historically always divided between its Greek (majority) and Turkish (minority) communities, it is now effectively two mini-states, following the Turkish invasion and occupation of the northern third of the island in 1974. In 1975 the Turkish Federated State of Cyprus was declared and then, in 1983, this renamed itself the Turkish Republic of Northern Cyprus. This Turkish 'state', however, has received no international recognition except from Turkey. The two 'states' of Cyprus are dealt with separately below.

REPUBLIC OF CYPRUS (Greek)
Area. 2,276 sq. miles (5,896 sq. km).
Population. (1995) 651,000.
Capital. Lefkosia (Nicosia) (177,451).
Other major cities. Limassol (136,741).
Language(s). Greek (official), Turkish, English.
Religion(s). Cypriot Orthodox 82 per cent, Maronite Christian 1.5 per cent, other 16.5 per cent.
Date of independence. August 16 1960 (from Britain).
GNP. (1993) $6,616,000,000, per capita $10,480.
Land and climate. A central plain with mountains in the south, the climate is temperate Mediterranean with hot dry summers and cool wet winters.

Agriculture

Agriculture contributes under 6 per cent to GDP and employs 12 per cent of the workforce. The principal crops are potatoes, vegetables, barley, grapes, olives and citrus fruits. Fruit and vegetables account for 25 per cent of exports.

Mining and manufacturing

There is no significant mining industry although minerals present in the island include copper, pyrites, asbestos, gypsum, salt, marble and clay earth pigment. Manufacturing contributes 12.6 per cent to GDP and employs just under 16 per cent of the workforce. The manufacturing sector has become increasingly sophisticated and covers clothing, food, cement, bricks and tiles, beverages, fabricated metals. Tourism makes an important contribution to the economy worth approximately $1.4bn a year. The Republic of Cyprus has assumed considerable importance during the 1990s as a centre for offshore registration by foreign companies and has become home for an estimated 19,000 such companies, many of them Russian, with up to 1 billion dollars a month being transferred, again principally from Russia. The per capita income places the Republic of Cyprus at the top end of the upper-middle-income group of countries.

TURKISH REPUBLIC OF NORTHERN CYPRUS
Area. 1,295 sq. miles (3,355 sq. km).
Population. (1995) 155,000.
Capital. Lefkosa (Nicosia) (41,815).
Other major cities. Gazimagusa (21,722).
Language(s). Turkish (official).
Religion(s). (as in Republic of Cyprus).

Date of independence. The Turkish invasion occurred in July 1974 and the Turkish Republic of Northern Cyprus was proclaimed on November 15 1983.
GNP. Circa $600,000,000, per capita $3,870.
Land and climate. Central plain and mountains in the north, a Mediterranean climate (as in the south).

Economy

A much smaller economy and population than for the Greek part of the island, with agriculture accounting for 11 per cent of GDP and mining and manufacturing for 9.3 per cent; the economy is substantially underwritten on an annual basis by Turkey.

Infrastructure

The United Nations provides a buffer zone between the Greek area (60 per cent of the island) and the Turkish area (35 per cent). There are also two British sovereign military base areas which account for the remaining 5 per cent of the land area.

There are 10,780km of roads of which 5,170km are paved; five ports – Famagusta, Kyrenia, Larnaca, Limassol and Paphos – and thirteen airports, ten with permanent runways of which seven are between 2,440 and 3,659m in length, serve the island. Telecommunications are first class in both parts of the island.

Political considerations and assessments

The chief political consideration is whether the de facto division of the island is to become a permanent political fact or whether by a compromise the two sides can create some form of federal or confederal system that will enable the island to operate as a single entity again. Despite political problems the people in the Greek part are well off and possess a relatively rounded economy; those in the Turkish part have only a third the level of prosperity as measured by per capita GNP but this still places them at the upper end of the upper-middle-income group of countries.

Should the division of the island into the two parts – Greek and Turkish – persist this, in effect, means the existence of two mini-states.

DJIBOUTI

Area. 8,950 sq. miles (23,200 sq. km).
Population. (1995) 586,000 (plus more than 100,000 Somali refugees in 1994–5).
Capital. Djibouti (450,000).
Other major cities. Ali Sabih (4,000), Tadjoura (3,500), Dikhil (3,000).
Language(s). Arabic, French (official), Somali, Afar.
Religion(s). Sunni Muslim 96 per cent, Christian 4 per cent.
Date of independence. June 27 1977 (from France).

GNP. (1993) $448,000,000, per capita $780.
Land and climate. A coastal plain and plateau separated by central mountains with a dry but torrid desert climate.

Introduction

This tiny, artificially created country of colonial times with a coastline of 314km on the Red Sea has three land neighbours: Somalia, Ethiopia and Eritrea. Its value is derived almost entirely from its strategic position at the railhead and port outlet for Ethiopia on the 307km jointly controlled railroad that links Addis Ababa to the sea. The port of Djibouti and the airport are both of international importance and French (Foreign Legion) forces have been stationed in Djibouti (at the 'disposal' of the government) since independence in 1977. The country has virtually no resources and cannot feed itself.

Economy

The economy depends upon Djibouti's position as an international port which serves Ethiopia as the outlet for that country's only railroad to the sea, and as a port of call for ships passing through the Red Sea. Its strategic position led France to create a permanent military base in Djibouti which was continued as a principal source of revenue to the little state after independence in 1977. Djibouti became a free port in 1981.

Agriculture contributes only 2.4 per cent to GDP; this is mainly concerned with livestock and live animals, including camels, are exported to Saudi Arabia. Other exports consist of vegetables and melons. Djibouti has to import most of its food requirements. Livestock is by far the most important aspect of the agricultural sector. Only 9 per cent of the land consists of meadows and pastures, the rest is desert and mountains. The only mining activity consists of producing materials for the local construction industry and salt from evaporation. There is a minuscule manufacturing sector which contributes about 3.6 per cent to GDP and consists of small-scale import substitution activities.

Infrastructure

Djibouti controls 97km of the Ethiopian railroad. There are 2,900km of highways of which 280km are paved. There is the one port of Djibouti (which is also the capital) and eleven usable airports of which two have permanent surface runways of 2,440 to 3,659m length. Telecommunications are adequate.

Political considerations and assessments

Subject to ongoing, low-intensity civil war between the majority Somali population and the minority Afars, and also a recipient country for refugees from its disturbed neighbours (in 1995 from Somalia), Djibouti's economic existence depends upon the base facilities it accords to France. In 1991 71.7 per cent of exports were designated as unspecified special transactions (which would largely have consisted of military arrangements). Otherwise, port dues and facilities are a further source of income derived from Djibouti's role as an entrepôt port. Apart from these activities, there are no prospects of Djibouti becoming economically self-sufficient. (An end to the civil war was negotiated during 1995.)

DOMINICA

Area. 290 sq. miles (750 sq. km).
Population. (1995) 72,100.
Capital. Roseau (15,853).
Other major cities. Portsmouth (3,621), Marigot (2,919), Atkinson (2,518), Mahaut (2,372).
Language(s). English (official), a French patois.
Religion(s). Roman Catholic 79.2 per cent, other 20.8 per cent.
Date of independence. November 3 1978 (from Britain).
GNP. (1993) $193,000,000, per capita $2,680.
Land and climate. An island of rugged volcanic mountains with a tropical climate that is moderated by the northeast trade winds. It has heavy rainfall.

Introduction

A tiny island of the Windward group in the eastern Caribbean, Dominica is overwhelmingly dependent upon its agricultural exports and has few other resources apart from rugged scenery that has still to be developed as a tourist attraction. The country is a member of the Commonwealth.

Economy

Agriculture accounts for 17.5 per cent of GDP (1994) and employs 31 per cent of the workforce. The main products for export are bananas (Dominica is dependent upon EU quotas for its banana exports), bay oil, vegetables, grapefruit and oranges. The one important manufacture is soap, made from coconut oil, and exported to neighbouring islands. It is not self-sufficient in staple foods and though its per capita income places it in the upper-middle-income bracket of countries it is still in receipt of aid for exports do not balance imports. There is a small mining sector that produces pumice and volcanic ash.

Political considerations and assessments

A mini-state whose future, in part, must depend upon the goodwill of larger trading groups or states. Its agriculture is subject to varying climatic conditions and in 1995 major hurricane damage virtually wiped out the banana industry which will be unable to recover for many years.

EQUATORIAL GUINEA

Area. 10,831 sq. miles (28,051 sq. km).
Population. (1995) 396,000.
Capital. Malabo (30,418).
Other major cities. Bata (24,308), Ela-Nguema (6,179), Campo Yaoundé (5,199), Los Angeles (4,079).
Language(s). Spanish (official), pidgin English, Fang, Bubi, Ibo.
Religion(s). Christian (mainly Roman Catholic) 88.8 per cent, traditional beliefs 4.6 per cent, other 6.6 per cent.
Date of independence. October 12 1968 (from Spain).
GNP. (1994) $142,500,000, per capita $350.
Land and climate. Coastal plains rising into hills; the islands are volcanic. The climate is tropical, hot and humid.

Introduction

This tiny country lies on the Atlantic coast of Africa sandwiched between Cameroon and Gabon; it includes the island of Bioko on which the capital, Malabo, is situated. Following independence from Spain in 1968 Equatorial Guinea became a byword for corruption and tyrannical rule under the notorious Macías Nguema until his overthrow by coup in 1979. Since that time the country has been ruled by a Supreme Military Council with a greater semblance of democracy. The economy, which was virtually destroyed under Nguema, depends upon agriculture: cocoa, coffee and wood products are the main exports.

Agriculture

The economy is almost wholly based upon agriculture, forestry and fisheries with subsistence agriculture predominating. Cash crops consist of cocoa, coffee and wood products (638,000cu m) and in 1994 cork and wood accounted for 35.6 per cent of exports, cocoa for 4.4 per cent. Principal staples are cassava, sweet potatoes, bananas, coconuts and palm kernels. The numbers of livestock are small with only 5,000 head of cattle. Agriculture accounts for 50.2 per cent of GDP and employs 57.9 per cent of the workforce. Timber and coffee come from the mainland (Rio Muni) and cocoa from the island of Bioko. Land use is divided between forested 46.2 per cent, meadows and pastures 3.7 per cent, agricultural land under permanent cultivation 8.2 per cent, other 41.9 per cent.

Mining and manufacturing

Although the only mining currently carried out consists of quarrying for building materials, a number of minerals are present in workable quantities; these include iron ore, lead, zinc, manganese, uranium, alluvial gold and molybdenum. Oil exploration offshore looks promising and export of natural gas products began in 1995.

Infrastructure

There are 2,460km of highways on the mainland (Rio Muni) and 300km on Bioko. Malabo and Bata are the country's two ports. There are three usable airports, two with permanent surface runways, one of which is 2,440m in length. Telecommunications are poor though adequate for government purposes.

Political considerations and assessments

Elections in 1993 gave the ruling Democratic Party of Equatorial Guinea (PDGE) 68 of 80 seats in the assembly but the election procedures were condemned by international observers. The country is heavily dependent upon international aid and debts in 1993 of $218,700,000 were a third as much again as the GNP.

FIJI

Area. 7,056 sq. miles (18,274 sq. km).
Population. (1995) 791,000.
Capital. Suva (69,665).
Other major cities. Lautoka (28,728), Lami (8,601), Nadi (7,679), Ba (6,518).
Language(s). English (official), Fijian, Hindi.
Religion(s). Christian 62.9 per cent, Hindu 38.1 per cent, Muslim 7.8 per cent, other 1.2 per cent.
Date of independence. October 10 1970 (from Britain).
GNP. (1993) $1,626,000,000, per capita $2,140.
Land and climate. The islands are mainly made up of volcanic mountains; the climate is tropical marine with only slight seasonal variations of temperature. Fiji is subject to hurricanes (November to January).

Introduction

A group of islands in Oceania, situated due north of New Zealand in the South Pacific (there are 332 islands altogether of which about 110 are inhabited), Fiji is a middle-income country whose economy is primarily agricultural and depends for the greater part of its foreign exchange earnings upon sugar exports and tourism. The fact that incomers from India threatened to swamp the indigenous Melanesian (Fijian) people was the stimulus for two coups in 1987 which led to the overthrow of the Indian-dominated government. The Constitution of 1990 ensures that seats to the House of Representatives are allocated on a racial basis so as to maintain the Melanesian majority.

Agriculture

Sugar is the principal crop and mainstay of the economy; in 1994 the sugarcane harvest came to 4,064,000mt and sugar accounted for 38.4 per cent of exports. Coconuts and copra are another export crop but the copra business is now in decline. The main food crops are cassava, rice, sweet potatoes and bananas. There is a small livestock sector, fishing is of growing importance and the catch in 1993 came to just over 31,000mt. There is a large subsistence sector and the islands are broadly self-sufficient in foods. Agriculture acounts for 22 per cent of GDP and employs 44 per cent of the labour force.

Mining and manufacturing

The mining sector is very small, confined to gold and silver deposits. In 1994 3,440kg of gold and 1,386kg of silver were mined. Gold accounted for 9.5 per cent of exports.

The manufacturing sector accounts for 12 per cent of GDP and employs 7.5 per cent of the labour force. Principal manufactures are refined sugar, cement, flour, stock feed, soap, coconut oil, beer and paint. Tourism attracts up to a quarter million visitors a year and receipts from tourists in 1993 came to $236,000,000.

Infrastructure

The government-owned Fiji Sugar Corporation owns 644km of narrow gauge railway. Out of 3,300km of roads, 1,590km are paved. There are 203km of inland waterways. Four ports serve the islands: Lambasa, Lautoka, Savusavu and Suva. There are 22 usable airports, two with permanent surface runways and one with a runway between 2,440 and 3,659m in length. There are good inter-island tele-communications and reasonable international links.

Political considerations

The dominant political problem, which came to a head in 1987, is that of racial tension between the Fijians and Indian immigrant community which at one time just became the majority. Now 50.4 per cent of the total population are Fijians while 44.2 per cent are Indian. Numbers of Indians emigrated following the events of 1987 so that Fijians emerged once more as the largest ethnic group in the country.

Assessments

Fiji is a middle-income economy with reasonable assets but no major resources.

THE GAMBIA

Area. 4,127 sq. miles (10,689 sq. km).
Population. (1995) 1,115,000.
Capital. Banjul (42,326 – Greater Banjul 270,540).
Other major cities. Serekunda (102,600), Brikama (24,300), Bakau (23,600).
Language(s). English (official), Mandinka, Wolof, Fula.
Religion(s). Muslim 90 per cent, Christian 9 per cent, indigenous beliefs 1 per cent.
Date of independence. February 18 1965 (from Britain).
GNP. (1993) $372,000,000, per capita $360.
Land and climate. The land consists of the flood plain of the Gambia river, but also includes some low hills; the climate is tropical with a hot rainy season from June to November and a dry cooler season from December to May. The country suffers from deforestation.

Introduction

This tiny country, 400 miles long and ten miles wide running from west to east into the bulge of Africa, is essentially confined to the banks of the river Gambia and, more than most African states, is the creation of colonialism. It is the smallest country on the continent and is completely surrounded by its far larger Francophone neighbour, Senegal, except for an 80km coastline on the Atlantic. There are no minerals or other resources and the people are dependent upon agriculture. The Gambia is among the world's poorest countries; it is not self-sufficient in food and is heavily dependent upon international aid. On December 12 1981 The Gambia and Senegal entered upon the Confederation of Senegambia but the experiment failed and the confederation was dissolved on September 30 1989.

Agriculture

Agriculture accounts for 18.9 per cent of GDP and employs 73.7 per cent of the workforce. The principal crops are groundnuts (the main export), millet, maize, rice, cassava and pulses. Livestock has not been developed; the national cattle herd stands at 414,000. The fish catch in 1993 was 20,479mt and fish and fish preparations accounted for 4.4 per cent of exports. The fishing industry could be considerably expanded. Groundnuts are the main export crop while cotton is also being developed as an export crop. Roundwood production in 1993 came to 958,000cu m. About a third of food requirements have to be imported. Land use consists of forested 14.5 per cent, meadows and pastures 9 per cent, agricultural land under permanent cultivation 18 per cent, other 58.5 per cent.

Mining and manufacturing

The only mining activity consists of the extraction of sand and gravel for local use. Manufacturing accounts for 5.8 per cent of GDP and employs 2.5 per cent of the workforce. The sector is very small and undeveloped; its principal products are processed foods including peanut and palm kernel oil, beverages, textiles, chemicals, non-metals, printing and publishing and leather. There is a growing tourist industry which concentrates upon visitors from Europe.

Infrastructure

There are 3,083km of highways of which 431km are paved; 400km of inland waterways and one port at the capital Banjul. There is one airport with a permanent surface runway of between 2,440 and 3,659m in length. Telecommunications are adequate.

Political considerations

An army coup of July 22 1994 toppled the government of President Dawda Jawara who had ruled the Gambia since independence in 1965 and presided over a democratic system. Gambian policy must always take account of its neighbour Senegal and close working relations with that country, whether or not in a federal relationship, are a necessity for viable survival.

Assessments

The Gambia is a tiny country of no resources dependent upon the goodwill of Senegal and international aid.

GRENADA

Area. 133 sq. miles (344 sq. km).
Population. (1995) 92,000.
Capital. St George's (4,439).
Language(s). English (official), French patois.
Religion(s). Roman Catholic 53 per cent, Anglican 14 per cent, Seventh Day Adventist 8.5 per cent, Pentecostal 7.2 per cent, other 17.3 per cent.
Date of independence. February 7 1974 (from Britain).
GNP. (1993) $219,000,000, per capita $2,410.
Land and climate. A volcanic island dominated by central mountains; the climate is tropical tempered by the northeast trade winds.

Introduction

This tiny Caribbean island illustrates most of the economic and political problems faced by mini-states whose economy depends upon a few traditional agricultural products while it is faced by huge and apparently permanent (comparative) unemployment. A political crisis erupted in 1983 when the prime minister Maurice Bishop (who had himself seized power in a coup) was murdered in a faction struggle. The suspicion voiced in Washington at that time of Cuban involvement in the island led to a US/Caribbean invasion to restore constitutional government. This episode illustrates the vulnerability of such tiny states. Grenada is a spice island and nutmeg and mace are its most important exports while tourism is its biggest foreign exchange earner. It is situated in the eastern Caribbean 150 miles north of Trinidad and Tobago.

Economy

It is essentially an agricultural economy producing spices and tropical plants. Agriculture accounts for 11.6 per cent of GDP and employs 14.3 per cent of the workforce. Bananas, coconuts, sugarcane, nutmeg, fruits, cocoa, mace are the main crops with bananas, nutmegs, cocoa beans and mace accounting for just over 40 per cent of exports. It is the world's second largest producer and fourth largest exporter of nutmeg and mace. Small-sized farms predominate. Tourism is the largest foreign exchange earner and brought in $58m in 1994. The manufacturing sector is undeveloped and industries are lightweight. The sector accounted for 6.9 per cent of GDP in 1993 and employed just over 7 per cent of the workforce. It is mainly concerned with food processing. The only mining activity is the excavation of gravel for local construction purposes.

Infrastructure

There are 1,000km of highways of which 600km are paved. The only port is St George's. There are three usable airports, one with a runway between 2,440 and 3,659m in length. There is an adequate system of telecommunications and an island-wide automatic telephone system.

Political considerations and assessments

The tiny size of Grenada's political structure make it vulnerable to internal overthrow or external intervention as the events of 1983 demonstrated. A stable political system should assist in the attraction of investment for small-scale industrial activity or to expand the tourist business; the island's scenery is one of its best assets. The per capita income of $2,410 places Grenada at the upper end of the lower-middle income bracket of countries.

GUINEA-BISSAU

Area. 13,948 sq. miles (36,125 sq. km).
Population. (1995) 1,073,000.
Capital. Bissau (125,000).
Other major cities. Bafatá (13,429), Gabú (7,803).
Language(s). Portuguese (official), Criolo, a number of African languages.
Religion(s). Traditional beliefs 54 per cent, Muslim 38 per cent, Christian 8 per cent.
Date of independence. September 10 1974 (from Portugal).
GNP. (1993) $241,700,000, per capita $233.
Land and climate. The land consists mainly of a low coastal plain which rises to savanna in the east. The climate is tropical, hot and humid, with a rainy season from June to November with southwesterly winds and a dry season from December to May when northeasterly harmattan winds prevail.

Introduction

This tiny West African country (one of Africa's several mini-states) is one of the poorest in the world and though it has a number of mineral resources their exploitation has to await finance to create a proper infrastructure. Meanwhile, existence is largely a question of agricultural subsistence. Guinea-Bissau has two neighbours – Senegal and Guinea – and a 350km Atlantic coastline. It achieved independence from Portugal in 1974 after a long, bitter liberation war and following a period of one-party rule became a multiparty democracy in the 1990s.

Agriculture

Agriculture and fishing are the primary activities and agriculture accounts for 45 per cent of GDP and employs 78 per cent of the labour force. The main crops are rice, fruits, sweet potatoes, cassava, plantains, cashews, millet, coconuts, vegetables, peanuts, sorghum, maize, palm kernels, sugarcane, bananas, copra and palm oil. The national cattle herd numbers 494,000. The main export crops are cashews (52.8 per cent in 1991), groundnuts 11.3 per cent and frozen fish 3.1 per cent. Timber is underexploited. The country is not self-sufficient in food but agricultural potential could be more fully exploited. Land use is divided between forested 38.1 per cent, meadows and pastures 38.4 per cent, agricultural land under permanent cultivation 12.1 per cent, other 11.4 per cent.

Mining and manufacturing

There are substantial mineral resources including a deposit of 200m tons of bauxite and a deposit of 200m tons of phosphates while there are possibilities of offshore oil; a good deal of prospecting has already been carried out by a number of foreign oil companies. The manufacturing sector is minuscule, primarily concerned with food processing and clothing.

Infrastructure

There is a relatively advanced road system, a legacy of Portuguese strategic considerations during the liberation war: 3,218km of highways of which 2,698km are bitumen surfaced. Bissau is the only port. There are fifteen usable airports, four with permanent surface runways of which one is between 2,440 and 3,659m in length. Telecommunications are poor.

Political considerations and assessments

One of the world's poorest countries, mainly dependent upon international aid, Guinea-Bissau has little chance of greater development without a major injection of capital to make the exploitation of its minerals a more viable proposition than it is at present.

GUYANA

Area. 83,044 sq. miles (215,083 sq. km).
Population. (1995) 770,000.
Capital. Georgetown (248,500).
Other major cities. Linden (27,200), New Amsterdam (17,700).
Language(s). English (official), Amerindian dialects.
Religion(s). Christian 52 per cent, Hindu 34 per cent, Muslim 9 per cent, other 5 per cent.
Date of independence. May 26 1966 (from Britain).
GNP. (1993) $285,000,000, per capita $350.
Land and climate. The land consists of rolling highlands, a low coastal plain and a savanna region in the south. The climate is tropical, moderated by the northeast trade winds with two rainy seasons (May to mid-August and mid-November to January).

Introduction

This small, ex-British territory on the mainland of South America is, on a per capita basis, the poorest country in the region. Heavily indebted and subject to constant IMF pressures to 'reform' its economy, it has suffered from a fall in demand for its two most important exports – bauxite and sugar. Known as the 'land of six peoples' for its mixed population, it has three land neighbours – Venezuela, Brazil and Suriname (with Venezuela claiming part of its territory in the west and Suriname in the east) and a Caribbean coastline of 459km.

Agriculture

Agriculture, forestry and fisheries account for 44 per cent of GDP with sugar responsible for half that figure at 21.2 per cent. Sugar has long been the country's most important product, employer and foreign exchange earner and in 1994 raw sugar output came to 256,700mt and accounted for 31.3 per cent of exports. Sugar exports depend upon quotas from both the USA and the EU under the Lomé Convention. The second agricultural export is rice and output in 1994 came to 233,400mt with rice accounting for 15 per cent of exports. There is potential for the expansion of fisheries; the fish catch in 1994 came to 38,200mt of which 8,200mt were shrimps or prawns and these accounted for 3.3 per cent of exports. Rum, an offshoot of sugar, provides another 2.7 per cent of exports. Staples, apart from rice, include coconuts, roots and tubers, plantains, bananas, oranges. Livestock is confined to the savanna country of the south and the national cattle herd is only 131,000 strong. Guyana is not self-sufficient in wheat, vegetable oils or animal products. Land use is divided between forested 83.2 per cent, meadows and pastures 6.2 per cent, agricultural land under permanent cultivation 2.5 per cent, other 8.1 per cent.

Mining

Bauxite, gold and diamonds are Guyana's three minerals. Problems of flooding and equipment have adversely affected the bauxite industry in recent years as have the effects of world overproduction so that bauxite is no longer as important a component of the economy as formerly. A total of 1,991,100mt of bauxite was produced in 1994 and bauxite accounted for 14.5 per cent of exports. Gold mining (Guyana was the original El Dorado of Sir Walter Raleigh) yielded 375,000 troy ounces in 1994 and accounted for 15.8 per cent of exports (higher in value than bauxite). The yield of alluvial diamonds fluctuates widely from year to year. There are no other minerals. Mining contributes about 21 per cent to GDP and employs 3.9 per cent of the workforce.

Manufacturing

Manufacturing only contributes 3.7 per cent to GDP although employing 11.8 per cent of the workforce. The main manufactures are flour, rum, beer and stout, cigarettes, refrigerators and pharmaceuticals. All imports require licences and there is a single-tier customs tariff. Goods from Caricom countries or for development purposes are normally allowed free entry.

Infrastructure

There is a single coastal railway of 187km, single track 0.914m gauge; 7,665km of highways of which 550km are paved; and 6,000km of inland waterways of which a total of 330km up the Berbice, Demerara and Essequibo rivers are navigable to ocean-going vessels. Georgetown and New Amsterdam are the country's two ports. There are 48 usable airports, five with permanent surface runways. Thirteen airports have runways between 1,220 and 2,439m in length. Telecommunications are fair.

Political considerations

During the 1990s, under the presidency of Cheddi Jagan (the one-time Marxist) Guyana began to liberalize its economy and in 1994 obtained another Enhanced Structural Adjustment Facility from the IMF while the Caribbean Group for Co-operation in Economic Development offered $320m in economic assistance. Guyana requires major international assistance. Despite many irregularities, Guyana maintains a democratic, multiparty tradition.

Assessments

The limited development options open to Guyana and over-dependence upon bauxite and sugar provide the country with little economic room in which to manoeuvre. In 1993 debts at $1,727,000,000 stood at six times GNP. There seems little prospect of much economic improvement in the foreseeable future.

KIRIBATI

Area. 313 sq. miles (811 sq. km).
Population. (1995) 80,400.
Capital. Bairiki (on Tarawa Atoll – urban Tarawa 25,154).
Language(s). English (official), Gilbertese.
Religion(s). Roman Catholic 53.4 per cent, Kiribati Protestant 39.2 per cent, Baha'i 2.4 per cent, other 5 per cent.
Date of independence. July 12 1979 (from Britain).
GNP. (1993) $54,000,000, per capita $710.
Land and climate. The group consists of low-lying coral atolls surrounded by extensive reefs. The climate is marine tropical, hot and humid though moderated by trade winds.

Introduction

This tiny country, the former British Gilbert Islands, consists of three groups of islands – the Gilbert Islands, Line Islands and Phoenix Islands – straddling the equator halfway between Hawaii and Australia. There are 33 islands altogether of which twenty are inhabited. Kiribati is a multiparty republic, a member of the Commonwealth and an ACP country.

Economy

The only important natural resource is phosphate and the island of Banaba is one of three great phosphate rock islands in the Pacific (the others are Makatea in French Polynesia and Nauru) although the mining of easily exploitable phosphates ended in 1979 (the year of independence). The economy relies largely upon the production of copra from coconuts and fishing. In 1993 the fish catch came to just under 30,000mt. Copra accounted for 67 per cent of exports in 1992. The rest of the economy is on a very small scale and Kiribati is dependent upon aid inputs to meet its requirements since exports are equivalent to only 25 per cent of imports. Most basic goods have to be imported.

MALDIVES

Area. 115 sq. miles (298 sq. km).
Population. (1995) 253,000.
Capital. Malé (55,130).
Language(s). Dhivehi (official), English.
Religion(s). Sunni Muslim 100 per cent.
Date of independence. July 26 1965 (from Britain).
GNP. (1993) $194,000,000, per capita $820.
Land and climate. These tiny islands are flat with no more elevation than 2.5m. The climate is tropical, hot and humid; the islands are subject to the dry northeast monsoon (November to March) and the wet southwest monsoon (June to August). Maldives is one of the world's states that stands at risk of being inundated should global warming lead to a rise in ocean levels.

Introduction

This archipelago of 1,200 coral islands grouped into nineteen atolls lying in the Indian Ocean southwest of the Indian sub-continent is one of the world's mini-states whose only natural resource consists of the fish in the surrounding sea. President Maunoon Abdul Gayoom won a fourth term of office in the elections of 1993. There are no organized political parties. Although politically stable and making reasonable progress within the limitations of its minuscule economy, Maldives must depend upon aid on a more or less permanent basis.

Agriculture

Agriculture contributes slightly under 21 per cent to GDP and employs 25 per cent of the workforce. Crops consist of vegetables, melons, coconuts, fruit, cassava, sweet potatoes, yams and copra. But these essentially subsistence-produced crops meet only 10 per cent of food requirements and most staple foods have to be imported. However, fishing makes the biggest single contribution to the economy. The fish catch in 1993 was 89,388mt and canned tuna, dried skipjack tuna and frozen skipjack tuna together account for about 51 per cent of all exports. Land use is divided between forested 3.3 per cent, meadows and pastures 3.3 per cent, agricultural land, under permanent cultivation 10 per cent, other 83.4 per cent.

Mining and manufacturing

Mining coral for construction contributes 1.8 per cent to GDP. Manufacturing contributes about 6 per cent to GDP and is principally concerned with fish processing, shipping, boat building, coconut processing, garments, woven mats, coir (rope), handicrafts. Apparel and clothing account for 16 per cent of exports. Tourism has been encouraged and earns about $146,000,000 a year.

Infrastructure

There are 9.6km of coral highway in the city of Malé, and Malé and Gan are the country's two ports. There are two airports, both with permanent surface runways between 2,440 and 3,659m in length. Telecommunications are minimal.

Political considerations and assessments

Maldives relies upon India for aid and training, for example the Maldivian army is trained by India which also sent troops in 1988 to thwart an attempted anti-government coup. More generally, Maldives will rely upon economic aid for its survival into the foreseeable future. Its dependence upon fisheries and tourism is enhanced by the fact that the islands lie athwart major world shipping lines.

MALTA

Area. 122 sq. miles (316 sq. km).
Population. (1995) 370,000.
Capital. Valletta (9,144).
Other major cities. Birkirkara (21,770), Qorimi (19,904), Hamrun (13,654), Sliema (13,514).
Language(s). Maltese and English (official).
Religion(s). Roman Catholic (official) 98.6 per cent, other 1.4 per cent.
Date of independence. September 21 1964 (from Britain).
GNP. (1992) $2,606,000,000, per capita $7,210.
Land and climate. Consisting of low rocky islands with flat but dissected plains and coastal cliffs, Malta enjoys a Mediterranean climate with mild wet winters and hot

dry summers. Fresh water is scarce and the islands depend increasingly upon desalination to meet requirements.

Introduction

The country consists of an archipelago whose three largest islands – Malta, Gozo and Comino – are inhabited. It lies between Sicily and Libya in the central Mediterranean. Malta has had a turbulent history as an island fortress, playing its last fortress role during World War II when, as a British base, it was repeatedly attacked by the German airforce. Malta became independent in 1964. It has few resources and the withdrawal of the British naval dockyard and military base in 1979 deprived the island of a major source of revenue. It concluded associate status with the European Community in 1970 and has applied to join the European Union. It welcomed the 1994 declaration of the European Council that the next phase of expansion would involve Malta (and Cyprus).

Agriculture

Agriculture contributes only 3 per cent to GDP and employs only 2 per cent of the labour force. Altogether Malta produces about 20 per cent of its food needs. The principal crops are potatoes, cauliflower, grapes, wheat, barley, tomatoes, citrus fruit, cut flowers and green peppers. Livestock consists of poultry, pigs and a small number of cattle. Fishing makes an important contribution to the overall economy. There are shortages in grain, animal fodder, fruits and other basic foods. Land use is divided between agricultural land, under permanent cultivation 40.6 per cent, other 59.4 per cent. Much of the land is infertile because of the limestone base.

Mining and manufacturing

Mining and quarrying covers the extraction of limestone and salt. Manufacturing with mining contributes about 27 per cent to GDP and employs the same proportion of the workforce. Electronics and textiles are the lead industries. The dry docks (the former British naval yards) are a major employer. Transport equipment, food processing, paper and publishing, chemicals and metal goods are the other important manufactures. Tourism contributes about $653,000,000 a year (1993) in revenues. Offshore service activities are of growing importance.

Infrastructure

There are 1,291km of roads of which 1,179km are paved; Valletta and Marsaxlokk are the two ports. Malta operates a large merchant marine fleet and a flag of convenience. There is one airport with a permanent surface runway between 2,440 and 3,659m in length. The telecommunications system is reasonable.

Political considerations and assessments

An offshore European island with an upper-middle income, Malta is in a halfway position between developed and developing and is in periodic need of aid, receiving economic assistance through the EU. The country operates a stable political multi-party system. Malta should benefit from full membership of the EU if this is achieved.

MARSHALL ISLANDS

Area. 70.07 sq. miles (181.48 sq. km).
Population. (1995) 56,200.
Capital. Majuro (Dalap-Uliga-Darrit, 14,649).
Other major cities. Ebeye (8,324).
Language(s). Marshallese and English (official).
Religion(s). Protestant 90.1 per cent, Roman Catholic 8.5 per cent, other 1.4 per cent.
Date of independence. October 21 1986 (from USA which administered the UN Trusteeship).
GDP. (1994) $88,800,000, per capita $1,640.
Land and climate. A series of low coral limestone and sand islands, the Marshall Islands lie on a typhoon belt and the climate is hot and humid with a wet season from May to November.

Introduction

This archipelago of tiny Pacific islands became independent from US administration (on behalf of the UN) in 1986 although they are currently dependent upon annual US aid injections equivalent to about two-thirds of budget requirements. A major controversy erupted during 1994 over proposals to use the Bikini and Eniwetok islands (which had been used for nuclear testing in the 1940s and 1950s and are estimated to be uninhabitable for 10,000 years) as dumping grounds for US nuclear waste. The principal source of income for the islands, apart from US aid, is tourism.

Economy

Agriculture and tourism are the two pillars of the economy. The main agricultural products are coconuts, cacao, taro, breadfruit, other fruits, pigs and chickens. The fish catch of about 12,000mt a year makes a substantial addition to food supplies. The islands are not self-sufficient in food. Tourism is the principal generator of foreign

351

exchange and employs 10 per cent of the workforce. There are phosphates deposits and possible deep sea minerals yet to be exploited.

Infrastructure

There are paved roads on the main islands. Majuro is the only port. The Marshall Islands operate a merchant marine flag of convenience. There are sixteen usable airports, four with permanent surface runways. The telecommunications system is fair.

Political considerations and assessments

Under the Compact of Free Association with the USA, the Marshall Islands receive $40m in aid a year; without this annual subvention the economy could hardly function. The World Bank has advised the government to structure the economy so that it takes account of a future when US aid ceases.

MAURITIUS

Area. 788 sq. miles (2,040 sq. km).
Population. (1995) 1,128,000.
Capital. Port Louis (142,850).
Other major cities. Beau Bassin-Rose Hill (94,299), Vacoas-Phoenix (92,072), Curepipe (74,738), Quatre Bornes (71,534).
Language(s). English (official), Creole, French, Hindi, Urdu, Hakka, Bojpoori.
Religion(s). Hindu 50.6 per cent, Roman Catholic 27.2 per cent, Muslim 16.3 per cent, Protestant 5.2 per cent, Buddhist 0.3 per cent, other 0.4 per cent.
Date of independence. March 12 1968 (from Britain).
GNP. (1993) $3,309,000,000, per capita $2,980.
Land and climate. A small coastal plain rises to a series of hills that enclose a central plain. The climate is tropical, modified by the southeast trade winds; the winter (May to November) is warm and dry, the summer (November to May) is hot, wet and humid.

Introduction

Originally colonized by the French in the eighteenth century, seized by Britain from France during the Napoleonic wars and peopled predominantly by Indians from India and Pakistan on the sub-continent, Mauritius became independent in 1968. It has made rapid strides to become one of the world's leading mini-states with an economy dominated by sugar, textiles, tourism and the shrewd development of an Export Processing Zone (EPZ). The island is located 900km east of Madagascar in the western Indian Ocean.

Agriculture

Agriculture contributes just under 9 per cent to GDP and employs just over 14 per cent of the workforce. Sugar has long been the principal product of Mauritius and about 90 per cent of cultivated land is given over to sugarcane. In 1992 sugar accounted for 25 per cent of exports. As an ACP country Mauritius benefits from EU sugar quotas. Smallholders produce tea in the highland areas (the green tea crop in 1993 came to 30,900mt, the black tea crop to a further 6,000mt) and this is the second export crop. Tobacco is the third cash crop though output only comes to 1,000mt. Food crops consist of maize, potatoes, bananas, pulses. There are small numbers of livestock – cattle, sheep and goats. The fish catch of 19,000mt could be increased; meanwhile, Mauritius imports substantial quantities of fish. Subsistence agriculture is on a very small scale and the island is a major net food importer, especially of rice. Land use is divided between forested 28.1 per cent, meadows and pastures 3.4 per cent, agricultural land, under permanent cultivation 52.2 per cent, other 16.3 per cent.

Mining and manufacturing

There are no minerals and no mining activity of any significance apart from sand for construction purposes and salt. Manufacturing, however, has been greatly boosted in the years since independence and accounts for 24 per cent of GDP and employs 36 per cent of the workforce. During the 1970s, fearful of over-dependence upon sugar, Mauritius developed an Export Processing Zone (EPZ) that offered attractive conditions under which investors could operate and concentrated upon labour-intensive activities. The most important of these deal with imported semi-manufactured products for re-export and clothing and textiles are by far the most important manufactures and account for 55 per cent of exports (1993). Apart from textiles, manufactures are principally concerned with sugar and other food processing. Tourism has been developed as an important industry, earning approximately $300,000,000 a year.

Infrastructure

Mauritius has 1,800km of roads of which 1,640km are paved. Port Louis, the capital, is the only port. There are four usable airports, two with permanent surface runways of which one is between 2,440 and 3,659m in length. There is a small but efficient telecommunications system.

Political considerations and assessments

A multiparty democracy that has worked well since independence although there is periodic labour unrest, Mauritius must depend for its future progress upon the development of its manufacturing base and particularly upon the expansion of its

EPZ. External investment is welcome. The country has no mineral resources and must continue to base its agriculture upon sugar production. Limited available land and a relatively high rate of population increase represent the two most obvious present restraints and long-term problems. Mauritius has kept its international debts to manageable proportions, less than 30 per cent of GNP, while its per capita income places it well into the upper-middle-income group of countries.

MICRONESIA

Area. 270.8 sq. miles, (701.4 sq. km).
Population. (1995) 105,000.
Capital. Palikir (on Pohnpei).
Language(s). English (official), Trukese, Pohnpeian, Yapese, Kosrean.
Religion(s). Christianity, various sects.
Date of independence. November 3 1986 (from USA which had administered the UN Trusteeship).
GNP. (1989) $157,400,000, per capita $1,595.
Land and climate. Stretching over hundreds of miles the islands are a mixture of high mountains and low coral atolls. The climate is tropical with heavy rains year round and the islands lie on the southern edge of the typhoon belt.

Introduction

One of the world's mini-states, the Federated States of Micronesia were a former UN Trusteeship administered by the USA until they achieved independence in 1986. Micronesia depends upon the USA whose aid is equivlent to two-thirds GDP. The islands are located in the North Pacific Ocean, three-quarters of the way between Hawaii and Indonesia and consist of four major island groups with a total of 607 islands.

Economy

Economic activity consists of subsistence farming and fishing. There are high grade deposits of phosphates but these are not being exploited. The islands offer major possibilities as tourist attractions except for their inaccessibility and lack of infra-structure or facilities. The geographical remoteness of the islands is a major impediment to their development. The primary source of revenue is US aid, accounting for 73 per cent of all revenues in 1990, while fees for fishing rights provided another 7.8 per cent. Under its Compact of Free Association with the USA, Micronesia was to receive US aid to the value of $60m a year for the period 1987 to 1991; $50m a year from 1992 to 1996; and $40m a year from 1997 to 2001. No aid is guaranteed beyond that date. There are four ports, five usable airports and adequate inter-island telecommunications for government purposes.

Future

The long-term prosperity and development of these islands would appear to depend upon the bounty of the USA.

PALAU

Area. 188 sq. miles (488 sq. km).
Population. (1995) 16,900.
Capital. Koror (10,500).
Language(s). Palauan and English (official).
Religion(s). Roman Catholic 40.8 per cent, Protestant 24.8 per cent, traditional beliefs 24.8 per cent, other 9.6 per cent.
Date of independence. October 1 1994 (from USA which had administered the UN Trusteeship).
GNP. (1994) $81,800,000, per capita $5,000.
Land and climate. A chain of 340 volcanic and coral islands stretching over 400 miles; the main islands are Babelthuap and Koror.

Introduction

Part of the US-administered Trust Territory of the Pacific Islands (established under UN auspices after World War II in place of former Japanese colonies), Palau had a dispute with the USA from 1983 to 1990 over the storage of nuclear waste. In November 1993 Palau formally approved the Compact of Free Association with the USA and became independent on October 1 1994. Part of the Caroline Group of islands, Palau lies due east of the Philippines between the Philippine Sea and the Pacific Ocean.

Economy

A minuscule economy with agriculture contributing 17 per cent of GDP and a tiny manufacturing sector, Palau is dependent upon US aid. Under the terms of the 1994 Compact of Free Association the USA will be responsible for Palau's defence for 50 years and Palau must not enter into foreign policy commitments contrary to US interests.

ST KITTS AND NEVIS

Area. 104 sq. miles (269.4 sq. km).
Population. (1995) 39,400.
Capital. Basseterre (18,000).
Language(s). English (official).
Religion(s). Protestant 76.4 per cent, Roman Catholic 10.7 per cent, other 12.9 per cent.

Date of independence. September 19 1983 (from Britain).
GNP. (1993) $185,000,000, per capita $4,560.
Land and climate. The islands are volcanic with mountainous interiors; the climate is subtropical tempered by permanent sea breezes with a rainy season from May to November.

Introduction

A federation of St Christopher (usually referred to as St Kitts) and Nevis, this mini-state was a British colony until 1983 and is one of the few islands in the Caribbean whose economy still largely depends upon the cultivation of sugar. It is a constitutional monarchy, recognizing the British sovereign as head of state. The 1995 elections resulted in the defeat of the People's Action Movement (PAM) by the St Kitts–Nevis Labour Party (SKNLP) following a period of political instability during 1994. St Kitts and Nevis is located in the eastern Caribbean Sea about a third the distance between Puerto Rico and Trinidad and Tobago.

Economy

The economy depends upon the production of sugarcane and agriculture contributes just over 7 per cent to GDP and employs nearly 30 per cent of the workforce. Sugar accounted for 37 per cent of exports in 1993 and in 1994 the sugarcane harvest 200,000mt. Staple crops are rice, yams, vegetables and bananas. Fishing potential has not been fully developed and most food has to be imported. The manufacturing sector contributes 11.6 per cent to GDP and employs 15 per cent of the workforce. Export-oriented manufacturing is of growing importance and includes small light industrial assembly factories which concentrate upon electronic goods, textiles and sports equipment. St Kitts and Nevis has developed a healthy tourist industry which earns about $65,000,000 a year and also depends upon remittances sent home by its nationals abroad.

Infrastructure

There are 58km of 0.76m gauge railway serving the sugar industry; 300km of roads of which 125km are paved; Basseterre (St Kitts) and Charlestown (Nevis) are the ports. There are two airports, one with a runway betwen 2,440 and 3,569m in length. Telecommunications including inter-island services are good.

Political considerations and assessments

With a per capita income in the upper-middle-income range St Kitts and Nevis no longer qualifies for World Bank concessionary loans. It is a stable mini-state which has balanced its assets to maximum advantage.

ST LUCIA

Area. 238 sq. miles (617 sq. km).
Population. (1995) 143,000.
Capital. Castries (urban area 13,615).
Language(s). English (official), French patois.
Religion(s). Roman Catholic 79 per cent, Protestant 15.5 per cent, other 5.5 per cent.
Date of independence. February 22 1979 (from Britain).
GNP. (1993) $480,000,000, per capita $3,040.
Land and climate. A volcanic, mountainous island with some broad fertile valleys; the climate is tropical, moderated by northeast trade winds with a rainy season from May to August. It is subject to hurricanes and volcanic action, deforestation and soil erosion.

Introduction

St Lucia is a former British colony which remained a constitutional monarchy after independence and recognizes the British sovereign as head of state. Bananas are the mainstay of the economy. There was unrest in the banana industry through 1993 and 1994 as farmers protested against the low prices paid by the St Lucia Banana Growers Association (SLBGA), leading the government of the United Workers' Party of Prime Minister John Compton to sack the SLBGA Board and raise the prices paid to farmers. St Lucia is located in the eastern Caribbean Sea, two-thirds the distance between Puerto Rico and Trinidad and Tobago.

Economy

Agriculture is the most important contributor to GDP, accounting for just over 12 per cent, but the sector is vulnerable to major fluctuations since it is over-dependent upon the banana industry which, periodically, is adversely affected by droughts and tropical storms. In 1993 bananas provided 48 per cent of all exports. Coconut oil is another agricultural export. Foreign investment has enabled St Lucia to create a manufacturing sector whose most important products (for export) are clothing, paper and paper board, and beer. Tourism makes a significant contribution to the economy and in 1993 receipts from visitors came to $221,000,000. Food for the tourist industry has to be imported. St Lucia receives substantial aid from Britain and France, principally for infrastructural development.

Infrastructure

There are 760km of roads of which 500km are paved. The island is served by two ports – Castries and Vieux Fort – and two airports, both with permanent surface runways of which one is between 2,440 and 3,659m in length. Telecommunications are reasonable with fair inter-island connections.

Political considerations and assessments

St Lucia is a mini-economy with few resources and over-dependent upon the one export, bananas; but it is building up a light industrial base and expanding its tourist industry.

ST VINCENT AND THE GRENADINES

Area. 150.3 sq. miles (389.3 sq. km).
Population. (1995) 112,000.
Capital. Kingstown (15,824).
Language(s). English (official), French patois.
Religion(s). Protestant 80.5 per cent, Roman Catholic 11.6 per cent, other 7.9 per cent.
Date of independence. October 27 1979 (from Britain).
GNP. (1993) $233,000,000, per capita $2,130.
Land and climate. St Vincent and the Grenadines are volcanic, mountainous islands; the climate is tropical with a rainy season from May to November.

Introduction

A British colony until independence in 1979, St Vincent and the Grenadines continued as a constitutional monarchy recognizing the British sovereign as head of state. The New Democratic Party (NDP) under Prime Minister James Mitchell retained power in the elections of 1994. Like the neighbouring island of St Lucia, St Vincent and the Grenadines depends upon the export of bananas for more than 50 per cent of its foreign exchange earnings. Otherwise, the main source of income is derived from the tourist industry. There is a constant high rate of unemployment. The islands are located in the eastern Caribbean Sea, three-quarters the distance between Puerto Rico and Trinidad and Tobago.

Economy

The economy is dominated by agriculture and agriculture depends upon the annual banana crop. Agriculture accounts for 16 per cent of GDP and employs 20 per cent of the workforce. In 1992 bananas accounted for 52.7 per cent of exports. Other export crops include ginger, arrowroot and coconuts. Staple foods are yams, mangoes, sweet potatoes and a variety of fruits. Small numbers of livestock are nonetheless important to the food supply. The fish catch is consumed locally. St Vincent and the Grenadines is not self-sufficient in food. The small manufacturing sector, largely consisting of food processing, textiles and metal and electrical products, accounts for 9 per cent of GDP and employs 7 per cent of the workforce. Tourism is of growing importance and contributes approximately $50,000,000 a year to the economy. The rate of unemployment ranges between 30 and 40 per cent, one of the highest in the Caribbean.

Infrastructure

There are 1,000km of roads of which 300km are paved. Kingstown is the one port and St Vincent and the Grenadines operates a merchant fleet flag of convenience. There are six usable airports, five with permanent surface runways of which one has a runway between 1,220 and 2,439m in length. A fair system of telecommunications includes links to neighbouring islands.

Political considerations and assessments

There is basically a one-crop agricultural system subject to the vagaries of such crop dependence although tourism and small-scale industries offer some additional outlets.

SÃO TOMÉ E PRÍNCIPE

Area. 386 sq. miles (1,001 sq. km).
Population. (1995) 131,000.
Capital. São Tomé (43,420).
Other major cities. (1981) Trindade (11,388), Santana (6,190), Neves (5,919), Santo Amaro (5,878).
Language(s). Portuguese (official), Fang.
Religion(s). Roman Catholic 80.8 per cent, Protestant (various sects) 19.2 per cent.
Date of independence. July 12 1975 (from Portugal).
GNP. (1993) $41,000,000, per capita $370.
Land and climate. An archipelago of volcanic, mountainous islands (São Tomé and Príncipe are the two main islands) with a hot humid climate and a rainy season extending from October to May.

Introduction

An archipelago of islands off the west coast of Africa, facing Gabon and straddling the equator, São Tomé e Príncipe was formerly part of the Portuguese African empire. It has few natural resources and its economy is largely built upon agricultural exports, principally cocoa. But the land is over-used and inadequate to meet the needs of the population and São Tomé e Príncipe, which is one of the world's poorest mini-states, is mainly dependent on international aid for its survival. It became a one-party state at independence but in 1990 adopted a multiparty constitution.

Economy

São Tomé e Príncipe is basically a one-crop economy, largely dependent upon earnings from cocoa production. The crop was developed in colonial times by the Portuguese and remained the economic staple after independence. However, drought as well as mismanagement since 1975 have reduced output to only half its former levels and in 1994 production totalled only 4,000mt. Even so, this accounted for 77 per cent of all exports. Other export crops include coffee, copra and palm kernels. Agriculture accounts for 28 per cent of GDP. There is a small manufacturing sector equivalent to less than 8 per cent of GDP but most manufactures as well as fuels have to be imported. The country is dependent on imports for 90 per cent of its food requirements. São Tomé e Príncipe relies upon annual aid inputs and now has debts which it cannot service; these are equivalent to over five times the GNP. The only economic alternative to agriculture lies in the country's tourist potential which the government is working to develop.

Political considerations and assessments

An army coup in August 1995 was reversed within days under pressure from international donors. São Tomé e Príncipe is a vulnerable mini-state and will remain dependent upon the goodwill of international aid donors into the foreseeable future.

SEYCHELLES

Area. 176 sq. miles (455 sq. km).
Population. (1995) 75,000.
Capital. Victoria (24,325).
Language(s). English, French and Creole (official).
Religion(s). Roman Catholic 88.6 per cent, other Chistian 8.5 per cent, Hindu 0.4 per cent, other 2.5 per cent.
Date of independence. June 29 1976 (from Britain).
GNP. (1993) $444,000,000, per capita $6,370.
Land and climate. Mahé, the main island, is granite with a narrow coastal strip but is otherwise rocky and hilly. There are other granite islands while the rest of the archipelago consists of flat coral islands or elevated reefs. The climate is tropical, marine and humid. The cool season is from May to September (the southeast monsoon); the warmer season from March to May is during the northwest monsoon.

Introduction

First inhabited by the French in 1770, and later ceded to Britain (1814), the Seychelles became independent in 1976 and in many respects has been able to demonstrate how a mini-state with few resources can, nonetheless, prosper if it learns how to maximize its advantages. The economy depends upon three main activities: the export of refined petroleum products from its refinery; tourism; and fishing. The country has had an uneasy political history since independence with the Seychelles People's United Party (SPUP) staging a coup against its coalition partners in 1977 to introduce a period of one-party rule under Albert René. However, under international pressure, the Seychelles returned to multipartyism in the early 1990s. Over the years several coups against the government have been attempted but thwarted, the most serious being that of 1981 which involved South African mercenaries. The Seychelles comprise an archipelago of approximately 115 islands (the main island is Mahé) ranging over 1 million square miles of the western Indian Ocean to the northeast of Madagascar.

Economy

The tourist industry employs about 30 per cent of the working population and provides up to 70 per cent of foreign exchange earnings; in some years more tourists than the total population visit the country. Seychelles has worked hard to create an attractive tourist infrastructure and aims at the upper end of the tourist market. Tourism contributes more than 17 per cent of GDP. Petroleum re-exports (refined products) accounted for 44.6 per cent of exports in 1994. The development of its extensive offshore fisheries and especially of canned tuna since 1987 has transformed the economy and in 1994 canned tuna accounted for 32.4 per cent of exports while other fish accounted for a further 5 per cent. The most important agricultural products are coconuts, copra and cinnamon bark each of which contributes to exports. But available land is strictly limited and a large proportion of food requirements have to be imported. A programme of reafforestation is making Seychelles self-sufficient in wood. The only mineral is guana with an average production of 6,000 tons a year. There is a number of small-scale, food-related industries (apart from tuna canning). Oil exploration is being conducted in the offshore waters and the country receives rent from the USA for its satellite-tracking station. International debts at $138,100,000 (1993) are equivalent to 30 per cent of GNP.

Infrastructure

There are 260km of roads of which 160km are paved. Victoria is the only port. There are fourteen usable airports, eight with permanent surface runways, one between 2,440 and 3,659m in length. Telecommunications are reasonable.

Political considerations and assessments

A mini-state facing all the problems of vulnerability and dependence that always trouble such tiny countries, Seychelles nonetheless has maximized its resources to give its population a reasonable living standard in the upper-middle-income group of developing countries. Its membership of the Indian Ocean Commission (with Comoros, Madagascar and Mauritius) through which it qualifies for substantial EU aid is of increasing importance to its development projects.

SOLOMON ISLANDS

Area. 10,954 sq. miles (28,370 sq. km).
Population. (1995) 382,000.
Capital. Honiara (35,288).
Language(s). English (official), Melanesian pidgin, (120 indigenous languages).
Religion(s). Christian 96.7 per cent, other (non-religious) 2.3 per cent.
Date of independence. July 7 1978 (from Britain)
GNP. (1993) $260,000,000, per capita $750.
Land and climate. The islands consist mainly of rugged mountains with some low coral atolls. The climate is tropical monsoon without extremes of temperature or weather. The islands are subject to typhoons though these are only rarely destructive.

Introduction

Stretching across 1,200 miles of the South Pacific Ocean to the east of Papua New Guinea, the Solomon Islands archipelago consists of seven main islands and a large number of smaller ones. Formerly part of the British Empire, the Islands became independent in 1978 and still retain the British monarch as head of state (represented by a governor-general). Agriculture is the mainstay of the economy although there are substantial mineral resources which have not yet been exploited.

Agriculture

Agriculture contributes just under 50 per cent to GDP and employs just over 27 per cent of the workforce. However, an even greater proportion of the population depends for its livelihood, at least in part, upon agriculture which is mainly subsistence except for forestry and fishing. Cash crops include cocoa, coconuts, palm kernels and timber. The fish catch at 33,000mt is the principal export and foreign exchange earner and in 1994 fish products accounted for 20 per cent of all exports. Roundwood production in 1994 came to 267,000cu m and wood products accounted for 56.3 per cent of the total so that fish and wood between them account for 76 per cent of exports. Palm oil, cacao beans and copra make up a further 13 per cent of exports. The main staple crops are rice, potatoes, vegetables and fruit, with cattle and pigs providing meat. The Solomon Islands are not self-sufficient in grains. Land use is divided between forested 91.5 per cent, meadows and pastures 1.4 per cent, agricultural land, under permanent cultivation 2 per cent, other 5.1 per cent.

Minerals

Gold is mined in small quantities and at present is the only mineral to be worked. The sector makes only a minimal contribution to the economy. However, there is a mineral-bearing area in Betilonga which has rich deposits of a number of minerals including gold, silver and copper. There is an estimated 10m ton deposit of phosphates on Bellona Island, asbestos on Choiseul, and high-grade bauxite on two other islands (Rennell and Vaghena). There are also deposits of lead, zinc and nickel. All these minerals await exploitation when finance and infrastructure have been provided.

Manufacturing

Manufacturing only contributes 3.7 per cent to GDP and employs under 10 per cent of the workforce. This includes fish processing, sawn timber manufactures, beer, soap, tobacco, garments and weaving, wood carving, fibre glass, boat building and leather work.

Infrastructure

There are 2,100km of roads of which 30km are paved. Two ports serve the Islands: Honiara and Kingi Cove. There are 29 usable airports, two with permanent surface runways of 1,220 to 2,459m in length. Telecommunications are minimal.

Political considerations and assessments

The Solomon Islands are a remote political and economic backwater the pace of whose development is unlikely greatly to change unless there is a worldwide surge in demand for minerals which could lead to the exploitation of the considerable resources which exist on the islands. In terms of accessibility and current world demand this does not appear likely in the foreseeable future. Debts are equivalent to just over one-third of GNP.

SURINAME

Area. 63,251 sq. miles (163,820 sq. km).
Population. (1995) 430,000.
Capital. Paramaribo (200,970).
Other major cities. Nieuw Nickerie (6,078), Meerzog (5,355).
Language(s). Dutch (official), English, Sranam Tongo (Creoles), Hindi (Suriname Hindustani), Javanese.
Religion(s). Hindu 26 per cent, Roman Catholic 21.6 per cent, Muslim 18.6 per cent, Protestant 18 per cent, other 15.8 per cent.
Date of independence. November 25 1975 (from the Netherlands).

GNP. (1993) $488,000,000, per capita $1,210.
Land and climate. The land consists mainly of rolling hills with a narrow swampy coastal plain. The climate is tropical, moderated by the trade winds.

Introduction

Suriname became independent from the Netherlands in 1975 and has had a troubled domestic history since that date, including military coups in 1980 and 1990 and a generally low intensity but continuing poverty-driven insurrection by the poorest sections of the population, especially those in the rural areas. In 1994 rebels occupied the Afobaka Dam (which supplies Paramaribo) and threatened to destroy it; they demanded the resignation of the government and better conditions for the rural areas. The economy is over-dependent upon bauxite and alumina which account for 70 per cent of exports. Suriname is located on the north coast of South America, sandwiched between Guyana and French Guiana; it shares a southern border with Brazil and has a northern coastline of 386km on the North Atlantic.

Agriculture

Agriculture accounts for 21.6 per cent of GDP and 21 per cent of the workforce. Agricultural commodities including fish (shrimps) and forestry products account for 25 per cent of exports. Principal crops are rice (which is the main staple with a surplus for export and represents 60 per cent of total farm output), bananas, palm kernels, coconuts, sugarcane, oranges, plantains, watermelons, cucumbers and cassava. The livestock sector is small scale with less than 100,000 cattle. Shrimps and forest products are of growing importance to the export trade. The country is self-sufficient in foodstuffs. Land use is divided between forested 94.9 per cent, meadows and pastures 0.1 per cent, agricultural land, under permanent cultivation 0.4 per cent, other 4.6 per cent.

Minerals

Mining means bauxite although small quantities of gold are also mined and there are deposits of iron ore and manganese, and small amounts of nickel, copper and platinum. Bauxite which is mainly turned into alumina accounts for about 50 per cent of exports. During the 1980s the bauxite mining area was several times disrupted by rebels in the civil war. In 1992 bauxite production came to 3,300,000mt while alumina production reached 1,573,000mt. There are oil-bearing sands in the Saramacca district and in 1992 Suriname produced 1,730,000 barrels of oil.

Manufacturing

Manufacturing contributes 14 per cent to GDP and employs just under 6 per cent of the workforce. Principal manufactures are alumina and relatively small quantities of aluminium, cement, sugar, palm oil, plywood, shoes, soft drinks, beer and cigarettes.

Infrastructure

There is a total of 166km of railroads of which 86km are 1.000m narrow gauge and 80km are 1.435m gauge; 8,300km of roads of which 500km are paved; and 1,200km of inland waterways most of which can be used by ocean-going vessels of up to 7m draught. The three main ports are Paramaribo, Moengo and Nieuw Nickerie. There are 39 usable airports of which six have permanent surface runways one of which is between 2,440 and 3,659m in length. International telecommunications are good and the domestic system is reasonable.

Political considerations and assessments

Suriname is an international backwater whose principal link with the wider world economy is through its alumina exports. The Dutch government cut off aid in 1982 and since that date the country has been troubled with internal challenges to the government by various groups drawn from the poorest, most neglected sectors of the population, principally from the rural areas. International debts stood at $138,000,000 in 1990. High unemployment (above 15 per cent) and growing divisions between the better off and the poorest pose major long-term problems.

SWAZILAND

Area. 6,704 sq. miles (17,364 sq. km).
Population. (1995) 913,000.
Capital(s). Mbabane (administrative) (38,290), Lobamba (royal and legislative).
Other major cities. Manzini (52,000), Nhlangano (4,107), Pigg's Peak (3,223).
Language(s). Swazi and English (official).
Religion(s). Traditional beliefs 20.9 per cent, Christian 7 per cent, other 2.1 per cent.
Date of independence. September 6 1968 (from Britain).
GNP. (1993) $933,400,000, per capita $1,050.
Land and climate. A land of mountains and hills with some sloping plains; the climate ranges from tropical to temperate.

Introduction

A conservative society largely controlled by the Dlamini family, Swaziland is a monarchy and power resides in the hands of the King and his council rather than in the two parliamentary chambers. The country became independent in 1968 and in 1973 King Sobhuza II suspended the constitution to rule directly; following his death in 1982 and a four-year period of regency King Mswati III came to the throne. A constitution of 1978 has yet to be presented to the people. Swaziland possesses one of the better balanced economies in Africa and is ranked among the lower-middle-income countries. It is a landlocked state, surrounded on three sides by South Africa and to the east by Mozambique.

Agriculture

Agriculture accounts for 13.4 per cent of GDP and employs 18.8 per cent of the labour force although a far higher proportion of the population practises subsistence farming. The main export crop is sugarcane, and sugar, which goes mainly to the EU, provides 25 per cent of exports. Other export crops are citrus fruits and pineapples which are canned and small quantities of cotton, tobacco and rice. Swaziland is not self-sufficient in grains. The country's manmade forests (a legacy of colonial times) account for 4 per cent of exports in the form of wood and wood products. The livestock herd includes 620,000 cattle and 434,000 goats. The main staple crops are maize, sorghum, groundnuts. Land use is divided between forested 6.9 per cent, meadows and pastures 62.2 per cent, agricultural land, under permanent cultivation 11.1 per cent, other 19.8 per cent.

Minerals

Minerals now only account for 1.6 per cent of GDP and employ 3.3 per cent of the workforce although they played a larger role in the economy before iron ore production stopped in 1978 and demand for asbestos declined in the face of growing health concerns. Asbestos (26,720mt in 1994) and diamonds (52,800 carats) are the principal minerals mined, apart from coal. Together they account for 3.9 per cent of exports. The mining of diamonds (mainly industrial quality) began in 1984. Swaziland has coal reserves of 1,000m tons (high grade, anthracite quality) and is currently mining at the rate of 100,000 tons a year. Coal represents a major long-term resource. Other minerals include clay, cassiterite, small gold deposits, quarry stone and talc.

Manufacturing

Manufacturing accounts for 29 per cent of GDP and employs 9 per cent of the workforce. The principal manufactures are processed foods, canned fruits, refined sugar, paper and paper products, machinery and equipment, non-metal mineral products. Nearly 50 per cent of Swaziland's products are exported to South Africa and about 96 per cent of its requirements come from the Republic.

Infrastructure

There are 297km of 1.067m gauge railway; 2,853km of roads of which 510km are paved; and 21 usable airports of which only one has a permanent surface runway of between 2,440 and 3,659m in length. The telecommunications system is generally adequate.

Political considerations and assessments

Swaziland is an intensely conservative society which, sooner or later, will have to face growing demands for greater democracy. At present the system is dominated by the King and his immediate advisers. Its landlocked position means that, to some extent, Swaziland must always be at the political/economic mercy of its two far larger neighbours. It is a member of the Southern African Customs Union (SACU) which provides 50 per cent of budget revenues and virtually all Swaziland's trade (imports and exports) passes through the Republic. Maputo in Mozambique is the nearest port but this was little used during the long years of the civil war in that country, although permanent peace there could see Swaziland switch some of its trade that way if only to escape over-domination from South Africa. The economy is relatively healthy and balanced and international debts at $217,800,000 (1993) are equivalent to only a quarter of GDP.

TONGA

Area. 289.5 sq. miles (749.9 sq. km).
Population. (1995) 100,400.
Capital. Nuku'alofa (21,383).
Other major cities. Neiafu (3,879), Haveluloto (3,070).
Language(s). Tongan and English (official).
Religion(s). Free Wesleyan 43 per cent, Roman Catholic 16 per cent, Mormon 12.1 per cent, Free Church of Tonga 11 per cent, Church of Tonga 7.3 per cent, other 10.6 per cent.
Date of independence. June 4 1970 (from Britain).
GNP. (1993) $150,000,000, per capita $1,610.
Land and climate. The islands are limestone or coral based and the climate is tropical, moderated by the trade winds.

Introduction

Tonga consists of an archipelago of islands lying some 2,200km north to northeast of New Zealand with a population of 100,000 people. Tonga is a constitutional monarchy, formerly part of the British Empire, which became independent in 1970. The basis of the economy is agriculture and fishing.

Agriculture

Agriculture accounts for 34 per cent of the GDP and employs 36 per cent of the workforce. Principal cash crops which between them account for 85 per cent of exports are squash, vanilla beans, fish, root crops, coconut products, cocoa, coffee, ginger and black pepper. Tonga is not self-sufficient in food and imports most of its requirements from New Zealand. Livestock numbers are on a small scale and the fish catch is only 2,500mt a year. Land use is divided between forested 11.1 per cent, meadows and pastures 5.6 per cent, agricultural land, under permanent cultivation 66.7 per cent, other 16.6 per cent.

Manufacturing

There are no minerals although coral and sand are quarried. Manufactures contribute 4 per cent to GDP and the sector employs 14.6 per cent of the workforce. Principal manufactures consist of food processing, chemical products, textiles, metal products, publishing and printing and furniture. Tourism is the second foreign exchange earner after agricultural exports and brought in receipts of $10,000,000 in 1993.

Infrastructure

There is a total of 272km of sealed (all weather) roads. Three ports – Nuku'alofa, Neiafu and Pangai – serve the islands. There are six usable airports one of which has a permanent surface runway between 2,440 and 3,659m in length. The telecommunications system is adequate.

Political considerations and assessments

Tourist receipts and remittances from Tongans abroad help keep the permanent trade deficit reasonably under control. Isolated and lacking any important resources, Tonga is unlikely to change its lifestyle or rate of development in the foreseeable future. International debts are equivalent to slightly less than one-third GNP and Tonga receives moderate aid injections from friendly donors.

TUVALU

Area. 9.25 sq. miles (23.96 sq. km).
Population. (1995) 9,400.
Capital. Fongafale (on Funafuti atoll) (3,432).
Language(s). Tuvaluan, English.
Religion(s). Church of Tuvalu (Congregationalist) 96.9 per cent, other 3.1 per cent.
Date of independence. October 1 1978 (from Britain).
GDP. (1990) $8,750,000, per capita $967.
Land and climate. Tuvalu consists of nine low-lying coral atolls. The climate is

tropical, moderated by the easterly trade winds. During November to March there are westerly gales and heavy rains.

Introduction

Tuvalu which is part of Oceania consists of a group of islands stretching over 1,000km that lie 3,000km east of Papua New Guinea in the South Pacific Ocean. Formerly a British colony, Tuvalu became independent in 1978 but continued to accept the British monarch, who is represented by a governor-general, as head of state. Fish represent the only resource.

Economy

There are no mineral resources and the main economic activities consist of subsistence agriculture and fishing. The main exports are clothing and footwear, copra, fruit and vegetables. The small size, lack of raw materials and remoteness of the islands mean they are unsuitable for tourist development. Government depends upon the sale of stamps and coins and remittances from workers abroad for its revenues as well as an annual income from a trust fund set up by Australia, New Zealand and Britain in 1987.

Political considerations and assessments

The main problem facing the government of Prime Minister Kamuta Laatasi in 1994 was to reduce the number of government workers (500 out of a total population of 9,300) and decentralize government departments from the atoll of Funafuti which with half the population was becoming short of land. Tuvalu is likely to remain one of the world's backwaters.

VANUATU

Area. 4,707 sq. miles (12,190 sq. km).
Population. (1995) 168,000.
Capital. Vila (19,400).
Other major cities. Luganville (6,900).
Language(s). Bislama, French and English (official).
Religion(s). Christian 77.2 per cent, Custom 4.6 per cent, non-religious, unknown, other 18.2 per cent.
Date of independence. July 30 1980 (from Britain and France).
GNP. (1993) $198,000,000, per capita $1,230.
Land and climate. Most islands consist of mountains of volcanic origin; the larger

ones possess narrow coastal plains. The climate is tropical, moderated by the southeast trade winds and subject to cyclones.

Introduction

As the Condominium of Britain and France from 1906 to 1980, the New Hebrides had a unique colonial experience with parallel British and French administrations duplicating one another. Nationalist demands for independence came to a head in the 1970s and in 1977 Britain and France agreed to grant independence in 1980, following a referendum. Vanuatu consists of an archipelago of some 80 islands with a total land mass of 4,707 sq. miles in Oceania, lying 5,750km southeast of Honolulu in the South Pacific. It is a republic with a unicameral legislature and a non-executive president. The main product and export is copra.

Economy

The economy is basically agricultural with copra (from coconuts) accounting for a third of exports followed by beef and veal, seashells, cacao beans and timber. There is also some coffee produced for export and a small fish catch. Land use is divided between forested 75 per cent, meadows and pastures 2 per cent, agricultural 11.8 per cent, other 11.2 per cent. Mining really only consists of quarrying coral reef limestone, crushed stone, sand and gravel although there are resources of manganese which have yet to be exploited. Manufacturing is small scale, for the domestic market – food processing, beverages, tobacco, wood products, fabricated metal products, paper, printing, publishing, non-metallic mineral products, handicrafts, textiles and leather.

Infrastructure

There are 1,027km of roads of which 240km are all-weather. The islands are served by four ports: Port-Vila, Luganville, Palikoulo, Santu. Vanuatu holds a flag of convenience register for foreign ships. There are 31 usable airports, two with permanent surface runways of which one is between 2,440 and 3,659m in length. Telecommunications are limited.

Political considerations and assessments

Small size has not prevented political instability in the coalition government. Vanuatu has few resources, a small tourist industry and a per capita income that places it in the ranks of the lower-middle-income group of countries. Debts at $39,400,000 (1993) are equivalent to 20 per cent of GNP. Vanuatu is unlikely greatly to change its economic status in the foreseeable future.

WESTERN SAMOA

Area. 1,093 sq. miles (2,831 sq. km).
Population. (1995) 166,000.
Capital. Apia (34,126).
Language(s). Samoan and English (official).
Religion(s). Christian (various denominations).
Date of independence. January 1 1962 (from New Zealand which had administered the UN Trusteeship over the territory).
GNP. (1993) $160,000,000, per capita $980.
Land and climate. Rugged interior mountains are surrounded by narrow coastal plains; the climate is tropical, rainy from October to March, dry from May to October.

Introduction

A former German colony, Western Samoa was occupied by New Zealand in 1914 and later became a mandate of the League of Nations and subsequently a Trusteeship Territory under the United Nations administered by New Zealand. It became independent in 1962. It is a parliamentary democracy and has maintained strong post-independence links with New Zealand. The islands are located halfway between Hawaii and New Zealand in the South Pacific. The economy is based upon agriculture.

Economy

The economy is based upon agriculture which accounts for 43 per cent of GDP and employs 63 per cent of the workforce. Coconuts, copra, desiccated coconut and coconut oil, taro and bananas are the principal exports. Other agricultural products are papayas, pineapples, mangoes, avocados. There are 1 million goats on the islands, pigs and a small number of cattle. Western Samoa is not self-sufficient in food. New Zealand is its principal trading partner. There are no minerals and manufactures are mainly concerned with food processing. The annual trade deficit is offset by remittances from Samoans working abroad. Debts are equivalent to 88 per cent of GNP.

Infrastructure

There are 2,042km of roads of which 375km are sealed. Apia is the port. There are three usable airports, one with a permanent surface runway between 2,440 and 3,659m in length. The telecommunications system is reasonable for its small size and includes 7,500 telephones.

Political considerations and assessments

A political and economic backwater of Oceania, Western Samoa depends upon its continuing good relations with New Zealand for aid and its principal market and source of imports.

APPENDIX: DEPENDENT TERRITORIES

There are approximtely 60 dependent territories round the world; most of these are very small, some are uninhabited, few have any important resources. In the majority of cases the term 'dependent' is an accurate description of their status since they have such tiny populations and such limited resources that it would be all but impossible for them actually to stand on their own. Instead, they receive substantial aid from the 'colonial' power, no matter how the relationship is described, and without such aid would be unable to survive except in great poverty. In a majority of cases the dependent relationship is mutually acceptable. They fall into a number of categories:

- Colonies picked up during the heyday of European imperial expansion that are content to remain so because of the tiny size of their economies and because the imperial power is willing to provide them with substantial subsidies. One or two, such as Bermuda (Britain) or Réunion (France), are relatively highly prosperous.

- Very small territories that were acquired by the imperial powers for potential strategic reasons but today are uninhabited.

- Territories of great strategic value when they were originally seized, such as Gibraltar, which, more recently, have acquired special importance because of a dispute (Britain and Spain over Gibraltar), their size or economic potential (Falkland Islands, Hong Kong).

- Pacific Islands which had particular strategic importance during World War II; today they may be uninhabited or still act as bases for US or other Western forces.

- One or two territories which are rich in minerals or are thought to be so: New Caledonia, Falkland Islands.

The majority of these territories are likely to remain dependencies into the indefinite future; two – Hong Kong and Macau – will shortly revert to China; and several are the subject of disputes – Gibraltar, Falkland Islands, New Caledonia.

American Samoa (USA)

Population (1993) 53,139.

Anguilla (Britain)

Population (1993) 7,006.

Aruba (Netherlands)

Population (1993) 65,117.

Ashmore and Cartier (Australia)

Uninhabited.

Baker Island (USA)

Uninhabited.

Bassas da India (France)

Uninhabited.

Bermuda (Britain)

Population (1993) 60,686.
Luxury tourist resort.

Bouvet Island (Norway)

Uninhabited.

British Indian Ocean Territory (BIOT) (Britain)

Strategic – US/UK military personnel.

British Virgin Islands (Britain)

Population (1993) 12,707.
Tourism.

Cayman Islands (Britain)

Population (1993) 30,440.
Tourism.

Christmas Island (Australia)

Population (1993) 1,685.

Clapperton Island (France)

Uninhabited.

Cocos (Keeling) Islands (Australia)

Population (1993) 593.

Cook Islands (New Zealand)

Population (1993) 18,903.
Agriculture.

Coral Sea Islands (Australia)

Three meteorological officers.

Europa Island (France)

Uninhabited.

Falkland Islands (Islas Malvinas) (Britain)

Population (1993) 2,206.
Sheep (oil under the continental shelf).
Dispute between Argentina and Britain.

French Guiana (France)

Population (1993) 133,376.
Fisheries and forestry.
French space station.

French Polynesia (France)

Population (1993) 210,333.
French base.

Gibraltar (Britain)

Population (1993) 31,508.
Tourism, offshore activities.
Strategic base – claimed by Spain.

Glorioso Island (France)

Uninhabited.

Guadeloupe (France)

Population (1993) 422,114.
Agriculture, tourism.

Guam (USA)

Population (1993) 145,935.
Strategic – US base.

Heard Island and McDonald Islands (Australia)

Uninhabited.

Hong Kong (Britain)

Population (1993) 5,552,965.
World-class trading entrepôt.
Reverts to China July 1 1997.

Howland Island (USA)

Uninhabited.

Jan Mayen (Norway)

Uninhabited.

Jarvis Island (USA)

Uninhabited.

Johnston Atoll (USA)

Uninhabited.
US base.

Juan de Nova Island (France)

Uninhabited.

Kingman Reef (USA)

Uninhabited.

Macau (Portugal)

Population (1993) 477,850.
Tourism.
Reverts to China December 20 1999.

Martinique (France)

Population (1993) 387,656.
Sugar and bananas, tourism.

Mayotte (France)

Population (1993) 89,983.
Agriculture, French aid.

Midway Islands (USA)

Uninhabited.
Strategic – US military personnel.

Montserrat (Britain)

Population (1993) 12,661.
Tourism.

Navassa Island (USA)

Uninhabited.

Netherlands Antilles (Netherlands)

Population (1993) 184,900.
Tourism, petroleum refining, offshore finance.

New Caledonia (France)

Population (1993) 178,056.
Possesses 25 per cent of the world's nickel reserves.
A referendum concerning independence is scheduled for 1998.

Niue (New Zealand)

Population (1993) 1,977.
New Zealand aid.

Norfolk Island (Australia)

Population (1993) 2,665.
Tourism.

Northern Mariana Islands (USA)

Population (1993) 48,581.
US aid.

Palmyra Atoll (USA)

Uninhabited.

Pitcairn Island (Britain)

Population (1993) 52.
Fishing, subsistence farming.

Puerto Rico (USA)

Population (1993) 3,797,082.
Strong mixed economy.

Réunion (France)

Population (1993) 639,622.
Agriculture (sugar).

St Helena (Britain)

Population (1993) 6,730.
British aid.

St Pierre and Miquelon (France)

Population (1993) 6,652.
Fishing, French aid.

South Georgia and South Sandwich Islands (Britain)

Uninhabited.
Strategic/biological station.

Spratly Islands (situated in the South China Sea)

Uninhabited.
Claimed in whole or in part by China, Taiwan, Vietnam, Malaysia, Philippines, Brunei.
Oil or natural gas may be present.

Svalbard (Norway)

Population (1993) 3,209.
Coal.

Tokelau (New Zealand)

Population (1993) 1,544.
Aid.

Tromelin Island (France)

Uninhabited.

Turks and Caicos Islands (Britain)

Population (1993) 13,137.
Fishing, tourism, offshore banking.

Virgin Islands of the United States (USA)

Population (1993) 98,130.
Tourism, petroleum refining.

Wake Island (USA)

Uninhabited
Strategic – US Air Force.

Wallis and Futuna (France)

Population (1993) 14,175.
Subsistence agriculture, aid.